D1827208

To Professor Jagdish Gundara

With deep gratitude & great respect

Terri Kim

12. 10. 2001

EAST ASIA: HISTORY, POLITICS, SOCIOLOGY, CULTURE

edited by
EDWARD BEAUCHAMP
UNIVERSITY OF HAWAII

A ROUTLEDGE SERIES

Forming the Academic Profession in East Asia

A Comparative Analysis

TERRI KIM

ROUTLEDGE
A MEMBER OF THE TAYLOR & FRANCIS GROUP
NEW YORK & LONDON/2001

Published in 2001 by
Routledge
A member of the Taylor & Francis Group
29 West 35th Street
New York, NY 10001

Copyright © 2001 by Terri Kim

All rights reserved. No part of this book may be reprinted or
reproduced or utilized in any form or by any electronic, mechanical, or other means, now known or hereafter invented, including
photocopying and recording, or in any information storage or
retrieval system, without written permission from the publishers.

10 9 8 7 6 5 4 3 2 1

*Library of Congress Cataloging-in-Publication Data is available
from the Library of Congress.*

ISBN 0-8153-4053-2

Printed on acid-free, 250 year-life paper
Manufactured in the United States of America

For my parents:
Professor In Whoe Kim and Professor Ok Sun Choy

Contents

Foreword
Robert Cowen

When I was a student, on my second course in comparative education, we had a look at 'education as a profession'. The topic reminded me of some of the ways of learning expected of me as a student in economics or in international law. There was a model, a principle, and the job of the student was to show knowledge of that, rehearse some difficulties, and then arrive at a reassertion of the explanatory power of the principle.

So this comparative education course was ok. Here was a simple model—professions performed an essential public service, the practitioners had esoteric knowledge, based on intellectual principles, a code of ethics, and the practitioners controlled entry to (and exit from) the profession and put service before profit. Here was the answer to an exam question, already half-written. All that was required was to feed in a bit of illustrative material from the United States or France on the situation of school teachers, contrast with the USSR, and serve up in good handwriting.

I still remember what happened later, when as a beginning student at the M.A. level, I suggested that the model was poor history and thus poor sociology; that it was an ideological statement that hid conflict over the control and distribution of knowledge; that it missed out the role of the State in the control of professions. I found myself in the middle of a very brutal fight. My teacher was asking how useful the model was as a measuring device in 'comparative education'. I was asking whether this kind of comparative education was good social science—though I did not realise that at the time and as students often do I lost the fight. I also lost something else. I had moved out from the role of being a good student. Clearly I was now a bit of a nuisance—reading books I should not have been reading. And if I wanted a career in comparative education, then I had clearly been politically very careless. But what I gained was immense—the beginnings of intellectual independence well before I started a Ph.D. I still find it a delight when a student, sustaining an interpretation with clarity and courage and determination, disagrees with something I had thought of as more or less true. So in this thesis of Dr. Kim's there come together some of the pleasures of university work: those of fresh interpretations and intense discussions and a great deal of lonely scholarship.

Retrospectively the pattern of how this work was created is reasonably clear. In real life as it was lived, we as supervisors were not always sure what we were doing. Nor were we always clear what was being argued by us or by the doctoral candidate. Good theses are often like that, despite what some of the books of advice say about how to get a Ph.D.

However there was a certainty. The future Dr. Kim was sure that this was her topic, a topic for her. She had begun to read and—far more rapidly than I had as a student—had formed a critical view of the existing literature. She then had the courage to outline her ideas on a large canvas, to do a risky thesis, one where a Ph.D. was not being guaranteed by a bit of competent fieldwork. She thought and she wrote. There was a huge excursion into post-colonial literature. There were displays of controlled bad temper—like the remorseless politeness of the British traffic police when they are confronted with something they do not like. Kim survived; indeed she fought back. She won her independence. Her viva was a polished performance—after some of the tutorials it was probably a bit of a relief and a bit of relaxation. But that was a while ago and that was the beginnings of making a young scholar.

Now the thesis is objectivated. It stands alone as text. It can be criticised. It will be. Her work is in the public arena. Let us hope she is not too distracted by criticisms of it and let us hope she does not spend a great deal of her professional career defending her doctoral thesis. Some academics do—and I am not thinking of Durkheim. There are other things to do, and other things to move on towards and already Kim is thinking of new topics and of some changes in her approach to this one.

In this work as it stands, she has made a good initial case for the historical and sociological contextualisation of analyses of professions. She has raised some interesting questions about the role of colonial states in the construction of professions. She has raised some good questions about the narrow line between the public interest and the need for some parts of the work of the academic profession to be left to academics. Clearly some of these themes come out of colonial oppression—the Japanese occupation of Korea was not kindly and the British occupation of Malaya while sometimes kindly was culturally overconfident and corrosive. The recovery from those colonialisms and the construction of the academic professions in those countries is a fascinating story that Kim tells well. The story is a dramatic one and sometimes, for example, in the search by Koreans for ways to claim their own educated identity, a moving one.

But for me it is the contrast—between Kim's story of tragedies and the contemporary academic profession in England—which captures my imagination. Certainly there are a lot of historical and comparative tragedies—the figures of Socrates or Heidegger. There are the Generals or Colonels in Argentina or Brazil or Greece and the universities. There are the university exiles and those who 'disappeared' or had their careers destroyed in times of McCarthyism, or fascism in Asia or Europe, or in the former USSR and Central and Eastern Europe. These are the high dramas of academic life and its relation to the state. The tragedies—the destruction of the mandarins—are there for us to explore and explain.

But what I would like to see now is more studies of banalities and the academic profession. What are the mechanisms of state surveillance of universities in 'democratic societies'? How corrosive is 'management' to and within university academic culture? What is the relationship between entrepreneurial or theoretical creativity and the bureaucratisation of teaching—where aims and objectives and expected learning outcomes have to be stated for each lecture-seminar? Does it make a difference if Paulo Freire or a visitor with a bit of paper and a check-list of behavioural expectations assesses your teaching?

The contemporary answer in many countries is, 'yes, it—management, measuring, public transparency—does make a difference'. Careful measurement of performance in universities is important because this sooner rather than later leads to improvements in the quality of university research and teaching and care for students and productive links with society and efficiency and effectiveness in the use of scarce resources, including public money and the ability of countries to compete in an international and globalised knowledge economy; and so on and so on. The ideology, in some countries, is fully developed. In what ways are this ideology and these banalities of surveillance leading to the destruction of the scholarships of teaching, of integration, of the application of knowledge, and of discovery about which Ernest Boyer writes so well? In what ways are the ideology and the surveillance leading to improvements in the power, elegance and impact of those scholarships?

I suggest we do not know. I suggest that much of the time we are asking the wrong questions—questions about trends and convergences—and collecting the wrong descriptions—descriptions of training systems or processes for the improvement of the academic profession, for possible transfer to other countries.

And indeed there is the core of the matter. Imagine Kim's comparative account of the social construction of the academic profession in parts of Asia—and the human tragedies and cultural discontinuities involved in that story—allied with the borrowing from, say, England of concepts and practices for the quality control of the university and the academic profession. Imagine the historical tragedies combined with the contemporary banalities. The imagining must be urgent: there is strong interest in policy circles in Japan, for example, in improvements in quality control of the universities. Senior Taiwanese visitors wish to discuss the same themes. In South Korea there is a powerful interest in the 'internationalisation' of universities—which on closer inspection seems to be quality control by other means.

Tacitus once wrote that the Romans in Britain made a desert (*solitudinem*) and called it peace. One contemporary version of that theme would be: how much banality can university systems stand? Kim's writing —on colonialism and the academic profession and on the contemporary controls on the university by the state in some countries—is a fine entry point for thinking about both propositions. The answers she gives in this work are disturbing. Were she now to extend her work to contemporary fashions in the international transfer of quality control practices in universities she might generate answers that were frightening.

Preface

The first version of this book was written as my doctoral thesis at the Institute of Education, University of London in 1998. The book traces the changing shape of the academic profession in (South) Korea and Malaya, Malaysia and Singapore, since colonial times.

This work tries to explain the different formations of the academic profession in modern East Asian university systems, with the argument that the colonial origins of the university systems have affected the postcolonial conditions of State-University relations in these East Asian countries; and the work aims at a comparative understanding of the shape, and the shaping, of the academic profession in the historical context of the different cultural and knowledge traditions of East Asia under international influences. In Korea, the formation of the modern academic profession was heavily influenced by Japan and the U.S.A.; in Malaysia and Singapore, by Britain. My comparative research interest in 'the academic profession' came also from a personal desire to understand something of the history of my family within the academic profession in Korea. Since the turn of the 20th century, Korea has undergone constant political upheavals and rapid social transitions in the process of colonisation and modernisation. My grandparents and many of my family members in the academic profession had studied in foreign universities—e.g. in Japan, U.S.A., China, Canada, and Germany—during and after the Japanese colonial period.

Currently my parents are university academics. Exceptionally, however, my parents deliberately chose not to study abroad and completed their higher degrees in Korea. My father was awarded the first 'Korean' Ph.D. in Education at Yonsei University in Seoul, Korea. He then pioneered the new academic "decolonisation" movement in Korea in the 1970s and 80s. Unlike my parents, I chose to study abroad. I went to England to study comparative higher education for both M.A. and Ph.D. degrees. In fact, I am the only person in my family who was awarded an "English" Ph.D.—

the first such Ph.D. in Comparative Education in Korea.

Thus, given my family's history and my own experience of the English university, my comparative inquiry began in both professional and personal curiosity about the social contexts, the political power, and the economic forces which have shaped the academic profession. To me, the academic profession in Korea seemed very different from the academic professions in countries with British colonial legacies, let alone in countries that have very European ideas about what a university academic is. I felt that the academic profession in Korea should be understood both comparatively and in a particular East Asian context.

In the existing literature, however, comparative studies of the academic profession often tend to stress comparison out of context and a convergence hypothesis. In this book, I wanted to explain a particular shape of the academic profession, as an historical object of transformation in the social dynamics of political and economic conditions in East Asia and international relations of the region.

The initial argument of my research was that the shape of the academic profession which has emerged by the contemporary period is a reflection of both the inherited models of higher education and their redefinition after the colonial period. The specific argument of this book is that the shaping of the academic profession in Korea, Malaysia and Singapore can be understood because of this colonial genesis and because the State formations of the colonial and postcolonial periods permitted only restricted social space for the university and academic autonomy.

Many debts had been incurred in composing this work. In particular, I should like to thank the Committee of Vice-Chancellors and Principals (CVCP), for having been honoured with an Overseas Research Scholarship at the Institute of Education for three years, from 1995.

I was extremely fortunate as a doctoral student to have two supervisors. They enabled me to understand the importance of a strong academic culture, of being at a major international academic centre to learn both comparative higher education and intercultural studies.

The intellectual and pedagogic charisma of Professor Robert Cowen, my supervisor, illuminated what the English model of liberal knowledge and cultivation can mean—when coupled with demands for precision of thought and excellence in writing. I also remain amazed by the quality of teaching in his fortnightly doctoral seminars. My special thanks are expressed to Professor Jagdish Gundara, my other supervisor, for his genuine personal concern for my progress and especially his invitation to think divergently and broadly about the themes in my thesis.

The excellent supervision and the very English apprenticeship I received from my supervisors were vital in forming my self-identity as an academic. Two years after my Ph.D., my comparative concerns for, and interest in, the university and the academic profession have become more realistic with some hands-on experience of teaching at universities in Korea.

Finally, I dedicate this book to my parents and grandparents on both sides, who were pioneers in the formation of the Korean academic profession. Without my parents' academic inspiration, loving encouragement and support during the entire period of my Ph.D., I would not have begun, nor been able to complete, this comparative research on the academic profession.

List of Tables

CHAPTER ONE

Introduction

The purpose of this book is to examine comparatively the formation of the academic profession in Korea and Malaya (and later South Korea, Malaysia and Singapore) from colonial times. The main argument is that the academic professions in these places have been affected by their colonial genesis and by the particular State formations in the three East Asian countries. The comparative analysis of this book thus takes account of the connections and disconnections between the colonial and postcolonial periods in the shaping of the academic profession.

The initial proposition of the book is that the Western notions of the 'idea' of the university, of the State and of the academic profession are not always appropriate ways in which to approach East Asia.[1] Part of the work of the book is to show why this is so, starting with the colonial period in Korea and Malaya. However, this book is not in itself an historical narrative.

This book is a comparative inquiry into the relations of the State and the university which define some of the dynamics of the social construction of the academic profession in the three countries. By investigating the different formations of the State and relations of the State and the University at different times, the book attempts to locate comparatively the forces shaping the academic profession in these countries.

To create its analytic frame—the theme of 'the shaping' of the academic profession—the book critically assesses the concept of the academic profession as this is treated in the existing literature, establishes ideal typical models of the university (through the writings of Newman and Jaspers and Confucius), looks at conventional views of the East Asian State, and by the end of Chapter Two sets out a way to think about the shape of the academic profession, without imposing on the analysis some of the assumptions made in the classic and recent literature on professions.

Chapter Three analyses the emergent academic profession in Korea and

Malaya, in the context of Japanese and British colonial policies. The colonial political, economic and cultural milieux in Korea and Malaya define variations in, and close some of the options for, the formation and the subsequent shape of those two academic professions.

Chapter Four looks at the academic profession in the postcolonial period, within the processes of decolonisation and 'indigenisation'. (Indigenisation is here taken to mean the political processes by which each State redefined the national culture against colonial legacies in a postcolonial context.) Subsequently, all of these three East Asian States have recently taken up the theme of 'internationalisation' of higher education and this theme is also incorporated in the analysis.

Thus the themes that run through the book are: (i) the continuing cultural legacy of the pre-colonial and the colonial origins of what became the academic profession in the post-colonial period; (ii) the role of the East Asian States as actors in defining, legitimating, and implementing the political, economic and cultural contexts within which the academic profession was shaped in the postcolonial indigenisation process; and (iii) the challenges of internationalisation and globalisation as contemporary influences on the academic profession.

The book, in its closing argument, will analyse the overlap and contradiction of the various State projects in the colonial and postcolonial shaping of the academic profession, including the redefinition of imported models of the university, and the consequent 'peculiar' shape(s) of the academic profession in these East Asian countries.

The next chapter will begin the task of sorting out ways to think about the social construction of the academic profession in the countries selected for analysis. However, before that effort at rethinking begins, it is important to explain why existing approaches in the literature are not, simply and directly, incorporated into the book.

There is a considerable literature on the academic profession in general, but the book begins in disappointment with this literature, notably with the Carnegie Commission Report and subsequent analyses of the Korean academic profession. Perhaps, as in most books, there is also a personal element. My own family for several generations has included academics. Currently, both my parents are academics. The conventional literature on the academic profession seems to me to capture little of the anxieties, tensions and social struggles within which the academic profession in South Korea, at least, has been formed.

So the book begins in both professional and personal curiosity about the social contexts, the political power, and the economic forces which have shaped the academic profession in different places. Is it really the case that the academic profession is everywhere becoming the same ('converging')? Is it really the case that university academics everywhere are working within the same 'idea of the university', although this is now under pressure from 'the market'? Is it really the case that these East Asian governments, as in North Western Europe (with some exceptions) or North America, have respected academic autonomy and freedom? And even if the academic profession is under pressure to be 'relevant and useful', why is this so and what does 'relevant and useful' mean in particular times and places?

Thus, the first issue in the book—reviewed in the remainder of this chapter—is what theoretical purchase does the existing comparative literature offer to clarify such puzzles about the academic profession? How useful and relevant in theoretical terms is the existing literature for examining the academic profession in the context of East Asia, especially during the times when the academic professions were in process of formation?

It will be suggested that some of the best existing analyses of the academic profession in the literature are not directly useful for this book.

The existing literature has examined the academic profession within the general concept of profession as this has been constructed in Western sociology. In the existing sociological literature on 'professions', 'a profession' is often specified through criteria such as cognitive base, institutionalised training, licensing, work autonomy, collegial control over entry and exit, and codes of ethics.[2] For example, according to Myron Lieberman, a profession "performs a unique and essential social service; is founded upon intellectual techniques; has a long period of specialised training; offers a high degree of autonomy both to the individual practitioner and to the occupational group as a whole; accepts responsibility for judgements made and acts performed within the scope of professional autonomy; puts emphasis upon the service it performs rather than the economic rewards that the practitioner gets; is a self-governing organisation of practitioners, and finally operates on the basis of a code of ethics."[3]

However, it is important to be clear, immediately, that this book is not asking and answering the question of whether "academics" constitute 'a profession' in such a traditional sociological sense.[4] In other words, this book does not set out to utilise as a *tertium comparationis* such a standard concept of profession. Such models are normally static and distract attention from the question of the dynamics of the construction of professions. Even where there has been some effort to tackle the issue of power, and to locate the State and its role in the construction of the professions, the work has remained at a high level of abstraction and does not close down the issue comparatively and descriptively.[5]

The existing literature on the academic profession itself falls into two groups. One group uses an explicit comparative approach.[6] The other group offers case studies e.g. of America or of Britain, with implicit implications for comparison.

Most comparative analyses of the professions in the existing literature focus on Anglo-American and European examples and Anglo-American issues. These local issues have been extended to the international level to conduct "comparisons"; for example, by academics in books, and by major agencies such as the Carnegie Foundation, the Rockefeller Foundation, and the Organisation for Economic Cooperation and Development (OECD).[7]

Among the analyses by academics[8], P. G. Altbach wrote on the academic profession as early as the 1970s, in his *Comparative Perspectives on the Academic Profession.*

The book deals with eight cases: Britain, Italy, Japan, Australia, Canada, Latin America, India and North America.[10] The rationale for selecting these countries is not explained. There is no common conceptual framing for the analysis of the national academic professions. Nor is there any suggestion of the need to conceptualise the academic profession differently in Asia, Europe, Latin America and North America.[11]

The main analytic theme of the volume is the Anglo-American concern with "academic drift" in the 1960s and 1970s, a period marked by rapid expansion of higher education in many countries.[12] The main issues identified in the book are that "...general economic problems have caused governments to cut back on funding for universities. Demographic and economic factors have caused a downturn in enrollment in the industrialised nations".[13] The issues regarded as central in this book thus stem primarily from Anglo-American contexts and concerns.

The book makes no effort to synthesise the issues discussed in each chapter in a comparative conclusion, a point which Altbach, as Editor, notes in his Introduction:

> Comparative analysis of higher education in general and of the academic profession in particular is rare, and difficult to undertake because of the many national differences involved and the expense of such research (see Altbach, 1977). The chapters in this volume are case studies of specific countries, and it is left to the reader to discern relevant comparison [sic].14

Thus, the book offers little, conceptually and descriptively, for the comparative analysis of the formation of the academic profession in other social contexts and other times.

Similarly, Burton Clark's comparative discussion in *The Academic Profession: National, Disciplinary, and Institutional Settings*[15] is limited to northwestern Europe and the United States. The countries in this volume are the United Kingdom, the Federal Republic of Germany, France and the United States. The rationale is that they are considered "the major international centres of learning". Although Burton Clark indicates that this book is an international comparison to explore the variety and uniformity of the academic profession, the main emphasis in the text is on the enormous variety in "American higher education".[16] The conceptual apparatus used for the comparative analysis of the academic profession in this book is based on three categories: nation, discipline and institution.[17] However, they are used only to analyse the structural foundations of the Western academic profession in the 1980s.[18] The book does not cover a wide range of time and space—and does not consider East Asia.

Among the work by the agencies, a wide-ranging comparison of the academic profession was made by the Carnegie Foundation in 1994 in its Report, *The Academic Profession: an International Perspective*. The fourteen countries included in the survey were Australia, Brazil, Chile, Germany, Hong Kong, Israel, Japan, (South) Korea, Mexico, the Netherlands, Russia [sic], Sweden, the United Kingdom, and the United States.[19] The point of the comparison:

> ... was to learn more about the condition of the professoriate from a larger perspective and, in the process, define priorities that could strengthen the academy worldwide....The result is, we believe, the most comprehensive view of the professoriate available today [1994].20

The Carnegie Foundation Report offers contemporary portraits of the academic profession in these fourteen countries through seven major themes: (i) the individual national contexts of the institutional framing of the professoriate; (ii) access to higher education; (iii) professional activities; (iv) working conditions of faculty; (v) governing the academy; (vi) higher education and society; and (vii) the international dimensions of academic life. Within these seven themes, the information provided in this report is analysed in two categories: (i) variations (e.g. on student access, teaching and research, and support for academic freedom) (ii) similarities among faculty (e.g. the need for better methods of evaluating teaching, a commitment to service to help solve societal problems, as well as concern over the governance of higher education).[21] The Carnegie Foundation survey offers, in these categories, substantial *descriptions* of the academic profession in the fourteen countries.

However, the weakness of the Report is its lack of theoretical foundation. The Report discusses differences and similarities among the participating countries on issues such as salary, job satisfaction, means of governance and evaluation. The Carnegie Foundation Report is concerned with the socio-psychological aspects of academic life, on the assumption that there are common characteristics of the academic profession across different cultures.[22]

This is empirical research—a survey—without an account of why the seven themes were selected. The Carnegie Foundation research does not provide a new typology of the academic professions in different countries and different time periods, nor does it provide a theoretical analysis of the "changing shape" of the academic profession in the respective countries. For the purposes of this book, the comparative usefulness of the Carnegie Foundation Report is mainly in its statistical information about the academic profession in 1994 in South Korea and in other participating countries.[23]

The Carnegie Report was however influential. It affected the work of

Sungho Lee[24], U. Teichler and F. Van Vught[25]; and the recent work of Anthony Welch, on the academic profession.[26] The work of Van Vught and Teichler concentrates primarily on Europe.[27] The work of Welch, however, is more interesting as he raises fresh concerns, although the work by no means solves the problem of how to look at the academic profession in East Asia.[28]

In the Special Issue of *Higher Education: the International Journal of Higher Education and Educational Planning* which he edited, Welch stresses in his editorial introduction the changing pedagogical traditions in the contemporary university.[29] He points out new relationships between teacher and learner, following the massive growth of higher education and the introduction of new technology in higher education.[30] Welch also edited another Special Issue on the academic profession (*Comparative Education Review* Vol. 42, No. 1, February 1998).[31] In the first article, 'The End of Certainty? The Academic Profession and the Challenge of Change', Welch reflects on the cases of the fourteen countries surveyed in the Carnegie Foundation Research. The article relies on data from the Carnegie Foundation Report, but Welch attempts to conceptualise the shifting culture of higher education in the context of globalisation.

He argues that the culture of the academic profession is shifting dramatically, with closer ties between the 'performativity' of higher education and national economic growth. Consequently, there is a widening breach between the professoriate and university administrators, with signs of a growing managerialism within universities, in which a technocratic logic of efficiency and economy prevails and collegiality succumbs increasingly to more hierarchical modes of decision making.[32] Welch also points out that the cult of efficiency in universities has been accompanied by increasing financial pressures.[33] As Welch notes, "In the name of accountability, academics have become subject to measurement by performance indicators. In the name of quality, academics' time is increasingly governed by the technology of total quality management (TQM) in which style can overwhelm substance".[34]

Overall, then, on Welch's argument, the academic profession is assailed by a managerial hierarchy, by a business ideology in universities, by economistic conceptions of education held by governments and profit-oriented industries related to higher education. The result is loss of tenure, loss of status in a context of cost-effectiveness and the prevailing notion of a "do more with less" culture.[35] Welch's analysis then is critical and thoughtful and takes up—nor least on the basis of information provided by the Carnegie Report—themes of the evaluative State and the entrepreneurial university and the shift in definitions of "quality" already opened up by scholars such as Berdahl, Clark, Cowen, Lewis, Neave, and Watson.[36]

However, there are three central difficulties with the categories of analysis used by the Carnegie Commission and by Welch.

First, the analyses of the Carnegie Commission and Welch tend to impose Anglo-American concerns as topics of relevance for comparative work. Second, their analyses use convergence assumptions, i.e. there is a world-wide convergence of the patterns of higher education. Thirdly as higher education systems are becoming the same, by extension the academic profession, and its concerns, are assumed to be becoming the same everywhere. However, this 'convergence' hypothesis—while it has some obvious contemporary evidence in its favour—makes it difficult to remain alert to the particular shapes of the academic profession in particular countries. Studies of the academic profession are being culturally decontextualised—paradoxically in the name of comparative education.[37] Contemporary studies of the academic profession are in danger of being ethnocentric—placing Anglo-American experience at the centre of the conceptual apparatus for thinking about the academic profession everywhere. Furthermore, if it is 'well known' via the empirical work of the Carnegie Commission survey that academics everywhere share the same concerns, or if it is 'well known' through the work of Welch that convergence around the themes of efficiency is occurring, then any other differences between academic professions are trivial. An imposition of Anglo-American interpretations of the 'significant issues' for the academic profession will have occurred, within an insistently contemporary comparative analysis. Such insistently contemporary analyses are ahistorical, and take a very short time perspective to 'understand' why things are as they are. The studies offer little comparative account of the social dynamics of how things *became* as they are. In contrast, in this book, it is argued that it is important to identify the historical context of specific political and economic conditions in particular countries which, even if in the end they produce some symptoms of 'convergence', can permit an *explanation* of apparent convergence.

It is the argument of this book that the *longue duree* of the struggles between the State and the university in these East Asian countries is a complex story of the social construction of different academic professions. Further, it is argued that to tell this tale with delicacy it is necessary to clarify conceptions of the State, the university and the social role of the 'man of knowledge', which are tightly related to particular histories of colonial and post-colonial State projects.

Thus, the central thrust of this book is to demonstrate that the academic profession is not the same everywhere and to illustrate comparatively why this is so. To begin this task a considerable excursion into concepts of the State and the university and the social role of the man of knowledge is necessary. The academic profession is formed at the intersection of the social struggles over these concepts and their institutionalisation. The book begins with the suggestion that concepts of the State, the university and the social role of the 'man of knowledge' are not the same everywhere—and that defining the shaping and the shape of the academic profession requires comparative attention to such major concepts and their changing institutionalisation, over time.

This then is the methodological perspective of this book. The emphasis on the comparative conceptualisation of the academic professions, and their location within their particular histories in time and space, leads to the avoidance of the classical methodologies of the comparative education of the 1960s and 1970s, which tended (with the rejection of Hans) to be ahistorical. Similarly the book has made the methodological choice to reject the normal models of 'a profession'. As argued, these models also tend to be ahistorical, and to disguise the struggles over power which occur in the creation of professions. The methodological perspective of the book begins in the outline of different conceptual apparatus, concentrating on university and state relations.

The next chapter will review classic 'ideas of a university' in Europe by Newman and Jaspers and in East Asia by Confucius to establish ideal typical models of the University in the English, German and Confucian traditions. This will—later—permit the highlighting of an 'East Asian' configuration of the university, and the East Asian academic professions.

NOTES

1. The concept of East Asia in this book is based on the geographic definition used in the existing literature. (For reference, see Berger, Peter L., and Hsin-Huang Michael Hsiao (eds). *In search of an East Asian Development Model.* New Brunswick, N. J.: Transaction Publishers, 1988; Berger, M. T. and D. A. Borer (eds). *The Rise of East Asia: Critical Visions of the Pacific Century.* London and New York: Routledge, 1997; Brook, Timothy, and Hy V. Luong (eds). *Culture and Economy: The Shaping of Capitalism in Eastern Asia.* Michigan, Ann Arbor: The University of Michigan Press, 1997; Murphey, Rhoads. *East Asia: A New History.* New York: Longman Inc., 1996.)

The geographic location of Korea; South Korea is conventionally defined as Northeast Asia and that of Malaya; Malaysia and Singapore as Southeast Asia. However, the concept of "East Asia" is currently used to denote the so-called NICs (Newly Industrialising countries) in both Northeast and Southeast Asian countries. For example, Berger and Borer noted "the rapid economic growth of East Asia (particularly Japan, South Korea, Taiwan, Hong Kong and Singapore) was already setting the region apart from the rest of the world by the 1970s. By the 1980s, the trend was seen to have spread southward to Thailand, Malaysia and Indonesia". (M. T. Berger and D. A. Borer (eds)., op. cit., p. 1) In their book "East Asia" was conceptualised as the Asia-Pacific region in the context of the political economic transition from the Cold War to the post-Cold War era. Timothy Brook and Hy V. Luong also used the concept of "East Asia" as a single unit that includes South Korea, Malaysia and Singapore, referring to the "remarkable expansion of capitalism in Eastern Asia". (T. Brook and Hy V. Luong (eds)., op. cit., p. 1)

2. Lieberman, M., *Education as a Profession,* Englewood Cliffs, N. J.: Prentice-Hall, Inc., 1956; Dingwall, R. and P. Lewis (eds). *Sociology of the Profession,* London: Macmillan, 1983; Bledstein, Burton J. *The Culture of Professionalism,* New York: Norton, 1976; Macdonald, K. M., *The Sociology of the Professions,* London: Sage Publications, 1995; Middlehurst, R. 'Professionals, Professionalism and Higher Education For Tomorrow's World' in F. Coffield (ed). *Higher Education in a Learning Society'* Durham: School of Education, University of Durham on behalf of DfEE, ESRC and HEFCE, 1995, pp. 34-44.

3. Lieberman, M., op. cit., p. 18.

4. Freidson, E. *Professionalism reborn: theory, prophecy & policy.* Chicago: University of Chicago Press, 1994; Siegrist, H. The Professions, State and Government in Theory and History, in *Government and Professional Education,* edited by T. Becher. Buckingham: SRHE & Open University, 1994, pp. 3-22; Torstendahl, R., M. Burrage (eds). *The Formation of Professions: Knowledge, State and Strategy.* London: Sage Publications, 1990.

5. By the extension of this general sociological definition of the professions, the historical formation of professions in relation to the State was examined notably by Magali Sarfatti Larson's *The Rise of Professionalism: a Sociological Analysis* and Terry Johnson's 'Expertise and the State' in *Foucault's New Domains* (edited by Mike Gane and Terry Johnson, London & New York: Routledge, 1993, pp. 139-152).
Larson, in *The Rise of Professionalism: a Sociological Analysis,* considers the professional phenomenon from a double perspective: first, "as structural elements of the general form of the professional project, and second, as specific resource elements whose variable import is defined by different historical matrices". (Larson, M. op. cit., 1977, p. 212) As structural elements, these characteristics appear in various combinations in all the modern professions. As resources, however, they are qualitatively different in different historical contexts and therefore they vary in import or "useableness". In tracing the historical formation of the professions, Larson considers the cases of Britain and the United States in the 19th century, in a Marxian perspective.
In the capitalist social formations of these Anglo-Saxon societies, Larson provides an account of the emerging significance of professional training and the need for public recognition of tested competence so as to objectify professional privilege and the market value of professional service. According to Larson, the creation of professional commodities, and their unified definition ultimately necessitated the State's monopolistic appropriation and organisation of a social system of education and credentialing. Larson notes that the relation of market value and specific professional services appears to be ideological, as "it functions more as an implicit justification for the prices of the professional commodity and for the privileges associated with professional work, than as the actual quantitative translation of "aver-

age socially necessary labour time" into market value." (ibid.)

On the other hand, Johnson analyses the profession by incorporating Foucault's concept of 'governmentality'. He suggests that the State forms, in the context of the exercise of power, systems of technique and instrumentality of governance. The power relations in governance are not a relationship of domination, but the probability that the normalised subject will habitually obey, through which the legitimacy of power in the modern state can be regenerated. Consequently, the rise of the modern professions is construed in terms of the process of the reproduction of the self-regulating subject to form the tacit agreement of government apparatus as defined earlier. The emergent cognitive and normative patterns of political authority have not only generated the popular legitimation underpinning the government apparatus, but also induced what Stanley Cohen has called a profound shift in the 'master patterns of social control'. (Cohen, S. *Visions of Social Control,* Cambridge: Polity Press, 1985; Johnson, T. 'Expertise and the State', op. cit., 1993.)

More recently, S. Slaughter and L. Leslie' *Academic Capitalism: Politics, Policies, and the Entrepreneurial University* used professionalisation theory (developed from Larson, M. S. *The Rise of Professionalism: A Sociological Analysis,* Berkeley: University of California Press, 1977) and resource dependence theory (developed from Pfeffer, Jeffrey, & Gerald R. Salancik, *External Control of Organizations: A Resource Dependence Perspective,* New York: Harper and Row, 1978; Brint, S. G. *In an Age of Experts: The Changing Role of Professionals in Politics and Public Life,* Princeton: Princeton University Press, 1994). For details, see Slaughter, S. & Leslie, L. L., *Academic Capitalism: Politics, Policies and the Entrepreneurial University,* Baltimore & London: The Johns Hopkins University Press, 1997.

6. For example, Harold J. Perkin, *Key Profession: the History of the Association of University Teachers,* London: Routledge & Kegan Paul, 1969; A. H. Halsey, *Decline of Donnish Dominion: the British Academic Professions in the Twentieth Century,* Oxford: Clarendon Press, 1992; H. R. Bowen & J. H. Schuster, *American Professors: A National Resource Imperiled,* Oxford: Oxford University Press, 1986.
Harold J. Perkin's *Key Profession: the History of the Association of University Teachers* is a historical investigation of the rise of the English university teacher to the key role in the reproduction of society and its mastery of the physical and social environment from about 1920 until 1969. However, it is argued that behind Perkin's term, key profession there is a standard set by the ideal-type of the profession forged in the Anglo-Saxon context.
A. H. Halsey's *Decline of Donnish Dominion: the British Academic Professions in the Twentieth Century* investigates the academic profession in Britain from the mid-1960s until the early 1990s. That is to say, the book covers the history of British higher education from the beginning of the period of expansion associated with the Robbins Report until the period of the Thatcher government, during which education was put at the top of the British political agenda. Halsey's examination relies

on his own surveys of the behaviour and opinion of the academic staff conducted in each decade during the time period. The surveys offer a systematic account of the changing disciplinary composition, material conditions, status, attitudes, orientations, and morale of the academic staff in British higher education. In short, the core of his research interest in the academic profession is sociological account of changes in the structure and functions of the academic profession since the Robbins Report.

H. R. Bowen & J. H. Schuster, *American Professors: A National Resource Imperiled* describes the conditions and major concerns of the 1980s related to the American academic profession. It provides a explicit taxonomy of the academic profession in America. In the introduction and the conclusion, the purpose of the book is indicated as offering policy advice to officials in the universities and the state governments. The book intends to warn against the future deterioration of quality of those in the academic profession, through the idea that the academic profession is likely to become less and less attractive for highly able young people, over the next twenty five years or so, from 1985 to 2010.

7. For example, see Clark, B. (ed). *The Academic Profession: National, Disciplinary, and International Settings,* Berkeley: University of California Press, 1987, which was initially sponsored by the Rockefeller Foundation; Boyer, E.L., Altbach, P.G., Whitelaw, M.J. (eds). *The Academic Profession: an International Perspective,* Princeton: The Carnegie Foundation for the Advancement of Teaching, 1994; Kogan, M. Moses, I. & El-Khawas, E., *Staffing Higher Education: Meeting New Challenges,* London: Jessica Kingsley Publishers, OECD, 1994; Blumenthal, P. et. al., *Academic Mobility in a Changing World: Regional and Global Trends,* London: Jessica Kingsley Publishers, 1996.

The book of M. Kogan, I. Moses, and E. El-Khawas, *Staffing Higher Education: Meeting New Challenges,* was published as the final report of a funded research project by the OECD in 1994, and offers another frame of reference for the Western academic profession in the contemporary period. The purpose of this book was to provide practical guidance for policy makers in higher education at both the system and the institutional levels in the OECD member countries. Unlike the other comparative books being reviewed, this book is not structured by national settings, but by common issues in the OECD member countries.

Themes used in this book are: (i) staffing, (ii) changing frameworks for the academic profession such as expansion, changes in funding, governance and management and evaluation of higher education, (iii) changes in the nature and forms of task required of academic staff (e.g. teaching, scholarship, research, consultancy, community service and administration), (iv) changes in staffing structures in response to new demands (e.g. increasing part-time appointments), (v) policies and practices: qualifications and staff development, implications of graduate education for academic staffing policies, conditions of service including tenure and length of appointment and salaries and other rewards. Thus, the book extends some academic issues raised in a limited number of OECD countries to the level of general key points related to "all OECD countries". (Among the OECD member countries, the book especially focuses on the cases of the U.K., the U.S.A., Canada, Australia and Northwest European countries such as the Netherlands and Germany. The Japanese case is not dealt with in a separate chapter, but is sporadically mentioned for comparison. The cases of Central and Eastern European countries are not separately dealt with either, even though differences with the Western European countries are strong in a region where the institutions of higher education were still run by a centralised bureaucracy.) However, this conceptual frame for the analyses of OECD member countries follows the major issues in Anglo-American contexts. The full conclusion of the book is:

University decisions on academic staffing have been broadly affected by changes in the external environment over the last few decades. As already discussed at length, these changes have included a tightening financial climate and the pressures of accommodating larger students numbers and participation rates. Another environmental change that has affected staffing decisions is a general move, in all OECD countries, towards a social policy of encouraging greater participation of women and ethnic minorities in all arenas of life. (ibid., p. 111)

8. Altbach, P.G. (ed). *Comparative Perspectives on the Academic Profession*, New York: Praeger Publishers, 1977; Clark, B. R. (ed). op. cit.; Kogan, M., Moses, I. and El-Khawas, E., op. cit.; Boyer, E. L., Altbach, P. G., and Whitelaw, M. J., op. cit..

9. Altbach, P.G. (ed)., op. cit.

10. There are a total of ten chapters in the volume and six chapters are allocated to the Anglo-Saxon professoriate: two chapters for the Canadian case, two chapters for the American case, one chapter for Australia, and one chapter for Britain. The book also includes separate chapters on Japan, Latin America, and India.

11. The terminology in this book is loose—with an emphasis on the concept of staff—"professor", "teacher", "lecturer", "academic staff", and "faculty". All these terms were used to describe the academic profession.

12. Ibid., pp. 1-7.

13. Ibid., p. 7.

14. Ibid., p. 6.

15. Clark, B. R. (ed)., op. cit.

16. Ibid., pp. 1-10.

17. Ibid., pp. 371-398.

18. Burton Clark suggests that disciplinary and institutional settings are essential categories to understand the academic profession in context to grasp the comparative significance of differences between stereotype and reality:

Large areas of similarity may still exist, but they ought to be found, not assumed. They ought to be induced from empirical observation, not deduced from traditional images and statements of personal preference. (ibid., p. 3)

For example, in Chapter Five, Guy Neave and Gary Rhoades offer a broad juxtaposition of the Anglo-American academic "profession" and the Western European academics as an "estate" to analyse the academic profession in the organisational and disciplinary settings. In Chapter Six, Tony Becher deals with the disciplinary context. He investigates the academic profession in the perspectives of (Western) sociology of knowledge, social studies of science, and the study of higher education. (Neave, G. & Rhoades, G., 'The Academic Estate in Western Europe' in B. R. Clark (ed)., op. cit., pp. 211-270.) The chapter deals with the core issues of Tony Becher's major book, *Academic Tribes and Territories: Intellectual Enquiry and the Cultures of Disciplines,* which was published in 1989. He shows the ways in which disciplines contribute to the shaping of the academic profession: (i) different forms of knowledge characterised as hard-pure, soft-pure, hard-applied, and soft-applied; (ii) how recruits are attracted and initiated, i.e. academic routes; (iii) the nature of social interaction within a field—so-called cosmopolitans and the locals in Gouldner's terms (For details, see Gouldner, Alvin W. "Locals and Cosmopolitans." *Administrative Science Quarterly* 1, no. 2 (1957): 281-306; 444-480; (iv) the type and degree of specialisation within it; and (v) the modes of change in international structures and external boundaries of fields and in the career lines of those in the academic profession. For details, see Becher, T., 'The Disciplinary Shaping of the Profession' in B. R., Clark (ed)., op. cit., p. 7 and pp. 271-303; Becher, T., *Academic Tribes and Territories: intellectual enquiry and the cultures of disciplines,* Bristol: The Society for Research into Higher Education & Open University Press, 1989.

19. Boyer, E., P. G. Altbach and M. J. Whitelaw (eds)., op. cit.

20. Ibid., pp. 1-2.

21. Ibid.

22. Ibid.

23. First, according to the Carnegie Foundation Research, the Korean academic profession is staffed mainly by males. The Korean case shows the second highest proportion of male faculty; of the surveyed academics only 13 % in Korea and 8 % in Japan were female.
Second, according to the Carnegie Survey, Korean academics along with Japanese

academics were the least content in terms of relationships between faculty and administration. However, the Koreans—50 % of the surveyed academics—showed stronger approval of the government's role in defining the overall purposes and policies for higher education than the Japanese—only 19% of the surveyed academics agreed. This opinion also contrasts with the case of the United States where only 10 % of the surveyed academics agreed.

Also, in Korea, as in the United States more than one-third of the academics agreed that there are political or ideological restrictions on what a scholar can publish, which is interpreted by the Carnegie Foundation Report as being a clue to governmental oversight in Korea and the pressure of "political correctness" in the United States. At the same time, 89 % of the Korean academics surveyed—the highest proportion among the fourteen countries participating in the Carnegie Research—agreed that there is far too much governmental interference in important academic policies. Only 3 % of the Korean academics disagreed.

Nevertheless, the majority of Korean academics (90 %) expressed the view that they are fully free to determine the content of the courses they teach. This is again the highest level of agreement among the surveyed countries—for instance, 62 % in the United Kingdom; 78 % in United States; 80 % in Japan.

The Carnegie analysis continues—somewhat interminably—along the same lines: reporting perceptions of academics about such issues as their status as opinion makers and the international experience of the academic profession.

In terms of academics' self perception of the social role of the academic profession, the Korean case also showed the highest level of agreement that academics are among the most influential opinion leaders in the country—63 % of Korean academics surveyed agreed and only 8 % disagreed. In contrast, there was 40 % agreement in Japan; 21 % in the United States and 11 % in the United Kingdom. Also, a high proportion of Korean academics agreed with a professional obligation to apply their knowledge to problems in society.

Some of the questions in the Carnegie Foundation Research are directly related to the level of international activities of the academic profession. For instance, academic mobility was lowest in Korea along with Russia. The perception of Korean academics of their students' experience of studying abroad was also the lowest level of frequency among the countries surveyed—1 % frequently; 11 % occasionally; 58 % rarely; 30 % never. In contrast, the case of Japan shows the highest level as 53 % frequently; 28 % occasionally; 14 % rarely; 5 % never.

In terms of the academic experience of serving as a faculty member at an institution in another country, however, Korean academics along with the Japanese were the second least experienced, next to the Brazilian academics—only 7 % of the Korean academics had served once or more overseas and 93 % had no such experience.

As a consequence of Korean academics' low level of international experience, as indicated in the Carnegie Report, the Korean academics showed strong agreement with the idea that a scholar must read books and journals published abroad, to keep up with developments in his or her discipline—as 96 % of the Korean academics agreed in the survey. Similarly in Japan, 93 % of the academics agreed; in contrast, however, in the United States, only 62 % agreed. There is a strong desire of Korean academics to make connections with scholars in other countries for their professional work—the second highest level (91%) next to the case of Chile (95%). In contrast, academics in the United Kingdom and the United States show the lowest level of enthusiasm for an international academic network—63 % and 55 % respectively.

24. As a Korean contributor to the Carnegie Foundation research, Sungho Lee published his own book in Korean, *The Korean Academic Profession* in 1992. His book provides a lot of detailed information about the Korean academic profession, contained in the same frame of analysis as the Carnegie Foundation research, which was constructed on the basis of surveys of the "opinions" of those in the academic profession.

It is suggested that a particular weakness of Sungho Lee's book is in the fact that his conceptual apparatus to analyse the Korean academic profession relies on the existing American frame of analysis. For instance, the existing "American" literature on the academic profession is quoted in every chapter. In addition, when there is no relevant information about the Korean case, Sungho Lee uses the American case as substitute without any clarification of why the American model needs to replace the Korean case in his analysis. There is no attempt to make a historical contextualisation of the shape of the Korean academic profession. Sungho Lee's book as a national report on the academic profession lacks comparative significance for this book. (For details, see Lee, Sungho. *Hankookeuy Daehack Kyosoo [The Korean Academic Profession]*. Seoul: Hack-ji Sa, 1992.)

25. Following the Carnegie Foundation Research data on the academic profession, *Inside Academia: New Challenges for the Academic Profession* edited by Peter A. M. Maassen & Frans A. Van Vught, Utrecht, The Netherlands: Centre for Higher Education Policy Studies (CHEPS), 1996, is especially focused on the analysis of the Western European academic profession in the changing conditions of higher education. The book deals with common issues of higher education mainly in the selected Western European countries, and the U.S.A. in the following three divisions: the academic profession, governance, and quality. Teichler's chapter included in the first part of this book is based on the 1992 Survey initiated by the Carnegie Foundation. Using some of the major outcomes of the Carnegie Foundation research, Teichler discusses general aspects of the academic profession in Japan, the U.S.A. and four Western European countries—Germany (only Western Germany), the Netherlands, Sweden and the United Kingdom (only England).

26. Thus, since the Carnegie Foundation Research Report came out, there has been a substantial increase in the literature on the academic profession: e.g. Sungho Lee's *The Korean Academic Profession* (1992), *Inside Academia: New Challenges for the Academic Profession* (1996) edited by Frans A. Van Vught, and two journals: *Higher Education, the International Journal of Higher Education and Educational Planning* Vol. 34, No. 3 October 1997 and *Comparative Education Review* Vol. 42, No. 1 February 1998 both of which are edited by Anthony Welch as Special Issues

on the academic profession.

27. U. Teichler, 'The Conditions of the Academic Profession: an international, comparative analysis of the academic profession in Western Europe, Japan and the USA' in Maassen, P. A. M. and F. A. Van Vught (eds)., op. cit., 1996, pp. 15-68.

28. For example, the Special Issue of *Higher Education: the International Journal of Higher Education and Educational Planning* Vol. 34, No. 3 October 1997 is a publication which follows the Carnegie Foundation Research on the academic profession. Articles included in the Special Issue were written by researchers who actually participated in the Carnegie Foundation Research. It is notable, however, that all of the ten contributors to the Special Issue are from the Western industrialised countries: Australia, U.S.A. and Germany and that they deal with the issues significant mainly in the industrialised world—e.g. internationalisation, academic mobility, gender issues, and changing working conditions of the academic profession.
In the Special Issue, non-Western cases—Japan and South Korea were compared in two articles which were written on the basis of the Carnegie International Survey of the Academic Profession. The article 'The academic research-teaching nexus in eight advanced-industrialised countries' by Esther E. Gottlieb & Bruce Keith, deals with some non-Western countries on the basis of the Carnegie Foundation Research Survey to examine the international dimension of the research-teaching nexus in the former West Germany, United Kingdom, Sweden, the United States, Australia, Israel, Japan, and South Korea. The article 'A victim of their own success? Employment and working conditions of academic staff in comparative perspective' by Jürgen Enders & Ulrich Teichler examines academic status and functions in Germany, the Netherlands, Sweden and England and in some subsections, the case of the Japanese academic profession appears.
It is notable that Japan is the most frequently included non-western country. However, the rationale for the occasional inclusion and exclusion of the Japanese case in the comparative analysis is not clear.

29. Welch, A. 'All change?: The professoriate in uncertain times' in *Higher Education: the International Journal of Higher Education and Educational Planning* Vol. 34, No. 3 October 1997, pp. 299-300.

30. In the new modes of pedagogy in higher education, the formerly defined physical space as the central feature of the traditional university has been extended by being incorporated into an electronic virtual space, where academic communication between scholars across continents is easily made without ever needing face to face contact. (ibid.)

31. There are five articles included in the volume. Two articles by Postiglione and Ehara examine respectively Hong Kong, and Japan in comparison with the United States. The data used in Ehara's article were from the Carnegie Foundation International Survey of the Academic Profession. Jürgen Enders looks at the

European dimension of academic staff mobility in his article, 'Academic Staff Mobility in the European Community: the ERASMUS Experience'. (Postiglione, Gerard A. 'Maintaining Global Engagement in the Face of National Integration in Hong Kong' in *Comparative Education Review,* Vol. 42, No. 1, February 1998, pp. 30-45; Ehara, Takekazu ' Faculty Perceptions of University Governance in Japan and the United States', op. cit., pp. 61-70; Enders, J_rgen, 'Academic Staff Mobility in the European Community: The ERASMUS Experience' op. cit., pp. 46-60.)

32. Welch, A. R. 'The End of Certainty? The Academic Profession and the Challenge of Change' in *Comparative Education Review* Vol. 42, Special Issue on the Academic Profession, February 1998, p. 9.

33. A fiscal crisis in academia has meant rising pressure for staffing flexibility and a decline in tenure rates. Currently, almost 40 per cent of U.S. academic appointments are part-time. (For details, see Slaughter, S. 'Introduction to Special Issue on Retrenchment' in *Journal of Higher Education* 64, May/June 1993, Quoted by Welch, A. R. op. cit., 1998.)

34. Said, E. W. *Representations of the Intellectual.* London: Vintage, 1994, Quoted by Welch, A. R., op. cit., 1998.

35. Welch, A. R., op. cit., 1998, p. 14.

36. Berdahl, R. O. et. al., *Quality and Access in Higher Education: Comparing Britain and the United States,*Buckingham: SRHE & Open University Press, 1991; Clark, B. R. *Creating Entrepreneurial Universities: Organizational Pathways of Transformation,* Oxford: Pergamon, Published for the IAU Press, 1998; Lewis, M. *Academic Quality in Higher Education: a Guide to Good Practice in Framing Regulations,* London: Council for National Academic Awards, 1992; Cowen, R. (ed). *The World Yearbook of Education: The Evaluation of Higher Education Systems.* London: Kogan Page, 1996; Neave, G. and F. van Vught. *Prometheus Bound: the changing relationship between government and higher education in Western Europe.* Oxford: Pergamon Press, 1991; Watson, K. et. al. *Educational Dilemmas: Debate & Diversity—Vol. 4: Quality in Education,* London: Cassell, 1997.

37. It should be noted here that theories of convergence do not speak to the ways in which higher education policies are translated into practice in the particular context of a country. The similarities of the shape of the academic profession in different countries may not be in causal relation with political and economic similarities.

CHAPTER TWO

Ideal Typical Models

The purpose of this chapter is to set out a fresh way to think about the shape of the academic profession. It will establish ideal typical models of the university and the State, through which the conventional views of the 'East Asian State' and the social role of the 'man of knowledge' can be critically reconsidered.

The chapter is organised in three subsections: the first two sections establish ideal typical models of the university and the State, and the last section of this chapter will outline a way to think about the East Asian academic professions since colonial times.

THE IDEAL TYPICAL MODELS OF THE UNIVERSITY

The main purpose of this section is to set up three ideal typical models of the university from the writings of Newman, Jaspers and Confucius.
The argument in this section is that despite their colonial origins, the universities of (and the academic profession in) Korea, Malaysia and Singapore have diverged from the European university models and academic professions of the late nineteenth and early twentieth centuries. Thus, an initial task is to clarify classical visions of "the university" in Europe.

To establish a base line for comparison a treatment is offered of the English and German universities, as ideal-typical models following the thinking of Newman and Jaspers. Then Confucius' idea will be reviewed as an ideal-typical model with potential relevance to the university in East Asia.

In these ideal typical models, three aspects are stressed: the nature of knowledge; university and state relations; and the concept of the academic. These three aspects begin to provide a conceptual frame of reference for investigating the formation of the academic profession in Korea, Malaysia and Singapore, not least by the contrasts which are offered by the

European models and Asian realities.

The first theme then is Newman's 'idea of the university', which is analysed on three dimensions: the nature of knowledge; university and state relations; and the concept of the academic.

Newman's Idea of the University

The nature of knowledge

There is already a considerable literature that discusses the English tradition of liberal education that was extended by Newman.[1] In this tradition of liberal education,[2] Newman offers a view of knowledge:

> There are two ways of using Knowledge, and in matter of fact those who use it in one way are not likely to use it in the other, or at least in a very limited measure. One way is philosophical and the other is mechanical; the one rises towards general ideas, the other is exhausted upon what is particular and external.[3]

This view of the nature of knowledge is at the centre of the tradition of liberal education.[4] Thus Newman differentiates education for liberal knowledge from instruction to acquire information:

> Education is a "higher" word than instruction; it implies "an action upon our mental nature, and the formation of a character"; it is individual and permanent, and is commonly spoken of in connexion with religion and virtue.[5]

Thus, in Newman's discourse, liberal forms of education are useful in the sense that education elevates the mind. Liberal education is about free speculation, breadth, and disinterest.[6]

Liberal education in the university, then, should enable persons to develop and articulate their ideas with eloquence, focus and clarity. An intellect cultivated through liberal education should bring power and grace to every work it undertakes: it should enlarge the mind.[7]

In the European Enlightenment tradition, Newman sets out his definition of the university "as its name professes" as a place for teaching "universal knowledge."[8] What he meant by universal knowledge is a principle or criterion of a non-exclusive epistemology (which includes theology as a science, through the Roman Catholic doctrine of God).[9]

Newman argues that universal knowledge pursued in liberal education enables students to interpret and systematise what they perceive. Therefore, universal knowledge through liberal education has powers which enable students to master any subject. Professional studies, in this regard, should never displace the Liberal Arts education at the university, for partial maps of knowledge are dangerous as well as inadequate.

In short, according to Newman, university education based on universal knowledge is distinct from instruction for a vocation or a profession.[10] The place for such learning is the university.

University and State relations[11]

In the Tractarian Movement, Newman was one of those who objected to the role Parliament took in the affairs of the university, which he regarded as a betrayal of the traditional alignment of the Church of England and Oxford University. Newman distinguishes the function of a university from that of the Roman Catholic Church. The university exists for liberal education, whereas the Church exists for the higher ends of true religious faith.[12]

Accordingly, the university is a place for gentlemen.[13] Newman defines the Gentleman[14] as a person possessing expedient earthly virtue through liberal education (while the Christian is a person of real moral virtue through the teachings, faith and practice of the Roman Catholic Church). In Newman's view, liberal education does not pertain to the ultimate good of a human soul in eternity but is limited to the domains of the 'natural man' and participation in human society.[15] The gentleman educated at the university should be connected with the whole world, not through all careers or occupations, but through leadership positions which are traditionally political or military.[16] Despite strong enthusiasm for the liberal influences of a university education, Newman also admits that truly gentlemanly behaviour can only be acquired in the surroundings of established 'society', which is linked to leadership in the State.[17]

Thus the exact relationship between the University and the Sate is left unclear, though there is a set of assumptions about the qualities of leadership required in government and the professions, expressed in the idea of "the gentleman". The fact that Newman stresses the importance of the relationship of the university (of Oxford) with the Church, and glosses over 'the problem' of the relationship with the State is taken to be important—the State, in Newman's view, and in an ideal-typical model of the 'English' university, should have a weak or very minimal relationship with the university, and thus with academics.

The concept of the academic

As in the case of university and state relations, Newman does not specify in detail the concept of an academic. However, Newman's concept of an academic is traceable by examining *The Idea of a University*, which reflects his former experience as a Tutor at Oriel College and as Vicar at Saint Mary's Church in Oxford.

The Oxford collegiate system was modelled on medieval monastic institutions,[18] and the unique English tutorial system helps to define the concept of the academic in the English context. In *The Idea of a University*, Newman perceived the university as a particular kind of community. The education of youthful scholars was more important than instruction alone.[19] The creation of a particular intellectual, linguistic or cultural environment was more important than academic achievement itself.[20]

Thus an academic was a member of an educative community. That community and those colleges were autonomous bodies, with their own statutes and privileges.[21] The colleges were autonomous corporations, governed in most cases by their Fellows. Heads of College were elected by the Fellows.[22] These are rather specific qualities for an academic, and are defined by the nature of the internal community.

In their external relations, the academic elite was drawn from the same background as politically powerful groups, and was later linked to them by wide-ranging networks such as the old school tie and freemasonry within the Empire.[23] It is notable in the English case that those in the academic profession—following Newman—were well integrated into the Empire so that they were not detached from the world of leadership, decision making and opinion-forming.[24] In line with Newman's idea of university education, up to the First World War, the paradigm of a university teacher in England was the Oxbridge college don; his aim was to produce not a book but a person.[25]

Thus, in an ideal typical model derived from Newman, the nature of knowledge in the English university is liberal knowledge, based on the classical literary canon, for cultivation, i.e. the enlargement of the mind. The university based on the English collegiate system is run by an autonomous community of academics, the Oxford dons who are devoted to the transmission of a tradition of high culture. Pursuing liberal knowledge for its own end is, therefore, the educational goal of the university.

Within the same categories as those used for Newman's *The Idea of a University,* the book will review Jaspers' *The Idea of the University*[26] in the next section to construct an ideal typical model of the German university.

Jaspers' Idea of the University

Jaspers had a rather different view of the nature of knowledge; university and state relations; and the concept of the academic.

The nature of knowledge

Very much within the German tradition and Kant's epistemology,[27] Jaspers' *The Idea of a University* starts with a classic statement: "The University is a community of scholars and students engaged in the task of seeking truth."[28]

Thus Jaspers argues that the university should be much more than a collection of different disciplines. Knowledge is represented by all sciences formed in unity, but subordinated to philosophy which clarifies the sense of truth and cognition.[29] Among the four faculties (i.e., theology, law, medicine and philosophy), only philosophy is ruled by reason, while the other academic disciplines are "ruled by the State".[30] In this view, professional knowledges and specialized learning can also contribute to knowledge as a whole, but only when they are acquired on the basis of philosophy.[31]

For the acquisition of knowledge as such, Jaspers suggests the importance of the three types of education: i.e. scholastic, apprenticeship-training and Socratic. According to Jaspers, the Socratic mode of learning is the best means to achieve the "substance of education",[32] for such teaching is concerned to promote the transcendence of limited concepts of knowledge into the unknown. It is the university that has unique responsibility for the provision of the Socratic mode:

> Its [the university's] principle is to furnish all the tools and offer all possibilities in the province of the intellect, to direct the individual to the frontiers, to refer the learner back to himself for all his decisions, to his own sense of responsibility.[33]

To locate his philosophical concept of truth as the basis for the unity of research and teaching at the university, Jaspers developed the Humboldtian tradition of university and state relations.[34]

University and State relations

Jaspers makes it clear that the university must possess intellectual power that compels the public mind to clarify its thinking and discern its proper objectives.[35] Jaspers finds the *locus* of the university in the *Rechtstaat,* a unique German concept to locate the university in the State. Through institutionalisation, the university becomes a state within the state: while some autonomy is granted to the university, there is also some state control over the correct functioning of the institution. Jaspers writes:

> The university exists through the good graces of the body politic. Its existence is dependent on political considerations. It can only live as and where the state desires.[36] The state makes the university's existence possible and protects it. The state is providing legal and material support for the university.[37]

Although Jaspers perceived that there are tensions between the university and the state, he believed that the state can prevent the university from developing forms of degeneration and corruption. He did not lose his trust in the state as a protector of the university and of academic liberties, in spite of his experience of Nazi Germany.[38] The university can "control the state through the power of truth not of force."[39]

He notes that the *raison d'être* of the university relies on spiritual confidence, not on an economic, or a social justification. Therefore, the aim of the university must be to train the inner being, a form of training attainable only by a few.[40] Jaspers approves of elite education. He justifies the selection of excellence by its eventual benefit for society as a whole.[41] However:

> the state should not treat the universities as if they were higher classical schools or schools of special sciences. On the whole the State should not look to them at all for anything that directly concerns its own interest, but should rather cherish a conviction that, in fulfilling their real destiny, they

will not only serve its own purposes, but serve them on an infinitely higher plane than [being]at the disposal of the state itself.[42]

However, as an inheritor of the Humboldtian tradition of the university,[43]
Jaspers also thought that the university should be established and controlled by the state: all its academic autonomy comes from liberties granted to it by the state.

The concept of the academic

As is the case of Newman, Jaspers' sense of the university was derived
from his own experience as a student and faculty member at the university. In *The Idea of a University*, Jaspers clarifies that the university is "a
community of scholars and students engaged in task of seeking truth"
through research, the transmission of learning and the transmission of culture.[44] The functions of the university—academic teaching, research and
cultural life—combine to form "the unity".[45]

However, Jaspers notes that "The idea of the university lives decisively
in the individual students and professors and only secondarily in the forms
of the institution".[46] "What counts is done by the individual teacher
between the four walls of his classroom where he is free and on his own."[47]
As an autonomous institution, the university unites professionally[48] people
who belong to smaller autonomous units.[49] To safeguard the academic
freedom and autonomy identified with *Bildung*, Jaspers opposed the power
structures of the German university department system. These structures of
the professorially dominated, subject based departmental system were
examples of divisions of knowledge rather than of wholeness.[50]

In summary, Jaspers identifies the nature of knowledge with the task of
seeking truth in a community of scholars and students. Philosophy is then
central in this task through the unity of research and teaching in the university. Jaspers expects reciprocal relations between the state and the university on the basis of trust. The State safeguards university autonomy.
Within this protection by the state, university academics can carry out the
task of seeking truth to influence the State, through the power of truth. In
the German tradition of *Bildung*, Jaspers emphasizes the importance of
integration of knowledge based on communication. The German academic is identified with his autonomy and privilege expressed in the term
Lehrfreiheit.

Newman's and Jaspers' ideas of a university have been used as criteria
to examine the formation of the non-European universities e.g. in the
United States, Japan, Korea, Malaysia and Singapore.[51] In other words, the
existing literature retains the European concepts of the nature of knowledge, university and state relations and the academics, as general frames of
reference even for non-European cases.

To reconceptualise the shape of the academic profession in (South)
Korea, Malaysia and Singapore, it is probably necessary to note that uni-

versities there were in different political, economic and cultural contexts from those of the European university. At the very least it is probably wise to rebalance these two European 'ideas of the university' by looking at an Asian version of 'the university'. This will be done by examining Confucius' idea of the university.

Confucius' Idea of the University

Confucius' idea of the university is examined in the same three categories: the nature of knowledge, university and State relations and the concept of the academic.

The nature of knowledge

It was during the Chinese Han era that a clearly defined Confucian schooling system merged. The Han Emperor, Wu Ti (154-87 B.C.) established formal lectureships in Confucian studies and provided government stipends for scholarly experts on the Five Confucian Classics.[52]

The Chinese Confucians—especially until the Ming pragmatist school of Wang Yang Ming—believed that there was a body of absolute truths, which combined moral principles with cosmological laws, and that this body of knowledge had been already understood and written down by the Confucian sages.[53] This scholastic belief in a body of absolute truths directed energy towards mastering classical writings and standard interpretations.[54] Therefore, Chinese scholarship was dominated by documentary studies that sought to observe and preserve the traditional conventions of the histories and the classics. Study of the Confucian canon was the most valued knowledge in the Confucian State, while astrology and calendar-making played a supporting role. Medicine ranked far down the list and the status of mathematics was even lower. Technology and applied science did not find favour in the Confucian World.[55]

In the Confucian tradition, knowledge is not important in itself; it must be practised, though not pragmatically. Given the emphasis on practising knowledge, some Confucian examination compositions demanded the application of general set rules to a particular situation or problem,[56] and through Chu Hsi's emphasis on self-discipline for the governance of men (*hsiu-chi cihh-jen*), neo-Confucian knowledge was accepted as an ideal for social order throughout East Asia wherever the neo-Confucian curriculum became established.[57]

Confucius, in the *Analects,* argued that learning is for the sake of the self.[58] The Confucian notion of *Tao,* the Way to acquire knowledge, is a basic axiom of Confucian learning stressing self-cultivation and self-realisation. Self-cultivation here means to determine one's proper position in the network of social relationships and to behave properly according to one's position.[59] However, the principle of self-cultivation was applied to everyone, from the ruler down to the common man, with the ruler obliged to set an example for all men of self-restraint, self-correction, and self-improvement.

In that sense, the central concern of Confucian knowledge is how to learn to be human. Learning to be human in Confucian thought is not simply learning the skills of a particular profession or becoming proficient in one specific task. The learning process is continuous and holistic in the Confucian tradition.[60]

In China and Korea, the State organised the education system to transmit this knowledge based on (Neo) Confucian orthodoxy, and subsequently to recruit into government service those who had best mastered the Confucian classics.[61]

University and State relations

In Confucius' view, education is a fundamental obligation of the Confucian State. Education is here taken to mean both the teaching of knowledge and the training of virtuous character. In principle, the Confucian State is responsible for public education.[62]

The Confucian education system was essential for the honest and efficient public administration of the Confucian State.[63] The Confucian examination system functioned to confirm a hierarchical concept of the cosmos and society, although in principle it also promoted upward social mobility based on merit.[64] Wilkinson explains that:

> The Imperial examination system to select the scholar mandarins represented a rational attempt to reward individual talent, yet the classical content of the examinations favoured certain families. As a result, the Chinese Confucian political elite did something to acquire new blood and still preserve an aristocratic aura. This aura was enhanced by an elaborate system of magical devices which government and education together developed.[65]

The Confucian education system provided political, social, ethical and even aesthetic norms in East Asian States such as China and Korea for over two thousand years.[66] Although the Chinese first developed Confucianism, the Koreans have been recognised as more thorough-going in the application of the tenets of Confucianism, through their own independent Confucian State since the 4th century.[67] The last Confucian State in Korea, Chosun, survived for 500 years (1392-1895). [68] In these five hundred years, education was a useful instrument to legitimise Confucian ideology. *Sung Kyun Kwan* served as a national higher education institution in Chosun from 1392. It was primarily a training institution for the higher civil service as was its predecessor, *Kuk Ja Kam* in Koryo (935-1392).[69]

It is noted here that the contemporary university entrance examination system and the civil service examination system in Korea have inherited Confucian ideas about university-state relations since the period of Koryo dynasty (918-1392). Also—as will later be shown—the modern routes to the academic profession in Korea resemble the traditional formations of

academic power groups generated by certain academic clans and their networks (which can be traced back also to the period of Koryo dynasty, 918-
1392). However, this still leaves unexplained the Confucian concept of the
academic.

The Concept of the Academic

As a consequence of the Confucian valuation of learning, being an academic has been highly regarded.[70] In the *Analects*, the Confucian gentleman
scholar, or sage, is not simply viewed as a person to perform an utilitarian
instrumental task.[71]

The Confucian concept of an academic is well captured in the ideal of a
noble man, which connotes one who does his best to effect harmony in
everyday life. The essence of the Confucian way of becoming a 'noble man'
lies in self-cultivation through learning and practice. This reflects
Confucius' faith in the perfectibility of human nature through self-effort.[72]
Thus, within Confucian educational philosophy, there is a strong optimistic
belief that human nature is perfectible through self-effort and thus, every
human being is potentially a sage. Although the highest personality in the
Confucian tradition is the sage-king,[73] Confucian educational philosophy
also embraces a principle of egalitarianism.[74]

However, Confucius advised that that the sovereign should be very careful in appointing a State mandarin; and in turn a great scholar who is prepared for State service should be also careful to select the sovereign who is
to employ him.[75] He must examine the conditions of the State, and the
character of the sovereign before he enters into government service. The
scholar mandarin should do what he believes to be right, even though his
policies may be contrary to the will of the ruler. When the man of knowledge comes into power, he displays his virtue and wisdom by using correctly his power and position in the State.

Thus, the ideal typical model of the Confucian academic is built on the
inseparable combination of morality and politics and in the nexus between
the self-cultivation of the ruler (sage-king) and the scholar mandarins and
the governability of the people.[76]

In the Confucian State, the role of the *sonbi*—the Korean word for the
Confucian gentleman scholar—necessarily involves participation in governance. When the *sonbi* is appointed as a scholar mandarin, he is called
sadaebu[77]—an honorific term for scholar-mandarin, referring to the possibility of movement between the role of scholar and that of the government
official. Government service was not a long-life profession and the
Confucian scholar mandarin could regularly change his role between the
educational and administrative departments of government.

In this ideal typical model, there is no visible tension in the two roles:
the scholar mandarin—*sadaebu*—in the government and the autonomous
academic—*sonbi*—in the university.[78] Through scholarship, the *sonbi* was

also a social leader. He stood at the top of society's four classes—scholars, farmers, artisans, and merchants—complementing the role of those engaged in farming, manufacturing and commerce.[79]

In summary, the ideal typical model of the Confucian academic is epitomised in the concept of a gentleman scholar, *sonbi*. The *sonbi* would discipline himself, govern his family wisely, "rule the country" and pacify the world.

It is noted here—and will be illustrated later—that the idea of the *sonbi*, as a Confucian gentleman-scholar, shaped the new academic profession in the modern private institutions of higher education in Korea during the colonial period.[80]

However, the next section will focus on the State. It is in the tension between the State and the University that much of the social construction of the academic profession takes place. It is important not to assume that conceptions of the State are the same in Western political thought and in the East Asian Confucian tradition. The next section will try to exemplify this point by contrasting the ideas of Locke and Confucius, in anticipation of the later examination of Korea, Malaysia and Singapore.

THE IDEAL TYPICAL MODELS OF THE STATES

In this book, the State is taken to be a major actor in shaping the academic profession. In this section, in reviewing three classic ideas about the State, the underlying assumption is that there may be a 'peculiar' shape to the academic profession in East Asia because the ideological concept of and the historical reality of a social space reserved for academic autonomy are of Western origin, and the East Asian States have not absorbed or respected this idea.

Thus, the purpose of this section is to examine concepts of the State and to consider theoretical ways to think about the modern East Asian State initially by contrasting Locke and Confucius. These two classic conceptions of the State are reviewed in terms of ideas about the origins of the State, the legitimacy of the State, and the obligations of the State to individuals.

In the classic conceptions of the State, the contrast between Locke's idea of social contract and the state of nature and that of Confucius remains remarkable.

Locke's Conception of the State

Locke rejected the Hobbesian notion[81] of a Great Leviathan, pre-eminent in all social spheres, and establishing and enforcing law according to the sovereign's will.

In Locke's opinion—in contrast with Hobbes—the origins of the State do not signal the transfer of all rights of a subject to the sovereign.[82] Sovereignty remains ultimately with the people. The legislative body enacts rules as the people's agent in accordance with the principles of the law of nature, and the executive power enforces the legal system.

The government rules, but its legitimacy is sustained by the 'consent' of individuals. The government of the Lockean State, by virtue of the original contract and its covenants, is bound by the law of nature and, therefore, bound to guarantee 'life, liberty and estate'.[83] Thus, the State's *raison d'être* is the protection of individuals' rights as laid down by God's will and as enshrined in law.[84] Should the law of nature be consistently violated by a series of tyrannical political actions, Locke contended that rebellion to form a new government might not only be unavoidable but just.[85]

In most respects it was Locke (rather than Hobbes) whose views laid the foundation for the development of liberal democratic States in northwest European and Anglo-Saxon countries. The Lockean model has become a particular version of the theory of the liberal State dominant in England and America, since the late 18th century, where the role of the State is perceived as one that both relies on and guarantees the operation of a free market in civil society.[86] Also, modern State formations in East Asia were affected by Western political ideas from the colonial period.[87]

However, there are non-Western ways to think about the State, which include Confucian ideas that certainly have implications for East Asia. The next section reviews Confucian conceptions of the State.

Confucian conceptions of the State

This section reviews the Confucian conceptions of the State in the same categories that were used for Locke: the origins of the State; the State's legitimacy; and the obligations of the State to individuals. As noted by Leonard Shihlien Hsü, "the age of Confucius was marked by political chaos, revolutionary movements, moral degeneration, the influence of corrupt demagogues in office, the grievances of common people against powerful militarists and landlords, the prevalence of pessimists or irresponsible hermits, and the domination of anarchism, extreme individualism, political transcendentalism, military despotism, selfish imperialism, and unethical mercantilism".[88] Confucian conceptions of the State, therefore, should be understood against this historical background. The contrast between the ideas and social reality is dramatic, but perhaps thereby more comprehensible. Confucianism stresses harmony.

Confucianism is a system of politico-ethical ideas, in which rules and principles for the guidance of private life are bound up with those for the regulation of the public careers of men entrusted with the responsibility of governing.[89] Thus, there is a close link between ethics and politics in the Confucian State.

Confucius perceived the State as a product of natural evolution and therefore it is only a part of society.[90] The State does not originate in a 'state of nature', nor does it take its legitimacy from a 'social contract'.[91] From the formation of earth to the development of the ethical State, there are eight steps of evolution symbolised by: Heaven and earth; material things; male and female; husband and wife; father and son; sovereign and subject; high and low; and propriety and righteousness. They signify, in order, the physical stage, the dawn of life, the dawn of man, the dawn of social life, the age of patriarchy, the political stage, the constitutional stage, and the moral stage.[92] The "Great Appendix" of the *Book of Change* emphasises these principles of relation and of sequence, according to which the State should be organised.[93]

Therefore, in the Confucian State, there exists an idea of government traceable ultimately to the idea of the family. The family is the foundation of social organisation in Confucian society and the State is regarded as a large family.[94] Good government means the maintenance of proper relationships, in accordance with the laws of nature, between the sovereign and the mandarin, the superiors and the subordinates, the officials and the people.[95]

Thus the Confucian State's legitimacy is based on the principle that the government should be established and should operate in accordance with "natural laws." A government which keeps in harmony with nature will flourish. Otherwise, it will decay. In the universe, heaven and earth are the basic relations; in society, husband and wife. The term "nation-state" (*kuo-chia*, in Chinese or *kuk-ga* in Korean) literally indicates 'state family'. In Max Weber's terms, the Confucian State is a "familistic state": the family is a miniature state; the state an enlarged family.[96] Both involve loyalty and filial piety.[97]

The fundamental Confucian ideas—loyalty and filial piety—are associated with admonishment. Children and subjects were encouraged to remonstrate, to make sure kings and fathers acted justly, thus preventing unjust acts by their superiors. In Confucius' view, when a ruler became unrighteous and unmindful of the welfare of his subjects, Nature herself would be outraged and would cry aloud for vengeance. The people could revolt against the undivine ruler. Thus, revolution was justified in theory.[98] On this dimension, Confucius' justification of revolution is similar to that of Locke. Revolution is justified in both the Confucian and Lockean conceptions of the State, when the law of nature is violated by the sovereign. The obligations of the State to individuals should follow the order of the Nature, and the aim of this relationship is the promotion of virtue.[99]

In the approach of the book to the modern East Asian State, it is initially accepted that the Confucian conceptions of the State may be more relevant for the analysis than the ideas developed by Locke in the Western political tradition. However, modern East Asian States were affected by Western political ideas and it will thus be necessary to trace the colonial formation of the modern State in East Asia later in this book. However, it is probably useful here to summarise the initial operational and strategic themes of this book after the opening discussions in this chapter.

WAYS TO THINK ABOUT THE ACADEMIC PROFESSION

This section will set out a way to test the arguments of the book. It is important to remember the point made in Chapter One: this book is not asking and answering the question of whether 'academics' constitute a 'profession' in one, now traditional, sociological sense.[100] This book will not set out to utilise the ideal typical model of profession in the existing literature on the sociology of professions (and professionalism) for the reasons already discussed.[101] Not only are such models normally structural-functional but, as was suggested earlier, the comparative analyses of the academic profession have maintained Anglo-European frames of analysis, as if they are universally applicable. As was suggested, there has been lack of an intellectually powerful literature on the comparative dimensions of the academic profession, not just in historical variation, but across the boundaries between the Anglo-European world and other parts of the world. The deficiencies of such models obscure a main theme of this book: the book seeks to explain comparatively the *social construction* of the academic profession in (South) Korea, Singapore and Malaya/Malaysia since the colonial period.

The main argument in this book is that the shaping of the academic profession in these three countries has been affected by its colonial genesis and by the particular State formations in the three East Asian countries. The State will be taken and analysed as a major social actor, in framing the academic profession in the colonial and postcolonial periods.

Thus, the book asks about the changing relations of the State, the university and the academic profession in the processes of colonisation and postcolonialism, and the formation of the academic profession—as an act of dynamic and historical social construction in these selected East Asian societies since the colonial period. In this argument, the book analyses the different definitions of the academic profession which have emerged by the contemporary period in the selected East Asian States against the inheritances of the colonial period.

To pursue the argument, three operational themes run through the book. The *shaping* of the academic profession is analysed through two themes: first, the values and visions of the State visible in the States' modernity projects; and second, the State's idea of the university perceived through struggles over institutional forms and valued knowledge.

The themes emphasise the political framing of the academic profession. The examination of struggles over the institutional forms of higher education will include the agencies that link the university and the State, the expansion and new patterns of higher education institutions—i.e. private vs. public, university vs. polytechnic, domestic vs. international—through which the academic professions have been defined since the colonial period. The analysis of valued knowledge in university education will be through the knowledge profile of the university system which implies a way of understanding of the expected social roles of the academic profession—including expectations about its economic role.

The third operational theme is the *shape* of the academic profession that resulted from these struggles. Initial definitions of 'shape' will include the entry routes and the consequent social composition of the academic profession, in terms of nationality (e.g. expatriates), ethnic-cultural identity, gender, and class; and the formal ranks, or hierarchy of the academic profession that reveal variants around foreign models imported since the colonial period.

Thus, the strategic themes of the book build towards an interpretation of the comparative social construction of the academic profession in the colonial and postcolonial time periods in three different social contexts. Chapter Three deals with the colonial period in which the emergent academic professions of Korea and Malaya under Japanese and British colonialism are examined. Chapter Four looks at the postcolonial period, to analyse the ways in which the academic profession in South Korea and Malaysia and subsequently Singapore was affected by the modernity projects of the newly independent States. The chapter shows how those efforts were affected by the colonial inheritance—and how far an escape was made from that history. Attention is also given to the contemporary changes of the last decade and the academic profession—its knowledge priorities, its internal structures, and its international relations—under pressures of regionalisation, globalisation and the new policies of 'internationalisation' of education in South Korea, Malaysia and Singapore.

Chapter Five, the Conclusion, will reinterpret the East Asian academic professions comparatively. The initial idea for the conclusion is that the East Asian States and their patterns of development over time have created differences in the three academic professions around the themes of:

- their social usefulness in the maintenance of cultural stability;

- their political usefulness as State technocrats;

- their economic usefulness as participants in business and State dominated Research and Development.

However, that is only an initial guess. These possibilities may be contradicted and other insights may be generated by the substantive analysis which follows in Chapters Three and Four.

NOTES

1. The tradition of liberal education is, in general, connected to Greek philosophy (and later, Christian epistemology). The ancient Greek ideals of living in the world remained powerful in 18th and 19th century England. The concept of liberal education in classical Greek philosophy is epitomised in the idea of a whole person, whose wholeness is 'natural' conforming to the order of the cosmos itself in balance and good order. The relevant literature on liberal education includes Bloom, A., *The Closing of the American Mind: How Higher Education Has Failed Democracy and Impoverished the Souls of Today's Students,* New York: Simon & Schuster, 1987; Rothblatt, S., 'Liberal education in the English-speaking world' in Rothblatt, S. and B. Wittrock, *The European and American University since 1800,* Cambridge: Cambridge University Press, 1993, pp. 19-76.

2. Newman refers to Cicero's view on knowledge to proclaim "Knowledge must be pursued for its own end". Newman himself writes:

Knowledge is called by the name of Science or Philosophy, when it is acted upon, informed, or if I may use a strong figure, impregnated by Reason. Reason is the principle of that intrinsic fecundity of Knowledge, which, to those who possess it, is its especial value....Knowledge, indeed, when thus exalted into a scientific form, is also power; it is a good; that it is, not only an instrument, but an end.

Thus tensions are established between 'liberal' and 'servile'; 'utility' and 'inutility'. (John Henry Newman, 'Discourse V. Knowledge its own end', in *The Idea of a University,* edited by Turner, F. M., New Haven & London: Yale University Press, p.84.)

3. Ibid.

4. S. Rothblatt had contributed to the contemporary literature of the last decade on this issue. For details, see S. Rothblatt, 'Liberal education in the English-speaking world', in Rothblatt, S. and B. Wittrock, op. cit. 1993, pp. 19-76.

In the Seventh Discourse, Newman compares the 'utility' of knowledge in liberal education to that of health:

Health is a good in itself, though nothing came of it, and is especially worth seeking and cherishing; yet, after all, the blessings which attend its presence are so great.....And so as regards intellectual culture, I am far from denying utility in this large sense as the end of Education, when I lay it down, that the culture of the intellect is a good in itself and its own end.... As the body may be tended, cherished, and exercised with a simple view to its general health, so may the intellect also be generally exercised in order to its perfect state; and this is its cultivation.

(Newman, J. H., 'Discourse VII. Knowledge Viewed in Relation to Professional Skill', in John Henry Newman, op. cit. pp. 119-120.)

5. John Henry Newman, 'Discourse V. Knowledge Its Own End' in John Henry Newman, op. cit., p. 85.

6. Rothblatt, S. & Wittrock, B., op. cit.

7. Newman notes that the student "has a new centre, and a range of thoughts to which he/she was before a stranger." It is evolution to a newness. The student's perception is of the permanency of ideas, which must imply their substance having stood the test of time: a university communicates them. It is, therefore, 'a process of enlightenment', a proposition that can be understood within the broad Enlightenment tradition of Europe. (Allington, Nigel, F. B and N. J. O'Shaughnessy, *Light, Liberty and Learning: the Idea of a University Revisited,* Oxford: The Education Unit, 1992, p. 31.)

8. John Henry Newman, 'Discourse II. Theology A Branch of Knowledge' in Newman, J. H., op. cit., p. 25.

9. More specifically, however, Newman regarded universal knowledge as a key to mandate the presence of theology as a science of sciences in the Catholic University in Dublin in his time. (ibid.)

10. Similarly, John Stuart Mill also wrote: "The university is not a place of professional education. Universities are not intended to teach the knowledge required to fit men for some special mode of gaining their livelihood. Their object is not to make skilful lawyers, or physicians, or engineers, but they are lawyers or physicians or merchants, or manufacturers; and if you make them capable and sensible men, they will make themselves capable and sensible lawyers or physicians." (For details, see Cavenagh, F. A., *James and John Stuart Mill on Education,* Cambridge: Cambridge University Press, 1931, pp. 133-134.)

11. There is a lot of literature on this theme, borrowing Newman's idea of a university, though the literature tends to extend loosely Newman's ideas. The general analyses of university and state relations in the existing literature are mixing Newman's idea with others—such as the Humboldtian research university—in a broad definition of the so-called 'Western university tradition'. This trend is particularly visible in the American literature on the university, e.g., Allan Bloom and Bruce Wilshire—due to the fact that the origins of the American university model followed the examples of the English liberal college and the German research university. (For details, see Bloom, A. op. cit.; Wilshire, B., *The Moral Collapse of the University: Professionalism, Purity and Alienation,* Albany: SUNY Press, 1990.)

To construct an ideal typical model of university and state relations through

Newman's *The Idea of a University*, it is important to understand that Newman originally wrote *The Idea of a University* for the Roman Catholic University in Dublin. Therefore, the general line of the nine Discourses in the book relates to the Church, not the State. Newman was from an evangelical Anglican family background. He took his undergraduate degree in 1820 and two years later became a fellow at Oriel College in Oxford. Then, he became vicar of St. Mary's, the Oxford University church. He was also involved in the Oxford Tractarian Movement which sought to establish the independence of the Church of England from the state's intrusions following the passage of the Reform Bill of 1832. During the Tractarian Movement in the 1830s, Newman became increasingly attracted to the Roman Catholic Church. He converted to the Roman Catholic Church in 1845 and was ordained as a Roman Catholic priest. In 1851, Archbishop Cullen asked Newman to come to Ireland to preside over the establishment of a Roman Catholic university in Dublin. One result of his academic work for the Roman Catholic university in Dublin was the essays that today compose *The Idea of a University*.

In *The Idea of a University*, there is no explicit, direct account of 'university and state relations' by Newman. Nevertheless, when considering Newman's experience at Oxford University, including the Tractarian Movement, it can be suggested that Newman's idea of the relations of the university to the state was actually linked to the debates about education in Oxford which had taken place earlier in the nineteenth century. (For details, see John Henry Newman, op. cit. 1996, pp. xi-xxxiv.)

12. Ibid., pp.126-164.

13. Allington, Nigel, F.B. & N. J. O'Shaughnessy, op. cit, 1992.

14. The concept of the Gentleman is based on the intrinsic harmony of 'natural man'. What goes to constitute a gentleman is described by Newman as follows: "the carriage, gait, address, gestures, voice; the ease, the self-possession, the courtesy, the power of conversing, the talent of not offending; the lofty principle, the delicacy of thought, the happiness of expression, the taste and propriety, the generosity and forbearance, the candour and consideration, the openness of hand". (Quoted from Guttsman, W.L. (ed). *The English Ruling Class*,London: Weidenfeld and Nicolson, 1969, 5-5 Breeding and Education, p. 210.)

15. Newman, J.H., 'Rise and Progress of Universities', *Historical Sketches, 3 vols.,* 1876, vol. 2., ch. 2. Requoted from Guttsman, W.L. (ed). op. cit., p. 210.

16. According to Newman, the function of a university education should be focused on the achievement of a particular expansion of outlook, a turn of mind, habit of thought, and capacity for social and civic interaction. (For details, see Newman, J. H. op. cit.; Rothblatt, S., op. cit., pp. 24-29.)

17. This theme has been notable in the English elite 'public schools' and the ancient universities of Oxford and Cambridge. In 19th century England, liberal education was available mainly for the privileged: leisured aristocratic classes who did not need to make a living, groups aspiring to high social position, and elites in government and the leading professions. In other words, the ancient universities continued the ethos of English public school education and close connections with the British civil service in the Empire and key professions. (For details, see R. Wilkinson's *Governing Elite: studies in training and selection,* 1969; The education of Asiatics in Great Britain, *Board of Education Office of Special Inquiries and Reports* Vol. 8, 1902; Perkin, H., *Key Profession: the history of the association of university teachers,* London: Routledge & K. Paul, 1969.)

This is a particularly English version of university and state relations. Exclusive education in the public schools and Oxbridge inculcated lifelong ways of thinking and acting fit for the elite class in the Empire. "It is generally accepted that public schoolboys ruled the British Empire, but our knowledge has not yet proceeded much beyond this generalization." (J.A. Mangan, *The Games Ethic and Imperialism,* Harmondsworth: Viking, 1986, p. 75.)

18. Ibid.

19. Newman, J. H., Discourse VI. in *The Idea of a University,* op. cit., 1996, pp. 91-108.

20. Ridder-Symoens, Hilde De (ed). *A History of the University in Europe vol II,* Cambridge: Cambridge University Press, 1996; Stone, L. (ed). *The University in Society vol I, Oxford and Cambridge from the 14th to the Early 19th Century,* Princeton: Princeton University Press, 1974.

21. In the 14th century, there were 5 colleges in Oxford, and 7 in Cambridge in England, along with 37 in Paris, 8 in Toulouse, 11 in Italy and 2 in Spain. In the 15th and 16th centuries, there were new colleges established such as King's College, Queen's College and Trinity College in Cambridge, and All Souls, Magdalen and Christ Church in Oxford. (M_ller, Rainer A., Chapt. 8. Student Education, Student Life in Ridder-Symoens, Hilde De (ed)., op. cit., p. 334.)

22. In the collegiate community, according to Rainer A. Müller, the colleges dominated university life:

Disciplinary regulations were severe and scarcely differed in the early modern period from the medieval rules. Latin was spoken in the college; studies were interspersed with devotional lessons, even during communal meals. Lectures were gradually transferred from the university to the college....The university retained responsibility for examinations and graduations. A specifically English aspect appeared in the second half of the 16th century—*the tutorial system.* This one-to-one relationship is peculiar to the English college and university system and was not practised so intensively in any other country. As academic supervisor he was also responsible for the morals and the finances of his pupil. The quality of education and study was thus directly dependent on the capabilities of the tutor. (Müller, Rainer A., op. cit.1996, p. 335)

In the European university systems, the collegiate system was not normal. While the closed collegiate system, the so-called *modus Parisiensis* was developed in England, in Germany (and Italy, eastern Europe and the Netherlands), there was hardly any significant development of the collegiate system in the university. The so-called *modus studendi*, the free student form of study was common in Germany. (For details, see Müller, Rainer A., op. cit. 1996, pp. 285-325; Engel, A., 'Emerging Concept of the Academic Profession' in Stone, L. (ed)., op. cit., 1974, p. 306.)

23. Ibid., p. 116.

24. Symonds, R., *Oxford and Empire: The Last Lost Cause?*, op. cit., 1986.

The academics retaining the elitist view of higher education became convinced that there was no incompatibility between a classical liberal education and a modern, competitive, scientific and industrial nation. (Stone, L., 'Education and Modernization in Japan and England' in *Comparative Studies in Society and History*, vol. IX, no. 2 (1966-7), pp. 208-232.)

25. Until the early nineteenth century, before the rise of the civic universities, the only prestigious teaching posts in England were in Oxford and Cambridge. At that time, college teaching was not a career post but only a temporary employment and not a definite and acknowledged career. (For details, see Ashby, E. *The Academic Profession*, Oxford: Oxford University Press for the British Academy, 1969.) The functions of the university are focused on producing through liberal education the gentleman, equipped by a self-conscious elegant amateurism and a slightly insular nationalism in the British Empire in Newman's times.

26. Jaspers' *The Idea of the University* was first issued in the 1920s, but the enlarged version, was published in 1947 when Jaspers was reinstated to his chair in the University of Heidelberg. Wyatt, J., *Commitment to Higher Education*, Buckingham: SRHE & Open University Press, 1990, p. 3.

27. In *Der Streit der Fakultaten*, Kant defends the position of the department of philosophy. For details, see Jaspers, K., *The Idea of the University*, London: Peter Owen, 1960.

28. Jaspers, K., op. cit., p. 65.

29. In Jaspers' view, the so-called "higher" departments in the German university

structure (i.e., theology, law and medicine) exist for the sake of the State. As these departments (of theology, law and medicine) are concerned with the kind of knowledge which is useful, they do not exist for their own sake, but serve practical purposes. Then, philosophy, the "lower" department, can be totally autonomous, epitomizing academic freedom in the university as a place to search for truth. (For details, see Buczynska-Garewicz, H., 'Jaspers and University Self-Governance' in Walters, G.J. (ed). *The Tasks of Truth,* Frankfurt am Main: Peter Lang, 1996, p. 120.)

30. Buczynska-Garewicz, H., 'Jaspers and University Self-Governance' in Walters, G.J. (ed)., op. cit., 1996, p. 119.

31. Ibid.

32. Jaspers, K., *The Idea of the University,* op. cit., pp. 50-51.

33. Ibid., p. 66.

34. Buczynska-Garewicz, H., 'Jaspers and University Self-Governance', in Walters, G. J. (ed)., op. cit., p. 117.

35. Jaspers, K., op. cit.

36. Ibid., pp. 132-44.

37. Ibid., pp. 121-122.

38. Walters, G.J. (ed)., op. cit., pp. 118-119.

39. Jaspers, K., op. cit., p. 135.

On this ground, the university is free so that it can act as an intellectual conscience to the state and carry the social role of improving humanity. Following the tradition of nineteenth-century German liberalism, Jaspers is suspicious of mass schemes of human renewal. Jaspers notes that "Seeking truth and the improvement of mankind, the university aims to stand for man's humanity *par excellence.*" (ibid., p. 145)

40. Jaspers, K., *Man in the Modern Age,* London: Routledge and Kegan Paul, 1951, pp. 108-109.

41. Wyatt, J., op. cit., 1990, p. 54.

42. von Humboldt, W., *Ideen zu einem Versuch die Grenzen der Wirksamkeit des Staats zu bestimmen,* Berlin, 1854. (Quoted by Nigel F.B. Allington & Nicholas J

O'Shaughnessy, op. cit., 1992, p. 27.)

43. Humboldt, as the founder of the University of Berlin and also a high-ranking civil servant responsible for education and culture in Prussia, was probably the major initial influence on the formation of the German idea of the university.

44. Jaspers, K., op. cit., 1960, p. 1.

45. Walters, G. J. (ed)., op. cit., p. 120.

46. Schilpp, P.A. (ed). *The Philosophy of Karl Jaspers,* New York: Tudor, 1957, p. 52. Requoted in Wyatt, J., op. cit., p. 55.

47. Jaspers, K., *Philosophy and the World,* Chicago: Regnery, 1963, p. 31; Wyatt, J., op. cit., p. 55.

48. In this German context, Jaspers placed great emphasis on the role of the university in educating for what he terms 'the intellectual professions', which deal with the condition of human life as a whole. (For details, see Wyatt, J., op. cit., p. 59.)

49. Ibid., p. 3.

In order to safeguard university autonomy, through which privileges and positions of the academic profession can be preserved against all changes, the German academic often used the concept of *Bildung. Bildung* is a pedagogic term reflecting nineteenth century German liberalism. It is often identified with the *Lehrfreiheit* of professors and the *Lernfreiheit* of students. In the German university, the concept of *Bildung* is found in slogans such as 'unity of research and teaching' and 'loneliness and freedom'. Ringer, Fritz K., *The Decline of the German Mandarins: The German Academic Community, 1890-1933,* Cambridge, MA: Harvard University Press,1969, p. 87. (For details of an analysis of the Humboldtian German university and mid-century changes in the concepts of research and science, see McClelland, C. E., *State, Society, and University in Germany 1700-1914,* Cambridge, 1980, pp. 101-232.)
With emphasis on a particular German concept of *Bildung,* Humboldt proclaimed that nothing is as important to a high-ranking civil servant. The German state, as a late developing nation state in 19th century Europe, required university-educated men to be equipped with 'official' nationalism to serve as civil servants of the new German State in this period. Fritz K. Ringer argued in *The Decline of the German Mandarins: The German Academic Community, 1890-1933,*that *Bildung* was also the single most important tenet of the German mandarin tradition. (For further details, see Rothbaltt, S. & Wittrock, B. (eds)., op. cit.; Burrage, M. & Torstendahl, R. (eds). *Profession in Theory and History: Rethinking the Study of the Professions in Europe and North America,* London, 1990.)

50. He made it explicit that no one discipline should command the community of scholars, because such domination might be an implicit denial of the wholeness of knowledge and hence a curtailment of truth. (For details, see Wyatt, J., op. cit., Chapt. 4. Karl Jaspers: The Idea of the University—Communication at the Frontiers, pp. 45-51.)

Jaspers saw here the importance of communication between academics, who share a sense of community in the university, as the essential element of academic freedom. For a shared sense of community and idea of unity—through communication between the university academics—Jaspers notes genuine basic differences between different forms of knowledge. In his view, awareness of the differences between different forms of studies helps each academic to know himself or herself better. (For details, see Jaspers, K., *The Idea of the University,* op. cit.

Jaspers emphasizes that the good teacher in the university must always be conscious of the independent existence of the student through dialogue (i.e. the Socratic method as mentioned earlier). The true teacher has to acknowledge the unknown and the unknowable effects of the learning process and this acknowledgement should lead to the admixture of open scepticism: "One of his (Man's) essential traits is to be changed by his cognition in incalculable ways". (For details, see Jaspers, K., *Philosophy and the World,* op. cit., p. 148; Wyatt, J., op. cit., Chapt. 4. Karl Jaspers: The Idea of the University—Communication at the Frontiers, pp. 45-51.)

As an existentialist, Jaspers doubted the power of education to transform society. In *Man in the Modern Age,* Jaspers warns that the 'culture' of modern man is acquired from a variety of sources, only one of which is formal education. In the rapidly changing social conditions of his time, Jaspers observed symptoms of the disintegration of education and its insecurity: disintegrated knowledge served by the all-too present panic of modern educators. Among the educators, Jaspers notes, some look back for old certainties, others concentrate on narrow training for skills, and others pursue constant experimentation. (For details, see Jaspers, K., *Man in the Modern Age,* op. cit., p. 105.)

51. For example, Morsy, Z. & P. G. Altbach (eds). *Higher Education in International Perspective Toward the 21st Century,* New York: UNESCO, 1993; Allington, Nigel, F. B. and N. J. O'Sahughnessy, op. cit., 1992; Rothblatt, S. & B. Wittrock (eds)., op. cit., 1993.

52. Nakayama, S. *Academic and Scientific Traditions in China, Japan and the West.* Tokyo: University of Tokyo Press, 1974, p. 51.

53. Dardees, J. W. *Confucianism and Autocracy: Professional Elites in the Founding of the Ming Dynasty* Berkeley: University of California Press, 1983.

54. Wilkinson, R. *The Prefects: British Leadership and the Public School Tradition,*

A Comparative Study in the Making of Rulers. op. cit., p. 162.

55. Ibid., pp. 53-54.

56. Kuo, P. W. *Chinese System of Public Education.* New York: Teachers College, 1915, pp. 34-35; Wilkinson, R. op. cit., p. 163.

The phrase, *hsiu-chi cihh-jen* (first cultivate yourself and then you can rule others) symbolises the importance of examining moral and philosophical aspects of knowledge and practising what one has learned. Neo-Confucian knowledge is grounded in values such as self-reliance, individual responsibility, family cooperation, and local self-governance. Kim, Kwang-ok, 'The Reproduction of Confucian Culture in Contemporary Korea' in Tu Wei-ming, *Confucian Traditions in East Asian Modernity,* Cambridge, Mass. & London, England: Harvard University Press, 1996, pp.205-206.

57. de Bary, W. T. *Neo-Confucian Orthodoxy and the Learning of the Mind-and-Heart.* New York: Columbia University Press, 1981, pp. 25-27.

58. The family is seen as an enriching and nourishing support system, a vehicle for the true realisation of the self in its centre. The self in turn must develop in its various roles within the family system. To do so in each case depends that facet of our humanity. Familiar relationships can degenerate into nepotism. Thus, true realisation of the self, which begins in the context of the family, requires that one also extend one's relationships beyond the familial structure, and so beyond nepotism, in order to relate meaningfully to a larger community. (For details, see Tu Wei-ming, *Humanity and Self-Cultivation: Essays in Confucian Thought,* Berkeley: Asian Humanities Press, 1979; Tu Wei-ming. Way, *Learning, and Politics: Essays on the Confucian Intellectual,* Singapore: Institute of East Asian Philosophies, 1989; Waley, Arthur, *Three Ways of Thought in Ancient China,* reprint. Garden City, N. Y.: Doubleday, Anchor Book, 1956.)

59. Mencius depicted the six stages of human perfection:

The desirable is called "good".
To have it in oneself is called "true".
To possess it fully in oneself is called "beautiful",
but to shine forth with this full possession is called "great".
To be great and be transformed by this greatness is called "sage"; to be sage
and to transcend the understanding is called "divine".

(Quoted from Tu Wei-ming, 'Sung Confucian Idea of Education' in de Bary, W. T. and J. W. Chaffee (eds). *Neo-Confucian Education: The Formative Stage.* Berkeley: University of California Press, 1989, p. 141.)

60. There are five types of knowledge Confucius saw as being crucial in the process of learning to become human. Each of these five areas is articulated in one of the Five Classics: *The Book of Poetry, the Book of Rites, the Spring and Autumn Annals, the Book of History*, and *the Book of Change*. During the later Han dynasty, the incorporation of the *Analects* and the *Book of Filial Piety* into the "Five Classics" made up the "Seven Classics" and then later *San Li* or *The Three Rites* and *San Chuan* or the *Three Commentaries* were added to the *Spring and Autumn*, to form the so-called "Nine Classics". The basic Neo-Confucian texts, the Four Books are the *Great Learning,* the *Doctrine of the Mean*, the *Analects,* and the *Mencius* are centrally concerned with self-cultivation of the person as the prospective bearer of leadership responsibilities. (For details, see Hsü, L. S. *The Political Philosophy of Confucianism, an Interpretation of the Social and Political Ideas of Confucius, His Forerunners, and His Early Disciples.* London: George Routledge & Sons, Ltd., 1932, pp. 14-20; Tu Wei-ming. *Confucian Ethics Today: The Singapore Challenge.* Singapore: Curriculum Development Institute of Singapore, Federal Publications, 1984, pp. 6-7; p. 14; de Bary, Wm. Theodore, 'Confucian Education in Premodern East Asia' in Tu Wei-Ming, (ed). op. cit., 1996, pp. 25-30.)

The Neo-Confucian doctrine was established on the premise that the nature of man is fundamentally good, but it is also a metaphysical system of thought that endeavours to find the roots of this premise in the natural order of the cosmos. Through deductive reasoning, Neo-Confucians divided all existence into two inseparable components, *li* and *ch'i*. *Li* is a patterning or formative element that accounts for what things are and how they behave, or normatively should behave, while *ch'i* is the concretising and energising element. The two are interdependent and inseparable. In this dualism, two distinct Neo-Confucian Schools developed further in Korea since the late 15th century: one giving primary emphasis to *li,* the other arguing the primacy of the role of *ch'i.* These different intellectual visions also competed for political endorsement in Korea. (For details, see de Bary, W. T. op. cit., 1981; Lee, Ki-baik. *A New History of Korea.* Cambridge, Mass.: Harvard University Press, 1985, p. 217.)

61. The traditional Confucian orthodoxy of knowledge system was ruled out by the establishment of the modern education system during the Japanese colonial period, which arguably contributed to the development of capitalism in South Korea. With the abolition of the *Yangban* (Confucian literati) class and the end of colonialism, economic growth and a bureaucratic meritocracy further transformed educational achievement into a major avenue of pragmatic upward social mobility. (For details, see Bedeski, R.E., *The Transformation of South Korea: Reform and reconstitution in the Sixth Republic under Roh Tae Woo, 1987-1992*, London & New York: Routledge, 1994, pp. 109-110.)

62. Particularly free universal education with no distinction of class, sex, or race. Accordingly, all types of schools—the local school, district school, provincial col-

lege, the national academy, and the imperial university—should be supported by the State. (*Analects,* Book XV, Chapter xxxviii., Requoted from Hsü, L. S., op. cit., p. 156.)

63. By the seventeenth century in China the State-supported schools in the capital could prepare men who had passed district examinations for degree examinations that would qualify them for government office. Although some private academies survived where learning was pursued for its own sake, almost all higher education was linked to preparation for government office. (For details, see de Bary, W. T. 'Chinese Despotism and the Confucian Ideal in the 17th Century' in Fairbank, J. K. *Chinese Thought and Institutions.* Chicago: Chicago U. P., 1957, p. 179; Wilkinson, R., op. cit., p. 130.) It was in the Sui period (581-618), the Confucian classics were explicitly designated as the basis of a revived civil service examination system; and in the T'ang, the examination and educational systems were linked in a more systematic fashion. (Nakayama, S., op. cit., p. 53.)

64. In spite of class distinction mainly based on lineage, the Confucian education system was open to commoners as well as aristocrats so that social mobility was made possible in principle. (For details, see de Bary, W. T., and J. W. Chaffee (eds). op. cit., 1989.)

In this sense, the Confucian examination system inspired both idealism and opportunism: it stimulated men to seek government service for its own sake, but by exalting family ties, it also legitimised the pursuit of public power for the prestige and security it conferred on the individual's clan. (Wilkinson, R., op. cit., 1964, pp. 156-157.)

65. The close link between Confucian education and governmental bureaucracy was marked by major rituals. As Wilkinson notes "Chinese [Confucian] education went further than the English public schools in making manners and ritual symbolic of virtue." (ibid., p. 139.)

Written examinations in Europe were apparently not held until the 18th century, the one given by Richard Bentley in 1702 being the first on record. As for the Chinese examination system, the French Jesuits who visited China in the early Ch'ing praised it highly. (Teng Ssu-yu, 'Chinese Influence on Western Examination Systems' *Harvard Journal of Asiatic Studies,* VII, 1943, p. 227.) Although a written examination was not employed in the selection of European government officials before the French revolutionary government adopted the practice in 1791, by the 19th century written tests—an adopted model of the Chinese civil examination system—were widely used in the recruitment of an administrative bureaucracy in the English colonial empire and elsewhere. (Nakayama, S. op. cit., p. 80).

66. As argued by R. Kent Guy, "knowledge and political power in the Confucian State were united, as scholars and rulers together defined the nature of imperial

authority and explored its limits." In the process of definition and exploration, it is argued that institutions of Chinese (and Korean) Confucian scholarships not only reflected ideas of government, they affected the government of ideas. (Guy, K. R. *The Emperor's Four Treasuries: Scholars and the State in the Late Ch'ien-Lung Era.* Cambridge, Mass.: Harvard University Press, 1987, pp. 1-7.)

In 18th century China, all scholar mandarins shared an orientation toward examination: "virtually everyone at court spent at least the first twenty-five years of his life studying for the examinations, and the next twenty-five years of his life evaluating others' efforts".

"By the eighteenth century, the skills required in examination taking were limited, but they had to be so firmly mastered that the pursuit of them could become an obsession. As the examinations became more competitive with the growth of population in the seventeenth and eighteenth centuries, ever finer distinctions separated successful from unsuccessful candidates, forcing examiner and examinee alike to concentrate on the most trivial aspects of the process. A second concern of court officials was the ability to produce polished literary compositions for formal occasions... Finally, all at court had at least to pay lip service to Sun dynasty interpretations of the classics, especially those by Chu Hsi (1130-1200) and his followers, for it was their work, repeatedly reprinted under official patronage, that formed the basis of state ideology and the examination system". (For details, see Guy, K. R., op. cit., pp.4-5.)

67. Korea initially adopted the Chinese Confucian system in 372 A. D. when the first Confucian educational institution, *Tae Hak* (the Great School) was established, through which a systematic Confucian governing structure of Korea began to develop. Korean Confucian scholars in Chosun never deviated from the traditions of Confucianism or the doctrines of *Chu-tzu*. (For details, see Yu, Kyun-ho, 'Characteristics of Korea's view of the outside world in the late Chosun period (1392-1910)' in Hirano, Ken'ichiro (ed). *The State and Cultural Transformation: Perspectives from East Asia*, Tokyo & New York & Paris: United Nations University Press, 1995, pp. 213-231. For details of comparison of Confucian administrative culture of Korea with China and Japan, see Kim, Mahn Kee, 'The Administrative Culture of Korea: A Comparison with China and Japan' in Caiden, Gerald E. And Kim, Bun Woong (eds). *A Dragon's Progress*, Connecticut: Kumarian Press, Inc., 1991, pp. 26-42.)

67. Although China, for centuries at a time, remained stable and united in the Confucian system, the period of Chosun governed by the Yi dynasty in Korea is more continuous than in China. During the period of Yi dynasty, Confucian scholars in Korea never deviated from the traditions of (Neo) Confucianism or the doctrines of *Chu-tzu*. Thus, it can be construed that the essence of the Confucian education system was better preserved in Korea than in China—especially Ch'ing dynasty. For instance, the Tang and Ming Dynasties each lasted nearly 300 years, the Sung 150 years; the Ch'ing, the last Imperial dynasty, for 250 years. (Wilkinson,

R., op. cit., 1964, pp. 164-176; Lee, Ki-baik, op. cit.)

68. In fact, Confucianism in the period of Silla (668-918) before the founding of Koryo dynasty had already won wide acceptance as a doctrine providing a unique moral basis for effective government. However, the criterion for official appointment then was social class. Therefore, there was no great need for an examination system by which to select state mandarins. (For details, see Lee, Ki-baik, op. cit., pp. 105-106.)

The systematic development of university and state relations in Korea started with the establishment of the National University *Kuk Ja Gam* of the Koryo dynasty in 992. Like a modern university, *Kuk Ja Gam* contained a number of colleges within it, namely the so-called Six Colleges of the Capital—University College *Kuk Ja Hak*, High College *T'aehak*, Four Portals College *Samunhak*, Law College *Yurhak*, Calligraphy College *Sohak* and Accounting College *Sanhak*, which had been created during Injong's reign (1122-1146). However, it was not a case of each offering a distinctive curriculum and there was a different stipulation of entrance qualifications, based on the aristocratic system of the time. (Lee, Ki-baik, op. cit., pp. 118-120)

As Ki-baik Lee explains "University College, High College, and Four Portals College all were places to study, principally, the sources of the Chinese tradition, such as the Five Classics, the *Classic of Filial Piety,* and the *Analects.* Their difference lay in the different entrance requirements for their students: University College admitted the sons of military or civilian officials of the third rank or higher, High College the sons of fourth and fifth rank officials, and Four Portals the sons of officials of ranks six and seven. Finally, sons of eighth and ninth rank officials, as well as of commoners, were admitted to the Law College, the College of Calligraphy, or the College of Accounting to study one of these technical specialties". (For details, see Lee, Ki-baik, op. cit., pp. 119-120.)

In the period of Chosun, the Confucian examinations for recruitment to government office were conducted at two levels, the licentiate or lower level and the erudite or higher level. The licentiate examinations were of two kinds: the Classics Licentiate Examination that examined candidates on the Four Books and Five Classics of China, and the Literary Licentiate Examination that tested skill in composing such Chinese literary forms as poetry, rhyme prose, documentary prose and the problem-essay. (For details, see Lee, Ki-baik, op. cit., pp. 180-181.)

69. Yu, Kun-ho. 'Characteristics of Korea's view of the outside world in the late Choson period (1392-1910)' in K. Hirano (ed)., op. cit.,1995, pp. 213-231.

70. Commercial activities and menial work are looked down on. The Confucian academic should represent an end in himself.

71. Tu Wei-ming, 'Sung Confucian Idea of Education' in de Bary, W. T., and J. W. Chaffee (eds)., op. cit., p. 141.

72. Confucius himself was a sage, but certainly not a king. In terms of power politics, he failed in the political arena. Confucius, therefore, was not the paradigmatic expression of the highest ideal within the Confucian tradition itself. (For details, see Tu Wei-ming, op. cit. 1984, p. 42.)

73. As earlier reviewed under university and State relations, Confucius emphasised that anyone who is virtuous and wise is qualified to be a State mandarin. In principle, a commoner may rise to the prime ministership in principle. (*Analects*, Book XVI, Chapters, xvii, xviii, xx, xxiii., Requoted from Hsü, L. S., op. cit., p. 85.)

74. Analects, Book XII, Chapter xxii, Requoted from Hsü, L. S., op. cit., p. 83.

75. Max Weber once argued, in *The Religion of China: Confucianism and Taosim,* that the highest ideal of a Confucian is to adjust to the world and submit to the established order. However, this is arguably a mistaken view that has easily led to a further misconception that the Confucian tradition is authoritarian. (For details, see Weber M. *The Religion of China: Confucianism and Taoism.* Translated by H. H. Gerth, New York: Free Press, 1964.)

As reviewed earlier, Korea has inherited a strong tradition of literary scholarship rooted in the Confucian tradition. The Confucian gentleman scholar is called *sonbi* in Korean. The Korean word *sonbi* refers to a person of knowledge and good bearing. More specifically it denotes a man of character or class who embodies the precepts of Confucianism. With good personal bearing, the *sonbi* is called *sagunja* in Korean—*sa* meaning "scholar" and *gunja* meaning "man of virtue" in the sense of an ideal man who embodies Confucian principles.

During the Chosun era (1392-1910), the authority of the Confucian gentleman scholar was immense. They had to be socially responsible and maintain their identity as "moral" leaders. The Confucian academic should not seek opportunities for personal gain according to the prescribed Confucian norms for being socially responsible as the Confucian gentleman scholar. Throughout Korean history, the *sonbi* have taken a leadership role. Korean history is full of examples of the *sonbi* model since the fourth century, which shows a revolvement of personal bearing and a moral sense of etiquette, right and wrong. However, it was in the Chosun period (1392-1895) that Confucian ideology was embraced as the supreme ruling principle of government in Korea. The *sonbi* played that role in modern times as virtuous and patriotic leaders in the struggle for political Independence from Japanese colonial domination. (For details, see Yu Kun-ho, 'Characteristics of Korea's view of the outside world in the late Chosun period (1392-1910)' in K. Hirano, op. cit., pp. 213-230; Korea Foundation, The Korea Foundation, *Korean Cultural Heritage Thought & Religion Vol. II,* Joungwon Kim (ed)., Seoul: The Korea Foundation, 1996, pp. 30-35.)

76. The Chinese ideograph *sa*, often used to refer to such gentlemen, means "scholar", and connotes a certain knowledge and skill required to be the State mandarin.

77. The scholar mandarin had to maintain a moral sense of his own origins and his ascension to and retirement from the government. He had to maintain a critical attitude and reject injustice and was not to concern himself with wealth and fame. It is for this reason that the hermit Confucian who did not ascend to a government position was sometimes even more respected. In this Confucian tradition, the *sonbi* was both the social conscience and the social intellect. In the ideal typical model of the Confucian academic and university- State relations, the *sonbi* denotes the autonomous Confucian scholar who cultivates his personal morality and at the same time acts upon it. He is a leader in society and an educator both to the general public, by carrying his beliefs into action, and to the ruler, by rectifying customs and administering government affairs in a just manner. (Korea Foundation, op. cit., pp. 30-35.)

78. Some *sonbi* were more akin to the commoners and could be called *sasoin*, gentlemen who are also commoners. This distinction shows that while the *sonbi* could rise to the ruling elite, they were also subjects. Yu, Kun-ho, op. cit., pp. 213-230.

79. Education in Confucianism is regarded the most important mechanism by which people become proper human beings so that occupations related to education such as a teacher or professor, have been always respected highly in Confucian societies. Therefore, the university academic profession is said to be the modern version of the most prestigious occupation in Korea. (For details, see Kim, Kwang-ok, op. cit., pp. 206-7.)

80. Hobbes viewed the role of the State as pre-eminent in political and social life. The origins of the State, in Hobbes' view start, with the *state of nature* and conceptions of the social contract. Hobbes introduced a 'thought of experiment' employing four interrelated concepts: state of nature, right of nature, law of nature and social contract. He imagined a situation in which individuals are in a state of nature. The *State of nature* is a hypothetical condition wherein there is no common power to restrain individuals, no law, and no law enforcement. Civilised man would want to get out of this condition, but simultaneously he also has natural rights which he wants to preserve, particularly the "Liberty each man hath, to use his own power, as he will himself, for the preservation of his own nature; that is to say, of his own Life; and consequently, of doing anything, which in his own Judgement, and Reason, he shall conceive to the aptest means thereunto". (Quoted from Hobbes, *Leviathan*, edited by C. B. Macpherson, Harmondsworth, Penguin, 1968, p. 189.)

Hobbes shows how individuals with their own divergent interests come to commit themselves to the idea that only a Great Leviathan or State or 'Mortall God' can articulate and defend the 'general' or 'public' interest—the sum of individual interests. (Hobbes, *Leviathan*, op. cit.; Dyson, K., *The State Tradition in Western Europe*, Oxford: Martin Robertson, 1980, Chapt. 7; Held, D. (ed). *States & Societies*, Oxford: Martin Robertson in association with the Open University, 1983, pp. 4-18.) In Hobbes' interpretation of the *state of nature*, there exists a tension between preservation of the liberty available in the state of nature and the fear of violence and war which that initial condition produces. This leads to an individual giving up power to a sovereign. The State has ultimate power vested in the sovereign as laid down in the legal system and through the capacity of the sovereign to enforce the law through the fear of coercive powers. It is powerful and capable of acting as a centralised force. The State, however, is not involved in their socio-economic activities, but only in establishing their form and codifying their functions. The legitimacy of the sovereign State is based on a social contract and its covenants, which represents 'the public'. Hobbes saw the State as self-perpetuating, undivided and ultimately absolute. The right of citizens to change their ruler was, accordingly, regarded as superfluous. (Held, D. (ed). op. cit., p. 7)

The obligation of the State to individuals is found in the Hobbesian concept of the unique political power created as a result of the relation of the sovereign to the subject, in which the position of 'sovereign' is a product of their social contract. In this relation of the State's sovereignty to individuals, men should in their own self-interest acknowledge full obligation to the sovereign. The sovereign State must be able to act decisively to counter the threat of anarchy, and must ensure the protection of all property. (ibid.)

However, Hobbes' views of the State were contested, especially in the areas of the State's constitutional role, coercive power, representation (in which a sovereign authority can claim to articulate the public interest without forms of democratic accountability) and legitimacy—how the Sate is considered just or worthy by its citizens. An alternative view of these positions was provided by Locke.

81. Dunn, J., *The Political Thought of John Locke*, Cambridge: Cambridge University Press, 1969, Part 3.

82. Ibid.

83. Held, D. (ed)., op. cit.,1983, pp. 4-18.

84. Ibid., p. 13.

The obligations of the State to individuals in the Lockean concept lie in the maintenance of law and order at home and protection against aggression from abroad. Given that the State is the regulator and protector of society, individuals are best able by their own efforts to satisfy their needs and develop their capacities in a process of free exchange with others.

85. In the development of the conceptions of the liberal democratic State, Jeremy Bentham and James Mill were the first advocates of liberal democracy. Held, D. (ed)., op. cit., 1983, pp. 4-18.

86. Hall, S., 'The West and the Rest: Discourse and Power' in Hall, S. & Gieben, B. (eds). *Formations of Modernity*, Cambridge: Polity Press in association with the Open University, 1992, pp. 275-332; Held, D. *Democracy and the Global Order: From the Modern State to Cosmopolitan Governance*, Cambridge: Polity Press, 1995.

87. Hsü, L. S. op. cit., 1932, pp. 24-25.

88. The most characteristic ideas of the Confucian political system were expressed in 'Higher Learning'. The Confucian principle of the political system is summarised as follows:

The illustrious ancients, when they wished to bring the highest virtues to the world, first put their states in proper order. Before putting their states in proper order, they regulated their families. Before regulating their families, they cultivated their own selves. Before cultivating their own selves, they perfected their souls. Before perfecting their souls, they tried to be sincere in their thoughts. Before trying to be sincere in their thoughts, they extended to the utmost their knowledge. Such extension of knowledge lay in the investigation of things and seeing them as they really were. When things were thus investigated, knowledge became complete. When knowledge became complete, their thoughts became sincere. When thoughts were sincere, their souls became perfect. When their souls were perfect, their own selves became cultivated. When their selves were cultivated, families became regulated. When their families were regulated, their states came to be put into proper order. When their states were in proper order, then the whole world became peaceful and happy.

(Quoted from Chang Hsin-Hai, 'Chinese Political Thought and the West' in *The Nation*, 3 May, 1922. Requoted from Pott, W. S. A. *Chinese Political Philosophy*, New York: Alfred A Knopf, 1925, pp. 57-58.)

89. Hsü, L. S. op. cit.1932, pp. 26-42.

90. Neither Confucius nor his disciples give any formal definition of the State. The existing Western literature shows that Confucian political thought does not have the idea of the State in Western terms. (For details, see Hsü, L. S. op. cit.; Pott, W. S. A., op. cit.)

91. *Book of Change*, Chapter ii, Requoted from Hsü, L. S., op. cit., pp. 33-36.

92. Ibid.

93. The family is regarded as a social unit, an educational unit, an agency of recti-fication, the primary school of training political capacity, and the smallest econom-ic unit in Confucian political unity. For details, see Hsü, L. S., op. cit., pp. 61-89.

94. *The Analects,* Book III, Chapters, x, xv. Requoted from Hsü, L. S., op. cit., p. 27.
Confucius thought that the State is the greatest of all social institutions in the preservation of proper social relations. The State is the central agency for the ruler to link human phenomena with natural phenomena for the good of man. The State should prevent conflicts with nature, and promote social and political progress by keeping harmony with natural forces. (*Book of Change,* The Great Appendix, Book I, Chapters vii-xi; Book II, Chapters ii-iii, xi-xii. Requoted from Hsü, L. S., p. 40; *Analects,* Book II. , Requoted from Pott, W. S. A., op. cit., p. 70.)

95.Weber, Max, *The Religion of China,* New York: Free Press, 1951.

96. In the Western understandings, however, filial piety has been often taken to be a complete subordination of individuals to the State's absolute power, i.e. an unquestioning loyalty to the sovereign. In this perspective, the nature of the East Asian State appears similar to that of the State of Hobbes: self-perpetuating, undi-vided and in an absolute position (i.e. above the rights of citizens). (For details, see Weber, Max, op. cit.; Pye, L. *Asian Power and Politics: The Cultural Dynamics of Authority,* Cambridge, Mass.: Harvard University Press, 1985.)

97. However, whoever secured the throne after the revolution would be regarded as Heaven's choice once more, and he and his descendants might continue to rule until they by their folly and selfishness seemed to have betrayed the trust imposed in them by Heaven. For details, see Hsü, L. S., op. cit.

98. *Analects,* Book VII, chapter vii, *Mencius,* Book VII, part ii, chapter ii, Requoted from Hsü, L. S., op. cit., pp. 114-127.

Following the order of Nature, the Confucian ruler is paternal and democratic. He is moreover responsible in detail for the welfare, both material and moral, of his people. Confucius considered philanthropy to be one of the most important obli-gations of the State to the subjects, in the sense of promoting economic welfare, and conducting an honest and efficient civil service. Old men should be honoured and respected and the aged, widows, orphans, unemployed, and other unfortunates should be taken care of by the State. The Confucian principles of public relief include: (I) the government should take care of those who are either too young or too old to work; (ii) the government should provide work for able-bodied persons who are out of employment; (iii) the government should take care of those who are physically disabled and who find it very difficult to make their own living; and (iv) the dependents upon public relief should work as much as they are able. The old should not only be supported by the government but should also be respected by the authorities. (For details, see *Li Chi,* Book XXI, Section I, 13, Book XXXVII, 24. Requoted from Hsü, L. S., op. cit., pp. 148-159.)

Confucius and his disciples are advocates of benevolent imperialism, that is, "the influence of the benevolent government should be extended throughout the world with unselfish motives either for the civilisation of undeveloped peoples or for the overthrow of tyranny." (Hs, L. S., op. cit., p. 126.) The proper conduct of public administration by the scholar mandarins selected in meritocratic principle is essential to the realisation of benevolent rule, as reviewed earlier through the ideal typical model of the Confucian University. (*Analects,* Book XII, Chapter xxii, Requoted from Hs, L. S., op. cit., p. 83.)

99. There have been discussions about the concept of the professions in sociological theory. Freidson, E. *Professionalism reborn: theory, prophecy & policy.* Chicago: University of Chicago Press, 1994; Siegrist, H. The Professions, State and Government in Theory and History, in *Government and Professional Education,* edited by T. Becher. Buckingham: SRHE & Open University, 1994, pp. 3-22; Torstendahl, R., M. Burrage (eds). *The Formation of Professions: Knowledge, State and Strategy.* London: Sage Publications, 1990.

100. For example, Dingwall, Robert and Philip Lewis (eds). *Sociology of the Profession,* London: Macmillan, 1983; Macdonald, K. M., *The Sociology of the Professions,* London: Sage, 1995.

CHAPTER THREE

The Colonial Period

The book examines, in this chapter, the shaping of the academic profession in the colonial period of Korea (1910-1945) and Malaya (1824-1957).

The first main argument in Chapter Three is that the academic profession in this period was constructed (or re-constructed) by the colonial States to meet the immediate needs of those States.

The second main argument is that the colonial States' conceptions of the university led to struggles over institutional forms and over what was valued knowledge. In Korea, Japan changed the existing Confucian conception of 'the university', but in Malaya, the British colonial State created the university.

The third main argument of the chapter is that the academic profession was shaped not only by the major historical forces and factors of colonialism and educational traditions which locate the first two arguments above, but that the academic profession was also shaped by a series of smaller struggles and subtler conflicts about social mobility and opportunity, which helped to define its shape.

The arguments will be tested in three sections follow from the operational themes specified in Chapter Two: (i) the values and visions of the colonial State which affected the formation of 'the university' and the initial shaping of the academic profession; (ii) the State's 'idea of the university', which led to conflict over institutional forms and valued knowledge; and (iii) the detailed patterning of the academic profession which resulted. The last section of Chapter Three is a concluding and comparative interpretation of both societies and both academic professions in the colonial period.

THE VALUES AND VISIONS OF THE STATE

The purpose of this section is to analyse the ways in which the academic profession was shaped in the Japanese and British colonial periods in Korea and Malaya.

Thus, the argument is that the initial shaping of the beginnings of the academic profession in these East Asian countries was directly linked to its colonial contexts, and to the different political, economic and cultural projects of the Japanese and British in Korea and Malaya.

The section begins with a comparison in Korea and Malaya of the colonising States' modernity projects—what are termed here the 'values and visions' of those States. Both the Japanese and British colonial States undertook, to their own agendas, the economic modernisation of their colonies. Politically and culturally, however, the Japanese colonial State's rule[1] in Korea was much more penetrating and more obviously repressive than that of British colonial power in Malaya.

The book will examine the case of Korea first and then that of Malaya, to show the emerging relations of the colonial State and university, and the initial framing of the shape of the academic profession.

Korea: Values and Visions of the State: The Japanese Colonial State's Modernity Projects

The book first looks at the Japanese colonial State's modernity project in Korea, within which a modern higher education system was created. These modern educational institutions were the initial *locus* of the embryonic academic profession in Korea. The main argument is that it is possible to show that the construction of a higher education system in Korea was directly related to Japanese colonial political, economic and cultural projects. The analysis begins with the collapse of the isolation of the 'hermit kingdom'.

The late nineteenth century was a turning point in international relations for Korea. Korea had to redefine its political and economic relations with the external world, while China was struggling to maintain its sovereignty against Western incursions, and Japan was involved in rapid industrialisation. Korea was affected by the maneuvering among the Chinese, the Japanese, and the Russians. After hundreds of years of isolation as an 'hermit kingdom', Korea was not prepared for the challenges from foreign powers.

Korea was pulled into the world system in 1876 with the Kangwha Treaty with Japan,[2] and thereafter was exposed to several foreign influences, but most notably influences from Japan which had defeated China in the Sino-Japanese War of 1894 and established its dominance in the Far East by defeating Russia in 1904.

The second challenge to Korea was initially domestic. The pro-Japanese governing elite in Korea initiated a reform in 1894, similar to the Japanese Meiji Restoration in 1868. Led by these pro-Japanese Korean innovators, the 1894 Reform (*Kabo Kyongjang*) brought a fundamental change in Korea's political, social and economic infrastructure—not least through

Korea's changing international relations.

During this reform period, Japan was already influencing the Korean modernity project,[3] and the new modern governmental structure. The State Council (*Uijongbu*) was reorganised. Subsequently, this was further reformed, resulting in a Cabinet (*Naegak)* composed of seven ministries— for foreign affairs, home affairs, finance, justice, education, defence, and agriculture, commerce and industry, with bureaux and sections in each.[4] The traditional Confucian examination system was also abolished in these reforms. As a consequence of the 1894 reform (*Kabo Kyongjang*), the Confucian institutions which had existed in Korea since the 4th century were transformed.[5] Korea began to be a modern State, under Japanese influence.

The political project of the Japanese colonial State was to locate Korea firmly within Japanese rule. After the Protectorate Treaty of 1905, even before formal colonisation, Japan put the Education Ministry of Korea under its control to begin to convert Korean schools into instruments of the imminent colonisation. Three years after that, Japanese citizens already made up one third of the teaching force in Korea.[6]

The initial steps toward colonisation involved political efforts to gain the collaboration of the Korean governing elite. Titles of nobility and cash payments were distributed to 3,645 Koreans.[7]

The Japanese colonial State was headed by the military from the beginning.[8] The first Japanese colonial Governor-General, Terauchi Masatake, was from the Japanese military and his control was characterised by repression,[9] which prohibited public assembly for 'any purpose' and drew up new regulations aimed at inhibiting Korean freedom of expression. All political activity by Koreans was banned.[10]

In this context, conformity was highly emphasised in schooling.[11] School instructions were delivered in military fashion and school rituals were militaristic.[12] All Japanese officials and teachers wore military uniforms and carried swords even at school, and students had to wear black uniforms and keep their hair very short as if they were in the army.[13] All textbooks were censored; any material which fostered Korean national pride was banned.[14]

Resistance followed. The Independence Movement in 1919 attacked Japanese colonial propaganda which included the false idea that the Korean people had willingly submitted to Japanese colonial rule; and accordingly world opinion became extremely critical of Japan's actions in Korea.[15] As a result, the Japanese colonial government reoriented its political agenda. Japan announced that it would abandon reliance on its gendarmerie police forces to govern Korea.[16]

However, the new policy was largely fraudulent. For example, up to the time Japan was forced from Korea in 1945, no civil official was appointed to the post of Governor-General and police organs were in fact expanded and the number of police personnel increased.[17] The political project and the means of its enforcement were uninterrupted.

The initial economic project of the Japanese colonial government was to use Korea as a base to supply human and physical resources in the Japanese struggle to catch up with the Western industrialised countries. In the course of its modernisation by Japan, Korea had to go through a fundamental economic transformation during the three and a half decades of colonial rule, but as a complementary part of the larger economic unit of the Japanese Empire rather than an autonomous, independent unit.[18] This economic transformation was deliberately planned and effectively carried out. The ultimate intention to make Korea a permanent part of Japan prompted heavy investment in the administrative infrastructure, communications, railroads, ports, and other physical facilities in Korea.

From the 1930s onwards, Korea was viewed as strategic base for Japanese military expansion into the Asian continent, as well as for the consolidation of Japan's concept of an East Asian Economy.[19] Thus, the Japanese expedited new industrial development in the northern part of the Korean peninsula (which is now North Korea) and continued the exploitation of agriculture in southern Korea for the Japanese.[20]

To facilitate the process of colonial industrialisation, the colonial administration intensified its direct control over the economy, relying on a tripartite apparatus made up of the business conglomerates (*zaibatsu*), the central bank and the administrative bureaucracy.[21] The Japanese colonial State stepped in to fill the role of an incipient entrepreneurial class in Korea. The large corporations formed to organise heavy industrial production were staffed by Japanese, especially at the upper levels. Small scale enterprises, owned or managed by Koreans, were strictly subordinated to Japanese rules.[22] In short, the Japanese modernised Korea's economy to benefit Japanese political and military interests.[23]

These processes, of the development of new modern industries in the colony, had an educational consequence: the establishment of a public education system and the promotion of literacy in Japanese. By 1935, 2,361 elementary schools existed in the country, averaging one in each county and enrolling 30 per cent of male children between the ages of 6 and 12 in school. By then a substantial number of Korean adults had also received public elementary school education.[24] This nation-wide distribution of Japanese elementary education in Korea was aimed at producing cheap and relatively unskilled manpower for the development of new industries within the Japanese Empire.[25]

The Japanese cultural project for colonising Korea meant the destruction of the older Chinese cultural influence on Korea. To disseminate the Japanese language, Japanese morality, Japanese customs, and practical, vocational skills, the Japanese colonial government in Korea developed a tight network of primary schools. At the post-primary level, the Japanese colonial government encouraged vocational training in particular, rather than academic education.[26] Similarly, within this cultural project, the Japanese colonial government imposed various regulations and ordinances to restrict any Korean effort to generate a national educational system during the 36 years of occupation,[27] by setting up a separate and unequal schooling system for Koreans.[28] Paradoxically, however, elementary education after colonisation (in 1910) expanded considerably.

The deliberate promotion of Japanese literacy and cultural influence in Korea also marks a process of the systematic devaluation of the Korean culture and language.[29] For example, Japanese Shinto was used as a cultural agent of political and military control in Korea. To achieve this aim, during the colonial period, practically every city, town, village and even schools had Shinto shrines where the spirits of the ancestors of the Japanese, especially of Amaterasu Omikami, the sun-goddess, were worshipped.[30] In 1935, the Japanese colonial State ordered all educational institutions, including Christian schools, to ensure obeisance of their students in Shinto shrine ceremonies. Governor-General Minami introduced the 'Japanization' policy (*kokoku shimminka seisaku*) into Korea in May 1936, which contained three principles: the clarification of the essence of the Imperial system; the oneness of the Japanese and Koreans, and Training for Endurance.[31] In 1937, he forced the "Oath of the Imperial Subjects" upon the Koreans to test the Korean reaction to his policy. There was a severe reaction, for example by the Christian (academic) community, against such usage of Shinto.[32] When Korea was liberated, practically all the main Shinto shrines were burnt.[33]

The Japanese cultural assimilation project in Korea was also shown in language policy. All textbooks were published in Japanese, even for the first primary grades. Between 1920 and 1930, the percentage of the population who could speak Japanese rose from over 2 per cent to over 8 per cent,[34] and proficiency in Japanese expanded: "Out of a total of eleven different types of schools in the colonial educational system, eight required almost total Japanese language comprehension."[35]

From the 1930s onwards until the end of the colonial domination, the Japanese economic absorption project and the cultural project for assimilation greatly intensified: Japan required a labour force that understood Japanese for the development of war industries in Korea in the 1930s.[36] Therefore, from the 1930s Japan laid even more stress on teaching the Japanese language and on vocational education, invoking the doctrine of "education for everyday life".[37] The abolition of Korean language courses followed. In 1940, Governor-General Minami ordered the abolition of Korean kin-names so that most Koreans had to adopt Japanese style family names.[38]

The overall consequence of these projects and the restricted definition of 'educational reform' was the establishment of a Japanese dominated schooling system. It is against this educational and political background that the colonial conception of the university, and the formation and initial shaping of the academic profession in Korea, will be reviewed later. However, first, a comparison with Malaya in terms of the British colonial modernisation project is offered.

Malaya: Values and Visions of the State: The British Colonial State's Modernity Projects

This section looks at the British colonial State's modernity project in Malaya, within which the higher education pattern for the colony was constructed and one version of the modern British colonial university was envisaged. The main argument is that the British colonial State's modernity project in Malaya was initially driven from economic interests. Overall, the political construction of British Malaya followed an economic opportunity; the development of the colony, economically, meant also immigration, and a new ethnic profile in Malay society—which in turn produced cultural and political consequences.

Subsequently an ethnically-separated colonial schooling system was created in the colony, which was soon followed by the construction of the English-medium higher education system, the locus of the embryonic academic profession in Malaya. The English-medium colonial schooling system enrolled the selected locals, regardless of ethnicity, who would be recruited to government office and to the future academic profession.

The analysis begins with the construction of the 'Malay States' as a British colony. 'Malaya' became the term for an area which then included the Federation of Malaya and the Government of Singapore. Before the formation of Malaya, Singapore was already under British control, from 1819, on the initiative of Sir Stamford Raffles who founded a trading settlement as a free port. The British dominance in the Malay Peninsula was acknowledged in 1824, by a treaty to settle territorial conflicts between the Dutch and British in Southeast Asia.[39]

By that time Singapore had already become a centre of business activities, attracting Chinese merchants. The Chinese extended their economic role in trading, industry and tin mining in the Straits Settlements.[40] As the prosperity of the region grew, the immigration of the Malay people from Sumatra and other parts of Indonesia continued, as well as Chinese and Indian immigration.[41] At the turn of the 19th century, a multi-ethnic pattern, with a strong Chinese community, was already visible in Singapore. This demographic trend continued. The Chinese constituted four-fifths of the population of Singapore by 1858.[42]

The British political project speeded up in 1895 when the Federated Malay States (Perak, Selangor, Negri, Sembilan, and Pahang) were formally constituted as the base for British governance of the major part of the Malay area. The other four States of present-day Peninsular Malaysia

(Perlis, Kedah, Kelantan, and Trengganu) did not come under British influence until 1909.[43]

After official colonisation, British rule gave the Malays their first experience of formal political unification, within the new multiethnic pattern of Malayan society. Traditionally, there was no historical concept of a unified 'Malay nation'. There was rule by Sultans. The indigenous Malays, *Bumiputera*,[44] lived in small, widely scattered settlements. The area which became Malaya was dominated by Islam from the 13th century, although there existed some cultural influences from India such as Buddhism and Hinduism.[45]

The British colonial political structures in Malaya were complex, combining direct rule over Penang, Malacca, and Singapore, indirect rule over the Federated Malay States, and looser supervision of the four other Malay states in the north. However, these components of Malaya were interconnected for the first time under British colonial rule in a single political entity. Politically, the British colonial project in Malaya was conducted through indirect rule. In governing Malaya indirectly, the British colonial State did not intend to alter the indigenous Malay and Islamic social structure. The British governed Malaya pragmatically.[46]

Since the British colonial political project in Malaya was the maintenance of a *de jure* Malay Sultanate and a *de facto* British Administration, there came an urgent need to create a new group literate in English for the colonial government's administration, against the context that before the introduction of the formal British colonial education system in Malaya, education was mainly religious, based on Islamic teaching, and confined to the aristocracy. Quran schools were the only educational institutions in Malaya.[47]

In the colonial educational system, the British established English-medium elite schools. The British colonial State especially favoured and sponsored high-ranking Malay aristocrats, who would be then selected as lower administrative colonial officers, while encouraging Malay commoners to be content with schooling in agriculture and the manual arts.

The intersection between English-medium elite schools and colonial government office in the longer term served as the training ground for the earliest governing elite in Malaya who would succeed British colonial government officials, as Malaya advanced to political independence.[48] However, the British colonial political project focused on 'divide and rule' in Malaya and was designed for securing the political stability necessary to exploit the economic resources in the colony.

The economic project of the British colonial State in Malaya was to develop a colonial export economy geared to the production of and trade in a few primary commodities such as natural rubber and tin.[49] It was for these economic reasons that the British established political sovereignty over the three Straits Settlements (Singapore, Penang, Malacca) in the 19th century.[50]

The British economic interest in the newly commercialised sectors of tin-mining and rubber in Malaya induced massive migrations of Chinese and Indians.[51] From the late 19th century until the 1930s, the British colonial government in Malaya actively encouraged mass immigration, which subsequently transformed the more-or-less homogeneous traditional Malay society into a heterogeneous multi-ethnic colonial society.[52] The ethnic diversity and separatism resulting from the British colonial State's economic projects became the initial condition of the colonial and post-colonial social composition of Malaya; and later Malaysia and Singapore.

The profitable economic system in Malaya was dependent on the success of the British colonial State's cultural project: to achieve social tranquility in multi-ethnic Malaya. Within this British cultural project, the three major groups, the Malay, Chinese and Indian lived in separate communities, engaged in different occupations, spoke different languages, practised different religions, attended different schools, and formed different social organisations.[53] The British colonial State projects consolidated the main role of the Malay aristocrats in government office, the role of the predominantly Chinese urban dwellers in business and trade, and the roles of the Malay peasantry and other Asian cultivators in the agricultural sector.[54]

Colonial educational policy followed the lines of the political, cultural and economic projects. British colonial education policy was to create a plural schooling system divided along ethnic and linguistic lines.[55] The result was a different education for the various ethnic groups.[56] The aim of this education to maintain order and stability was well articulated by Sir George Maxwell:[57]

> The aim of the Government is not to turn out a few rather well-educated youths, nor yet numbers of less well-educated boys; rather it is to improve the bulk of the people and to make the son of the fisherman or peasant a more intelligent fisherman or peasant than his father had been, and a man whose education will enable him to understand how his own lot in life fits in with the scheme of life around him.58

This aim was consistent with the British political principle in Malaya of 'minimum interference' in the affairs of Malay commoners.

Accordingly, there developed two main types of schools in Malaya during the British colonial period: the vernacular schools and the English-medium schools. The aim of Malay vernacular education was stated in the Annual Report on Education for 1921:

> Malay vernacular education has broadly three functions to perform: (a) to teach the dull boy enough reading, writing and arithmetic to help him keep his accounts with the village shopkeeper or his employer; (b) to prepare the intelligent boy for that English education which is necessary if he is to aspire to well-paid business or Government posts; (c) to give the

bright boy with a bent for manual work the groundwork for prosecuting such work profitably.59

The aim of English-medium education for the selected Malays was to produce skilled labour with English literacy, such as junior clerks for the administrative service and for employment in commercial houses. Although it was suggested that a sound liberal education should be offered, in practice the English-medium schools in Malaya were vocational.[60]

The systemic development of British colonial English education for the purpose of government recruitment of civil servants began with R. J. Wilkinson, who was appointed as the new Federal Inspector of Schools in 1903. He proposed "the establishment at a suitable locality in the FMS of a residential school for the education of Malays of good family, and for the training of Malay boys for admission to certain branches of the Government service."[61] On the basis of his proposal, the Malay College of Kuala Kangsar was established in 1905, modelled after English public schools as 'the Malay Eton', to cater mainly to the children of Malay rulers and chiefs. This social distinction was made an integral part of the college policy. The college became a major producer of future administrative elite members.[62]

The indigenous demand for an English (higher) education was denied by the British because of fear of over-education and the migration of rural Malays to towns to seek modern occupations which would violate the social balance intended in the British colonial projects.[63]

While the British colonial government established and maintained Malay and Tamil vernacular schools, the Chinese immigrants established and maintained their own vernacular schools. For the Chinese schools, the British colonial government did not provide financial aid—such schools were often the seat for the propagation of Chinese nationalism and communist activities.[64] The British colonial government was perturbed about the rapid expansion of the Chinese schools in Malaya and never trained any teachers for the Chinese schools. As announced by the Governor, Sir Cecil Clementi Smith, in 1933, the British colonial government took up a definite position to support only Malay education.[65]

The three separate vernacular education systems in Malaya continued along with the English-medium education system up until the end of the Japanese occupation in August 1945. In December 1945, the Secretary of State for the Colonies announced in the House of Commons that "the main aim of the Government as regards the political future of Malaya after its liberation will be the development of its capacity for self-government within the Empire."[66] The gradual process toward independence and the idea of a role for education in the invention of the new Malay national identity meant discussion of the establishment of a university in Malaya.

As reviewed so far, the Japanese and British colonial States established formal education systems in Korea and Malaya but on discriminatory principles. In both cases, the basic discriminatory pattern of schooling was initially marked by the languages of instruction and differential governmental sponsorship. Both the Japanese and British States established the University in their colonies, as the apex institution of elite mobility on the top of such discriminatory educational routes. In such colonial social and educational contexts, the respective colonial States implemented their 'idea of the university'. The book examines the Korean case first, and then the case of Malaya.

THE STATE'S IDEA OF THE UNIVERSITY: STRUGGLES OVER INSTITUTIONAL FORMS AND VALUED KNOWLEDGE

Korea: The Japanese Colonial State's Idea of the University

The main argument in this section is that the colonial State's modernity projects in Korea was soon substantiated by the importation of the Japanese version of the modern university, a variant on the Western tradition. The Japanese colonial State's 'idea of the university' stressed Western knowledge and its practical use, but the Japanese State saw no need for the conventional 'idea of the university' as this had been expressed for example by Newman or was later expressed by Jaspers. In Korea, the Japanese emphasis on 'Western' (useful) knowledge also meant a replacement of Confucian knowledge.

Such Western knowledge as was imported was anyway censored by the Japanese in the colonial situation.[67] Despite this, the Japanese colonial period (1910-1945) was named 'the Modernisation Era' of Korean history by Japanese historians.[68] Thus, in terms of types of valued knowledge, there was first a shift from Confucian classics to Western knowledge.

However, the concept of academic autonomy, implicit in the structural arrangements for the creation of 'modern Western knowledge' in 'the university' was distorted by the colonial condition of Korea. The Japanese colonial State did not acknowledge the autonomy of academics. Academic autonomy in the public sector of higher education was erased by the colonial modernity projects discussed earlier.[69]

However, despite impediments and limitations, academic autonomy did survive in the private sector in Korea. This often produced tension between the State and the academics of the private sector. It was also through the private sector that a Korean academic ethos was preserved and Western knowledge was directly transmitted by Western expatriate (missionary) scholars. The idea of the social role of the autonomous man of knowledge survived within private institutions.

Both Korean and Western expatriates sought ways to resist the colonial State's regulations which restricted academic autonomy and freedom. For instance, proscribed Korean books were disseminated secretly and underground classes in Korean history and culture were conducted at Yonsei University.[70] Police arrested students who were found to possess notes from such classes.[71] For instance, the Korean Language Society composed of Korean academics in the private sector led a campaign to conserve and develop the native language. Leading members of the society "were arrested and put on trial during World War II especially for the heinous crime of compiling a dictionary."[72]

The effort to reassert national independence and the civic university movement, led by Korean intellectuals to claim academic freedom and to expand higher educational opportunity for Koreans, eventually hastened the promulgation of the Kyung Sung Imperial University Ordinance in May 1923.[73] The Japanese colonial government finally established Kyung Sung Imperial University in 1926, as the only authorised national university in Korea during the whole colonial period.[74] Thus, this university was under tight Japanese control. In contrast, the private institutions, which had to be called junior colleges (*Jeonmun Hakyo*) during the colonial period, were the only academic locus available for Korean scholars. (Such private institutions would eventually become the bases for the leading universities of the independence era.)

Overall, Japanese colonial education policy for higher education never changed its aims: to educate Koreans to perform supporting roles for Japanese bureaucrats and technicians. Japan directed its efforts toward creating a higher education system in Korea which emphasised the technical, the practical, and the militaristic.

The consequence of this Japanese view of 'the university' was, basically, that Korea could not establish a university of its own in the colonial period. The agency which linked the institutions of higher education (both public and private) and the Japanese colonial State was simple and, in some ways, symbolic of this fact. The higher education system was under the direct control of a military Governor.

Nevertheless the story is not as simple as that. The story will be elaborated—and the struggle over the shaping of the academic profession better illustrated—by concentrating on three issues: the basic institutional pattern of Korean education as a whole; the institutional forms of higher education; and the issue of what would be taken as valued knowledge in higher education. The issues are of course inter-linked. The basic institutional pattern affected who could get into higher education; the institutional forms affected the shape of the academic profession; and the struggle over valued knowledge defined what the emergent academic profession would study.

The basic institutional pattern

The Japanese colonial State's discriminatory educational policy in Korea began with the Korean Educational Ordinance of 1911,[75] which fixed the period of schooling as only eleven or twelve years for Koreans.[76]

The Education Ordinance of 1911 by the Japanese Governor-General indicates that the essential principles of education in Korea "shall be the making of loyal and good subjects by giving instruction on the basis of the Imperial Prescript concerning education."[77] Accordingly, the Japanese colonial Governor-General in Korea imposed strict regulations on the qualifications of teachers, the standard of buildings, and the facilities which all types of educational institutions were permitted.

One consequence was a marked disparity between the proportion of Koreans and Japanese receiving education, and between the 1920s and the 1940s, the expansion of secondary education continued to lag far behind primary education. Dong notes:[78]

> In 1920 one out of about six Korean students in primary schools, that is, common schools, had a chance of secondary education within Korea but...twenty years later only one of 30 primary school students in Korea could obtain a secondary education in Korea.79

At the end of World War II, only 2 per cent of the Korean population over 14 years of age had completed secondary school. Of all students enrolled in the school system at that time, 93 per cent were in the primary grades.[80]

To sustain this educational system, the Japanese established teacher training colleges. Other semi-professional schools to train Korean medical and legal assistants were also established. However, graduates of vocational secondary schools were not eligible for admission to higher education. This Japanese education policy in Korea consequently expanded the number of Korean students studying overseas.[81]

On the top of formal schooling which consisted of six years of primary school and five years of secondary, the Japanese colonial State defined a higher education system. The expansion of this higher education was necessarily limited by the State's control over the educational base—the schooling system.

In their higher education reforms, the Japanese created a public sector (Kyung Sung Imperial University, Government Normal Schools for teacher training, and Vocational and Technical Educational Institutions including professional schools[82]) and permitted a private sector of higher education—notably Christian missionary institutions founded by Americans and other private higher educational institutions established by Korean nationalists. The Japanese colonial State's education policy which limited the expansion of higher education, and academic autonomy within that, led to major tensions over the institutional forms of higher education. The tensions were a struggle over the formation of the academic profession itself, in Korea.

The institutional forms of higher education

The struggle over institutional forms was the tactical version of what the concept of the university was to be. The Japanese wanted the university to the useful, for the reasons discussed earlier. The concept of academic autonomy was not a major issue in the Japanese colonial State's idea of the university—in the sense that the Japanese did not recognise it for Korea.

In the higher education system newly constructed by the Japanese colonial State, there was a distinction between the university (of specific utility for the Japanese State's colonial project) and the Colleges (of various types); there was a distinction between the public and the private.

Within the new colonial higher education system of Korea, *Sung Kyun Kwan*, the Confucian institution of higher learning founded in 1398, had to be closed down in 1911.[83] By Ordinance, the authorisation to award degrees by Korean institutions, such as the Soong-sil Academy created by the former Korean Government in 1907 and Ewha Academy which was established in 1910, was annulled.[84] At the same time, a large number of private institutions set up by Koreans had to be closed. The movements to establish new civic universities by the Korean nationalists were further suppressed. As a result, the number of private institutions decreased from 2,080 in 1910 to 689 in 1920.[85]

However, there was a continuing struggle with the private sector. When a revised regulation was promulgated in 1915 to reinforce control over the private institutions, the Federal Council of Missions in Seoul protested against the regulation. This paved the way for the authorisation of Chosen Christian College (later Yonsei University) which was managed by a Foundation of missionaries from the U.S.A. and Canada.[86] Also, Severance Medical College, later annexed to Yonsei University, was granted a charter. However, the effort to upgrade junior colleges run by the missionaries to the level of degree awarding institutions ended unsuccessfully.[87]

Japanese colonial education policy continued to block Korean initiatives to establish their own educational institutions. For example, in November 1922, 46 national leaders organised a preparatory committee to discuss establishing a civic university. In the following year, a committee had a meeting at the YMCA in Seoul to raise funds and organise local chapters. Both efforts were stopped. The consequence was that there emerged a higher education system—and an embryonic academic profession in Korea—which had at its centre the discriminatory principle of nationality. This is illustrated by higher education enrollment figures:

Table 1
Higher Education Enrollment in Korea by Nationality in 1925

School Level	Nationality	Enrollments	Per Ten Thousand Population	Ratio
Colleges	Koreans	1,020	0.55	1:26
	Japanese	650	14.24	
University	Koreans	89	0.05	1:109
	Japanese	232	5.46	

Source: Lee, Ki-baik, *A New History of Korea*, Cambridge, MA.: Harvard University Press, 1984, p.367.

The Japanese colonial State continued to limit the opportunity for higher education for Koreans even after the establishment of Kyung Sung Imperial- University.[88] As shown in the Table above, in the colleges the proportion of Koreans to Japanese was 1:26, and at the university level it was well over 1:100. In 1941, as Henderson points out, the number of Koreans in all kinds of higher education made up less than 1% of college-age youth.[89] Quotas governed the enrollment of Koreans: 12% in the natural sciences and 37% in the humanities and social science fields.[90] Throughout the colonial period (1910-1945), the ratio of Korean students enrolled in higher educational institutions did not exceed 0.2 per cent of the whole student population in Korea.[91]

More specifically at Kyung Sung Imperial University itself, there was a strict enrollment regulation based on nationality:[92]

Table 2
Number of Students at Kyung Sung Imperial University
(1924-1943)

Year	Number of Students		
	Korean	Japanese	Total
1924	44	124	168
1930	183	335	518
1936	129	307	439
1943	335	444	779

Source: Kwan Lee, 'Past, Present and Future Trends in the
Public and Private Sectors of Korean Higher Education',
in *Public and Private Sectors in Asian Higher Education
Systems: Issues and Prospects,* Hiroshima University, p. 53.

As indicated in the Table above, the imbalance between the Koreans and Japanese enrolled in the university marks an expansion of educational facilities in Korea for the benefit of the Japanese colonial residents in Korea. For Koreans, Kyung Sung Imperial University only existed to produce a highly selected 'pro-Japanese Korean elite' who would serve the colonial State afterwards[93]. That is, Kyung Sung Imperial University was a *Japanese* institution in higher education.

As indicated, there were the other forms of State higher educational institution. These institutions produced a useful, if subordinate, skilled workforce through teacher training in the Government Normal Schools, and through vocational and technical training in Industrial Schools.

The following Table shows the number of higher educational institutions and of students during the colonial period:

Table 3

Types and Number of Schools and Student Enrollment

Year\ no. of students	1911		1919		1931	
Schools	Schools	Students	Schools	Students	Schools	Students
Normal Schools	-	-	-	-	3	1,669
Industrial Schools	20	961	25	2,843	54	13,236
Colleges	5	409	8	901	13	2,825

Source: *Annual Report on Administration of Chosun 1930-32*, Government General of Chosun, Keijo, Dec. 1932, p. 73.

Since teacher training, i.e. the training of native teachers in the colony, was considered urgent and important for the running of the colonial education system, the Normal Schools for teacher training were all Governmental. Private individuals were not permitted to establish such institutions.

A Government Normal School was started in Seoul in 1921 with a five-year general and a one-year special course.[94] By 1932, public Normal Schools had been founded in all other provinces. However, those public Normal Schools in each province were soon abolished and the Government Normal Schools in Seoul, Haeju, and Taeku were enlarged and improved to meet the increasing need for training teachers.[95]

The Japanese colonial State deliberately made the teaching profession prestigious within its new colonial schooling system. In the colonial period, a schooling system based on Western models was organised at the national level and school diplomas soon became recognised as the major guarantee to enter the upper social strata of the colony.

The new political and economic significance of gaining a school diploma in the colonial period here clarifies one role of modern Western knowledge in the colony—it obliterated the Confucian educational pattern that had sustained the Korean political and economic infrastructure since the 4th century. In this process, teacher education expanded towards the end of Japanese rule. The number of Korean students then exceeded 10,000. However, the number of Korean faculty members in the teacher training institutes remained small until the end of the colonial period: there were only 32 Koreans among the 362 faculty members in the fifteen teacher education institutes.[96]

The third institutional form encouraged by the Japanese was the vocational and technical educational institutions. These again were to provide a useful and skilled group of workers. These institutions included the technical middle school, having a course of three or four years, and higher vocational education after 1915 was provided for those over 16 years of age who had graduated from a higher common school, or who had received schooling of an equal standard for three or four years.[97]

Given the urgent necessity of disseminating industrial skills in Korea, the

Japanese colonial government, at the beginning of 1909, established the governmental Han-sung High School and the Pyong-yang High School—both industrial schools.[98] The standard of the Industrial School was between primary and higher education and the stress was on practical skills. Apart from those of college grade, there were 140 vocational and industrial schools, mostly elementary industrial schools, with the others being concerned with agriculture, commerce and fishing.

Other useful skills, e.g. in the fields of Law, Medicine, and Science and Technology, were also taught in government colleges. In 1932, there were five such government colleges: Kyung Sung Law College, Kyung Sung Medical College, Kyung Sung Technical College, Suwon Higher Agricultural Dendrological School, and Kyung Sung Higher Commercial School.[99]

These vocational and technical institutions had been initially created as part of a Korean modernisation effort, before colonisation. With their take-over by the Japanese, their location in the public higher education system became fixed: that is, they lost the potential dynamic to expand, later, into technological universities. Such a process was characteristic elsewhere (e.g. the Land Grant colleges of the USA, or British technical institutes).

However, the struggle for a higher education system with its own Korean dynamic continued in the private sector, intersecting with earlier Korean government efforts.

Korean initiatives to establish modern higher educational institutions go back to the pre-colonial 19th century, and the Korean government's efforts to modernise the nation. In the process of creating a new education system, the Korean government, before colonisation, had established modern higher educational institutions such as *Kwang He Won* (the House of Civilised Virtue), which made the first beginnings in medical education in 1885 and *Yugyong Kongwon* (the Royal English School) in 1886.

Simultaneously, there was a significant contribution from Christian missionaries via private institutions of higher education and their subsequent expansion before Japanese colonisation. From the pre-colonial period, the Christian missionary institutions had contributed to promoting equality of educational opportunity, regardless of gender or socio-economic background.

For instance, Western medical education was provided by missionary institutions. In 1888, Severance Medical College, a medical school for the training of doctors, was attached to the American missionary hospital established in 1886. In this provision of Christian education, girls were also admitted to schools for the first time in Korea. Ewha Women's College (later Ewha Women's University) was founded in 1886 by Scranton, an American missionary in Korea, and became famous as the largest women's university in the world. By 1908, twenty-five Christian mission schools had been created by the missionaries, and of them about half were girls' schools.[100]

Other missionary colleges included Chosun Christian College which was founded by the Presbyterian Church in 1886 and developed into Yonsei University and became one of the leading private universities in Korea. This and Ewha Women's College were the oldest, most prestigeous institutions and contributed to producing major Korean academic leaders.

According to a 1926 survey,[101] the following higher education institutions had been created and were managed by Protestant missions:

Table 4

Private Missionary Institutions of Higher Education in Korea in the Colonial Period

Names of the Private Institutions	Student Numbers
Chosun Christian College (earlier named Yonsei University)	250 (men)
Union Christian College	150
Ewha Women's College	70 (women)
Severance Medical College (Later annexed to Yonsei University)	62
Methodist Theological Seminary	165
Presbyterian Theological Seminary	150

Jayasuriya, J.E., *Education in Korea - a third world success story*, Seoul: Korean National Commission for UNESCO, 1983, p. 36.

Thus, the private sector of higher education in Korea eventually surpassed the public sector in numbers of institutions[102] and people, both academic staff and students, even though the Japanese colonial State's official position was to repress the growth of higher education, and to place the private sector of higher education under the direct control of the government.

Overall, under Japanese colonial rule, the surviving private institutions served as the main locus of the Korean academic profession in the colonial period. Against the State's position which stressed the Japanese colonial conception of the university, the private institutions played a significant role in shaping the first generation of the modern Korean academic profession even during the colonial era.

The tensions over institutional pattern of higher education examined so far indicate the Japanese colonial State's idea of the university. Another form of the tension in terms of the colonial State's idea of the university was a struggle over types of valued knowledge.

Valued Knowledge

The book examines valued knowledge in the colonial higher education system as an indicator of the State's idea of the university. Especially in a colonial situation, it is argued, valued knowledge is politically legitimated by the State, and this affects the cultural and epistemological framing of the academic profession.

Thus, this section examines the struggle over valued knowledge by noting the continuity and discontinuity of Confucian influence on the cultural valuation of knowledge, the Korean "double importation" of Western knowledge via Japan, the languages of instruction and learning, and the consequence of these changes for the embryonic academic profession in Korea.

As indicated earlier, the Confucian tradition of knowledge was broken in the Japanese colonial education system in Korea. The Japanese State still used the former Confucian mechanism for recruiting government officials of Korean nationality on the basis of State examinations. However, the knowledge to be tested in State examinations altered from the Confucian tradition to an amalgam of Japanese cultural literacy and Western knowledge, when the Japanese created the new schooling system.

For example, the subjects tested in the entrance examination of Kyung Sung Imperial University included Japanese language, writing, Chinese reading, foreign language comprehension (English or German) and its translation into Japanese, Mathematics, Western History, and Japanese History.[103] This curriculum was used in the selection of the civil service and offered possibilities for upward social mobility.[104] The Japanese State's promotion of new types of knowledge in the colonial period strengthened the already changed cultural valuation of knowledge in Korea which had been first initiated by the indigenous Korean "Enlightenment Group" [*Gaehwapa*] of the 1880s.[105]

In the pursuit of modernity, the Japanese colonial State's economic project was based, as reviewed earlier, on imported Western knowledge and applied technology. The Western knowledge regarded as useful by the Japanese State was then diffused through the government-dominated public higher education system in Korea and its authority was accepted in the colonial context. In this sense, the redefinition of knowledge was a reprise of the earlier Korean struggle for 'modern knowledge'.

Arguably, however, in terms of the borrowing of Western knowledge, the Japanese colonial State in Korea provided an *indirect* channel to Western knowledge for Koreans. For instance, the Japanese colonial government sent able Korean students to Japan, and not to Western countries (whereas Japanese students and scholars were sent to the Western world to absorb directly the knowledge needed for modernisation).[106] Only a privileged minority among Koreans had the opportunity to receive higher education, in colleges and universities in Japan and the U.S.A.[107] In the colonial period, the Japanese idea of the university was articulated with the episte-mological support of the German concept of *Staatwissenschaft* ("the study of the State") in both Japan and Korea.[108] Despite the double importation into Korean academe via Japan, Western (especially German) knowledge has had significant influence on the shaping of the academic profession in Korea since the colonial period.

Types of knowledge valued at the university since then have followed the 'normal' hierarchy—with Law and Medicine as prestigious subjects. Kyung Sung Imperial University in the beginning had only two faculties: the Faculty of Laws and Literature (offering four courses: Law, Philosophy, History and Literature) and the Faculty of Medicine. The Faculty of Engineering was added only later in 1938.[109]

However, the curriculum at Kyung Sung Imperial University was biased against science and technological subjects. According to Chang Yun-Shik,[110] one reason is that highly skilled Japanese in the fields of science and technology emigrated to Korea to undertake the industrial development of Korea. Thus, there was no urgent need to provide advanced knowledge in science and technology in the Imperial University in Korea. A second rea-son is that the Japanese political project put an emphasis on the moral aspects of higher education in the colony to foster the loyalty of Koreans to the Emperor.[111] The curriculum at Kyung Sung Imperial University, therefore, mainly concentrated on humanities rather than advanced tech-nological training in the colonial period.

Thus, although there was some emphasis on relatively low level voca-tional preparation (in teacher training, and in the vocational technical fields), there was also weak support for studies in the pure sciences and Western Philosophy; and a very low status for Theology in the knowledge hierarchy of the university in Korea. Noting the new prestige given to prag-matic fields of knowledge in the colonial period, prospective Korean aca-demic candidates were likely to study applied sciences and vocational tech-nical knowledge at low or intermediate levels.[112]

The German influence on the Japanese concept of useful Western knowl-edge and its double importation to Korea can be also understood in terms of the changing international relations of Japan with Britain and the United States, after the Japanese full-scale invasion of China in 1937 and the attack on the United States in 1941. Japan started controlling severely (and sometimes banned) the importation of Anglo-American texts in 1938. Thereafter until the end of the colonial period, it was not permitted, for example, to teach about the ideas of B. Russell and J. S. Mill at Yonhee (Yonsei) College from May 1938 till the end of the colonial period (1945).[113]

The doubly imported Western knowledge was also taught in a translat-ed medium. For example, at Kyung Sung Imperial University, the medium of instruction was entirely Japanese. However, in the private institutions, it was Korean. Even Western expatriates let alone Korean academics at Yonhee (Yonsei) College, for example, could deliver lectures in Korean at least until 1940. (After March 1940, despite the low proficiency of academics in the Japanese language, all lectures had to be given in Japanese.)[114] New criteria, set up by the colonial State then, for the appointment of academic staff included proficiency in the Japanese language.[115] Overall, acquisition of the Japanese language became essential for a successful academic career in Korea during the colonial period:

> Knowledge of Japanese rose from 0.6 percent of fifteen million in 1913 to over 15 percent of twenty-five million Koreans in 1945, or from ninety thousand to some three and a half million speakers. Every intellectual knew Japanese, and many schooled in the last decade of the regime [1936-1945] came to read, if not speak, it better than they did Korean.116

For the purpose of assimilation, the Japanese colonial State imposed regulations to ban teaching Korean Geography, Korean History and Christian Theology in private higher educational institutions. As indicated earlier, all text books used in the private sector had to be scrutinised by the Ministry of Education of the Japanese colonial State in Korea.[117] Ethics, Japanese and English were taught as the core subjects in the curricula of all types of tertiary institutions.[118]

Nevertheless, Korean academics in the private sector sought ways of evading regulations. As indicated earlier, Korean history, literature, and language as part of Oriental History classes were taught secretly by distinguished Korean scholars such as Chung In-bo, and Choi Hyun-bai at Yonsei University.[119]

The overall colonial formation of valued knowledge reviewed so far reflects the Japanese State's idea of the university in Korea. The book suggests that the function of 'the university' was subordinated to the colonial State's projects, and thus knowledge for its own ends in Newman's terms, or *Bildung* in the German tradition, were not transmitted in Korea. The cultural valuation of knowledge as self-cultivation in the long Confucian tradition was further weakened. As reviewed in Chapter Two, the educated man in the Confucian era was identified with the practice of the Confucian virtues, possession of a good knowledge of the Confucian Classics and acquisition of Chinese letters as the medium of literate communication and calligraphic skills. This definition of the educated man changed in the colonial period.

To become an educated man, it was essential to acquire Western knowledge, imported either directly from the West, or, more often, via Japan.[120] The acquisition of the Japanese language became a major definer, even more than English, of an 'educated man' in Korea.[121] In this way, the tradition of Confucian knowledge, which used to be 'official knowledge' in Korea for over 500 years, was broken. This was very different from the case of British Malaya, which is the theme of the next section.

Malaya: The British Colonial State's Idea of the University

This section examines the ways in which the British colonial State articulated its 'idea of the university' in Malaya, through the colonial government's decision to unite the diverse forms of existing higher education institutions and to promote types of knowledge that would be valued in the future University of Malaya.

The main argument is that the British colonial State's idea of the university was built up, gradually, long after Raffles' vision of a native college in Singapore.[122] Thus, the following section will consider first the British colonial State's idea of higher education (rather than 'the university') in Malaya during the colonial period.

The British colonial State provided higher education in Malaya only through the English language. English-medium schooling was open to all ethnic groups so that English higher education in Malaya could bridge the gap between the various ethnic groups—they could share a common curriculum and language. However, while English-medium education at the secondary and tertiary level fostered participation in society by all ethnic groups, vernacular education at the elementary level, as indicated earlier, reinforced the three different ethnic identities through their languages of instruction.

The provision of vocational education at the tertiary level was also tightly linked to the economic value of English education. In a sense, every English-medium school in Malaya was a commercial or vocational school, as it was attended mainly by children who studied the language for its commercial value and not as a form of mental discipline or as a contribution to their liberal educational development.[123] The Kynnersley Commission appointed in 1902 to examine the English-language education system concluded that the training of efficient clerks must be regarded as perhaps the most important work to be performed by English schools.[124]

Thus, tertiary education institutions in Malaya were not only established late, but in Newman's terms, were *mechanical, particular* and *external*.[125] This difference in vision was noted as late as 1939 in the Memorandum of Professor H. J. Channon, who had been a member of the McLean Commission.[126] In 1918, on the commemoration of the centenary of Singapore, the Committee led by Sir George Maxwell was:

> ...unanimously of the opinion that the most suitable memorial [for the centenary] is a Scheme which will provide higher education for the people of Malaya and Singapore with a view to preparing the foundation upon which a university may in the course of time be established. There appear to be three steps: first, the establishment of technical and higher grade schools; second, the provision of Science and Arts Colleges; and third, the University itself, residential, teaching and examining, with powers to confer degrees in Science and Arts.127

This proposal was confirmed and implemented by the Firmstone

Committee of 1919, which recommended the establishment of Raffles College. The college was to meet the most urgent need for more qualified teachers, and to offer facilities for training in technical and scientific subjects to the increasing number of the colonised who desired to be better qualified for commercial and economic work. The official opening of Raffles College was on 22 July 1929.[128]

After the establishment of Raffles College, however, there was no further expansion of higher education in Malaya for some time. A persistent official concern in British Malaya was that the spread of education in Malaya should not produce a population of educated unemployed, which had been and was a problem in British India.[129] Thus, in British Malaya, educational institutions at the tertiary level were mainly for teacher training and technical and agricultural studies.[130] In consequence, Raffles College and the King Edward VII School of Medicine established in Singapore were the only institutions of higher education available in British Malaya until 1949.

However, there was a steadily increasing demand among the graduates of Raffles College and the School of Medicine for British conferment of their degrees in Malaya. To review the growing demand and need for local universities in the colony, the Secretary of State appointed a commission on Higher Education in Malaya (called the McLean Commission after its chairman Sir William McLean) in 1939, "to survey the existing arrangements for higher education, general and professional, in Malaya, and to consider in the light of local needs and conditions whether they require extension, and if so, in what directions and by what methods."[131] The Commission recommended the merger of Raffles College and the King Edward VII College of Medicine into a university college.[132]

However, due to the outbreak of the War and the subsequent Japanese occupation, the decision to establish a university could not be carried out until the late 1940s.[133] After liberation from the Japanese, a Commission on Higher Education in Malaya (known as the Carr-Saunders Commission after its chairman, Sir Alexander Carr-Saunders) was appointed in 1948 to proceed with the recommendations made in 1939 by the McLean Report.[134]

The impulse to development was from Great Britain, and the task, though officially approved and financed, was promoted by the British universities.[135] The early 1940s saw an overall review of the problem of university development in the British Empire and of the extent to which the universities of Great Britain could help in its solution. This was stressed by H. J. Channon, who had been a member of the McLean Committee (as well as an Advisory Committee on Native Education in Africa.)[136] Professor H. J. Channon suggested a long-term scheme to develop the colonial university:[137]

> In the realm of higher education, the universities provide a common ground for all the peoples; nothing but gain can result if advantage is taken of this fact. These views are in no sense imperialistic in the old and

selfish sense. If we are sincere in our belief in the value of education and in our professed wish to help the colonial peoples to maturity, one step of the greatest value would be to endeavour to bring university institutions of the Colonies into active relationship with the university system of this country [Great Britain].138

There was no pre-colonial tradition of academic autonomy in Malaya, equivalent to the Confucian concept of the autonomy of the scholar mandarin.[139] Thus, the English concept of academic autonomy was directly introduced from Britain into the academic profession in Malaya. This concept of university autonomy and academic freedom took root. The McLean Commission in 1939 urged the development of a strong British academic tradition in the colonies, a recommendation that the Inter-University Council for Higher Education in the Colonies accomplished.[140]

The idea of the university proposed by the Commission on Higher Education in Malaya (the Carr-Saunders Commission) in 1948 was fundamentally a transplant of a British civic university in its constitution, standards and curricula and social purpose.[141] Sir Alexander Carr-Saunders, the Chairman of the Commission and also the Director of the London School of Economics and Political Science, expressed a British views of the university at that time:

> In our view, it is a proper function of universities to prepare students for entry into the higher professions... It is only common sense to hold that those who have enjoyed a prolonged education at the expense of the community should, as the outcome of it, be able to render special service to the community, and the method of performing such service is nowadays mostly by exercising some high professional skill. But it is not enough to arm graduates with the ability to exercise such a skill; it is also the aim of a university education to enlarge the sphere of interest, to sharpen sensibility, to quicken perspectivity, and to deepen sympathy. In other words university education should be liberal as well as vocational, general as well as special. It is the essence of our view that there is not insuperable antagonism between the special and the general, the vocational and the liberal, in the sphere of education.142

Thus, the discussions drew on British experience of universities. For instance, in terms of the insulation mechanism between the State and the University, the McLean Report in 1939 had considered whether a new University of Malaya should be controlled by the Government, or largely financed by the Government but having an independent Governing Body.[143] The Commission noted the current practice in Great Britain, where the Universities and University Colleges were not under the control of the Board of Education. Government grants went through the University Grants Committee, a Committee appointed by the Treasury and largely composed of members who previously held University positions to the institution. The UGC, furthermore, exercised very little control over the policies of individual universities.[144] In this practice there was a very strong

English tradition that "University education should not be controlled by the State, partly because it was believed that in this way freedom of development was best secured and partly because only by such a method were the necessary [academic autonomy and] freedom of thought guaranteed".[145] In this sense, the idea of the university, initially explored by the British in Malaya, followed the cultural principles of Newman examined in Chapter Two.[146] In replicating the British model, academic staffing, governing structure, curriculum, examinations and degree awarding procedures in the University of Malaya were all arranged and controlled externally by the British, through the University of London.[147] In practice, however, the 'idea of the university' in British Malaya mainly focused on recruitment to the colonial government service and vocational training.

In terms of implementing the university framework in the new University of Malaya, the colonial State's conception of a university fitted with the British scheme of gradual changes in the postwar era. A university would make good Britain's promise to train the people under her rule to hold responsible positions in the administration and government. The offer of a university came late.

Thus, for much of the colonial period, the British were not concerned with the university, but with the theme of social control and vocational education including teacher education, in the context of the colony. The themes were politics and economics—and only secondarily and later universities and academic freedom. However, given the early separate provision of English-medium education by the British colonial State as the colonial elite mobility channel in Malaya, there was no clear endogenous struggle over the institutional forms of higher education for socio-economic upward mobility. The lack of endogenous educational struggle itself may reflect the success of the British 'divide and rule' principle in governing the colony. There was no strong pressure within Malaya to create a university, until the probability of political independence of Malaya became clear. In the following section, the book will look at the basic institutional patterns of colonial education constructed in British Malaya during the colonial period, which reflects the slow colonial progression forwards constructing a university in Malaya.

The basic institutional pattern

It has already been suggested that the priority of British colonial education policy in Malaya was to establish at the elementary level a secular Malay education system. Second level education in British Malaya was provided for the colonial training of local teachers who could teach modern Western knowledge, instead of Koranic subjects in the Malay vernacular schools.

Thus, from as early as 1864, the British colonial government was greatly concerned about teacher training in Malaya, where many of the teachers and even headmasters lacked proper training or experience which would fit them for their work.[148] Overall, the function of the teacher training college was basically to run efficiently the already established and divided vernacular schooling system in Malaya. Other forms of secondary and tertiary education institutions were limited to vocationally oriented training, such as medical training, and technical and agricultural studies.

The skilled-labour needs of Singapore's public sector and predominantly European-owned and managed private sector were met by the specialised colleges established by the British in Peninsula Malyasia. For instance, the Lemon Committee of 1918 recommended the establishment of a technical school near Kuala Lumpur to teach subjects such as mechanical, electrical and civil engineering, and surveying; the establishment of an agricultural school also near Kuala Lumpur; and the opening of trade schools to children who could follow instruction in Malay.[149] Following these recommendations, a Technical and an Agriculture College were set up, in 1925 and 1931 respectively, to meet these needs within the colonial State's economic projects.

The Windstedt Committee on Industrial and Technical Education of 1925 further marked the British colonial government's interest in promoting vocational training in Malaya. This Committee recommended that industrial and technical education in Singapore was not only feasible but necessary; and emphasised the pressing demand for English-speaking trained clerks, assistant surveyors, technicians and assistant engineers.[150] Simultaneously, however, there was a consistent effort to prevent the Malays from being 'over-educated', following the British experience in India. It is against this background that the construction of the institutional forms of higher education, and the university, should be understood.

The institutional forms of higher education

As already indicated, the first significant higher education institution in Malaya was a medical school established in Singapore in 1905, which was renamed King Edward VII Medical School in 1912. The objective of its establishment was to train local men[sic] to meet the growing demand for Assistant Surgeons and General Practitioners among the native and immigrant population.[151] By 1936, the College provided courses in dentistry and pharmacy as well.[152]

Raffles College was established in 1929 as the second university-level institution in Malaya. Unlike the College of Medicine, Raffles College was not a government institution, though it received financial support from the British colonial government. Also, unlike the medical college, whose standards were recognised early by the medical world in Great Britain, the standards achieved at Raffles College long remained without adequate recognition in the British Empire. Its status was autonomous, controlled by a council on which the government was represented, while academic matters were in the hands of the senate.

With the expectation that it would be the nucleus of a future university, one of its major functions was to meet an urgent need for qualified teachers for secondary schools.[153] Its early years were made difficult by a major economic depression, so that by 1934-35 it had only eighty students, but from then on steady growth took place.[154] The College offered diploma courses in arts and science subjects and catered predominantly for children of the urban English educated middle class and the sons of the upper ranks of Malay society.

Overall, opportunities to enter higher education in British Malaya were limited, particularly for the Malays. The British colonial government also confined higher education in Malaya to teacher training and technical and agricultural fields to produce a useful workforce as reviewed earlier.

The establishment of a University in British Malaya came in 1949, not far from the political independence of Malaya. As indicated earlier, it was during the War that thought about the establishment and development of universities in the British colonial territories grew.[155]

Following the British pattern of university government, the McLean Report recommended that the Governing Body of the University College in Malaya should be a Council; that the academic affairs of the College be advised upon by a Senate, which in turn would be assisted by three Faculties. His Excellency, the Governor of the Straits Settlements and the High Commissioner of the Federated Malay States was the patron of the new College. It was also recommended that the Government's contribution to the income of the new College should be made "in some such manner as that adopted by the University Grants Committee in Great Britain as has been already done in part for Raffles College."[156]

After the establishment of the Kuala Lumpur branch, the University of Malaya started to be run by two largely autonomous divisions of equal status, one in each territory. Under the new arrangements, the University of Malaya in Kuala Lumpur and the University of Malaya in Singapore each had a Principal, a Divisional Council and a Divisional Senate.[157]

Thus, following the recommendations made by the Carr-Saunders Commission in 1948, the University of Malaya began, on 8 October 1949, with 645 students in three faculties: 168 in the Faculty of Arts and 82 in Science from Raffles College and 395 students in the Faculty of Medicine from the College of Medicine. Other faculties came later—e.g. Education in 1950, Engineering in 1955, Law in 1957, and Agriculture in 1960. The university situated in Singapore served the needs of both Singapore and the Federation of Malaya for the next ten years.[158]

Unlike other British colonial universities (e.g. in Sri Lanka, Nigeria, Ghana and the West Indies), which first had to be constituent colleges of the University of London before becoming universities in their own right, the University of Malaya was able to acquire degree granting status immediately after its establishment.[159]

To meet the growing demand of the rapidly expanding education system, a Teacher's Training College was established in Singapore in 1950. The Singapore Polytechnic was established in 1958 to provide for growing technical and vocational needs. In 1955 the Muslim College was established in Kelang, Selangor. In 1956, the Nanyang Chinese University was established by the Chinese community of both Singapore and Malaysia to meet the demand for Chinese-language school graduates in Southeast Asia for higher education, to preserve Chinese culture and to keep Chinese education independent. Nanyang University in Singapore was a community-financed Chinese university with money from the Hokkien Huay Kuan Association. However, it adopted the US system of credit hours and provided courses in less expensive subjects in the humanities and social sciences.[160]

The late development of higher education in British Malaya meant a limited expansion of institutions of higher education. Teaching was in English. While there were some struggles over knowledge patterns among the academic expatriates, there was a relative lack of local pressure over the types of knowledge to be valued and taught in the university. Broadly speaking, the patterns of knowledge valued in the University of Malaya were 'British'.

Valued Knowledge

In the colonial period, the book argues, the same types of knowledge required in the English university system were also transmitted in the University of Malaya, but liberal education in the University was less intensive and at a much lower level than that in England. This knowledge transmission was to train an indigenous elite in English and ultimately to recruit them to the colonial administration office and business and commerce, rather than to cultivate the mind through liberal knowledge for its own end, as in Newman's model.

Overall into higher education in Malaya there was a strong vocational theme though with strong English cultural overtones. For the University established in 1949, the Carr-Saunders Commission directly imported the knowledge pattern of the London School of Economics. For instance, social work courses in the LSE were introduced to the University of Malaya, linked to a newly established Social Welfare Department in the colonial government. [161] In the degree structure set out in the Carr-Saunders Report, economics would be the prime subject, combined with other subjects—e. g. political science, law and sociology.[162]

However, this initial knowledge pattern in the Faculty of Arts was soon questioned and caused some tensions among the faculty members in the University of Malaya.[163] The University of Malaya began with three faculties: Medicine, Arts and Science, which enrolled total 645 students—395 in

Medicine, 168 in Arts and 82 in Science. Philosophy was a new subject introduced within the administrative control of the English Department. It was a success and was made a separate department from the 1954/55 session. The Science Faculty in the University of Malaya included Physics, Chemistry and Mathematics which were moved from Raffles College, and two new departments, Botany and Zoology, were opened. The Departments of English, Economics, History and Geography at Raffles College were transferred to the new university. The Faculty of Medicine has the longest history of all the Faculties in the University of Malaya, going back to 1905. The Faculties of Medicine and Law continued to enjoy high status in the knowledge hierarchy in the University in Malaya. The Arts Faculty in the University of Malaya developed a trilogy of Chinese Studies, Malay Studies and Indian Studies.[164] With these departments, the University approximated to Raffles' dream of making Singapore a centre for the study and spread of knowledge of Asian languages, culture and civilisation.

In reality, however, the academic expatriates who were resident in the colonial territory did not become part of the local community. Noting that the professor in a colonial university faced difficulties, such as the poor standard of the undergraduate students, limited staff, having no post-graduate students, and an emphasis on teaching, Channon suggested:

> Leaving aside the questions of teaching and research there is an equally important aspect of the work of the staff to consider. If we are to develop universities in the colonies, their vital objective at this stage must not be the production of large numbers of men and women with no more than a highly specialised technical knowledge; it should be the production of smaller numbers who, while they must be adequately prepared for their future professional livelihoods, must go further and be prepared for wider service.[165] [italics in the original]

Thus although the cultural valuation of knowledge in the University of Malaya officially adopted the model of the University of London, to embrace the rhetoric of 'liberal education', the actuality of academic working conditions in the colony made the full implementation of this high ideal very difficult.

There was a struggle among the academic "expatriates" over the knowledge profile of the University of Malaya, but there was no conspicuous contestation about knowledge paradigms between the colonised and colonisers in British Malaya. It is possible that the British "divide and rule" principle in the colony prevented a potential educational conflict, especially over language issues in the multi-lingual structure of primary, secondary and higher education in Malaya. The medium of university education to transmit the valued knowledge was taken to be English, only without major dissent.

THE SHAPE OF THE ACADEMIC PROFESSION IN THE COLONIAL PERIOD

This section argues that the formation of the two academic professions begins with the shaping of the formal education system in the two colonies. The school system as a whole was the first layer in the formation of routes into the academic profession, and shaped its social composition in terms of race/ethnicity, gender, social class and religion. The ranks, or hierarchy of the academic profession, also reveal the impact of foreign models. Both however can be understood as marking shifts in the principles of meritocracy in the two colonial societies.

In both Korea and Malaya, academic recruitment was distinguished from that of other professions such as Law and Medicine which included local candidates, who were either trained in the colonial system of professional education, or qualified overseas. In contrast, the two colonial university academic professions were filled with colonial expatriates directly recruited from Japan and Britain.

The embryonic academic profession in Korea in the colonial period, however, requires some additional interpretation. This is because of the special role of Japan as an *Asian* 'modernizer' and because of the legacy of the Confucian academic tradition in Korea. The Confucian academic tradition was influential in shaping the academic profession in the private sector of higher education, which recruited Korean scholars as well as expatriates during the colonial period.

Thus, in the colonial period, there were three major educational routes into the academic profession in Korea: Japanese (colonial State) institutions; private institutions (nationalistic or American missionary); and foreign educational routes (mainly Japanese and American). As indicated earlier, private institutions, by law, could not be referred to as "universities". Nevertheless, they were already perceived as institutions of higher education by the Western expatriates.[166] Within the three possible routes to the academic profession in Korea in the colonial period, the first generation of the "Korean" academic profession benefited most from the private sector.

The argument for the Malayan part is that the first generation of the academic profession in Malaya was mostly Western expatriate—either British or white British colonial expatriate. As discussed earlier, colonial educational provision in Malaya was divisive through the four different strands of education: English, Malay, Chinese and Tamil. Against this complexity (of a linguistically divisive colonial education system), the main formation of the nascent academic profession in Malaya was through the English-medium educational system. Within these descriptors, the book will first discuss Korea and then Malaya.

Korea: The Shape of the Academic Profession

This section examines the shape of the academic profession in Korea against the earlier analysis of the Japanese colonial State's values and visions for 'modernising' Korea, and its idea of the university, and the struggles over the institutional forms of higher education and which knowledge should be valued in the colonial period.

The colonial shape of the academic profession was clear by the end of colonial period. The number of higher educational institutions established in Korea was estimated 28 as reported in 1942: Kyung Sung Imperial University, 20 *Jeonmun Hakyo* [junior colleges] and 7 Professional Schools. The number of Korean students enrolled was 3,546 in 1943,[167] and the number of academic staff which included Japanese nationals in higher educational institutions by April 1945 was estimated as 908.[168]

These simple figures hide major struggles over the institutional forms in this period in the public and the private sectors. The formation of the academic profession in Korea was schizophrenic. As indicated, there were sharp differences between public and private institutions on issues of academic freedom, the direct or indirect importation of Western knowledge and differences in the language of instruction and resistance (or acceptance) of the Japanese cultural project. Both the public and private systems broke with the Confucian legacy, and many Koreans accepted the chance of social promotion in the new structures. Within the bifurcation of the institutional forms of higher education, the academic profession in the private sector retained Western missionaries, and indigenous Korean nationalistic scholars. In contrast, in the public sector, especially the academic profession in Kyung Sung Imperial University was dominated by the Japanese through Kyung Sung Imperial University and thus fully incorporated into the State's projects. Other types of public institutions of higher education are also noted as one of the major entry routes to the future Korean academic profession. Thus, some of the embryonic academic profession in Korea was being formed in teacher training, and vocational and technical institutions in the public sector.

These summary points can now be expanded against the themes, in the colonial period, of the cultural continuity and discontinuity of Confucian assumptions about academic mobility and the new opportunities and blockages, outside and inside Korea, for the academic profession.

The emphasis, in other words, as promised as the start of the book, is less on a photograph of the academic profession (its numbers, and so on) and more on the cultural, economic and political struggles shaping it.

The Confucian Legacy and Entry Routes to the Academic Profession

In Korea, the academic profession in Korea was not a new invention by the Japanese colonial State but it was partly shaped by shifts away from the Confucian tradition. Mobility opportunities in the colony involved the use by Koreans of shamanistic adaptations to the tensions between Confucian knowledge, Japanese knowledge and Western knowledge.

In the colonial period, the former single academic route to scholar mandarin status was destroyed. The modern academic profession in Korea emerged from the cultural inheritance of the idea of the Confucian literati and the emergence of the new (colonial) idea of the academic technocrat. The initial shape of the academic profession was affected by the socioeconomic advantages open to those who were engaged in the new modern economy established in Korea by the Japanese colonial State.[169]

As the Confucian system had already been abolished in 1894 before colonisation in 1910, it was not difficult for the Japanese colonial State to construct a new class structure legitimated by the new cultural valuation of Western knowledge. The Korean government officials in the pre-colonial period were new elites in the sense that they were all influenced by Western Enlightenment ideas and eager to adopt the Japanese model of modernisation. Even the former Confucian elites in Korea, who eventually became politically dissident intellectuals, while serving as academics in the private sector of higher education during the colonial period, were also affected by Western conceptions of "modern societies".

Arguably, however, there was some continuity in the Korean academic elite composition in the colonial period. According to Duck Kyu Jhin, the newly recruited government officials in the colonial period were mainly from the old Confucian pre-colonisation, ruling class background.[170] In his examination of the Korean political history of elite mobility from 1860 to 1950, Duck Kyu Jhin argued that the colonial mode of recruitment of the elite cadre was directly linked to the long established Cofucian State system.[171]

Although the colonial education system replaced the Confucian system when Confucian knowledge became irrelevant (in terms of the State's modernity project), the Japanese colonial State kept the Confucian mechanism of State sponsorship and academic selection for civil service recruitment in Korea. The Confucian idea that society is divided into the rulers and the ruled, which had dominated Korean society for over five centuries, was sustained in the newly formed colonial class structure. Both government officials and scholars had been almost exclusively recruited from the *yangban* elite in the Korean Confucian State.

However, along with the abolition of the Confucian State's examination system, the former distinctions between *yangban* and commoners were also eliminated from the processes of government recruitment.[172] This made it possible to open the ranks of officialdom to the man of talent irrespective of social background.[173]

The Japanese colonial State effectively used the educational incentive for upward socioeconomic mobility. The colonial State gave full scholarships to those in teacher training, and also upgraded their educational certificates to the same level as higher education diplomas. Education became regarded primarily as an effective means for upward mobility, accepting the traditional aspiration to government service, but de-linking it from social class background in Korea. As illustrated in Chapter Two, the position of the scholar mandarin (which guaranteed power and wealth) had been attainable through the formal academic route sanctioned by the Confucian State,[174] and was now established and approved by the Japanese colonial State.

However, while maintaining the Confucian mechanism of educational selection for government service, the Japanese colonial State broke the position of the former Korean ruling class, the *yangban* who had been the scholar mandarins. It was mainly Japanese nationals who were recruited to the academic profession in the State institutions and to high ranking positions in the government service, as the Korean *yangban* used to be in the Confucian State. Thus, although the Japanese colonial State maintained the older selection mechanisms to recruit colonial civil servants, there was no State-sponsored, systematic routes open for Koreans to enter the academic profession in the new institutional forms of higher education under the direct surveillance of the Japanese colonial State. This affected the shape of the meritocratic principle in the colony. The official tradition of a meritocratic principle in the selection of scholar mandarins in Korea has always triggered the commoners' desire to attempt social mobility whenever possible. In the new structure, the shamanistic culture of Korea, which gave a high level of adaptability in the social dynamics of Korea, became more effective in the colonial routes. According to In Whoe Kim, the shamanistic culture has been tested throughout the historic turbulence of the colonial experience in Korea.[175] According to Kim's analysis, Korean shamanistic values, characterised by strong adaptability for survival, include situation-oriented and life-oriented attitudes, and an opportunistic cultural code of ethics.[176] However, the Korean shamanistic values are identified with the commoners' culture against the virtues of the high culture of the Confucian literati in Korea.

It can be suggested that the colonial social mobility based on 'meritocratic' educational principle enhanced the diffusion of this shamanistic adaptability, which had been especially associated with the commoners. In the colonial period, the formerly dominant cultural code of practice and the definition of excellence inherited by the Confucian literati class became absorbed in the newly legitimated, situation-oriented, opportunistic cultural code in the colonial State's social promotion system. All Koreans were now commoners in the sight of the Japanese colonisers. In the colonial circumstances, the only possible way for Koreans to climb up the social ladder was to attain a higher education diploma authorised by the Japanese colonial State.

This principle was soon applied to the academic recruitment of Koreans.

This shift in the cultural form and usage of the meritocratic principle—present in Confucianism and also embedded in the older tradition of shamanistic culture, and newly defined by the Japanese—became culturally part of the formal entry routes to the academic profession.

Formal Entry Routes to the Academic Profession

The formal entry routes to the academic profession in the colonial period were mainly three: Kyung Sung Imperial University, the private sector of higher educational institutions, and overseas higher educational institutions, mainly in Japan and the United States.

As indicated, the Japanese colonial State controlled the shaping of the academic profession in Kyung Sung Imperial University by recruiting only Japanese expatriates to professorial positions. It also intended to expand Japanese domination of the academic profession in the private sector for the purpose of assimilation.[177] For Koreans, formal entry routes to the academic profession in the public sector were almost closed due to official educational discrimination during the colonial period—part of the assimilation policy of the 1930s.

Within this assimilationist pattern, the indigenous Korean academic profession during the colonial period survived with difficulty in the private sector, which had continued to expand after the abolition of the Confucian academic route in the 1894 *Kabo* reform. It was the limited educational opportunity of Koreans during the colonial period and the blockages in the State system which strengthened the private educational sector. More than half of the Korean students enrolled in higher education studied in private Korean institutions. The basis of this pattern in the lack of State provision of education is shown through the Annual Reports of the Japanese Government-General in Korea. Overall, in 1935, 5.5 per cent of the total Korean population, i.e., about one third of the children of school age, were educated in Japanese primary schools; 0.1 per cent of the total Korean population were enrolled in Japanese secondary schools and about the same number in the Japanese professional schools. From such a system, only a small number of Koreans were able to receive higher education. Of these, most entered private institutions.[178]

Thus, from a restricted general educational base, the private sector of higher education was the main formal entry route to the academic profession for indigenous Korean scholars in the colonial period. The Kyung Sung Imperial University graduates were also recruited to the academic profession in the private sector: both for secondary and higher educational institutions. As examined by S. E. Joung,[179] their real preference was to enter government office by passing the Japanese Sate examinations. As suggested earlier, this reflects the legacy of the Confucian valuation of the state-mandarin position.

The other main route into the academic profession for Koreans was

overseas. The foreign academic routes chosen by Koreans to obtain a higher degree were mainly through Japan (where discrimination against them
was ironically less severe than in Korea) and the United States.[180] In 1931,
3,639 Korean students were enrolled in schools (at all levels) in Japan,
while as many as 493 were studying in the United States. The majority of
them were college students.[181]

Overall, the embryonic academic profession in Korea was formed
through private academic routes available both locally and abroad, rather
than through the public educational routes provided by the Japanese colonial State.

This pattern however hides the detailed social composition of the emerging academic profession, which also echoes the newly emerging socio-economic stratification in the colony. The next section focuses on the social
composition of the academic profession (in terms of nationality, religion,
gender and social class in the colonial period).

Social Composition of the Academic Profession

As indicated, professorships at Kyung Sung Imperial University were
given only to the Japanese nationals. At Kyung Sung Imperial University,
there were one Korean lecturer, three Korean assistants among 39 professors, 13 associate professors, 8 lecturers, 13 assistants in 1941.[182] Kyung
Sung Imperial University appointed two Korean scholars in 1929, Dr. Ko
and Dr. Yoon, both educated in Japan, as associate professors in Medical
Studies. However, Ko resigned within two days and Yoon transferred his
post to Severance Medical School within Yonhee (Yonsei) College a year
after the appointment. In the private higher education institutions, the
majority of academics were Koreans, but especially those who were
Christians and adherents of the United States. The two were interrelated,
as Chon-Sik Lee has explained:

> The peculiar fact that Korea had become the colony of a non-Western
> power differentiates Korean nationalism from any other colonial nation-
> alism. Whereas most of the colonial nationalists around the world looked
> upon the Western powers, or the white race as a whole, with at best sus-
> picion and at worst hatred, the Korean nationalists looked upon the
> Western world as the pioneer of liberalism and a new civilisation (espe-
> cially after the country became subjugated by Japan).183

The Western academic world was perceived favourably by Korean academics, but the social structures in which they worked were heavily influenced by the Japanese.

As indicated earlier, the new class structure in Korea which emerged during the colonial period was the product of the Japanese colonial State's
modernity project. Therefore, a large portion of the new modern sectors in
Korean industry was occupied and controlled by the Japanese. Most
Japanese in Korea were highly selected immigrants, in the sense that much

of the Japanese migration was affected by the Japanese economic project in Korea.[184] The Japanese in Korea were skilled and professional personnel, seeking opportunities in colonial administration and economic expansion. According to Yun-Shik Chang, more than 80 per cent of the Japanese in Korea, who were gainfully occupied, were in the non-agricultural sectors in both census years of 1930 and 1940.[185]

Thus, the class and occupational structure was altered during the period of the rise of new industries in Korea, between 1930 and 1940. The Japanese in the civil service and the professions were estimated as 40. 6 % in 1930 and 27. 5 % in 1940.[186] That is, the number of Japanese in government occupations and in the professions decreased in percentage terms, although the actual numbers engaged in the same categories increased by 30 per cent. The number of Koreans in the (lower ranks of) government and in the professions such as law, medicine and secondary school teaching increased by 57 per cent.[187] Since the modern industrial sector was dominated by Japanese immigrants, these were the only possible professions available for Korean college graduates during the colonial period.

In fact, however, the opportunity for Koreans to enter the teaching profession was already unequal to that of the Japanese, as by law, only Japanese could be principals of educational institutions in the public sector. Thus, the Japanese were central in the social composition of academic personnel in higher education in the colonial period. By 1945, the last year of the colonial period, "close to one-third of the elementary school teachers, two-thirds of the high school teachers, and the majority of college and university professors" were Japanese.[188] Korean academics were also paid less than Japanese, sometimes only half as much according to the Japanese colonial State's regulations.[189]

The academic profession in the private sector was also occupied by the foreign educated—though these included Korean nationals. As innovative nationalist leaders infused with Western knowledge, the Korean academics in the private sector played a role, often as discussants, in modernising Korea in and after the colonial period. Leading Korean academics in the colonial period, such as Kim, Whal-ran (at Ewha Women's College) and Baik, Nak-jun (at Chosun Christian College), were notably the graduates from the private institutions of higher education.[190] Their leadership affected the reorientation of Korean society after Liberation, regardless of gender difference and other elements of the social composition of the academic profession.

However, the social composition of the academic profession in Korea was gradually affected by the Japanese colonial State's determination to increase the number of Japanese in the academic profession even in the private sector. A deliberate quota system based on nationality was used in academic recruitment.

By 1931, at Yonhee (Yonsei) College in the private sector, among 40 members of the academic staff, there were a Canadian Principal Dr. O.R. Avison, an American Vice-Principal, H. H. Underwood, the Korean Chancellor, Yu, Erk-kyum, and Korean Chairpersons of all departments. Altogether, there were 8 Americans, 27 Koreans, 4 Japanese, 1 Canadian at Yonhee College at that time.[191] From the late 1930s, however, Japanese academics further benefited from State-sponsored recruitment, and obtained extra legal and financial privileges, regardless of the divisions in the higher education sector. Thereafter the Japanese colonial State developed an extreme version of academic control for the assimilation project in Korea, in line with Japan's involvement in wars until the end of the colonial period. In that period, a new Japanese educational regulation imposed on the private institutions a new quota system to recruit and appoint Japanese academics to senior ranks. In consequence, the social composition of the academic profession in the colonial period in Korea was defined particularly by nationality.

Through a new national and legal basis for academic recruitment in the colonial condition, there emerged a new model of academic ranks within the academic profession. The official model of the university academic in the colonial period was the Japanese professorship, which was initially based on the German model. On the other hand, the academic profession in the private sector of higher education in Korea followed the American model. The ranks of the academic profession in Korea also appeared in the two patterns according to the divisions in the higher education sector: the public and the private. That is, the public sector followed the Japanese model, whereas the private sector followed the American model.

Notwithstanding this and the Japanese direct influence on Korea, the book argues that the shape of the academic profession in Korea (and South Korea after Independence) did not follow any single model. In fact, the shape of the academic profession in Korea, and later South Korea, is characterised by a rather complicated mixture of models: the traditional Confucian model of the scholar mandarin as a persistent legacy of Korean culture; the German model indirectly inspired by the Japanese professorship; and the Anglo-American model directly influenced by American missionaries in the private sector of higher education.

Overall, there were also several important colonial routes into the "embryonic" academic profession (that would be eminent in the post-colonial period). The Government Normal School for teacher training was an important route into the future academic profession, as most tertiary education institutions would be upgraded, after Korea became liberated from Japan.[192] Another important route into the embryonic academic profession was provided by vocational, technical and professional schools in the colonial period. These tertiary-level institutions of a lower academic status—apart from the medical college—provided practically-oriented education such as agriculture and vocational-technical studies.

The special financial aid and career sponsorship provided for the graduates of the Japanese colonial teacher training, vocational, technical and professional institutions continued in the independence period, leaving significant effects on the character of Korean education after Liberation.[193] While the Japanese colonial State did not recruit Koreans to the academic profession in the Kyung Sung Imperial University at all, the graduates of the Kyung Sung Imperial University were privileged in access to the academic profession in the private sector of higher education.

In summary, it is suggested that the embryonic Korean academic profession was already being shaped by the Japanese colonial State's control over the meritocratic principle in education, which was fundamentally defined by nationality. As professorships in Kyung Sung Imperial University were open to the Japanese only, the private sector of higher education was alternative the most favoured by the Korean academic candidates for a professional career then.[194] Accordingly, as Korean nationals, both those who entered the colonial State sponsored system (especially notable in teacher training, as well as Kyung Sung Imperial University) and those who went through the private educational routes (often extended to higher degree courses overseas, especially in the United States and Japan), sought an academic career in the private sector.[195] The cultural shape of the meritocratic principle in framing the Korean academic profession can be understood on two dimensions: first, the continuity of the Confucian tradition of high social respect for scholars in Korea, and second, the specific colonial context which produced anti-colonial and nationalist attitudes.

For comparison, the following section will examine the shape of the academic profession in British Malaya.

Malaya: The Shape of the Academic Profession

This section examines the shape of the academic profession in Malaya, which resulted from the British colonial period.

Malaya, unlike Korea, had no institutionalised university tradition. There was only the colonial State's route into the (embryonic) academic profession in Malaya. In terms of creating the new academic profession after the foundation of the University of Malaya in 1949, the British colonial State was the major actor in Malaya. Between 1949 and 1958, the staff increased from 58 to 195.[196]

However, it is argued that (as in the case of the Japanese in Korea) the British in Malaya did not provide, formally, entry routes into the academic profession for the colonised. As indicated earlier, the academic profession in the University of Malaya and other English higher educational institutions in the colony recruited mostly expatriate academics from Europe and British Commonwealth countries during the colonial period.[197] Given the long-established tradition of English education in the colony and its authority as the only channel of colonial elite mobility, it is suggested that there was no great endogenous struggles to change the meritocratic principle in academic recruitment culturally.

With these arguments, this section examines the formal entry routes to the (embryonic) academic profession and then the subsequent social composition of the academic profession in British Malaya.

Formal Entry Routes to the Academic Profession

The British colonial education system was the first potential route into the academic profession in Malaya. As indicated, before the introduction of the formal colonial education system in British Malaya, education was mainly religious, based on Islamic teaching and confined to the aristocracy.

However, since the colonial education system was based on different languages of instruction following ethnic lines, future access to the academic profession in Malaya would differ by the level of participation of ethnic groups in English-medium education.

The extent of education in colonial Malaya was limited. Education for the majority of the indigenous Malay people was "education not aspiring above instruction in gardening, simple carpentry etc. to train a child to be satisfied with forms of unskilled manual labour for which there was a constant demand".[198] It should be noted, however, that in the postcolonial period, vernacular schools would be upgraded to that of higher level educational institutions. Those newly upgraded vernacular higher educational institutions were then able to provide more opportunities for academic recruitment to those educated in the vernacular languages. (e.g. the Malay academics in the National University of Malaysia).

The British colonial State needed indigenous elites, selected from the English-medium institutions, for the colonial civil service. The British imperial recruitment system of the Malay Administrative Service (MAS) and the Malayan Civil Service (MCS) through formal education was newly introduced in Malaya, where a Confucian model of a State bureaucracy did not exist.[199] The function of the English-medium colonial higher education system to produce vocationally trained men for governmental posts. This led to the maintenance of the status of the traditional elites. In other words, the traditional Malay status structure effectively absorbed the emergence of the bureaucratic elites as a group in Malay society. The graduates of higher educational institutions in the colonial period became either teachers in the urban-based English schools or lower echelon staff members of the Malayan Civil Service (which in time became the breeding ground for Malaya's first two generations of political leaders.[200])

The major routes into the embryonic academic profession in British Malaya were the King Edward VII College of Medicine; Raffles College in 1929; and the University of Malaya. In the Medical School in Singapore, the staff consisted mostly of part-time lecturers drawn from the

Government Medical Service, the Royal Army Medical Corps, and the ranks of the general medical practitioners of Singapore before 1920. When the College needed to recruit an adequate full-time staff from about 1920, some Asian graduates of the College were recruited as academic assistants or lecturers in the College.[201]

The graduates of Raffles College mainly served as teachers in the English medium secondary schools. The College produced a small number of recruits for the lower echelons of the administrative ranks of the Civil Service in the Straits Settlements and Malaya.[202] The expatriate academic staff in Raffles College were given new contracts to serve in the new University of Malaya.[203]

In terms of academic staff recruitment, the University of Malaya continued its pre-war practice of using the services of the Association of Universities of the British Commonwealth for recruitment. (In contrast, the new colleges in other British territories could take full advantage of the Inter-University Council. The IUC enlisted as members of selection committees those in British universities with expert knowledge of any subject in which there was a vacancy).[204]

As Channon indicated, there was difficulty in recruiting adequate staff for the colonial university in British Malaya:[205]

> As a result, the men who are appointed to the academic profession in colonial universities often have neither the outlook nor the experience necessary for the carrying out of their work. There are, of course, exceptions to be found in occasional men who possess either the spirit of adventure or something of the missionary spirit which is most frequently found among members of the medical profession. Speaking generally, however, the men appointed are relatively young graduates of our universities; they have perhaps obtained a Ph.D degree after pursuing two or three years of post-graduate study and during this time they will have carried out a certain amount of lecturing and in science subjects, of laboratory teaching, while some few will be men of more experience. They are, however, as a body ill-equipped for the work which will fall to them.[206]

According to Channon, the scope of the duties of those in the academic profession in Malaya was too narrowly defined by their official status which was equivalent to that of the colonial civil servant. Academic expatriates regarded their entry to the higher institutions in Malaya as entry into the British colonial government service.[207] Channon notes that "the one section of the Malayan Report with which our secretary disagreed was that in which proposals were made to try to provide intellectual stimulation for the members of the staff by changes in the practice regarding leave and the provision of substitutes; he regarded such a proposal as impossible, because it would result in the staff of Raffles College receiving treatment different from that of government officers. This attitude of a man of considerable seniority in the Malayan Civil Service is indicative of Malayan administrative opinion as a whole".[208]

The consequent social composition of the academic profession, in this context, is the theme of the next section.

Social Composition of the Academic Profession

English-medium education in Malaya followed the English educational model of cultivation as noted in Chapter Two. For the colonised, regardless of ethnic difference, to become literate in English meant the possession of a promising qualification for posts in the (colonial) government office and other clerical, white collar occupations.

As indicated, British educational policy in Malaya held most Malays back from the advanced learning which might have transformed their life opportunities.[209] While encouraging Malay commoners to be content with schooling in agriculture and manual work, the British colonial State favoured high-ranking Malays with Western education and preference in government jobs.

The majority of students attending the English-medium Schools were non-Malays, because English-medium education was available in urban areas. Thus, only a few urban and privileged Malays were able to benefit from English-medium schooling in the colonial period.[210] In addition, the British government imposed on the Malays prerequisites to enter the English-medium schools. Unlike other ethnic groups—the Chinese and Indians who were permitted to begin their education in English in English-medium schools—only the Malays had to receive a four-year vernacular education as a prerequisite for admission to an English school.[211] This reveals one aspect of the British colonial State's 'divide and rule' principles in Malaya. Thus, the tripartite divisions within the colonial education system, which derived from the British colonial State's projects, impeded the social mobility of indigenous Malay commoners.

The role of the State-sponsored English medium educational stream was fundamental in upward social mobility, which influenced the formation of the embryonic academic profession in British Malaya. Furthermore, the academic profession in Malaya was a new creation within the emerging new class structure related to ethnic divisions in education and in the economy in the colonial period.[212] However, in the advent of Independence, when the British colonial State finally considered the extension of English language instruction for the future of a United Malayan Nation through a new education system, the academic profession in Malaya was to be more available to the English-educated Chinese than the indigenous Malays.[213]

The fact that there was some recruitment of those educated in the colony through the English language to the lower administrative posts in the civil service helps to explain the willingness of many Chinese parents to arrange for their children to receive an education through the English language.[214]

As a result, the English-educated Chinese outnumbered the Malays and Indians. As early as 1901, the Chinese were 60 per cent of English-school enrollment in the Straits Settlements, which was the major place to receive English education at that time. By 1938, 80 per cent of students in English-medium primary and secondary schools were Chinese.[215] This movement of Chinese into the middle and upper echelons of a modernising economy continued through the early years of Independence.[216] Subsequently, the Chinese dominated major branches of the professions, and commerce and clerical work, because of the benefit of English-medium education in the colonial period.[217]

The Chinese from the English education stream would replace expatriates as university staff, in the post-war period of educational reconstruction, preceding the political independence of Malaya. Thus, among the local personnel in the University of Malaya, Chinese graduates of Raffles College were especially notable.[218]

The academic ranks in the University of Malaya followed the British model. In consequence, the shape of the academic profession in Malaya was a copy of the British civic university model as initially conceptualised by the British Commission chaired by Sir Cyril Asquith. Despite the emergent surface features, the University of Malaya was operated in heavily dependent relationships with the British in terms of admissions, curriculum, examinations, and academic staff profiles. Overall, it is suggested that the academic profession in the University of Malaya was shaped by the expatriates who struggled to define their academic role on the British model and simultaneously to handle their colonial civil servant position in the Malay Civil Service.

Unlike Korea, there is no strong evidence in Malaya that the academic profession in the colonial period was the most favoured and sought-after career, next to government service. Given the absence of the Confucian tradition of a scholar-mandarin culture in Malaya and the newly recognised commercial benefits from English education and Western knowledge, there were no strong cultural supports for the (re-)emergence of a scholarly mandarin group in the colonial—and indeed the postcolonial society—of Malaya.

THE CONCLUSION TO CHAPTER THREE

Chapter Three was organised in three parts. The first two parts were about the shaping of the academic profession, through the values and visions of the colonial States, and the States' 'idea of the university'; and through the struggles over institutional forms and the knowledge valued in higher education. The third part of the chapter illustrated the consequence: the shape of the academic profession—its entry routes, its social composition, and its internal ranks in the colonial period. Overall, this chapter has attempted to understand the *shaping* of the modern academic profession in the Japanese colonial State in Korea and the British colonial State in Malaya; and to show the *shape* which resulted in each case.

In concluding this chapter, there is a stress on the strategic similarities and the differences in detail between the Japanese and British colonial shaping of the academic profession, and a comparative interpretation of both the shaping and the shape of the two academic professions.

The Shaping of the Academic Profession in Korea and Malaya

Values and Visions of the State: Japan and Britain compared

In Korea, the values and visions of the Japanese colonial State focused on political control, economic modernisation, and the cultural assimilation of Korea as a part of the Japanese Empire. The Japanese colonial projects in Korea were affected by three facts. First, Japan was a new coloniser, borrowing heavily from Western examples of colonisation and modernisation. Second, Korea was geopolitically significant to Japanese imperial expansion in North East Asia. Third, Japan's long historical and close relations with Korea in which Japan had been a borrower (from an ancient civilisation) were now inverted in the new colonial relation with Korea. During the thirty six year colonial period (1910-1945), the Japanese colonial project in Korea focused on cultural assimilation and economic modernisation, and was carried out with great intensity and directed by military Governors. Korea was subordinated to Japanese militaristic expansion, imperialistic modernisation, and the inversion of cultural superiority.

In contrast, the values and visions of the British colonial State in Malaya were mainly focused on the economic dimension, on the basis of indirect political rule and divisive cultural policies, for a longer period of colonisation (1824-1957). The British colonial projects in Malay were affected by the fact that, unlike Japan, Britain was an old experienced coloniser. Geopolitically, Malaya was not an important military base of the British Empire, but had an economic value from the beginning of colonisation.

The British economic interest in Malaya led to Chinese and Indian migrations for work in large-scale rubber cultivation, the tin mining industry in the Federated Malay States, and commercial development through in the free-trade areas of Singapore and Penang.[219] Consequently and subsequently, the heterogeneous culture formed by the new immigrants necessitated a major effort by the British to maintain political stability in Malaya. One controlling mechanism of the British colonial State was the differential provision of education according to ethnic and linguistic divisions. The British colonial State's educational domination and penetration in Malaya was affected by earlier British colonial experience in India of the possible ill-effects of over-expansion of higher education and English instruction.

The Colonial State's Idea of the University: Japan and Britain compared

It is suggested that the colonial States' efforts to relate the university to State projects in East Asia should be explained by the respective colonial conditions of Japanese Korea and British Malaya. In these colonial conditions, the State's 'idea of the university' was defined narrowly. In both Japanese Korea and British Malaya, the colonial formation of 'the university' was functional and pragmatically orientated.

The university was used as a means of social control by the two States. At the individual level, the university was a place of opportunity to gain future socio-economic benefits in the colonial system. In other words, 'the university' was introduced in the colonial condition to provide higher level *training*, under the colonial State's control, and had strong economic value to the colonial State and to the individuals able to take advantage of the new structures.

The universities of Japan and Britain were different from the higher education systems in the colonies, but sent some basic messages about institutional forms and valued knowledge. In Japan itself, the State's idea of the university took institutional form in the establishment of Tokyo Imperial University in 1877, which followed the Prussian model in terms of state and university relations.[220] In its Japanese adaptation, the Imperial University started with the four faculties of Law, Humanities, Sciences and Medicine. This, and later Japanese Imperial Universities, functioned like higher professional training institutions to serve the State's needs by producing highly skilled professionals and government officials.[221] The Japanese Imperial universities also carried strong cultural messages, e.g. 'revere the Emperor'.

The Imperial University in Korea was established in 1926 with the same principles, forming an elite group for the systemic development of Korea and stressing Japanese culture and obligations to the Japanese State. As indicated, Kyung Sung Imperial University catered mainly for the Japanese residents in Korea and only a third of the highly selected students were from a Korean background.[222] Thus, the establishment of Kyung Sung Imperial University was a part of the Japanese assimilation colonial project in Korea to serve the direct demand of the increasing number of Japanese residents in Korea for university education and to meet the colonial State's need to recruit from the Imperial University a small number of the Korean elite for the lower ranks of the government.

In short, Kyung Sung Imperial University was a major symbol of the Japanese colonial assimilation project. Throughout the colonial period, the Japanese colonial State did not permit the establishment of another university. In contrast, in Japan, there were 7 Imperial Universities at the time of the establishment of Kyung Sung Imperial University, and altogether there were 49 universities, including 15 government universities, 2 public universities and 25 private universities by 1940.[223]

As in the Japanese case, the British colonial higher education project was influenced by the British 'idea of the university' even though in British Malaya, a University did not exist until 1949. However, the idea of the university had been discussed by the British earlier, especially in 1918, the centenary year of Raffles' arrival in Singapore. To commemorate Raffles' initial idea of the university for the natives in the colony, the British government appointed the Maxwell Committee to enquire into the advisability of higher education in Malaya. Subsequently, Raffles College was established in 1929, as a higher educational institution at the top of the English-medium education system. The college followed the English model of public school education.

One major form of the provision of higher education in the two colonies was teacher training, to provide teachers for the colonial education systems. Even before formal colonisation, the Japanese had begun to influence the Korean Government's teacher training college, *Kyung Sung Sabum Hackyo,* established in 1895, by sending trained Japanese teachers to Korea. The British colonial government also started training local teachers for English schools in Malaya as early as 1864. In contrast, however, it should be noted that British teacher training 'at home' started being systematically organised only from 1902.[224]

Paradoxically, the British government also implemented a State education system for the colonised in Malaya much earlier than for the people at home.[225] Britain, as the dominant colonising power in the world then, did not feel any urgency to establish a State education system through which to control its own people. To run the Empire, Britain used the public schools and ancient universities, which cultivated imperial leaders to manage its colonial domination abroad.[226]

However, the British colonial State found it necessary to develop early a formal education system to 'divide and rule' the colonised people in Malaya, and in other colonies. A small selected elite among the colonised could be trained in the English-medium higher educational institutions. The colonial elite who won the Queen's Scholarships had a chance to receive university education in Britain. Thus, for the systemic support of the British political project in Malaya—the 'divide and rule' principle in Malaya—the British colonial State established and controlled a State education system in the colony.[227]

The British colonial State did not make any efforts to create a new colonial university in Malaya until the Second World War. It was only during the early 1940s that the British government started to review the conditions of Malaya (as well as other overseas colonies) to assess if and when they would be capable of some self-government, within the British Empire.

In that sense, the actual impetus to university construction and development in Malaya was from the British government directly.[228] The British government carefully planned ways to establish the University of Malaya by appointing Commissions on higher education in Malaya—the McLean Commission in 1939 and then the Carr-Saunders' Commission in 1948. This was a technique borrowed from 'home'.

As with Japan in Korea, the British used their own cultural and institutional example of a university. The British colonial State's idea of the University of Malaya was formulated on the basis of the civic universities in Britain, following the recommendations of the Commission on Higher Education in the Colonies, chaired by Lord Justice Asquith, who was then the Vice-Chancellor of Birmingham University.[229] In 1945 the Asquith Commission recommended a programme for the development of university education in the British territories, on the view that "it is essential that colonial universities should be autonomous in the sense in which the universities of Great Britain are autonomous".[230]

To establish a new university in Malaya, the British colonial government in Malaya relied on the recommendations of the Higher Education Commission appointed from Great Britain, whose members were from the British universities. The new University of Malaya was set up and organised partly on the model of the University of London, especially Carr-Saunders' model of the London School of Economics.

The fascinating thing here is that both the Japanese and the British exported not only their 'idea of the university' but the modalities of their establishment. The Japanese State used its model of the Imperial University and the British their model of the civic university. The Japanese-created university in Korea was in response to an abrupt political crisis, and was a decision made by a small elite in Japan and the implementation was through a military governor. The British used a series of Committees and Commissions over a period of time (at least from 1918) and this approach is reminiscent of the major Commissions which, in the nineteenth, and later in the twentieth century, have been used to reform British higher education and the academic profession 'at home'.

Struggles over institutional forms & valued knowledge: Japan and Britain compared

As illustrated above, both colonial States established only one State University throughout the colonial period: Kyung Sung Imperial University in 1926 and the University of Malaya in 1949.

In the case of Korea, there were serious struggles over the expansion of the private sector of higher education led by indigenous Korean intellectuals and Western missionaries. The civic university movements by indigenous Korean academics were the expression of a Korean nationalism stressing Korean culture and the idea of a 'Korean University'.

In British Malaya, higher education was provided only within English language educational institutions and was framed by the British economic and political needs in the colony. Unlike the Korean case, the indigenous demand for university education in Malaya was mainly related to the economic value of English-medium education to individuals, rather than the promotion of a Malay national culture. The lack of national aspiration for indigenous higher learning in Malaya may, perhaps, be linked to the fact that before the colonial period there was no indigenous political unit to form a 'Malayan' nationalism.

In both Japanese Korea and British Malaya, the early forms of higher educational institutions were mainly vocationally-oriented training institutions, for medical training, teacher training, and technical and agricultural studies. These institutional forms of higher education were the colonial States' 'idea of the university', before the actual establishment of the colonial universities.

For the small local elite who were selected to enter the colonial university, what was offered in the university curriculum was in content and form that of the colonial powers: i.e. the domestic curriculum of Japanese and British higher education. The knowledge to be diffused by the institutions was Western in both Korea and Malaya. The colonial higher educational institutions promoted certain types of Western knowledge useful in the control of the physical and material environment of the colonies—such as medicine, agricultural studies, science and applied technology. The Korean case included the unique position of Japan as a coloniser, when Japan herself had to absorb Western scientific knowledge and transmit it to Korea.

Overall, in both cases, the colonial higher education curriculum destroyed or marginalised local educational traditions. In other words, the types of knowledge valued in colonial higher education contradicted both the Korean and Malayan indigenous culture of learning—the Confucian and the Islamic knowledge traditions. In the Confucian tradition, knowledge was sought to understand men's relations with the cosmos and, in human relationships, to establish a harmonious social order. Similarly, knowledge in the Islamic tradition was aimed at defining men's relations with God, through which the social orders were established. In these traditions, academic technique was to learn by rote. Truths rested on authority, not on scientific observation or enquiry. In both colonies, higher education largely discarded these traditions. Useful, 'Western', knowledge became prestigious, and the main epistemic canon for the academic profession.

The common types of knowledge valued in the colonial university in Japanese Korea and British Malaya were law, medicine, and the social sciences. These types of knowledge promoted under the respective colonial States resemble the traditional hierarchy of the university faculties which developed in Europe. However, in both Japanese Korea and British Malaya, the particular colonial relations between the State and university generated a new cultural valuation of agriculture, engineering and applied sciences and technology and their location in the university hierarchy of faculties soon became significant.[231]

In both Korea and Malaya, the language of instruction in the University was that of the colonisers. In Kyung Sung Imperial University, it was entirely Japanese, and in the University of Malaya, it was entirely English.

There were, however, differences in ways in which the Japanese and the

British promoted the language of the colonisers. In Korea, the use of Japanese was officially imposed on the school curriculum by the order of the military Governor at the time of the establishment of the colonial State's schooling system. Subsequently, the use of the Japanese language became dominant as the only medium of school instruction at all education levels and even in private sector higher educational institutions, especially after 1938 when Japan was fully engaged in war.

In contrast, in Malaya, English was one of the four languages of school instruction. The colonial education system used English, Chinese, Malay, and Tamil. This linguistic division of schooling was not challenged during the entire colonial period. As the official language of the British Empire was English, university education was only available in English for a selected local elite in Malaya in the entire period of colonisation.

This linguistic requirement in the colonial university affected the initial definition of the academic profession in Korea and Malaya. Proficiency in Japanese (in Korea) and English (in Malaya) became the gateway to upward social mobility in the colonial period. Knowledge of Japanese (in Korea) and English (in Malaya) was essential in university academic staff recruitment—only those with the "literacy" of the colonising powers could enter the academic profession in the university. Thus, the colonisers' language, imported and imposed as the language of university education in the colonies, became the language of academic social mobility, in the colonial period and in Malaya for some time afterward.[232]

The colonial university was the locus of an academic discourse through which the imported Western knowledge was (translated in the case of Japanese Korea) diffused in the language of the colonisers. The Japanese State emphasised the importance of learning Western languages, especially English and German, in the elite secondary schools of Japan. As a Japanese colony, Korea had to adopt this Japanese language policy. Consequently, the teaching of English and German was also included in the Kyung Sung Imperial University curriculum. But there also existed discrimination against Koreans in that curriculum. For instance, foreign languages were taught only for the first two years of Kyung Sung Imperial University education whereas they were taught for three years even at the secondary schools in Japan.[233] The university examinations taken after two years in Kyung Sung Imperial University, however, did not include a German language test but only English.[234] Overall, in both Japan and Korea, the Japanese Imperial Universities promoted the English language as the official vehicle for the local elite to gain access to modern professional knowledge.

Nevertheless, it was the Japanese language that gave the new Korean academic elite access to the academic profession, as well as other professions and government office in the modern career pyramid in the colony.[235] For Korean academics in the private sector of higher education, learning

English was the way to acquire modern knowledge directly from the West. This split was paralleled by the split in academic disciplines: academic disciplines in Korea were borrowed simultaneously from both Japan and the United States. On the other hand, in Malaya, the imported knowledge pattern was simply the British model.

These epistemic patterns developed in the colonies meant that, unlike the traditional Western university reviewed through the ideas of Newman and Jaspers in Chapter Two, the colonial university could not develop its own mission. The colonial State took the initiative in defining the ontological stance of the university as well as in linking the academic mission of the profession to the colonisation projects. The university academic profession in the colonial era was formed to serve what the colonial State expected to produce through higher education.

Thus, the colonial origins of the university in both Korea and Malaya meant new conceptions of the university. Even though the "classic" models of the university in Western Europe and North America were introduced into East Asia by expatriate academics during the colonial period, the classic 'idea of the university' could not survive in the particular colonial contexts of the State and university relations. As a consequence, the shape of the academic profession in the colonial period was different from Western models.[236]

The Shape of the Colonial Academic Profession: Japan and Britain Compared

The models of the professor in Korea and Malaya were imported from the colonising countries: Japan and Britain. Subsequently, however, the actual shape of the academic profession in the colonies then diverged from the original model imported from the colonising metropolitan countries, as the colonial origins of the university justified the subordination of the academic profession to the State. There was a lack of academic autonomy and freedom for those in the academic profession in the colonial period.

This disparity between the ideal model of the professor and the colonial reality caused a tension (and confusion) in the academic profession. The tension was two-fold.

First, there was a tension in the nature of the profession between that inherited from the Confucian model of 'man of knowledge' in the case of Korea, and another imported from Western models in Korea and Malaya (and subsequently, South Korea, Malaysia and Singapore.)

Second, there was a tension in the disparity between the imported ideal conceptions of the academic in the Western European tradition and the actual role of the academic profession in the colonial condition: to be immediately useful. The visibility of the State's control over the academic domain and its specific, pragmatic use of the results of academic work developed early in the colonies. These tensions do not disappear. It will be the work of Chapter Four to show how these tensions continued in the post-colonial period. However, this will be traced within the same lines of analysis: what were (and are) some of the selected forces *shaping* the academic profession in South Korea, and Malaysia and Singapore; and what were (and are) the consequences of these forces for the *shape* of the academic profession?

Both the Japanese and British colonial States created meritocratic principles to define entry routes to the (embryonic) academic profession. Broadly speaking, the most conspicuous meritocratic principle in Japanese Korea was defined by nationality, whereas in British Malaya, it was defined by language. In Korea, there were tensions between those from the public route sponsored by the Japanese colonial State and those from the private route sponsored by Korean nationalists and by American Christian missionary organisations. However, the colonial condition privileged those from the Japanese academic route in academic staffing. This trend would become reversed after political independence, which came with the sudden collapse of the Japanese Empire and the new American influence in South Korea, along with a recovery of the Korean national academic tradition.

In Malaya, the academic recruitment route into the University of Malaya was exogenous: most academic staff members were mainly expatriates recruited overseas within the British Empire. In the colonial period, there was little endogenous contestation in Malaya to construct alternative academic routes and to invent a new knowledge tradition (such as the revival of Islam and Confucianism). This struggle in Malaya was still to come after the start of the indigenisation process during the postcolonial period. This is partly because the decline of the British Empire came gradually, unlike the postcolonial condition of Korea.

NOTES

1. During the 36 years of colonial rule, the Japanese Governor-General in Seoul ruled the peninsula as an integral part of Japan's imperial system. Korea was annexed and Japan's political suppression of Koreans was thorough and far-reaching. After annexation, Japan introduced Western forms of modernisation rapidly in the economic sphere so that there suddenly occurred a serious dislocation of traditional economic and social structures in Korea. (For details, see Kim, C. I. Eugene. & D. E. Mortimore (eds). *Korea's response to Japan: the colonial period 1910-1945*. Michigan: The Centre for Korean Studies, Western Michigan University, 1977.)

2. Lee, Ki-baik, *A New History of Korea*, Cambridge, Mass.: Harvard University Press, 1985.

3. Ibid.

4. Ibid.

5. Eckert, Carter J., Ki-baik Lee, Young Ick Lew, M. Robinson, E. W. Wagner, *Korea Old and New. A History*. Published for the Korea Institute, Harvard University, Seoul: Ilchokak, 1990, pp. 222-247.

6. Lee, Won-ho, 'The Modern Educational System Came the Hard Way to Korea', *Koreana*, 5, No. 2, 1991, p. 28.

7. "Altogether six marquises, three counts, twenty-two viscounts and forty-five barons were created and each of them received a [financial] grant." Thereafter, Japan began to interfere more and more in Korean affairs, and finally formally annexed Korea as a colony in 1910. (For details, see Andrew J., *Modern Korea*, Institute of Pacific Relations, 1944, p. 45; Requoted from Meyer Weinberg, *Asian-American Education: Historical Background and Current Realities*, Mahwah, N.J. & London: Lawrence Erlbaum Associates Publishers, 1997, p. 75.)

8. In 1920, for instance, a law required that the Governor-General in Korea must be either a general or an admiral. (For details, see Dong, W. 'Japanese Colonial Policy and Practices in Korea, 1905-1945: A Study in Assimilation', Doctoral Book, Georgetown University, Washington, D.C., 1965, p. 190; Requoted from Weinberg, M. op. cit., p. 79.)

9. Lee, Ki-baik, op. cit., p. 314.

10. Ibid.

11. Ibid.

12. Ibid.

13. McGinn, N. F., Snodgrass, D.R., Kim, Y.B., Kim, Q.Y., *Education and Development in Korea*, Cambridge, Mass.: Harvard University Press, 1980.

14. Lee, Won-ho, op. cit., p. 28.

15. Lee, Ki-baik, op. cit., p.346.

16. The March First Movement was the greatest mass movement in Korean history. It began with the promulgation of the Declaration of Independence by the thirty-three representatives of the Korean people. Those thirty-three prominent Koreans were religious leaders from various organisations (e.g. Chondogyo, Christian, Buddhist, and others). The opening lines of the declaration read as follows, in a translation made shortly after the event:

We herewith proclaim the independence of Korea and the liberty of the Korean people. We tell it to the world in witness of the equality of all nations and we pass it onto our posterity as their inherent right. We make this proclamation, having behind us five thousand years of history and twenty millions of a united loyal people. We take this step to insure to our children, for all time to come, personal liberty in accord with the awakening consciousness of this new era. This is the clear leading of God, the moving principle of the present age, the whole human race's just claim. It is something that cannot be stamped out, or stifled, or gagged, or suppressed by any means. (Source: Lee, Ki-baik, *New History of Korea*, op. cit).

The March First Movement was entirely peaceful. The demonstrations for independence continued across the whole country. According to Japanese public records, more than two million Koreans directly participated, in more than 1,500 separate gatherings, in all but seven of the country's 218 county administrations. The demonstration quickly spread even to Manchuria, to the Russian Maritime Territory, and to other overseas areas. Japan coped with these unarmed peaceful demonstrations with the police, army and navy. The Japanese set fire to schools and churches, and private dwellings. The reports issued by the Japanese authorities record 46,948 demonstrators arrested, 7,509 killed, and 15,961 injured, while as many as 715 houses were destroyed or burned, along with 47 churches and two schools. However, in reality, the numbers in all these categories probably exceeded those officially reported. (For details, see Lee, Ki-baik's *New History of Korea,* op. cit.)

A consequence of the March First Movement was that new Japanese colonial Governor-Generals would be appointed as civilian officials, and the gendarmarie police system would be abandoned, demilitarising police operations in Korea. (Lee, Ki-baik, op. cit., p. 346.)

The Japanese Annual Report on Administration of Chosen 1918-1921 shows the Japanese government's new official position: "The main points of the reform lay in the appointment of either a civil or military official as Government-General, the change of the gendarmerie system into that of an ordinary policy system, the ensuring of non-discrimination between Japanese and Koreans, and the raising of the Korean people to the same standards as that of the Japanese, by means of a cultural policy." (Government General of Chosen, *Annual Report on Administration of Chosen 1918-1921,*Seoul, 1921. Requoted from Adams, Don & Gottlieb, Esther E., op. cit., p. 13.)

17. Lee, Ki-baik, op. cit.

18. Chang, Yun-Shik, 'Planned Economic Transformation and Population Change' in C. I. Eugene Kim & Doretha E. Mortimore (eds)., op. cit., p. 53.

19. Ibid., p. 60.

20. "Unlike most colonial powers, Japan located heavy industry in its colonies, bringing the means of production to the labour and raw materials... By 1945, Korea proportionally had more railroad miles than any other Asian colonies of Japan..." The establishment of new industry in the North was related to the Japanese political agenda to expand its power over Chinese and Russian territories. Thus, under Japanese colonial rule, the traditional self-sufficiency of the Korean economy was broken. (For details, see Cummings, Bruce, *The Two Koreas*, Foreign Policy Association, May-June 1984, p. 24; Requoted from Meyer Weinberg, op. cit. p. 76.)

21. Kim, K. S., 'From neo-mercantilism to globalism: the changing role of the state and South Korea's economic prowess' in M. T. Berger and D. A. Borer. (eds). *The Rise of East Asia: Critical Visions of the Pacific Century*, London & New York: Routledge, 1997, pp. 81-105.

22. Weinberg, M. op. cit. p. 76.

23. The modernisation process took place during Japanese rule. Nevertheless, it can be construed that it would have taken place anyway without the Japanese presence, as both indigenous forces and missionary influences were already moving in that direction, when the Japanese made their intervention.

24. Chang, Yun-Shik, op. cit., p. 60.

25. For instance, Kim Yun-hwan notes that the wage level of the average Korean worker in the colonial period was about 50 per cent lower than that of the Japanese worker in Japan, which was already very low by international standards. The average Japanese worker in Korea itself received twice as much as the average Korean worker. Moreover, Korean wages actually decreased between 1930 and 1940 by about 8 per cent. (For details, see Kim, Yun-hwan, *Han'gukui nodongmunje yon'gu* [Studies on Labour Problems in Korea] Seoul, 1967, p. 77; Takahashi, Kamekichi *Kendai Chosen Keizairon* [A Study of the Current Korean Economy] Tokyo, 1935, pp. 429-432; Suzuki, Masabumi, *Chosen Keizai no Kendankai* [The Current Stage of Korean Economy] Seoul, 1939, pp. 297-305. Requoted from Chang, Yun-Shik, op. cit., p. 62.)

26. Ibid.

27. Dong, W., op. cit., pp. 629-652.

28. During 1912-1942, for example, the inequalities were quite sizeable:

Expenditure per Korean students as a percentage of expenditure on Japanese students:

1912	55.5	1930	40.4
1915	67.2	1935	39.6
1920	58.3	1940	19.3
1925	54.4	1942	27.6

(Sources: Dong, W. op. cit., p. 385.)

The number of students per teacher was increasingly unequal toward the later stages of the colonial period:

Korean Schools		Japanese Schools
1912	27.9	31.7
1913	31.5	30.2
1940	73.2	35.3
1942	73.1	35.9

(Sources: Dong, W. op. cit., p. 385.)

The Japanese colonial State defined education for Koreans narrowly so that any non-formal education outside the schooling system became illegitimate and, since then, it has been common to identify "education" only with formal schooling in Korea.

29. Ibid.

30. Kang, Wi Jo, 'Religion and Politics under Japanese Rule' in Kim, C. I. Eugene & Doretha E. Mortimore (eds)., op. cit., p. 115.

31. Son, In-su, *Hanguk Kundae Kyoyuksa* [A Modern History of Korean Education]. Seoul: Yonsei University Press, 1971, p. 221.

32. Ibid.

33. Kang, Wi Jo, op. cit., p. 118.

34. Dong, W., p. 354.

35. Vacante, Russell A., *Japanese Colonial Education in Korea, 1910-1945: An*

Oral History, Doctoral book, State University of New York at Buffalo, 1987, p. 106; Requoted from Weinberg, M. op. cit.

36. Lee, Ki-Baik, op. cit., p. 368.

37. Ibid.

38. In 1945, Governor-General Koiso ordered the setting up of the National Youth Training Organisation which was to prepare for compulsory military service. The youth organisation for both Koreans and Japanese in Korea had 3,245 branches throughout the nation, including 2,461,883 Korean members who were watched by 23,146 Japanese members. (For details, see Kang, T. H. 'The changing nature of Korean Confucian personality under Japanese rule' in Kim, C. I. E. and Mortimore, D. E. (eds)., op. cit., pp.308-309.)

39. The British took Penang in 1786 before its purchase of Singapore in 1819. The islands of Singapore and Penang, together with certain areas on the mainland, forming the so-called Straits Settlements, came under the Presidency of Bengal until 1867 when they were transferred to the Colonial Office. The greater part of the mainland belonged to either the Federated or the unfederated Malay States. However, before the expansion of the British power, the area was under the control of the Dutch East India Company (from 1641) and then the Dutch government (from 1682). Before the Dutch and British colonial expansion, the Malacca region (in what is now Malaysia) was captured by the Portuguese as early as 1511. In 1824, the Dutch and the British settled conflict over colonies by agreeing to Dutch control of the East Indies and British control of the Malay peninsula. In 1896, the British established the Federation of Malay States. During the war time (1941-1944), the British Malay territories were occupied by the Japanese. (For details, see Simone, V. and Thompson A. Feraru. *The Asian Pacific: Political and Economic Development in a Global Context.* London: Longman Group Ltd., 1995, pp. 32-59.)

40. Lamb Alastair, 'Early History' in Wang, Gungwu (ed)., *Malaysia: a survey,* Singapore: Donald Moore Books, 1964, p. 105.

41. Chai, Hon-Chan, *The Development of British Malaya 1896-1909,* Oxford: Oxford University Press, 1964.

42. The result of the migration of Chinese and Indians during the colonial period was that at the time of independence the Malays constituted slightly under 50 per cent of the population. (For details, see Simone V, Thompson A. Feraru, op. cit., p. 55.)

From the early trading period in the region, when the significance of Singapore in commercial terms became clear, Raffles called for the establishment of a college in

Singapore, which would be 'a monument of light'. He said, "[college] education must keep pace with commerce in order that its benefits may be ensured and its evils avoided... Shall we not consider it one of our first duties to afford the means of education to surrounding countries and thus render our stations not only the seats of commerce but of literature and the arts?" (*Report of the Commission on University Education in Malaya*, 1948, p. 134. Requoted from Carr-Saunders, A. M. *New Universities Overseas*. London: George Allen & Unwin Ltd., 1961, p. 20.)

Raffles believed in the advantages of educating "the sons of the higher order of natives" rather than those of the lower ranks alone. He wanted the higher educational institution to be "under the immediate control and supervision of Government," but did not expect it to be fully Government-supported, as the native chiefs were expected to contribute to its support. (Raffles, Lady. *Memoir of the Life and Public Services of Sir T. S. Raffles*, 1830, p. 79 of Appendix, Quoted in Wong Hoy Kee, F. and Ee Tiang Hong. *Education in Malaysia*. Kuala Lumpur: Heinemann Educational Books (Asia) Ltd., 1975, p. 37.)

In 1822, when Raffles began to make arrangements for the actual establishment of the institution, it was proposed to:

> ...include a native professor in each of the three principal languages, Malay, Bugis and Siamese, with an assistant in each department, and four extra teachers in the Chinese, Javan, Burman and Pali languages. The course of education will be the requirements of such of the above languages as the students may select, together with Arabic; and in the higher classes the Roman characters and English language will be taught, together with such elementary branches of general knowledge and history, as their capacity and inclination may demand. (Raffles, Lady. op. cit., p. 34. Quoted in Wong Hoy Kee, F. and Ee Tiang Hong, op. cit., p. 38.)

However, this plan by Raffles to establish a college failed.

The successors of Raffles held different ideas about the type of education appropriate for the colonised who "have not yet attained that state of civilisation that would benefit from the enlarged system of education held up by the Singapore Institution." (Wong Hoy Kee, F. and Ee Tiang Hong, op. cit., p. 39.) As noted by Carr-Saunders, "there was no one who had the understanding or energy to carry out Raffles' plans." (In consequence, the remnants of the Raffles' foundation were taken over by the government which used them to found a secondary school with the title, the Raffles Institution in 1903. Nevertheless, Raffles remained as an important pioneer who first conceived one colonial vision of a University in Malaya. But before that, 'Malaya' had to be formed. For details, see Carr-Saunders A. M. op. cit., p. 21.)

43. Ibid.

44. The term *Bumiputera* literally means 'son of the soil' and refers to the Malays and other indigenous people of the country, although, the origins of the Malays of today were also as immigrants from southern China in about 300 B.C. (For details, see Lamb Alastair, 'Early History' in Wang, Gungwu (ed)., op. cit., p. 105.)

45. Gullick, J. M., *Indigenous Political Systems of Western Malaya,* London: The Athlone Press, 1965.

46. This *laissez-faire* policy in Malaya diminished the political antagonism of the indigenous Malay people against British colonial authority. As noted by Snodgrass, "The British then were even expected to be the protector of indigenous Malays *vis-a-vis* the new immigrant groups during the colonial period." (Snodgrass, Donald R., *Inequality and Economic Development in Malay*sia, Oxford: Oxford University Press, 1980, p.20; For further details, see also Chai, Hon-Chan, op. cit.)

47. Most of teachers in those Quran schools had little more than an elementary knowledge of Islam and were strongly influenced by indigenous magical beliefs and local traditions. (Hashim, R. *Educational Dualism in Malaysia: Implications for Theory and Practice.* Kuala Lumpur: Oxford University Press, 1996.)

The traditional education of a normal Malay child was informal. For aristocratic families, tutors were employed, a number of whom were Malay school masters, trained in the Straits Settlements, or Arab scholars. Young aristocrats did not attend the same Quran classes as village boys and instead were tutored privately at home. It has been suggested that they cultivated the gentlemanly manners of the Islamic tradition and an aristocratic bearing that differentiated them from the ordinary populace. (Committee on Malay Education. *Report of the Committee on Malay Education, Federation of Malaya.* Kuala Lumpur: The Government Press, 1951.) The literacy rate among Malay aristocrats was not high, because letter writing was considered unworthy of a nobleman and there were trained professional scribes. A written script for the indigenous Malay language did not exist anyway. The scribes were not numerous enough to form a literary or scholarly class in the traditional Malay region, and they were confined by custom and by restricted opportunities. (For details, see Stevenson, R. *Cultivators and Administrators: British Educational Policy towards the Malays, 1875-1906.* Kuala Lumpur: Oxford University Press, 1975.)

48. Before the British colonial period, Malaya had already experienced other European influences such as the Portuguese and the Dutch. However, it was in the period of the British domination (1786-1957) that the territory of Malaya was constructed as a convenient base for the British to trade in that region.

49. Stevenson, R. op. cit.

50. The Straits Settlements were regarded as outposts of the East India Company

and prospered. The free trade policy made Singapore, as a centre of the trading nexus, an immediate economic success. As indicated earlier, the Chinese played an active economic role in trading, industry and tin mining from the early trading period. (Ibid.)

51. Chai, Hon-Chan, op. cit.

52. By the end of the colonial period in 1957, the rate of natural population increase in Malaya was about 3.5 % per annum, which was one of the highest in the world. (For details, see Young, K., W. C. F. Bussink and P. Hasan, *Malaysia: Growth and Equity in a Multi-Racial Society*, Baltimore: Johns Hopkins University Press, 1980, pp. 97-99.)

53. Simone V and Thompson A. Feraru, op. cit., p. 55.

54. In the period of Japanese occupation during the World War II, however, this ethnic division of political, economic, and cultural practices in Malaya was interrupted. The period of Japanese occupation saw a reversal of British colonial governance based on ethnicity in Malaya. While the Malays and Indians accepted the occupation with more equanimity, and actively cooperated with the Japanese in many cases, Chinese received the harshest treatment by the Japanese and provided practically all the underground opposition. In this period, the rise of the Chinese worker from coolie status was temporarily checked by the Japanese occupying forces. Thus, the Chinese became deprived of some previous forms of employment, thousands of Chinese retreated to a near-subsistence existence on the jungle's fringe. In 1947, the list of ten leading Chinese occupations included padi planting and fishing for the first and only time in Malaya. (For details, see Snodgrass, Donald R., op. cit., p. 39.)

55. Stevenson, R., op. cit.

56. Committee on Malay Education. *Report of the Committee on Malay Education, Federation of Malaya*. Kuala Lumpur: The Government Press, 1951.

57. He chaired the committee set up to enquire into the advisability of higher education in Malaya in 1918—the centenary of Raffles' arrival. (For details, see *Report of the Maxwell Committee to consider and report on a Scheme to commemorate the Centenary of the Founding of Singapore*, 1918.)

58. *Chief Secretary's Report, Federated Malay States, 1920*, Quoted in Hashim, Rosnani, op. cit., p. 45.

59. Chelliah, D. D., *A History of the Education Policy of the Straits Settlements*, Kuala Lumpur: Government Press, p. 78.

60. English medium schools started in the British Malay States as early as 1864. The first English school was established in 1864 when Johor opened the Tanjung Petri School (later renamed Johore Free School) at the request of its ruler. But the official government English education school in the British Malay States began following the Pangkor Treaty of 1874 which formalised British protection for the State of Perak. These English schools were the Grant-in-Aid English schools, established and maintained by missionary bodies with financial aid from the British government. These English schools were called 'Free'schools, "not because they did not charge fees but because no restriction of race, creed, or colour was placed on the admission of pupils". The English Free Schools existed earlier in the Straits Settlements. Chief among them, with the Penang Free School (1816), were the Raffles Institution, originally named the Singapore Free School (1823), and the Malacca High School, originally the Malacca Free School (1826), the Kuala Lumpur Victoria Institution (1894), and the Taiping King Edward VII School (1906). (For details, see Francis Wong Hoy Kee & Ee Tiang Hong, op. cit., pp. 13-19.)

61. Hashim, R., p. 49.

62. Ibid., pp. 49-50.

63. The British policy to keep English education under control was first formulated in India and became a persistent preoccupation amongst British colonial officials in other British colonies. At the lower level of education in the British colonies, native languages were used as the medium of instruction. This was due to British anxiety about the potentially 'seditious' indigenous people in the colonies after English education. (For details, see Loh, Philip Fook Seng, *Seeds of Separatism: Education Policy in Malaya 1894-1900*, Kuala Lumpur: Oxford University Press, 1975.)

According to Maxwell's memorandum to the Advisory Committee on Education in the Federated Malay States:

"When he has reached the older age, the Asiatic product of an English school inevitably looks down upon manual labour. With the education of Standard VI only, he is unfit for employment in any office, and infallibly becomes a malcontent. He is bitterly aggrieved by an educational system which fits him for nothing, and he becomes a potential seditionist."

'Memorandum on the Educational Policy of the Straits Settlements and Federated Malay States' by Sir George Maxwell, 31 December 1932, in *Straits Settlements: Original Correspondence 1838 to 1940*, Vol. 585, Great Britain, Public Record Office, London, Series CO273, Quoted in Loh, F. S. P. op. cit., p. 105.

64. For details, see Fenn, William P. & Wu, The Yao, *Chinese Schools and the Education of Chinese Malayans,* Kuala Lumpur: Government Press, 1951; Purcell, Victor. *The Chinese in Malaya*, London: Oxford University Press, 1948.

65. "The British colonial government ... decided in 1876 not to support the Tamil or the Chinese vernacular schools mainly because English was the administrative and commercial language of the country, and Malay was the lingua franca and the language of the race whose interests they felt it was their duty to safeguard." Quoted from Francis Wong Hoy Kee and Ee Tiang Hong, op. cit., 1975, p. 12. (For further details, also see Doraisamy, T. R. et. al., *150 Years of Education in Singapore,* Singapore: Teachers' Training College, 1969, p. 32.)

66. As a way toward the national independence, post-war educational reconstruction in Malaya focused on creating a new schooling system to unify the three peoples, on a new inter-racial basis, to build a common national identity.

At that time it was suggested that the existing separate vernacular schools should be replaced by a single type of primary school common to all—the National School, where all pupils would be taught English and Malaya for six years. At the end of the course the best of them would proceed to post-primary schools in which instruction would be available only in English. The National School would be administered and financed in part by a local education authority, 'having its roots in the local community.' (For details, see *Report of the Committee on Malay Education,* Federation of Malaya, 1951, Chapter XII; Francis Wong Hoy Kee & Ee Tiang Hong, op. cit., p. 49.)

67. Lee, Ki-baik, op. cit.

68. Lee, Kwan, 'Past, Present and Future Trends in the Public and Private Sectors of Korean Higher Education' in Research Institute for Higher Education, Hiroshima University, *Public and Private Sectors in Asian Higher Education Systems: Issues and Prospects,* 1987, pp. 49-70; Son, In-su, op. cit.

69. Adams, D. and E. E. Gottlieb. *Education and Social Change in Korea.* New York & London: Garland Publishing Inc., 1993.

70. Yonsei University, *The 100 Year History of Yonsei University*, Seoul: Yonsei University Press, 1987.

71. Vacante, R. A. "Japanese Colonial Education in Korea, 1910-1945: An Oral History", Doctoral Book, State University of New York, 1987, pp. 300-301; Requoted from Weinberg, M. op. cit., p. 78.

72. Eckert, C. J., K-b Lee, Y. I. Lew, et. al. op. cit., 1990, p.294.

Another example of the struggle for autonomy by the academics in the private sector is found in the aftermath of the Independence Movement on 1 March 1919. (7,000 demonstrators were killed and 52,000 were imprisoned. (For details, see Lee Ki-baik, op. cit..) Even after the Independence Movement was brutally quelled, the 1920s saw a series of strikes at educational institutions designed to raise and resolve grievances. These included demands for the appointment of Korean principals, universal compulsory education, the use of the Korean language in textbooks, the building of more colleges and universities, and the acceptance of the right to have student meetings in high schools. National independence was the unspoken text of the demands. As indicated earlier, toward the end of the colonial period (1938—1945), there was no academic autonomy and freedom in the academic profession. These characteristics of higher education in Korea were aggravated by Japan's involvement in wars in that period. The Korean academics in both the public and private sectors of higher education had to serve the needs of the war effort. For example, to meet technical requirements, courses in the liberal arts were reduced in number or eventually dropped from the curriculum. Secondary and higher educational institutions were required to send students to work on war production as Japan needed a large labour supply, additional soldiers, and more technicians and it forced college students into military service. (For details, see Adams, D. & Gottlieb, E., op. cit, p. 16; Hung Kyu Bang, *Japan's Colonial Educational Policy in Korea, 1905-1930,* Doctoral book, University of Arizona, 1972, p. 205; Requoted from Weinberg, M. op. cit., p. 79.)

73. Lee, Ki-baik, op. cit., p. 353.

74. Ibid.

75. The Education Ordinance proposed to educate Koreans to be loyal to the Japanese Emperor according to the spirit of the Imperial Prescript on Education, which was founded on Confucianism, so as to strengthen the foundations of imperial rule. Later in 1916, it was further specified in the Teacher's Manual that there should be the cultivation of moral character among young Koreans on the basis of "loyalty and filial piety" the two pillars of Confucian ideology. (For details, see Son, In-su, op. cit., p. 102.

76. In contrast, the period of schooling in Japan was fifteen to seventeen years at that time. (Lee, Kwan, op. cit., p. 52.)

As indicated earlier, even before the annexation of Korea in 1910, the Japanese government began to bring all education under its direct control. From 1906, the Japanese Resident-General in Seoul began issuing edicts for the re-organisation of the Korean education system. The theme of control was made visible early. In 1911, addressing a conference, Governor General Terauchi made the following statement

The number of students in Korean private schools now amounts to more than

200,000—more than the number of students attending common elementary schools operated by the government... It is your duty to maintain surveillance lest textbooks compiled by the Ministry of Education of Old Korea be used at schools. (Sohn, Pow-key (ed). *The History of Korea,* Seoul: Jung-min Sa, 1970, p. 251.)

77. *Chosen Education Ordinance of 1911.* Cited by Underwood, H. H., *Modern Education in Korea*, New York, 1926, p. 191.

78. Dong, W., op. cit., pp. 425-426

79. The Table below shows the disparity between the Korean and the Japanese education enrollments at levels before higher education:

Table A
Education Enrollment in Korea by Nationality in 1925

School Level	Nationality	Enrollments	Per Ten Thousand Population	Ratio
Elementary	Koreans Japanese	386,256 54,042	208.20 1,272.35	1:6
Boys Higher Schools	Koreans Japanese	9,292 4,532	5.01 106.70	1:21
Girls Higher Schools	Koreans Japanese	2,208 5,458	1.19 128.50	1:108
Vocational Schools	Koreans Japanese	5,491 2,663	2.96 62.70	1:21
Normal Schools	Koreans Japanese	1,703 611	0.92 14.39	1:16

Quoted from Lee, Ki-baik, op. cit. p.367.

80. Mason, E.S., Kim, M.J., Kim, K.S. and Cole, D.C., *The Economic and Social Modernization of the Republic of Korea*, Cambridge, Mass., Harvard University Press, 1980, p. 344.

81. In 1921, for instance, the number of Korean students were 902, almost twice the number of Korean students enrolled in local institutions of higher education. For details, see Joung, S. E. "*Kyung Sung Je-kook Dae-hack* [A Study of the Characteristics of Kyungsung Imperial University]", Doctoral book, Department of Education, Yonsei University, Seoul, December 1997, p. 13.

82. Mason, E.S., Kim, M.J., Kim, K.S. and Cole, D.C., op. cit., p. 346.

83. Son, In-su, op. cit., pp. 176-177.

84. Lee, Kwan, op. cit., p. 52.

85. Ibid.

86. Ibid.

87. Ibid.

88. Henderson, G., *Korea: The Politics of the Vortex*, Cambridge, Mass.: Harvard University Press, 1968, p. 89.

89. Ibid.

90. Vacante, Russell A., op. cit., p. 76; Requoted from Weinberg, M. op. cit., p. 77.

91. Joung, Sun Ei. "*Kyung Sung Je-kook Dae-hack* [A Study on the Characteristics of Kyung Sung Imperial University].", op. cit., 1997, p. 14.

92. Ibid.

93. Ibid., p. 18.

94. Government General of Chosen, *Annual Report on Administration of Chosen 1930-32*, Seoul, December 1932, p. 72.

95. Republic of Korea, *Korean Overseas Information Service*, Seoul: The Government Press, 1994, p. 13.

The Government Normal School in Seoul was recognised as the best institution of its kind in Korea during the Japanese colonial period. The staff consisted of eight Koreans and nine Japanese, and the total number of students were 256. The graduates of the school were to be all engaged as teachers in Government and public common schools. Students who received teacher training at Normal Schools were granted a fixed sum of money to subsidise their expenses and in return they were to follow the teaching profession after graduation. (Government General of Chosen, op. cit., p. 113.)

96. Kim, In Whoe, '*Hankook Kyoyook: Kwager, Hunjae, Mirae* [Korean Education: its past, present and future]' in *Sa Sang* Vol. 1., 1989, p. 286.

97. Government General of Chosen, op. cit., p. 74.

98. Lee, Ki-baik, op. cit.

99. Kyung Sung Medical College was first established before the annexation as a department of the government hospital and in 1910, when Korea was colonised, it was transferred to Japanese colonial administration. It trained men in Western medical knowledge. Kyung Sung Law School was initially established by the Korean government before the annexation of 1910 to train judicial officials. After annexation, however, the college was reorganised to offer special courses in law and economics. Kyung Sung Technical College was established in 1905 by the Korean Government to produce managers for the industrial and engineering development of *Chosun* (the former name of Korea). After annexation in 1910, Kyung Sung Technical College came under Japanese colonial control and offered courses in applied chemistry, civil engineering, architecture, and mining and weaving. Suwon Higher Agricultural Dendrological School offered training in agriculture and forestry. The school was originally attached to the Model Farm at Suwon and was opened in 1906 and reorganised after annexation. Kyung Sung Higher Commercial School had its origin in the Kyung Sung branch of the Oriental Association School established in 1907. In 1921 it was reorganised and in 1922 was transferred to colonial government control. (Government General of Chosen, op. cit.)

100. Jayasuriya, J. E., *Education in Korea—a third world success story*, Seoul: Korean National Commission for UNESCO, 1983, p. 29.

101. Ibid. p. 36.

102. The overall development of the private sector against that of the public sector colleges during the colonial period is as shown in the following Table.

Table B

Development of Junior Colleges (1910-1945)

Year	Classification	No. of Colleges	Students
1912	Public	10	93
	Private	0	0
1919	Public	4	474
	Private	2	111
1923	Public	5	1,061
	Private	3	445
1931	Public	5	1,202
	Private	8	1,623
1940	Public	8	2,350
	Private	10	2,871
1943	Public	9	3,033
	Private	10	4,025

Source: Kwan Lee, op. cit., p. 53.

103. Joung, S. E. op. cit., p. 71.

104. This was a major shift, but one which had begun in pre-colonial Korea. Before the modern State came into being in Korea, mastery of the Confucian literary classics was the only legitimate qualification to be a scholar mandarin. Until the early colonial period, the legacies of the Confucian academic knowledge tradition in Korea were still influential in the private sector, which was however becoming open to the teaching of Western knowledge. Some Confucian institutions survived until the final annulment of Confucian institutions in 1929. (For details, see Lee, Ki-baik, op. cit.)

105. Yu, Kun-ho, 'Characteristics of Korea's view of the outside world in the late Chosun period (1392-1910)' in Hirano, K. (ed). *The State and Cultural Transformation: Perspectives from East Asia.* Tokyo & New York & Paris, United Nations University Press, 1995, pp. 226-28.

Kim Ok-kyun, Park Yong-hyo, and Yu Kil-jun led the Enlightenment Group in Korea, and entered the political arena with the slogan "civilization and enlightenment" in the 1880s. After learning abroad even before the opening of the Korean ports in 1876, members of the group argued that the foremost task for the survival of Korea was to expel Chinese influence from Korea. The group also issued a periodical, *Hansong Sinbo* in 1883. Through the journal, the group affirmed the values of Western civilisation and proposed "Oriental truth be equipped with Occidental techniques". In his inaugural address, Yu Kil-jun stated the political position of the Enlightenment Group:

Our purpose is to enlarge the knowledge of our people. All things ranging from moral self-training and household management to international politics are changing day by day. We are determined to help our people liberate themselves from their bigoted customs, direct themselves toward the trend of civilization, eliminate evil practices, return to right reason, abandon inconveniences, adopt what is useful, and promote our cultures.

Yu Kil-jun urged people to absorb knowledge not only of Western natural sciences but also of Western political systems, economic production, and commerce so that they could 'abandon inconveniences and adopt what is useful' from a utilitarian standpoint. (Yu Kil-jun, *Yu Kil-jun Chonso,* vol.5, Seoul: Ilchogak, 1971, p. 161. Requoted from Yu, Kun-ho, op. cit., p. 226-27.)

106. As discussed earlier, in Korea, it was the private education sector that opened a direct path to Western knowledge for Koreans.

107. Kim, Sung Hack. *Seokoo Kyoyookhack Doip-ey Kiwon-kwa Chungae [The Origins and Development of Western Educational Studies in Korea].* Seoul: Mooneum-sa, 1996, pp. 194-219.

108. Ryee, J.C., 'Republic of Korea', in Uchida, T. (ed). *Political Science in Asia and the Pacific: Status Reports on Teaching and Research in Ten Countries,* Bangkok: UNESCO Regional Office for Education in Asia and the Pacific, 1984, p. 52.

109. Lee, Kwan, op. cit., p. 53.

110. Chang, Y.-S. 'Planned Economic Transformation and Population Change' in C. I. E. Kim, C. I. E. and Mortimore, D. E. (eds)., op. cit., p. 80.

111. Ibid.

112. The Japanese filtering of the German academic influence on shaping the knowledge profile in Korea was also notable in the field of political studies during the colonial period. In Japan, political studies in its early stage of development were heavily influenced by German scholarship, and Korean political science was influenced by the Japanese interpretation of the German tradition of politics. (Ryee, J. C., 'Republic of Korea', in Uchida, T. (ed)., op. cit., p. 53.)

Another example of the double importation of Western knowledge in Korea is found in the field of economics. Although Korean economists in the academic profession in the colonial period were recruited in the private institutions, such as Yonhee (i.e. Yonsei) and Bosung (i.e. Korea) Colleges, they were initially trained by Japanese economists (in Kyung Sung Imperial University in Korea, or in Japan) who were predominantly influenced by Marxian theory. Therefore, rather surprisingly, the early development of Korean economics in the colonial period followed the

Japanese interpretation of Marxian economic theory.

Some Japanese economists, though a minority in number, went to Europe and the United States in the early 20th century and studied economics of the kind developed by such economists as Cournot, Jevons, Walras, Marshall and Keynes. Some of their books and articles were translated in Japan to form eventually the foundation for the post-World War II development of modern economics in Japan. However, this line of orthodox economics made no impact on the development of economics in Korea during the colonial period. No major Korean economists from the Japanese colonial academic institutions did any research within orthodox economic theory, and this, in due course, had effects on the Korean economics profession. (Han, S. S., 'Republic of Korea', in UNESCO (ed). *Economics in Asia; Status Reports on Teaching and Research in Nine Countries*, Bangkok, UNESCO, 1985, p. 325.)

Following the German notion of *Staatwissenschaft*, the Faculty of Law and Literature at Kyung Sung Imperial University conducted a wide range of research giving priority to Korea-related fields. Thirty seven published research projects out of fifty nine (about 64 %) by 1941 were directly related to Korea: e.g. Korean politics, law, economics, history, language, literature, religion, customs, etc. However, the authors of the published research works were (with one exception) all Japanese during the colonial period. (Joung, S. E. op. cit., p. 99)

113. Yonsei University. op. cit., p. 249.

114. Ibid., p. 248.

115. Yonsei University, op. cit., p. 190.

116. Henderson, Gregory, op. cit., p. 90.

117. Yonsei University, op. cit., p. 162.

118. For instance, the six departments at Yohee (Yonsei) College—Humanities, Theology, Maths and Physics, Business Studies, Agriculture, and Applied Chemistry—had to include these three subjects in their curriculum regardless of the differences in the academic disciplines. The knowledge profile of the Department of Humanities at Yonhee College in 1921 included Ethics, Japanese, English, English literature, History, Geography, Mathematics, Biology, Astronomy, Physics, Chemistry, Educational Studies, Chinese literature, Philosophy, Psychology, Music, and Physical Education. It should be noted here that although Yonhee College was founded by American Christian missionaries, Bible Studies had to be excluded from the curriculum according to the Private School Regulations which the Japanese colonial State enacted from March 1915. (Ibid., pp.163-168.)

119. Among the publications by missionary academic expatriates were: *Modern Education in Korea* by Underwood in 1926 and *Democracy and Mission Education in Korea* by J. E. Fisher in 1928, *History of the Korea Mission Presbyterian Church U.S.A., 1884-1934* by H. A. Rhodes. (For details, see Yonsei University, op. cit., 1985, pp. 197-202.)

120. Many of the educated men in Korea then had to learn Western knowledge in addition to the Confucian knowledge, which they had already acquired through a different educational channel, separate from the official one, i.e. the (colonial) State education system. (For details of the transmission of Western knowledge in Korea during the colonial period, see Kim, Sung Hack. *Seokoo Kyoyookhack Doip-ey Kiwon-kwa Chungae [The Origins and Development of Western Educational Studies in Korea]*. op. cit., 1996)

121. Adams, D. & Gottlieb, E. E., op. cit.

122. His vision was an:

...Institution in the nature of a native college which shall embrace not only the object of educating the higher classes of the native population, but at the same time affording instruction to the officers of the Company in the native languages and of facilitating our more general researches into the history, condition and resources of these countries. (Raffles, Lady, *Memoir of the Life and Public Services of Sir T. S. Raffles,* London, 1830, p. 79; Requoted from Wong Hoy Kee, F. and Ee Tiang Hong. op. cit. p. 83.)

This vision of Raffles had to wait for more than a hundred years to be realised. The establishment of Raffles College in 1929 was the nucleus of the future university in Malaya. However, the actual introduction of university education was not encouraged in British Malaya until the British colonial government finally judged the colony was about to attain self-government, and the end of the colonial phase was at hand.

123. This trend had already been noted in the Annual Report for the year 1899:

In Malaya as in India there is often a cry for more vocational instruction with complete disregard of the fact that our schools are all too vocational and utilitarian, and that the greatest fault is that they are not promoting genuine culture. Parents and schoolmasters are compelled by the economic conditions of modern life to train the pupils primarily to earn a livelihood.

(*Report of the Kynnersley Commission of Inquiry into the System of English Education in the Colony of Singapore.* 1902. Quoted in Wong Hoy Kee, F. and Ee Tiang Hong. op. cit., p. 33.)

124. Ibid. Quoted in Wong Hoy Kee, F. and Ee Tiang Hong. op. cit., p. 34.

125. Allington, Nigerl, F. B. & N. J. O'Shaughnessy, *Light, Liberty and Learning: the Idea of a University Revisited,* Oxford: The Education Unit, 1992, p. 31.

126. He made a contrast between the condition of higher education in Malaya with the traditional concept of the English university:

The fundamental principles underlying the conception of university education have not been adequately appreciated. A university should not be, as it has so often and dangerously been, a mass production vocational machine through which are passed, regardless of their future livelihoods, students of indifferent mental calibre but of great capacity for memorising facts... Even if the institution was conceived at the start on a more enlightened basis, in the shortest of time it becomes a vocational training centre and little else. Once this idea of its functions has arisen, there is little or no hope of recovery; the university institution exists in no more than name, for the real justification for its existence has been forgotten. The very danger which it was sought to avoid has been brought into being.

(Channon, H. J. (Jan. 1941). 'Some Observations on the Development of Higher Education in the Colonies: Memorandum' by Professor H.J. Channon [Extract], *Imperial Policy and Colonial Practice 1925-1945, Part II: Economic Policy, Social Policies and Colonial Research,* S. R. Ashton and S. E. StockwelL (eds), London: HMSO, Series A, Vol.1, 1996, pp. 293-294.)

127. *Report of the Maxwell Committee to consider and report on a Scheme to commemorate the Centenary of the Founding of Singapore,* 1918. Quoted in Wong Hoy Kee, F. and Ee Tiang Hong, op. cit., p. 44.

128. Wong Hoy Kee, F. and Ee Tiang Hong. op. cit., p. 44.

129. British colonial education policy can be dichotomised as English schooling for a native elite and vernacular school education for native masses. This divisive British education policy was applied to both the Indian and Malayan systems. (For details on the Indian case, see Edwards, M., *British India*, New York: Taplinger Publishing Company, 1968.)

130. Aziz, U. A., S. B. Chew, K. H. Lee, and B. C. Sanyal. *University Education and Employment in Malaysia.* Paris: IIEP, 1987, p. 76.

131. *Report of the McLean Commission on Higher Education in Malaya,* 1939, p. 1.

132. This new college would continue to award the medical diploma, but there was to be a Board of Examiners in England which would grant diplomas to students in

arts and science, which indicates some failure to appreciate the standards of university education already reached at Raffles College at that time. (*The Report of the Carr-Saunders Commission on University Education in Malay*, 1948, p. 134.)

133. In 1929, the Secretary of State for the Colonies suggested the possibility of a University in Singapore, which was referred to in the Legislative Council, where it was assumed that in the course of time a University for Malaya would be established. The McLean Commission was formed in 1939 "to survey existing arrangements for higher education, general and professional, in Malaya; and to consider in the light of local needs and conditions whether they require extension and, if so, in what direction and by what methods. To report upon the present work of Raffles College, Singapore, and on any additional developments that may seem desirable." (Quoted from Wong, F. H. K., and Yee Hean Gwee. *Official Reports on Education: Straits Settlements and the Federated Malay States 1870-1939*. Singapore: Pan Pacific Book Distributors, Ltd., 1980).

134. *Report of the Carr-Saunders Commission on University Education in Malaya*, op. cit.,1948.

135. Carr-Saunders, A. M. *New Universities Overseas*. London: George Allen & Unwin Ltd., 1961, p. 15.

136. After visiting Malaya in 1939, Prof. Channon presented a critical comment on the condition of higher education in Malaya which had been shaped on the basis of *ad hoc* colonial policies. (Carr-Saunders, A. M. op. cit., p. 29.)

137. Channon, H. J. (Jan. 1941). op. cit., p. 300.

138. Ibid.

139. As discussed in the Korean case, ideally the Confucian scholar mandarin enjoyed the highest prestige, to be followed in the descending order by the farmers, artisans, and merchants. This social structure was consolidated in Confucian Korea at least for 500 years. On the other hand, in Confucian China, the acquisition of wealth provided merchants with a degree of social mobility which enabled the most successful of them to displace farmers from second place in the traditional hierarchy, framers in practice being relegated to the lowest social status. In the highly commercial environment of Singapore, merchants have come to wield the greatest power and influence since the colonial period and hence to enjoy the highest prestige among the Chinese. This point has been made by Wang Gungwu 'Traditional Leadership in a new nation: The Chinese in Malaya and Singapore' in Alisjahbana, S. Takdir (ed) *The Cultural Problems of Malaysia in the Context of Southeast Asia*, Kuala Lumpur: The Malaysian Society of Orientalists, 1966, pp. 172-73; Purcell, V. op. cit., 1965, p. 73; Wilson, H. E., *Social Engineering in Singapore: Educational Policies and Social Change 1819-1972*, Singapore: Singapore University Press,

1978, pp. 12-15.

140. Selvaratnam, V. 'Change amidst continuity: University Development in Malaysia', in Altbach, P. G. and Selvaratnam, V. (eds). *From Dependency to Autonomy: The Development of Asian Universities*, Dordrecht: Kluwer Academic Publishers, 1989, p. 194.

141. The Commission recommended in 1948 the amalgamation of the Medical College and the Raffles College as the nucleus of the University of Malaya in 1948, as a degree granting, English-medium, residential institution in Singapore. (For details, see *Report of the Carr-Saunders Commission on University Education in Malaya*, op. cit., 1948.)

142. Ibid., p. 11.

143. Ibid.

144. Report of the Commission appointed by the Secretary of State for the Colonies on Higher Education in Malaya (The McLean Report) in Wong, F. H. K., and Gwee, Y. H., op. cit., pp. 143-146.

145. Report of the Commission appointed by the Secretary of State for the Colonies on Higher Education in Malaya (The McLean Report) (Ibid., p. 146.)

146. The McLean Report admits that the success of this British university system "depends on the possession by the academic staff of freedom of thought unencumbered by external direction. It is a system which exerts a powerful force on everyone concerned with it to give of his best for the corporate good. Each is, however, free to contribute in his own way." (Ibid.)

147. Carr-Saunders, A. M. op. cit.; Ashby, E. *Universities: British, Indian, African: a study in the ecology of higher education*. Cambridge, MA: Harvard University Press, 1966, pp. 206-343.

148. Various types of teacher training for both English-medium schools and Malay vernacular schools were provided by the colonial government: e.g. Normal Classes for pupil teachers at Raffles' Singapore Institution from 1872, Training Classes at Raffles Girls' School, Singapore and the Government Girls' School, Penang, and the Sultan Idris Training College, Perak, established to train vernacular Malay teachers in 1922. However, the Sultan Idris Training College was the only tertiary institution available for students from Malay vernacular schools. (Tregonnig, K. G. 'Tertiary Education in Malaya: Policy and Practice 1905-1962' in *Journal of the Malaysian Branch of the Royal Asiatic Society*, Vol. LXIII, No. 1, 1990, pp. 1-14.)

149. *Report of the Lemon Committee on Technical and Industrial Education in the*

Federated Malay States, Kuala Lumpur: Government Press, 1918.

150. Wong Hoy Kee, F. and Ee Tiang Hong, op. cit., p. 34.

151. In 1916, the Diploma of the College was recognised by the General Medical Council of Great Britain, and its graduates were allowed to practise anywhere in the British Empire. The name was changed again in 1921 to the King Edward VII College of Medicine and its license in medicine and surgery was recognised by the General Medical Council of Great Britain. (Turnbull, C. M., *A History of Singapore, 1819-1975,* Kuala Lumpur: Oxford University Press, 1977, p. 120.)

152. Stedman, Joann Bye, *Malaysia,* American Association of Collegiate Registrars and Admissions Officers, International Education Activities Group, 1986, p. 55.

153. 'Report of the Commission appointed by the Secretary of State for the Colonies on Higher Education in Malaya (the McLean Report)', 1939, in Francis H. K. Wong and Gwee Yee Hean, op. cit., p. 143.

154. Francis H. K. Wong and Gwee Yee Hean, op. cit.

155. According to the McLean Report in 1939, the demand for a local university was not unanimously supported by all sections of the population. "While the Chinese and Indians were generally in favour of it, it was said that the Malays, particularly those in the Federated Malay States, were not in favour. The Europeans, though not opposed to the idea, did not consider that the time was ripe enough for the establishment of a university." (ibid.)

156. Report of the Commission appointed by the Secretary of State for the Colonies on Higher Education in Malaya (The McLean Report) in Wong, F. H. K., and Gwee Y. H. op. cit., p. 155.

157. *The National University of Singapore 1996-7, General Information,* Singapore: Singapore University Press, p. 2.

158. Lee, E. and Tan Tai Yong. *Beyond Degrees: The Making of the National University of Singapore.* Singapore: Singapore University Press, 1996, pp. 117-118.

159. *Report of the Carr-Saunders Commission on University Education in Malaya,* op. cit., 1948.

160. Ibid.

161. In postwar Britain, the dominance of the Labour party under Attlee's Prime Ministership signalled the beginnings of the welfare state in Britain which was to have an impact on the British colonies as well. Lee, E. & Yong, T. T., op. cit., p. 90.

162. The Carr-Saunders Commission in 1948 was also concerned with the nature of the degree courses: i.e. should they be general degree courses or honours degree courses? The Commission suggested that "the admission to honours courses should be very carefully controlled and as an interim measure, there should be special courses of an honours standard (if not full-fledged honours courses) in addition to pass and general degree courses. (For details, see Wong, F. H. K. and Gwee Y. H. op. cit., p. 143; Lee, E., and T. T. Yong. op. cit., p. 82.)

163. For instance, the debate between Silcock as acting Vice-Chancellor and Dean of Arts and Professor C. N. Parkinson, who had been recruited to the Raffles Chair of History. Silcock wanted the teaching of economics to include some economic history, a move which was envisaged by Carr-Saunders. Silcock planned to give courses on the Industrial Revolution and its effects on the development of trade with non-industrialised countries. Parkinson objected strongly to this basically economic approach to history. Silcock gave in, and in the 1953/54 session, the course on English economic history was abandoned by the Economics Department. (For details, see Lee, E. & Yong, T. T., op. cit., pp. 88-89.)

164. Ibid., p. 93.

165. Channon, H. J. (Jan. 1941). op. cit., p. 296.

166. Yonsei University, op. cit.

167. Chung, Hwan-kyu, 'A Study on the Establishment of Seoul National University in Usamgik' Doctoral book, Department of Education, Yonsei University, Seoul, 1997, p. 64.

168. Werth, Richard. 'Educational Developments under the South Korean Interim Government' in *School and Society* Vol. 69, No. 1793, 1949.

169. Jhin, Duck Kyu, 'A Study on the Power Structure of the Korean Political Society', Doctoral Book, Dept. of Political Science, The Graduate School, Yonsei University, Seoul, 1977.

170. Ibid.

171. Ibid.

172. Through the reforms of 1895, the social class status system became in point of law, totally abrogated. (For details, see Lee, Ki-baik, op. cit., pp. 182-188 and pp. 290-294.)

173. Ibid.

174. In contrast, physical labour, or involvement in any kind of commercial or productive activity was degrading. Thus, there was severe competition for the position of State mandarin. According to the Confucian visions of the State and education, as reviewed in Chapter Two, low ranking, rural and provincial quasi-aristocrats and even commoners, in principle, were not excluded from entry to the national examination for selecting State mandarins in Korea. However, it was closed both *de facto* and *de jure* to the socially stigmatised lowborn, such as slaves, actor-entertainers (*kwangdae* and *sadang)*, the outcasts (*paekchong)* who hereditarily worked at such occupations as butchering, tanning, and wickerwork and others. (For details, see Kim, Terri, 'Korean Higher Education: an Interpretation and a Comparison, MA Dissertation, University of London, Institute of Education, 1992, pp. 54-63.)

175. Kim, In Whoe, *Hankook Moosock Sasang Yonku* [A Research on Shamanistic Ideology in Korea], Seoul: Jipmoon-dang, 1988.

176. Ibid.

177. Joung, S. E. op. cit.

178. Government General of Chosen, op. cit., 1921.

179. Joung, S. E., op. cit., pp. 130-142.

180. Ibid.

181. Lee, Ki-baik, op. cit., pp. 368-369.

182. Joung, S. E. op. cit., p. 99.

183. Lee, Chon-Sik, *The Politics of Korean Nationalism,* California: University of California Press, 1963, pp. 277-278.

184. Except for the Japanese immigrants in Korea, alien populations residing in Korea were insignificant in their number and in their participation in the economy. The size of the Japanese population was not very large, remaining in the neighbourhood of one per cent of the total population in Korean territory throughout the colonial period: 444,340 in 1925; 527,016 in 1930; 619,005 in 1935; 707,337 in 1940; and 708,448 in 1944. For details, see Chang, Y.-S. Planned Economic Transformation and Population Change. in Kim, C. I. E. and Mortimore, D. E. (eds)., op. cit., pp. 66-79; ft.27.

185. Ibid., pp. 53-84.

186. Ibid.

187. Ibid., p. 80.

188. Lee, Sung-hwa, 'The Social and Political Factors Affecting Korean Education, 1885-1950', Doctoral Book, University of Pittsburgh, 1958, p. 152; Requoted from Weinberg, M., op. cit.

189. Dong, W., op. cit., pp. 423-424 and ft. 65; Weinberg, M., op. cit., p. 79.

190. Han, Sung-jin, 'Korean elites under the U.S. military governance', M.A. Dissertation, the Graduate School of Education, Yonsei University, Seoul, 1986, p. 29.

191. Yonsei University, op. cit. p. 193.

192. Chung, H. K., op. cit.

193. Lee, Ki Baik, op. cit.

194. In 1920, more than half of the Koreans sponsored by the Japanese colonial government to study in Japan were recruited to the teaching profession and government officials after their return to Korea. (Kim, Sung Hack. op. cit., p. 209.) Among 1,312 Koreans who studied in Japan between 1909 and 1923, only 2 people were in the Industrial sector; 289 (22%) were in the Agricultural sector; 284 (21.6%) were unemployed; 177 (13.5%) had a teaching career in the educational sector; 140 (10.7%) were recruited as government officials; 119 (9.1%) worked in banking and private companies; 103 (7.9%) in commerce. (For details, see Kim, Sung Hack, op. cit., pp. 209-211)

195. Kim, Sung Hack. op. cit., pp. 199-219.

According to Kim, there were 541 Korean students studying in the United Stated between 1910 and 1918, but 20 per cent of them graduated from universities. Between 1921 and 1940, there were 289 Korean students in the States and 65 per cent of them graduated. Altogether, there were total of 296 Koreans who graduated from American universities during the colonial period. (Ibid. p. 218) Many of them were from the Christian missionary educational institutions in Korea and majored in Theology and Educational studies as well as Medicine, Science, Engineering in the United States. (Ibid. p. 216)

The number of Koreans who graduated from higher educational institutions in Japan steadily increased from 1920: 54 in 1917; 120 in 1926; 394 in 1935; and 529 in 1937. Those self-financed Koreans who went to Japan for higher degrees favoured Law, along with Politics and Economics. In contrast, those who were sponsored by the Japanese colonial State to study in Japan were studying very different fields—such as Agriculture, Engineering, Business and Medicine. (Ibid., p.

206)

Overall, the Korean academics educated in the United States formed a group competing against those educated in Japan. However, the American educated academics were relatively disadvantaged in professional career prospects in the public sector. Even nationalistic educational institutions in the private sector preferred Japanese educated candidates to the American educated. (Ibid., p. 219)

It was estimated in 1924 that there were 56 Korean academics who had studied in Germany. The range of fields in which they studied varied: e.g. Economics (8), Law (6), Medicine (6), Philosophy (3), Literature (3), etc.. (Ibid., p. 218).

196. The number of students also increased from 645 to 1,615. Of the students in 1958, 63 per cent were Chinese, 11 per cent Malay, 14 per cent Indian, 7 per cent Ceylonese, 2 per cent Eurasian and 3 per cent were 'other races'. For details, see Carr-Saunders, A. M. *New Universities Overseas,* op. cit., p. 61.

197. Ashton, S. R. and S. E. Stockwell (eds)., *Imperial Policy and Colonial Practice 1925-1945, Part II Economic Policy, Social Policies and Colonial Research,* London, HMSO, 1996.

198. *Great Britain, Public Record Office, London.* Series CO 717, Federated Malay States: Original Correspondence 1920 to 1940, Vol. 53, Technical Education Committee Report, 21 October 1925, p. 8. Requoted from Loh, F.S. P., op. cit., p. 104.

199. The State mandarin culture introduced by the British would survive to connect the Malay intelligentsia to the post-colonial political arenas of Malaysia and Singapore. For example, the first and second Prime Ministers of Malaysia, Tun Razak and Tun Hussein Onn with prestigious and wealthy ancestral backgrounds benefited from English education, as did Lim Yew Hock and Lee Kuan Yew, the first and second Chief Minister of Singapore. Unlike the first two Prime Ministers in Malaysia, Datuk Seri Mahathir bin Mohamad was the first commoner Prime Minister with no aristocratic ancestry or family wealth and with a local educational background. He symbolised the new Malaysian technocrat in the political arena.

200. Lim, T. G. 'Malaysian and Singaporean Higher Education: Common Roots but Differing Directions', in Lee, A. H. (ed) *East Asian Higher Education, Traditions and Transformations,* Oxford: Pergamon, 1995, p. 70; Tham Seong Chee. *Malays and Modernization: A Sociological Interpretation.* Singapore: Singapore University Press, 1977, pp. 98-101.

201. Chelliah, D.D., *A History of the Educational Policy of the Straits Settlements with Recommendations for a New System Based on Vernaculars,* Kuala Lumpur: The Government Press, 1947, p. 119.

202. Selvaratnam, V., *Innovations in Higher Education: Singapore at the Competitive Edge*, Washington, D. C.: The World Bank, 1994, p. 102.199. Lee, Edwin & Tan Tai Yong, op. cit., p. 86.

203. Carr-Saunders, A. M. op. cit., p. 173.

As noted by Carr-Saunders, this had the incidental advantage of spreading knowledge of the overseas institutions and their needs widely in British university circles. (Ibid.) For instance, L. A. Sheridan, formerly of the Queen's University, Belfast, was appointed to the chair in Law, when a four-year law degree course with honours began under the supervision of the Arts Faculty in the University of Malaya. In the Department of Engineering, Professor C. A. M. Gray, formerly of Sydney University, was appointed the first Professor of Engineering in 1954. (Lee, E. and T. T. Yong, op. cit., p. 92; p. 95.)

204. For instance, "scholars who had already achieved distinction in their own subjects for 45 years or were committed to their universities were too old to be newly recruited to the colonial university academic profession. On the other hand, able young men were unwilling to surrender academic ambitions by leaving the first class facilities available in Britain and by losing contact with their fellow workers in their own subjects". For details, see Channon, H. J. (Jan. 1941), op. cit., pp. 295-296.

205. Ibid.

206. Channon, H. J. op. cit. p. 295.

207. Ibid., p. 294.

208. Loh, P. F. S. *Seeds of Separatism: Education Policy in Malaya 1894-1900.* Kuala Lumpur: Oxford University Press, 1975, p. 24.

209. Ibid.

210. Loh, F.S. P., op. cit., p. 2; p. 105.

211. Ashton, S. R. and S. E. Stockwell, *British Documents on the End of Empire.* London: HMSO, 1996.

212. Wong Hoy Kee, Francis and Hong, Ee Tiang, op. cit.

The recruitment situation for the government posts in Malaya was that "the British recruited all the upper branches of the service by Englishmen and the lower by Eurasians and Chinamen from the Colony and by men from India and Ceylon" and as discussed above, the percentage of Malays recruited to the colonial administrative service remained low. (*Minutes of Conference of Residents,* March 1804. Cited by Steven, Rex, op. cit. p. 145.)

213. Yen, C-h. *A Social History of the Chinese in Singapore and Malaya.* Singapore: Oxford University Press, 1986.

214. In comparison, the Malays were only 5 percent of the pupils in English-medium boys' schools in the Straits Settlements in 1901. (For details, see Loh, Fook-Seng, Philip, op. cit., p. 51.)

215. Ibid.

216. For instance, sixty two per cent of craftsmen and production process workers were Chinese. (For details, see Loh, Fook-Seng, Philip, op. cit.)

217. For instance, Goh Keng Swee who was an arts graduate of Raffles College in 1940, became an economics tutor at Raffles College and later he went on to administrative service in the Department of Social Welfare. Lim Tay Boh, also a Raffles College graduate in 1934/35, won a scholarship to study in England and in 1940 became the first local lecturer ever to be employed, at the college. (For details, see Lee, E. and T. T. Yong, op. cit., p. 90.)

218. Until the end of the nineteenth century, tin-mining in the Malay States was very largely a Chinese enterprise. The labour force was predominantly Chinese. After the introduction of the large expensive tin-dredge into Malaya in 1912, the Chinese dominant tin industry was taken over by European management. In 1900, Malaya was producing more than half of the world's supply. The tin industry in Malaya was responsible for a substantial proportion of Chinese immigration. The rubber industry was developed in Perak, Selango, Negri Sembilan and Johore, where communications were good. By 1920 the annual exports from Malaya had reached the half of the world's supply at that time. The large-scale rubber cultivation induced a large scale immigration from South India. Penang and Singapore were important entrep?ts for free trading in the region. (For details, see Wong Hoy Kee, F. and Ee Tiang Hong, op. cit., pp. 25-30.)

219. Joung, S. E. op. cit.

220. Ibid, pp. 35-40.

221. Under the Japanese rule, formal schooling in Korea was different from that in Japan until the 1921 education reforms. Before 1921, the schooling system for Koreans consisted of 4 years of primary school, 4 years of secondary school before tertiary education, whereas that in Japan consisted of 6 years of primary school, 5 years of secondary school. After the reforms, the duration of primary education and secondary education in Korea became the same as in Japan.

222. Joung, S. E. op. cit., p. 34.

223. Andy Green notes that in England, "an integrated national education system was not properly consolidated until Balfour's Act of 1902, which created the local education authorities and brought all sectors of education under a unified adminis-trative structure... Teachers were poorly qualified and mostly untrained. There were no legal requirements regulating entry into teaching in England... In 1860, there was less than one certificated teacher per school, and the number of pupil teachers still outnumbered trained teachers by three to two in 1875". (Quoted from Green A. *Education and State Formation: The Rise of Education Systems in England, France and the USA.* New York: St. Martin's Press, Inc., 1990. p. 8, and pp. 22-23.)

224. The British domestic education system was not systematically organised until the early 20th century. As argued by Green, the British industry developed early without the systematic control of the State, the formal education system was not established as early as in Europe where the State made an effort to link industry and educated labour through the State's control over the educational process. (For details, see Green, A. op. cit.)

225. Rich, P. J. *Elixir of Empire.* London: Regency Press Ltd, 1989.

226. However, the types of education that received the direct attention of the British colonial State only included the Malay vernacular schools and the English-medium schools, even though there were two other types of vernacular schools for the Chinese and Indian immigrants in Malaya. Seeing the Chinese and Indians as immi-grants in Malaya at that time, the British colonial government was relatively indif-ferent to their schools.

227. Carr-Saunders, A. M. op. cit.

228. Ashby, E. op. cit., 1966; Carr-Saunders, A. M. op. cit.

229. *Report of the [Asquith] Commission on Higher Education in the Colonies,* 1945, p. 34.

230. In both Japanese Korea and British Malaya, medical studies was already avail-able through higher educational institutions before the official establishment of the university. In short, the colonial university in both cases gave priority to vocation-ally oriented, practical, professional Western knowledge.

231. In this aspect, both the Japanese and British colonial ideas of the university embodied an explicitly "linguicist" structure and ideology. As examined in Chapter Three, the colonisers shaped the future academic profession, at both the individual and the societal levels, and also at the supranational level, through language(s). "Linguicism" is the ideologies and structures which are used to legitimate, effectu-

ate and reproduce an unequal division of power and resources (both material and non-material) between groups which are defined on the basis of language (i.e. of their mother tongue).

As noted by Phillipson the acceptance of the "native" into the colonial order implies the adoption of the language of the coloniser and rejection of indigenous liguistic and epistemic values. This colonial intention behind the establishment of higher educational institutions or the university in the colonies is disclosed in the notes by a French colonialist, George Hardy:

To transform the primitive people in our colonies, to render them as devoted as possible to our cause and useful to our commerce...the safest method is to take the native in childhood, bring him into assiduous contact with us and subject him to our intellectual and moral habits for many years in succession, in a word to open schools for him where his mind can be shaped at our will.(Phillipson, R. op. cit., p. 343.)

(For details, see Phillipson, R. 'Linguicism: structures and ideologies in linguistic imperialism' in Skutnabb-Kangas, T. & Cummins, J. (eds). *Minority Education.* Clevedon: Multilingual Matters Ltd., 1988, pp. 339-358.)

232. Joung, S. E., op. cit., pp. 64-67.

233. Report of the (Asquith) Commission on Higher Education in the Colonies, 1945, p. 34.

234. However, in the longer term, the Japanese colonial language policy did not leave a deep impact on the post-colonial formation of an intellectual elite in Korea. It was replaced by the power of English that has been extended and further consolidated after the official end of the colonial era.

235. As briefly reviewed through Newman's and Jaspers' ideas of the university earlier in Chapter Two, the modern ideas of the university stemmed from the historical universities in Europe which initially developed like the craft guilds of the university cities, private corporations of teachers and students formed for the purpose of educating men (no women at that time), who wished to become lawyers, physicians, teachers or priests. At their inception, therefore, universities were teaching institutions whose activities were directed towards the training of high-level manpower, and the subsequent careers of many of their graduates comprise important parts in the history of Western Europe. The older European universities in the first place were international institutions drawing their teachers and students beyond the national boundaries. Although it was realised that the university was a local asset, so that city administrators and national governments endeavoured to retain and develop the university within their territory, the universities *per se* did not direct their activities to merely local aims. Each of them produced graduates to serve all

the countries of Western Europe, and there was specialisation. For instance, Bologna was outstanding in legal studies, Paris was pre-eminent in theology, and Salerno in medicine.

The ancient European universities taught in Latin, the international language of scholarship at that time. Thus, the whole body of knowledge was available only to the person who had made himself master of Latin. Academics of every university then shared the common cultural heritage of Europe and also students were required to familiarise themselves with the common cultural knowledge before commencing the specialised studies for professions.

In the European tradition, the university was in large measure the interpreter of the national culture, and to some extent, the conscience of Western Europe. The merchants of Antwerp sent a delegation to ask the theologians of the University of Paris whether it was sinful to make a profit from speculation. The Pope himself sought the advice of the Canon Lawyers at Bologna.

In this way, the university, with its professors and doctors, had become the final authority in the community on academic, legal and spiritual traditions. Its voice was independent of political government and its opinions were founded upon knowledge.

The university also assumed the role of a pioneer in research and the discovery of new knowledge, which has been a particularly strong in the German model. After the country became a unified nation-State in 1870, German universities began to place emphasis on research in many fields of pure and applied science, as a significant agency for economic development of the country. This inquiring spirit of research in German universities had been transmitted to other academic disciplines and spread to universities in other countries all over the world.

The three functions—teaching, the conservation and re-interpretation of accumulated knowledge and continuous research for the enlargement of mind—are still recognised as fundamental to the university's role. Regardless of different university histories, academic structure, and political philosophy, it can be contended that every university in every country of the world has inherited these three functions. (For details, see Haskins, C. H., *The Rise of Universities*, Ithaca, New York: Cornell University Press, 1957; Ridder-Symoens, Hilde De (ed). *A History of the University in Europe vol I, II*, Cambridge: Cambridge University Press, 1996.)

CHAPTER FOUR

The Postcolonial Period

The book examines, in this chapter, the postcolonial shaping and shape of the academic profession in South Korea (1945-1997) and Malaysia (1957-1997) and Singapore (1965-1997). The chapter has three sections. Each section deals with one of the three operational themes specified at the end of Chapter Two and used in Chapter Three.

It was concluded in Chapter Three that the different styles of the colonial States' modernity projects were important for explaining the social construction of the academic profession in Korea and Malaya. This chapter argues that the colonial legacy of State and university relations continued to remain influential in the postcolonial *shaping* of the academic profession in South Korea, Malaysia and Singapore. The Independent States in East Asia continued to give priority to the technical and vocational functions of the university. The State continued to play a role in systemising and controlling teacher training and vocationally-oriented university education in the postcolonial period.

In this period, the respective East Asian States also defined their modernity projects with a strong emphasis on the legitimation of the political sovereignty of the new government; the rapid industrialisation of the national economy; and the creation of a new indigenous national identity. The East Asian universities were involved in the postcolonial State's modernity project of nation-building. However, unlike the colonial period, the postcolonial academic professions were mainly shaped by indigenous political forces and domestic economic concerns.

In the postcolonial Independence period, the East Asian pursuit of rapid industrialisation borrowed human capital theories developed in North America and Western Europe during post-war reconstruction.[1] The universities in East Asia were considered the most important locus of human resource development for rapid industrialisation.[2] Thus, the relations of the East Asian State and the university, especially for the State's economic projects became even tighter in the postcolonial period than in the colonial period. Furthermore, the international academic links established in the colonial period offered a reprise—with variations—of the cultural impact of the colonisers on the shaping of the academic profession, within new institutions.

With these themes and arguments, this chapter will first concentrate on the shaping of the academic profession, which resulted from the respective East Asian States' idea of the university and the struggles over institutional forms and valued knowledge. Then the actual shape of the academic profession will, as in Chapter Three, be described, mainly through the themes of the 'meritocratic principle' defined and used by the respective East Asian States in academic recruitment routes and the consequent social composition of the academic profession. This chapter concludes with a comparative analysis of the three academic professions in the postcolonial period.

VALUES AND VISIONS OF THE STATE

In the post-colonial era, the 'nation-state' system which originated in Europe spread widely. However, the newly independent East Asian States carried out their own modernity projects with the aims of indigenising colonial education. Thus, both the shaping and the shape of the modern academic professions in East Asia were still connected with the modernity projects of the respective States, although these projects were new. Paradoxically they drew on older cultural traditions (such as Confucianism and Islam) as well as the new idea of 'the nation'. The States' sponsorship and subsequent supervision of schooling and higher education became pervasive.[3]

To test these arguments, the book will first look at the process of indigenisation and development of the respective East Asian States. The book will examine the case of South Korea first and then those of Malaysia and Singapore.

South Korea: Values and Visions of the State: The Independent State's Modernity Projects

Immediately after Liberation, Korea experienced national partition between the North and the South, symbolising the beginnings of the Cold War after 1945. Politically, the State's project in South Korea in the postcolonial period focused on maintaining national security and developing the Republic of Korea as a democratic and capitalist nation-state. This political project of South Korea began under the influence of the United States, after political independence and national partition in 1945. The South Korean alliance with the United States was consolidated after the Korean War ended in 1953.[4]

The anti-communist stance of the U.S. military government in the South was a decisive factor in the making of the new Republic of Korea. The North Korean communist threat made it possible and easy to legitimate strong nationalistic, authoritarian, and military governance. The American military regime's immediate concern was to suppress the labour movements mobilised by a variety of groups with socialist sympathies,[5] while the land reforms initiated by the U.S. military government led to the virtual elimination of the land-owning class as a political force.[6]

In this new political context, however, it is argued that the newly independent government in South Korea, like the American military government, maintained the political, and economic infrastructure of the Japanese colonial State.

The rise of a modern bureaucratic State in Korea occurred under Japanese colonial governance and the newly independent State in South Korea inherited this structure and continued a high level of political centralism and bureaucracy, and a low level of differentiation between the political and the socio-economic. The continuing development of the bureaucratic structure in Korea was possible because the conservative political elite in Korea who had cooperated with the Japanese colonial state remained in political power even after Independence.[7]

However, South Korean politics were volatile, which produced governance by the military.[8] In 1961 General Park Chung Hee was able to institutionalise an authoritarian and interventionist regime by following the Japanese model of the Meiji Restoration (*Ishin*). Under the argument of national 'revitalisation' (*Yushin*), the Constitution was amended to legitimate and consolidate the dominance of the executive and one-party rule.[9]

Park sought a way to restore the State's legitimacy and authority within the Confucian political ideal of loyalty to the State. Simultaneously, the State denounced those aspects of traditional Confucianism which produced economic retardation. Park's vision for the country was based on Korean nationalism and the economic advance of non-communist industrialised societies. National partition, war, poverty and threats of social chaos were the immediate stimuli to building a strong state in South Korea. Thus, overall, the State's priority in the modernity project was national security and economic growth.

From the establishment of the Third Republic after the military revolution in May 1961, Korea made considerable progress in building a strong nation with economic modernisation through consecutive Five-Year Economic Development Plans.[10] Economic growth was made possible by cooperation between the government and the private sector (although the *chaebol*—i.e. conglomerates—were guided by government). Park's leadership of the so-called "developmental state"[11] proved effective for economic growth, but stunted political progress towards democracy. The combination of strong government and high economic growth led to serious tensions in society.

Nevertheless, economic growth was taken to be more important than 'democracy' until the end of Park's authoritarian government (1961-1979). The State's modernity projects, in the period of the Chun regime (1980-1987) focused on political stability and economic growth.[12] There were difficulties. Although the South Korean economy grew at an average annual rate of 8.5 per cent during the period 1962 to 1984, South Korea suffered inflation, and instability caused by constant political friction.[13] The departure of President Chun in 1987 was followed by a wave of labour and student unrest. The subsequent years of rapid democratisation under President Roh saw a surface transition from long-term authoritarian rule to political liberalisation.[14]

Roh sought political legitimacy for his regime by winning the support of the middle class. Politically, he tried to contain the potentially explosive forces in favour of 'democratisation from below'. Grass-roots labour movements were targeted for containment. His reformist measures proved to be unpopular. Economic growth, the perennial source of legitimacy, was erratic in this period. Domestically, the rising demand for democracy forced the State to pay more attention to social welfare and equity between 1987 and 1992. However, the conglomerates (*chaebol* in Korean, *zaibatsu* in Japanese) increased their political power, becoming more independent and resistant to government control.[15]

Thus, politically, and apart from the obvious crisis of the Korean War and a divided nation, the period of 1950 to 1990 saw severe political tensions, oscillations in the forms of governance and a continuing and urgent search for political legitimacy—which included tight surveillance of the universities. The political legitimacy of the various regimes was typically sought through promises of economic growth—according to the World Bank report released in 1994, Korea's per capita GNP growth rate was recognised as the world's highest during the 1985-1992 period.[16] Subsequently, the political turning point in South Korea came in 1992, after three decades of authoritarian military governance, with the new civilian government led by Kim Yong Sam.[17]

Economically, the South Korean State's modernity project stressed rapid economic growth through export-oriented, outward-looking, industrial development. State-led economic development started in the 1960s by relying heavily on foreign aid and borrowing.[18] An important part of the capital needed was foreign, though this was not direct foreign investment; the capital was controlled by the State, within its own strategic economic plans.[19] This was an interventionist, state-led economy, rather than an economy based on market principles, especially in the early stage when the country was trying to catch up with the industrialised world.[20]

The State-guided economic development of South Korea was a close replica of the Japanese economic pattern, including the strong role of conglomerates (*chaebol*). State support for strategic industries started with labour-intensive sectors in the 1960s, moving on to capital-intensive and skill-intensive sectors in subsequent plans. The industries targeted for support ranged from iron, steel, ship buildings to chemical sectors, sophisticated electronics, information technology products, and automobiles by the 1980s.[21]

A general weakening of the overall performance of the Korean economy was signalled by wage increases, high inflation, currency crises and rising imports within ongoing trade liberalisation in the 1990s. Yet, the South Korean State still maintained its bureaucratic apparatus[22]—despite an economic mandate for liberalisation and decentralisation, the subordination of business to the State remains unchanged.

Culturally, the South Korean State project since political independence has been linked to America. The influences included American educational aid since political independence from Japan.[23]

The second theme in the cultural project of the South Korean State was the military government's use of Confucian values to define the national culture of South Korea. According to President Park Chung Hee:

> Just as a home is a small collective body, so the State is a large community... One who does not maintain a wholesome family order cannot be expected to show strong devotion to his state... A society that puts the national interest above the interests of the individual develops faster than one which does not.[24]

The cultural project stressed the mission of 'national revitalisation (*Yushin*)', a mission captured in the Charter of National Education,[25] proclaimed by Park Chung Hee in 1968. The Charter of National Education has shaped the educational ethos of South Korea. Since the proclamation of the Charter, the Ministry of Education has taken various measures to embody its spirit at various levels of the schooling system. For example, at the upper secondary and tertiary level of education, the Ministry of Education incorporated a course of 'national ethics' in the curriculum from 1970.[26]

However, an unanticipated consequence of the expansion of higher education in Korea was that universities became the centre of political dissent within an authoritarian culture. At the primary and secondary school levels, there exists a Confucian approach to learning with a strong dose of indoctrination. However, at the tertiary level, extracurricular activities in university life in Korea have included politics, normally anti-government politics.

Overall, while rapid economic development has been the basis of the military regime's claim to political legitimacy in South Korea since 1961,[27] culturally, political leaders have utilised the Korean people's traditional instincts for collective identity and group conformity for survival throughout historical turbulence and the pursuit of modernity. Nevertheless, political conflict has been considerable and regimes unstable.

It is in this context that the effort to use the university and the academic profession in the construction of Korean society—and the South Korean State's idea of the university—should be understood in the postcolonial period. However, first, the following section will examine the values and visions of the Malaysian and Singaporean States through their modernity projects in the postcolonial period.

Malaysia: Values and Visions of the State: The Independent State's Modernity Projects

Politically, the most visible colonial heritage in the postcolonial period in Malaysia was the ethnic divisions underpinning Malaysian political and economic structures. The substantial impediment to national integration at political independence was that ethnic divisions in Malaysia were marked in geography, employment and educational structures.[28] The Malaysian State is thus often identified as an ethnic State in the existing literature.[29] In this sense Malaysia is a state in which major controlling values draw on ethnic nationalism.[30] The Malaysian State's political modernity projects in the postcolonial period can be understood in this context of ethnocultural identity (through which the shaping of the academic profession will also be outlined later).

In 1957, the Federation of Malaysia gained political independence within a constitutional framework that institutionalised the special position of the *Bumiputera*.[31] Unusually Malaysia did not go through conflicts between the former colonial-trained administrators and the new independent nationalist political leaders.[32] However, ehthnonational politicisation and tensions continued throughout the 1960s, especially after Bahasa Malaysia (the Malay language) became the official national language in 1967.

The role of the first Prime Minister, Tengku Abdul Rahman, was crucial in setting the new political style after Independence. Tengku's political leadership was gentle and deflective on ethnic issues, reflecting his Malay aristocratic and English educational background, which was further refined by many years of living in London.[33] He did not attempt to diminish the ethnic distinctions, by cultural assimilation, to create a single Malaysian national culture. Instead, he preserved the British colonial legacy of the "divide and rule" principle, insisting that each community should take care of its own affairs, according to its own cultural norms.[34]

His approach, however, turned out to be unsuccessful, as indicated by the ethnic riots of May 13, 1969. Subsequently, he stepped down and his deputy, Tungku Abdul Razak, took over and was one symbol of the New Economic Policy era in 1970.[35] The ethnic riots were the major trigger for the inception of the NEP, through which a policy of "positive discrimination" was devised in favour of *Bumiputeras* in all dimensions of the State's modernity project.[36] In other words, the State's modernity project within the NEP has focused on a fundamental alteration of ethnic balance to locate the *Bumiputeras* at the core of the social structure.[37]

Economically, the Malaysian State stressed the NEP goals of economic growth and social equity, introduced in the period of the Second Malaysia Plan (1971-75). The NEP (which continued in five-year plans until 1990) has stressed the active participation of the *Bumiputeras* in corporate ownership via state enterprises.[38] The New Economic Policy was the economic dimension of the cultural and political drive to assert the "Malayness" of Malaysia—principally by the insistence on a common national language, Bahasa Malaysia, and on the national ideology (*Rukun Negara*), which stresses the special privileges of the Malays written into the Independence Constitution of 1957. The national ideology defines the privileges of the *Bumiputeras*, through the operation of reserved status or quotas for Malays in university admissions and recruitment. In the higher civil and diplomatic services, a 4 to 1 ratio of Malays to non-Malays was required.[39] The political justification of Malay ethnic privilege underpinned all dimensions of the State's economic modernity projects after the start of the NEP. Within the successful legitimation of the political subordination of the non-Malay ethnic groups to the *Bumiputeras*, the economic project of the Malaysian State has been State-driven industrialisation.

Since the mid 1980s, the Malaysian pattern of rapid economic growth through export-led industrialisation has officially followed the examples of other East Asian economies such as Japan and South Korea.[40] Through the Industrial Master Plan (1986-1995) and the Fifth Malaysia Plan, a science and technology policy underpinned strategies for manpower development and industrial growth which stressed the need for a considerable self-sufficiency in industrial technology.[41] In 1991, the government announced the New Development Policy (NDP) and Vision 2020[42]:

> ...Vision 2020 makes it perfectly clear, and we must have it perfectly clear in our minds, that we must be a "developed country in our own mould." Modernisation is not westernisation or Japanisation or Easternisation or Asianisation. The land that must be fully developed by 2020 must be uniquely modern, i.e. in keeping with the progress that the world has made in every field by then and yet remain distinctly and uniquely Malaysian...[43]

The contemporary values and visions of the Malaysian State have stressed 'Look East', privatisation, deregulation, and a (relatively) open and liberalised economy.

The expansion of the private sector and export-led economic growth[44] in the contemporary Malaysian State indicate its strategy of internationalisation in education and in the economy. Mahathir Mohamad perceives the private sector of higher education as "the primary engine of growth",[45] for the development of human resources.[46]

Culturally, the Malaysian State's modernity project has focused on establishing a new national education system as a crucial mechanism to meet Malaysia's manpower needs and in particular to train *Bumiputeras* for the professions as well as to spread the national language which since 1982 has been the medium of instruction in all types of schools (except in Sarawak).[47] To correct the disparities in occupational patterns between the Malays and the non-Malays, a new single national education system was advocated, to integrate the existing education streams inherited from the colonial period. The State's projects also included a number of specific steps that placed the Malays eventually in favoured positions for access to higher education and advanced employment sectors.[48] The privilege of the Malays was, for instance, evinced in the National Language Bill of 1967, which made Bahasa Malaysia the sole official language and the Malay Certificate of Education (MCE) obligatory for overseas study.[49] In July 1969, Tun Razak, as Director of the National Operations Council, announced a policy to make Malay the effective national language, at all levels of education, by the immediate conversion of English medium schools to the Malay medium so that the university education system would also be effectively converted to Malay by the mid-1980s.[50]

Since the mid 1970s, Islamic revivalism has been also notable in the Malaysian State's cultural project.[51] UMNO (United Malays National Organisation) leaders have tried to revitalise traditional Islam to unify the Malays in the multi-cultural context of Malaysia and simultaneously to promote economic development in the Western capitalist sense: "modernising without sacrificing its (Islamic) values."[52]

In the context of economic development, the Islamic theme can also be understood within the emphasis by the Prime Minister on the East Asian work ethic and values in the Fourth Malaysia Plan from 1981. The Prime Minister Mahathir Mohamad urged the nation to look to both Japan and South Korea for "inspiration, methods and skills" in order to increase Malaysian economic progress.[53] He defined such an effort as crucial to national development, and promulgated the "Look East Policy" (LEP).[54] The Look East Policy outlines the new visions and values of the Malaysian State and advocates deliberate severance of its former association with the West, by establishing new links with Japanese and Koreans in education and training programmes, as well as in enterprises and construction projects:

> Whatever you used to do before with the West I think you should also do with the East. That is the Look East Policy. And if you have learnt all the bad work ethic of the West before, it is about time you learn [sic] some of good work ethic of the East... Look East means we should resort to other sources than just the West and this doesn't mean that we are going to give up the West entirely. What is good in the West, we will still follow, but here is a source of ethical values, systems and everything else which are

useful to us. So why shouldn't we make a deliberate effort to acquire this from the East?[55]

In the "Look East" policy emphasis is given in education to "inculcating discipline, moral values and work ethics,"[56] as well as Islamic precepts,[57] while priority is attached to courses in business, commerce, science and technology to meet the need for manpower in the industrial sectors.[58] Overall, the Malaysian State's cultural project in the postcolonial period has focused on the consolidation of a new Malay-centric, national unity through educational, religious and language policies. The NEP in 1970, after the May 13 ethnic riots in 1969, had far reaching effects on political, socio-economic and educational developments in Malaysia. The strains of inter-ethnic relations, especially between the Malays and the Chinese, resulted in the consolidation of the Malay language as the sole medium of instruction and emphasised Islamic culture within the national culture. The *Bumiputera* policy within the NEP directed successively the Education Policy and the National Language Policy, through which the replacement of English-medium education with Malay began. By 1984, all English-medium educational institutions in Malaysia were converted to Malay-medium institutions. The new Malaysian version of national unity has emphasised the politics of cultural autarky, which contradicts to some extent the government's economic project of internationalisation and which has created new intra-ethnic strains among the nation.

This issue will be revisited later through an analysis of the State's idea of the university. First, in preparation for a comparative analysis, the following section will look at the Singaporean State's values and visions.

Singapore: Values and Visions of the State: The Independent State's Modernity Projects

The contemporary Singaporean State in the 1990s is marked by a small population of just under three million, which is plural in ethnic composition: the Chinese are 77%; Malays 14%; Indians 7%, and 2% are 'others'.[59] Despite the State's policy of ethnic integration since Independence, distinctions still remain which reflect the colonial legacy of vertical cleavages of race, language, religion and culture. However, the average literacy rate in 1990 reached 90.7%, with 46% being literate in two or more languages.

Singapore became a sovereign city State after leaving Malaysia on 9 August 1965. The main political feature of the post-war period in Malaya and Singapore was the organisational and ideological strength of the independence movement, which came after the failure of two attempts to form, first, an alliance with the Malayan-based Chinese entrepreneurial class, and then a coalition with the Malay ruling class. According to Tremewan, the political achievement of Lee Kuan Yew was the transformation of the

People's Action Party from an anti-imperialist party based on the Chinese mass to a party of the non-communist, pro-British, English-speaking, post-independence capitalist class.[60] The first generation of the PAP in Singapore was composed of nationalists who were anti-colonial, anti-communist, English-educated and trained in the United Kingdom—all of them had tertiary education (in Raffles College, later the University of Singapore) and four of them had advanced training in the United Kingdom.[61] They belonged to the professional middle-class, who joined the PAP in their mid-thirties.[62]

Politically, Singapore carried out its own nation-building programmes initially with two purposes: to combat the communist threat and to maintain racial harmony. Following the British pattern, Singapore developed a parliamentary democracy after Independence (although it has recently amended the constitution to create an executive Presidency). The promotion of economic development was politically necessary to enhance commitment to Singapore and to reduce such competing loyalties as race, language, and religion.[63]

For the purpose of political integration, the government introduced national (or military) service, and also used the education system. Entrance to university was made conditional on a political suitability certificate issued by the internal security police. Individual dossiers were also maintained on all students by the State security authority, which would be consulted at the time of employment.[64] The government also restricted individuals, groups, organisations and the mass media, especially the Press, from sensationalising and exploiting racial, linguistic, and religious issues.[65]

To carry out these projects successfully, the newly Independent Singaporean government has been run on the principles of meritocracy and efficiency to attract the "best and the brightest to join the Singapore Civil Service (SCS) and also to minimise corruption".[66]

To promote the meritocratic principle underpinning Singapore's modernity project, the State has maintained its control over the national education system through which the criteria of merit are defined. The education system has been the only route to upward mobility—a Confucian theme.[67] Singapore, as a Chinese dominated multi-ethnic city-state, has also consistently emphasised Chinese Confucian values to develop a "National Ideology".[68] To create ideological legitimacy, based on the notion of "Chinese" Singaporeans, the government fostered the use of Mandarin, and Confucian ethics in religious education. From 1984, every student in Singapore had to study religious education—which included Confucianism, Islam, Hinduism, Buddhism and Christianity—as an examination subject in secondary schools.[69] Most Chinese pupils chose to study Confucian ethics.[70] The use of religious education had a political purpose: to consolidate hierarchical, patriarchal familial relations as well as induce conformity in the citizens.[71]

The White Paper for Shared Values announced in January 1990 praises the concept of government by "honourable men" (*junzi*) as a Confucian ideal that fits Singaporean society and its needs.[72] The Singaporean State's 'National Ideology' is described as 'key', 'shared' or 'core' values, common to the major ethnic and religious groups in Singapore which are Asian rather than Western in nature. The shared values are: (i) the nation before community and society above self; (ii) the family as the basic unit of society; (iii) community support and respect for the individual; (iv) consensus not conflict; and (v) racial and religious harmony.[73]

Given the multiethnic structure of the Singaporean State, however, the Confucian movement at the national level has had to be conciliatory and use terms such as "national ideology" and "shared values". Meanwhile, a Confucian political ideology has persisted as a core value underpinning the Singapore's modernity project in its political and cultural dimensions.

Economically, the Singaporean State's modernity project has stressed rapid development. Even before independence from Malaya in 1965, the PAP government in Singapore made it clear as early as 1959 that its education policy would give strong emphasis to science and technology in education to equip youth with skills, aptitudes and attitudes for employment in industry.[74]

From an entrepôt economy in the colonial period, Singapore was transformed into an entrepôt-manufacturing economy, with the growth of international banking and tourism added to this new economic framework. Since Independence in 1965, particularly after 1967, there was a cumulative annual GNP growth rate of about 14% per annum until the mid-1970s.[75] The economy grew by an average of 10% a year from 1978 to 1982. The contribution of manufacturing and commerce grew in significance while the financial and business services sector contributed 20.9% to GDP by 1980.[76]

The Singaporean government, after creating political stability and independence and the legitimacy of the government, has achieved a successful economic transformation from a resource-poor developing country into an Asian "dragon" and a 'High-performing Asian Economy'.[77] In consequence, Singapore has received the status of an "advanced developing country" from OECD, with a per capita GNP in 1995 of US$24,614 (an increase of nearly 26 times since Independence).[78] At the beginning of the 1990s, the Singaporean State entered its fourth phase of modernisation "to attain the status and characteristics of a first league developed country within the next 30 to 40 years."[79]

To carry out the economic project, State control of national education, with an emphasis on bilingualism, technical training and English proficiency, has been important. The aim of the tightly-controlled educational process in Singapore includes the selection of an English-educated technocratic elite.[80]

To increase the economic productivity of human resources[81], the PAP government has introduced a Gifted Education Programme for the most talented 8 per cent, and the best educational resources were directed to them. Simultaneously, more funds were allocated to tertiary education. Consequently, total enrollments in universities and colleges rose by 49.4 per cent, and in technical and vocational institutes rose by 7.5 per cent from 1979 to 1983. In the same period, engineering course enrollments rose by 2,014 at the National University of Singapore and by 10,232 at Singapore Polytechnic.[82]

Within its meritocratic education principle, the PAP has held the view that there can be no distinction between majority rights and minority rights, although it officially has kept the multi-racial policy of the right of all racial communities to order their own affairs in culturally appropriate ways. Just as in Malaysia the multi-racial policy had been used against the Chinese interest, it was turned against the Malays in Singapore, when Singapore no longer had to accommodate the Malay politics of the peninsula. In Lee Kuan Yew's words, "we must expend our limited and slender resources" on "no more than five per cent" of the population (who happen to be overwhelmingly Chinese middle and upper middle class).[83] The overt meritocratic selection procedure from the primary level has promised social upward mobility only through educational competence. Despite blockages for ethnic minorities and the working class, the State's meritocratic ideology has inculcated a strong sense of unity and conformity.[84]

Culturally, given the British colonial legacy of a multi-ethnic profile in the population, the Singaporean State has fostered pragmatic, multiethnic and meritocratic cultural values to shape many aspects of Singaporean life. In developing a local culture rooted in the people's Asian backgrounds (which is however strongly dominated by the overseas Chinese cultural heritage) the use of English in Singapore is a salient feature of the State's cultural project. Catherine Lim points out, "While the status of English in the post-independence Third World declined or was reversed *vis a vis* the native languages, in Singapore it went on from strength to strength, until today, it is the language that enjoys the highest status and support among the nation's 2.6 million people".[85]

There are four official languages (English, Chinese, Malay and Tamil) in multi-racial Singapore. In practice, however, English dominates the institutional life of the nation. It is the language of government, of administration and employment. It is the medium of instruction in all the schools and tertiary institutions. English extends across all ethnic groups and socio-economic levels in Singapore.[86]

In this cultural context of Singapore, the use of English should be understood within a pragmatic ideology.[87] The Education Minister Dr. Tony Tan has emphasised:

> We do not wish to be a pseudo-Western society. While we need to learn
> and use English to master technology and enhance our competitive edge
> in the international business community, we should not let the use of
> English override the importance of keeping our links to our cultural roots
> strong and healthy.[88]

The PAP government was concerned that under the onslaught of
Western permissiveness, the English-educated Singaporeans might lose
their Asian cultural identity and values, especially the English-speaking
Chinese. Malays were less likely to lose their culture because of their rural
based cultural heritage. In 1974, the PAP government launched its
Education for Living (EFL) and Civics courses in primary and secondary
schools, aiming to instil Asian (Confucian) moral values of thrift, filial
duty, obedience to authority and loyalty to the government.[89]

Overall, as noted by Clammer, Singapore's cultural project is "the exal-
tation of the philosophy of pragmatism", which needs to be seen in the
context of an "anti-ideological stance and technocratic politics, of posi-
tivism in the social sciences and of the commodity fetishism of the materi-
alistic consumer society."[90] Overall, the Singaporean State's cultural project
has focused on legitimating and sustaining an extreme version of pragmatic, meritocratic principles in economic development since decolonisation,
and subsequent independence from Malaysia.[91]

Thus, it can be suggested that in all three societies, the State has been the
major actor in defining the national culture. The next section will analyse
the role of the university in reinforcing such processes.

THE STATE'S IDEA OF THE UNIVERSITY: STRUGGLES OVER
INSTITUTIONAL FORMS AND VALUED KNOWLEDGE

This section examines the social construction of the academic profession
through the Independent States' 'idea of the university'; and the struggles
over institutional forms and valued knowledge.

In the Independence period, the new States recovered, within the university system, some of the knowledge traditions which had been devalued
in the colonial period. In South Korea, Sung Kyun Kwan University was
reopened to revitalise parts of the Confucian epistemic tradition which had
been disturbed by the Japanese colonial modernity projects.[92] In Malaysia,
the International Islamic University was established to develop Malay-
Muslim academic culture.[93] In Singapore, the Nan Yang Technical Institute
was established, reviving the Chinese identity of the Nan Yang University,
which had been already amalgamated into the National University of
Singapore in 1980.[94]

It is argued here that in the postcolonial period the university systems
grew rapidly but within the particular political ideology of each particular
East Asian State: for example, in South Korea, within the political ideolo-

gy of the Cold War period. However, there were continuities in the ways in which the universities worked, for a while, following the models inherited from the colonial period.

Second, it is argued that the types of knowledge taught in the university curriculum reveal the new cultural valuations of knowledge in the new economic and cultural projects. However, the colonial legacy of vocationally-oriented, practical knowledge was still maintained in these post-colonial East Asian States. The socio-economic prestige given to the pragmatic value of knowledge has been continuously promoted by the stress on economic development. For example, Technology, Applied Sciences, and Business Studies are regarded as important in all these East Asian States. The English language has always been the most important medium of higher education for direct acquisition of Western knowledge in Malaya; Malaysia, and Singapore, and, to a lesser extent, in South Korea. Therefore, the acquisition of English has been significant in the entry routes to the academic profession in universities in East Asia.

Third, there is a growing alertness to new international networks in higher education in the contemporary decade, which is affecting the academic profession in East Asia. The so-called 'internationalisation' of higher education, as noted by OECD Reports[95] includes concerns about the international trade in professional services and transnational educational mobility. English-speaking countries in the West are keen to export their educational programmes and these East Asian countries are now prepared to franchise some of these programmes.[96] The programmes promote among local academics certain types of knowledge and skills useful for participation in international networks and the programmes also carry values, such as efficiency, competitiveness, and acceptance of the importance of the English language, which have been transmitted to the East Asian university systems.

Amid these international trends, this book argues that beneath the surface similarities, there are continuing historical forces in the particular contexts of East Asia, which have re-formed the idea of the university. In the following sections, the book examines the cases of South Korea, Malaysia and Singapore, in that sequence.

Korea: The State's Idea of the University

The university system under the U.S. Military Government (1945-1948) had clearly defined political and economic purposes, which included converting Koreans to the American conception of democracy and providing useful skill training.[97]

In the education system as a whole, schools became coeducational and the school curriculum was thoroughly revised. The new textbooks were written in Korean (*Han'gul*), disseminating democratic principles and ideas about scientific method. Instructional emphasis was placed on problem-solving and learning-by-doing. Comprehensive high schools and second-ary-level vocational-technical schools were created, while academic sec-ondary schools received less attention.[98] However, higher education was the main focus of educational reforms at this time.

As a result of the rapid educational reforms under the U.S. military gov-ernment's supervision for three years (1945-48), the Korean university sys-tem was newly constructed. After the Korean War (1950-53), American aid again played an important role in developing university education in Korea. American aid went to the improvement of undergraduate faculties and the development of graduate level programmes in public administra-tion, agriculture, and medicine.[99]

Nevertheless, the Korean academic profession in the newly organised university system still reflected many aspects of the former Japanese model. As in the Japanese colonial education tradition, the university system of South Korea was still under the direct control of the Ministry of Education. The government continued to fix the number of students permitted to enrol, to set fee levels, and to control the administration of the universities by various means (often financial). Until 1971, it was even necessary for universities to obtain the government's permission before awarding a doc-torate and Korean students were subject to strict controls by the Education Ministry which limited overseas study as well.[100]

As in the colonial period, the postcolonial South Korean State also tried to control the rapid expansion of the private sector of higher education. The first governmental intervention over expansion came with the 1955 Presidential Decree on the Establishment of Colleges and University Standards.[101] The number of academic staff and students in the university sector increased rapidly in the first three years after political independence, as shown in the following Table:

Table 5

The Number of University Students and Academic Staff

Year	No. of University Students	No. of Academic Staff
1945	7,110	753
1946	10,315	1,170
1947	25,813	2,775
Increase(%) 1945/46	45	55
1946/47	103	137
1945/47	184	268

Source: Werth, R. 'Educational Development under the South Korean Interim Government' in *School and Society*. April 30 1949, Vol. 69, No. 1793.

In the rapid expansion of the university system, the government was worried about the politicisation of the university students, who were participating in protests, often violent, against government policies.[102] The government tried not only to curb the expansion of higher education, but also to reduce the excessive demand for higher education, by shifting high school enrollment from academic to vocational courses and expanding vocational counselling.[103]

The South Korean State's idea of the university in the postcolonial period still focused on the practical function of university education for economic development. In other words, like the Japanese colonial State, the new South Korean State continued to emphasise vocational and technical education within the formal school system. As part of the State's economic project within Five-Year Economic Plans from 1962, the Ministry of Education placed much emphasis on the promotion of science and technical education.[104] For instance, the Ministry established ten junior technical colleges in 1963 to produce technicians for industry.[105]

In another reflection of the colonial legacy of the State's 'idea of the university', the Korean government maintained its monopoly of teacher training. The Education Law in the postcolonial period maintained the colonial philosophy of teacher training, in terms of educational uniformity and conformity and aimed to keep the supply of teachers under government control.

Within this condition of political subordination and social control, similar to the colonial practice in many aspects, the postcolonial period saw numerous higher educational reforms by the Ministry of Education. For instance, the Ministry of Education under the Park Military Regime created a new preliminary college entrance examination system in 1968 to check the expansion of higher education, to control the types of knowledge tested at entry to higher educational institutions, to prevent "unfit high school graduates from entering colleges" and to restrain "the reckless quantitative expansion of higher education institutions".[106] This new national examination system was a mechanism for the government's quality control of higher education in South Korea. The Ministry of Education's view was that "it has gone a long way in achieving the expected result of up-grading higher education.[107] The Ministry of Education then enacted a series of radical reforms in higher education. The "Rearrangement Plans of Higher Education" (1961-1963) were primarily aimed at improving the quality of higher education, especially in the fields of education, science and technology. The reforms included the establishment of new 2-year junior colleges of education for training elementary school teachers, and 5-year vocational higher professional schools for training advanced level technicians in various fields; and governmental intervention in the university entrance examination system, in authorising enrollment quotas and tuition fees. Within a subsequent series of reforms, the "University Experimentation

Programme" was introduced in 1973. This employed external criteria to judge the quality of higher education and to support selectively those institutions which met the external criteria, by providing subsidies or allowing them more autonomy.[108]

Although the *Yushin* Constitution under the Park regime guaranteed in a vaguely worded clause, the "independence and political impartiality of education", in reality, the South Korean university system was under close government supervision, as were the staff and students themselves.[109] When the Emergency Measures were proclaimed under the *Yushin* system in the 1970s, academic autonomy and freedom, already limited, diminished even further. Any criticisms of the government and its policies were prohibited under Park's *Yushin* system.[110]

In consequence, uniformity has been important in both the public and private sectors of higher education, regardless of the different conditions of individual institutions. For instance, with the exception of Seoul National University, which has its own Ordinance, all national universities are under the Education Act, supervised by the Ministry of Education. This means each national institution does not have its own "charter". Private institutions of higher education come under the control of the Private School Law, which emphasises restrictions and rules rather than autonomy, as in the colonial period.[111]

In short, the South Korean State's idea of the university is expressed in the State's intention to use the output of the higher education system, which is also planned and managed directly by the Ministry of Education. As indicated, in spite of the rapidly expanding industrial and social demand for university graduates, the Ministry of Education managed to impose a rigid enrollment quota on all types of higher educational institutions, including the private sector.[112]

In a new effort to decentralise the higher education system, the Korean Council for University Education (KCUE) was established in 1982 as an insulation mechanism between the Ministry of Education and four-year colleges and universities.[113] In May 1988, the Advisory Council for Educational Policy was inaugurated with 60 members, all of whom are specialists in education.[114] In 1993, to promote the government's initiative in educational reforms, the Commission on Education Reform was organised as a Presidential Advisory Council.[115]

Overall, the growth of higher education has not been the result of governmental design and sponsorship in South Korea. By the late 1970s, the supply of university graduates did not meet the rising industrial demand for skilled manpower. The increasing economic demand for university educated workers and continued governmental restrictions on the enrollment quota further intensified the social demand for higher education. As a consequence, the university entrance examination, which was also controlled by the government, became extremely competitive—and a major social issue.[116]

To solve the problems caused by the severe competition for access to university education, the South Korean government made an ad hoc decision to enlarge the enrollment quota of university students. The new Educational Reform on 30th July 1980 opened up a new direction for higher education in the Fifth Republic under Chun, Doo Hwan (1981-1987). The key policy measures included a 30 per cent increase in enrollment quotas in the name of the "Graduation-Quota Policy". The status of teachers' colleges was also upgraded. The courses in the Air and Correspondence University were extended from two-years to four years. Junior Technical Schools were given College status. Entrance examinations by individual universities were replaced with a standard national examination, called the High School Achievement Test.[117]

Reflecting the State's idea of the university of the time, higher education reforms in Chun's Regime still narrowly focused on economic development. To meet the strong demand for higher education on both individual and national levels, an additional 30 per cent and 15 per cent of secondary school graduates started being admitted to universities and junior colleges, respectively, from 1980. By 1986, almost 38 per cent of the school-age population were attending higher educational institutions.[118] This drastic change in the university enrollment ratio, however, could not solve the problem. The university admission rate was 22 per cent of all applicants in 1990 with 37 per cent reapplying after being rejected in previous years.[119] The graduation-quota system which had been implemented from 1981 to 1987 was again replaced by an admission quota system.[120] There has been always a severe competition for places especially at Seoul National University and a few prestigious private institutions such as Yonsei and Korea University in the pyramidal structure of the higher education system. Furthermore, as a subsequent effect of the sudden enlargement of the university enrollment ratio in the existing university facilities, there were worries about a overall deterioration of academic quality in university education, not least because the student-teacher ratio became high after the "Graduation-Quota Policy" in 1980.[121]

Overall, while the Korean university system has continued to produce the literate, skilled manpower which the State wanted for the national economy, the university system as a whole has been always under-funded, but paradoxically regulated by the government. Universities in the private sector receive very little funding from government and depend largely on tuition fees,[122] at the level of 80 per cent of the total budget, compared with 38.7 per cent in the U.S.A. and 60 per cent in Japan. In the private sector of higher education, the staff-student ratio has increased from 1:19.7 in 1971 to 1: 40 in 1993.[123]

It is in this context that new concerns have emerged about internationalisation and globalisation. The State's idea of the university has been newly articulated. For instance, the President's Commission for Education Reform pointed out the importance of internationalisation in its May 1987 Report. "For the enhancement of national academic standards and the advancement of arts and sciences," the Commission wanted to:

> (i) increase exchanges of academic staff from foreign universities at the individual institutional level; (ii) strengthen support for international academic conferences; (iii) establish international links with foreign universities and promote joint research projects; (iv) support international research activities of professors and professional researchers; and (v) strengthen the role of institutions as a medium for exchanging international arts and science research.[124]

The Ministry of Education and the Korea Research Foundation have operated programmes to foster internationalisation of higher education at the governmental level. The Korean Council for University Education and individual universities have also tried to promote internationalisation of higher education.

Simultaneously, the primary concern of government higher education policy in the 1990s has again been the qualitative improvement of higher education. To ensure excellence in higher education, the general direction of higher education policy in South Korea is following the Anglo-American pattern to promote competition among higher educational institutions and to provide selective support for those which are outpacing the others.[125]

In this context, selective institutions are expected to enjoy a greater degree of university autonomy, particularly with regard to enrollment quotas. Since 1992, the evaluation and accreditation system has been used to measure a university's ability to provide quality education.[126] Within the new formal evaluation and accreditation system, the degree of university autonomy has become contingent on individual institutions' capacity for self-management and adjustment of tuition fees and enrollment quota, which would be measured through the process of evaluation.[127] The government's stated purpose for this new mechanism for quality control was to liberalise, diversify and encourage specialisation with the university system.[128] The autonomy of university management is then conditional upon the results of evaluation (whose techniques has been borrowed directly from English and American market-oriented university management systems).[129] The consequence is the existing gap between "haves" and "have nots" among universities in South Korea is expected to increase further—a feature which is reminiscent of the colonial period.

The South Korean State's idea of the university as reviewed in Chapter Three was initially formed by two major exogenous influences, through the Japanese importation of the Prussian and German conceptions of the university, and directly through the American missionary educational institutions. The public and private sectors of higher education in the colonial period represented not only "haves" and "have-not" but also different foreign cultural traditions of the university. After political independence, the South Korean State sought to define its own idea of a university system fit for the new project of independent nation-building. A new university system was reconstructed in South Korea overtly on the basis of the American ideas of the university during the period of the USAMGIK (the United States Army Military Government in Korea) between 1945 and 1948. Nevertheless, there was a surviving colonial legacy from the Japanese and German ideas of the university. These were still influential among South Korean university academics. The different university traditions influenced the struggles over institutional forms of higher education and valued knowledge, which are examined in the following section.

Institutional Forms

The current educational system in Korea had its beginnings in the late 1940s after political independence from Japan. At that time the Republic of Korea adopted to a great extent the educational structures of the United States: six years of primary education, three years of junior high school, three years of senior high school, and four years of college. However, vocational/technical education was influenced by the German and Japanese systems of education.[130]

The overall patterns of the new university system in the postcolonial period reflected a mixed model based on the Japanese colonial tradition and newly adopted American educational patterns. The National University Plan, issued by the American Military Government, recognised Seoul National University in August 1946. Seoul National University was a reorganisation and integration of the former Kyung Sung Imperial University and nine professional schools formerly sponsored by the Japanese colonial government. In the same year, three private higher educational institutions, the Yonsei Professional School, Bosung Professional School and Ewha Hak Dang were upgraded to become, respectively, Yonsei University, Korea University, and Ewha Women's University.[131] Thus, at the time of the establishment of the Republic of Korea in 1948, there were 4 universities (Seoul National, Yonsei, Korea, and Ewha), 23 independent colleges (3 national, 4 public and 16 private), 4 junior colleges (all private) and 11 miscellaneous schools of collegiate standing, with a total enrollment of 1,265 faculty members and 24,000 students.[132]

As an addition to this pattern, the Korean government sought to create a new advanced science research institute to sustain national development after its economic take-off in the 1960s. Subsequently, the Korean Institute of Science and Technology (KIST) was founded in 1966, under an agreement between the Presidents of South Korea and the United States,[133] especially for the development of high technology in engineering, science and research which had become a major priority in South Korea at that time.[134] KIST soon gained a reputation as the "think tank" of science and industry in Korea and was linked to the Korean Advanced Institute of Science

(KAIS) established in 1971.[135] KAIS contributed to reducing the brain drain, by providing Korean academics and students in the science fields with incentives to study and work in Korea.[136]

By 1989, there were a total 536 institutions of higher education in South Korea: 104 national, 3 public and 429 private institutions. Among 536 institutions, there were 104 universities and colleges: 22 national, 1 public and 81 private institutions. The number of universities, colleges and other higher educational institutions (teachers' colleges, junior colleges, etc.) went from 19 in 1945 to 85 in 1960 to 556 by 1990.[137] More than four-fifths of them were private. The following Table shows the overall types of higher educational institutions in South Korea as of 1992:

Table 6
Higher Educational Institutions, 1992

Classification	Institutions	Departments	Students	Teachers
Junior College	126	1,538	404,996	8,518
Teacher's College	11	350	16,504	719
College & University	121	4,315	1,070,169	32,287
Graduate School	335	3,418	96,577	-

Sources: Korean Overseas Information Service, *Facts about Korea,* Revised and Condensed Edition, Seoul: Samhwa Printing Company, Republic of Korea, 1993, p. 77.

Overall, the postcolonial period was marked by the rapid expansion of the higher education system especially in the private sector, as in the colonial period. In this postcolonial pattern of expansion of higher education, the theme of the continuities and discontinuities in the types of valued knowledge is the concern of the next section.

Valued Knowledge

It is argued that since 1945 and the three-year American Military Government, the USA has continued to be actively involved in the South Korean political economy and influential in shaping the knowledge profile of the South Korean university system. The (military, economic, cultural and) academic influence of the United States in South Korea was significant in defining the types of knowledge valued in university education during the first 25 years after liberation.

For example, the importance of the acquisition of English increased. American approaches in various academic disciplines were directly introduced to Korean academics by U.S. educational aid and scholarly exchange programmes and they affected academic development in South Korea. Like the Japanese, the American military government also offered teacher training and established the American Language Institute to promote English, as part of American educational aid.[138]

Japanese approaches through German scholarship which used to be dominant in Korea were soon replaced by American scholarship in the postcolonial period. Don Adams notes that there "was a violent repudiation of everything Japanese. Nearly all traces of Japanese language and literature were eliminated from curricula. Japanese books and works of art were burned or otherwise destroyed."[139] Nevertheless, the Japanese language continued to be regarded as a very useful academic medium for Korean university academics. They could conveniently rely on Japanese publications and translations of Western knowledge that were often more easily accessible through neighbouring Japan than a direct importation of knowledge from the West.[140]

Although on the official level it was necessary to devalue the use of the Japanese language after decolonisation, by 1971 Japan's investments in South Korea had become almost twice as large as those of the United States.[141] Accordingly, the use of the Japanese language has gradually increased in South Korea. In the schooling and examination system, the Japanese language started being taught again and was used as part of educational selection and job recruitment. By the contemporary decade, learning Japanese has become almost as significant as learning English.

Besides the continuing significance of the American and Japanese languages as the most important medium of knowledge transmission in Korea since the colonial period, the fields of economics, business studies and advanced technological fields (e.g. computer science) gained importance with the fast growth of the Korean economy in the postcolonial period. Accordingly, talented academic candidates were attracted to these fields.[142]

The following Table shows the pattern of academic disciplines developed in the university curriculum, which marks the types of knowledge valued and promoted by both the government and by recipients of higher education:

Table 7

Number of Students of College and Universities by Course[1] in 1997

Academic disciplines	The Total Number of Students	Number of Female Students
Humanities	190,724	103,634
Social Sciences	352,047	108,266
Natural Sciences	614,796	133,670
Medical & Pharmacy	48,822	20,839
Arts & Physical Education	99,000	56,029
Teacher Education	63,072	41,301

Source: Ministry of Education. *Education in Korea 1997-1998.* Seoul: Ministry of Education, Republic of Korea, 1998, p. 68.

In response to the economic modernity project, with its stress on manufacturing industries, the university enrollment quota for engineering and science education was fixed at a higher level than that for humanities and social science education. The ratio was 57:43 in 1997.[144]

While each university was in principle free to choose its own curriculum, a number of subjects, specified by the government, had to be taken by all students before they could graduate. These subjects included the Korean language and history, "national ethics", an introduction to philosophy, and physical education.[145]

It is suggested here that the South Korean definition of an educated man—the 'man of knowledge'- in the postcolonial period continued to be identified with the acquisition of Western scientific knowledge and English and Japanese languages. In a continuing colonial reflection of the Japanese cultural valuation of knowledge, academic excellence in Korea was also linked to the colonial notions of pragmatic usefulness, conformity to the group and an alertness to the needs of the State.

Similar propositions will be reviewed in terms of the State's idea of the university in Malaysia and Singapore in the following sections.

Malaysia: The State's Idea of the University

In the postcolonial period, the Malaysian State's projects for national unity and integration altered the existing ethnic imbalances in primary and secondary education.[146] It was much later that the Malaysian State started its direct intervention in university education.[147]

Higher education in the early postcolonial period developed slowly in comparison with primary and secondary education. However, in 1962, a committee was set up to review the arrangements for higher education in Malaysia. The recommendations of the committee were made in the *Report of the Higher Education Planning Committee*[148] (HEPC Report) in 1967. The HEPC Report became the guideline for the expansion of higher education in Malaysia during the Independence period until 1985. The Report made it clear that the Malaysian development of higher education should prepare manpower for economic development.[149]

However, the need to use education as an instrument for greater social equity and national unity was not considered in the Report. Two years later, in 1969, there came a drastic revision of higher education policy. The background of the education reform was that, towards the late 1960s, there was increasing Malay-Muslim dissatisfaction about the lack of opportunities for a university education in which Bahasa Malaysia was not yet the language of instruction. Accordingly, the State amended the university system, which was perceived as a crucial access point into the expanding modern sector.

To rectify ethnic imbalances in the University of Malaya, a Committee, chaired by Dato' Dr Abdul Mjid Ismail, made five recommendations in

1971.[150] First, the University was required to commit itself directly to a policy of ethnic representation and the composition of its student enrollment would reflect the ethnic composition in the country. Second, the University was required to increase the admission of Malay students in faculties with poor Malay representation. Third, students from rural areas would be provided with assistance and tuition, especially in the sciences. Fourth, the criteria for admission would include other factors besides the Higher School Certificate (HSC) results. Fifth, more scholarships in the science fields would be awarded to Malay students so as to rectify the ethnic imbalance in the sciences.[151]

Following these recommendations, the Malaysian State began to increase the numbers of *Bumiputeras* in higher education. The State provided the Malays with special residential schools and privileged access to institutions of higher education, through fixed quotas and financial sponsorship.[152] This was followed by new quotas for recruitment into the civil service.[153] The *Bumiputeras* were supported through special governmental scholarships for science and technological studies endowed by the Majlis Amanah Rakyat or the Peoples Trust Council (MARA).[154] As a result, a ratio of three science to two arts and humanities graduates in secondary schools was achieved. Also, specialised universities in science, agriculture and technology were established and began to develop postgraduate courses in these fields in response to the five-year economic plans.[155]

As the University of Malaya was unable to play its recommended political and social role alone, the State established new universities to train more Malays in modern professions such as medicine in the 1970s.[156] The National University of Malaysia was established in 1970. The National University has become the apex institution "to act as the centre of the national education system and development with the Malay language as the medium of instruction".[157]

In the period of the Second and Third Malaysian Development Plans (1971-1975;1976-1980), Malaysian ethnic politics emphasised the role of the educational system for promoting national integration and unity through:

> the continued implementation, in stages, of Bahasa Malaysia as the main medium of instruction at all levels; the development of personality, character and good citizenship and the promotion of moral discipline through curricular and extra-curricular activities; narrowing the gap in educational opportunities between the rich and poor, and among the various regions and races in the country.[158]

Thus, the State's idea of the university was incorporated into the State's new vision of restructuring society under the New Economic Policy (NEP) which was introduced in 1971. This prioritised a greater intake of Malays for science and technological education than other ethnic groups in the university system and the creation of a Malay entrepreneurial class in the economic sector. In fact, however, universities still remained peripheral to scientific research relevant to national development in Malaysia.[159] Most of the early significant research on national products such as rubber and oil palm was undertaken by specialised research institutes while the universities were playing the role of trainers and teachers of scientific manpower.[160]

The Malaysian State's idea of the university can be defined on the basis of its political and economic visions. On the surface, the development of higher education in Malaysia was related to the State's consideration of equity in general. However, it is notable that the State has defined the poor and the disadvantaged groups mainly as indigenous Malays.[161] The implementation of the NEP resulted in denying places in the universities to qualified Chinese candidates. The number of applicants, regardless of race, for limited places in the universities has been steadily increasing in absolute terms. In the 1970s, some 250,000 students were enrolled in the pre-university classes each year while the universities could only take some 20,000 students annually.[162] In the severe competition for university admission, the fixed quota system along racial lines became scandalous, in the view of the Chinese community. The initial proposal to establish a Chinese-medium university (known as Merdeka University) in 1967 and the subsequent Merdeka University campaign which continued up until 1982 showed the long term Chinese struggles in Malaysia to secure their own position against the national education policy.[163]

Furthermore, the Malaysian State's idea of the university after Independence diminished university academic autonomy. Enloe notes that:

> A government in the throes of a civil war, as was the Kuala Lumpur government at the time of the first important education reports, is intent above all to reduce the spheres of autonomy within its jurisdiction, whether that autonomy breeds mere fence-sitting or active resistance.[164]

The diminution of academic autonomy in the postcolonial period has often been attributed to the national priority to establish racial and religious harmony in the country.[165]

Constitutionally, however, all universities in Malaysia are classified as a statutory body and the academic staff of a university are categorised as members of that statutory body and are governed by a special set of rules. The rules and regulations governing the academic staff of the Universiti Sains Malaysia, for instance, were given in the 1977 Report of the Cabinet Committee.[166]

Nevertheless, a considerable degree of governmental control has been maintained over the university system. The State's control was visible through its large subsidy—nearly 95 per cent of the recurrent and developmental costs of universities and colleges—as well as legislative enactment such as the College and Universities Act of 1971.[167] On that basis, the Ministry of Education could exercise control over the establishment of institutions, student enrollments, staff appointments, curricula and the financing of universities and colleges.[168]

Thus, the State has directed the overall development of higher education in Malaysia within a new vision of Malay-centred national unity and economic development. According to Jasbir Singh and Henna Mukherjee, the National University represents the "culmination of the aspirations for Malay privilege in the newly unified Malaysian education system".[169]

However, the State's idea of the university in Malaysia—focused on creating a considerable professional and middle class represented by the *Bumiputera* since the inception of the NEP in 1971—has been only partially realised. In 1957, the *Bumiputera* occupied only 3 per cent of the professional and technical and administrative/managerial occupational categories. The proportion of the *Bumiputera* grew to 4.8 per cent by 1970 and to 6.1 per cent in 1980. In other occupational classifications, the *Bumiputera* percentages also increased.[170]

To develop a competitive industrial economy in Malaysia, the Malaysian government has emphasised the urgent need to build competence in key technologies such as automated manufacturing, advanced materials, electronics, biotechnology and information technology.[171] R&D programmes in these new and emerging technologies are now prioritised in university education. Since 1985, new multi-disciplinary research institutions and consulting agencies have been established within universities. Yet, it is anticipated that universities will carry out only about 22 per cent of planned research and development, while focusing mainly on teaching and training scientific and research manpower.[172] The tertiary education and training programmes in the Seventh Plan period (1996-2000) are expected to produce not only manpower which is knowledgeable, highly skilled and computer literate, but also imbued with discipline, high moral values and a strong work ethic.[173]

In all these endeavours, the private sector is intended to be an active partner in complementing the efforts undertaken by the government.[174] The University and University Colleges Act of 1971 was amended in 1995, enabling public institutions of higher learning to be corporatised.[175] Corporatised universities are to be allowed to borrow money, enter into business ventures, set up companies, and acquire and hold investment shares. The most frequently cited rationale for corporatisation in Malaysia is the need to free the university from the cumbersome bureaucratic processes of the civil service.

According to Molly N. N. Lee, however, the real thrust that has induced corporatisation is the increasing social demand for higher education following the introduction of universal secondary education.[176] As a solution to meet the demand for higher education, the Malaysian government turned to the market and the private business sector. The full implementation of the corporatisation exercise is expected to solve the current problem of outflow of experts and experienced lecturers from public higher educational institutions. Nevertheless, the government policy direction and objectives will still control the overall development of the higher education system.[177]

As reviewed so far, the Malaysian State's idea of the university was developed within the frame of a centralised bureaucracy initially created by the British colonial State. The Malaysian State after independence perceived the role of the university as central in the process of economic modernisation as well as decolonisation. Subsequently, the postcolonial State's idea of the university in Malaysia emphasised a new indigenous shape for the academic profession, by promoting the upward social mobility of indigenous Malays and stressing Islamic values, and Asian cultural values in general. However, it can be argued that it was the Malay ruling elite, rather than the Malay mass, that benefited most from the new positive discrimination in the NEP era.[178] Against these propositions, the following section examines further details of the new institutional forms of higher education and the types of knowledge valued in university education in Malaysia.

The Institutional Forms

In 1959 the University of Malaya (UM) was established in Kuala Lumpur, grew rapidly and became an autonomous national university of the Federation of Malaya in 1962. In 1965, when the Federation of Malaya split into two countries, Malaysia and Singapore, the University of Malaya in Kuala Lumpur kept the name of the original university and the original division in Singapore changed its name to the University of Singapore (now the National University of Singapore).

By 1963, 11 institutions of higher education had been established in Malaysia: one university, one technical institution, seven teacher training colleges, and two other specialised institutions. In the higher education sector, 80 per cent of institutions are public and 94 per cent of student enrollment was in the public institutions.[179]

In October 1967, the MARA Institute of Technology was established to offer courses leading to the award of its own diplomas and the diplomas/degrees granted by professional bodies in the United Kingdom in the fields of Accountancy, Applied Sciences, Administration and Law, Art and Architecture, Business and Management, Computer Science, Statistics and Actuary, Engineering and Land Surveying, Hotel and Catering Management, Library Science, and Pre-University Studies. The MARA Institute of Technology originated from the Dewan Latehan Rural Industrial Development Authority which was established in 1954 to prepare young Malays to participate in commerce and industry. This training centre was regarded as the first major government initiative to introduce Malays to the world of business and the various professions, on the basis of the *Bumiputera* policy, using the same positive discrimination principles as university education. In 1974, the advanced diploma issued by the MARA Institute of Technology became equated to an honours degree.[180]

Four more universities were established from the late 1960s. The University Sains Malaysia (University of Science, Malaysia) was established in 1969, Universiti Kebangsaan Malaysia (the National University of Malaysia) in 1970, and both the University of Agriculture in Serdang and the University of Technology in Kuala Lumpur, were established in 1971. The University of Agriculture evolved from the College of Agriculture in Serdang (established in 1931) and the University of Technology originated from the Technical College in Kuala Lumpur which has existed since 1925.[181]

In 1983, the International Islamic University (IIU) was founded in Petaling Jaya, Selangor, in response to the resurgence of Islam in the region. In the same year, a Japanese cultural centre was also set up in the University of Malaya, an effect of the Look East Policy promulgated by the Prime Minister Mahathir at the inception of the fourth NEP in 1981. Universiti Utara Malaysia (UUM) or Northern University of Malaysia was established in 1983. By 1986, the number of universities was seven; six of them were fully sponsored by the Malaysian government and one (the Universiti Islam Antarabangsa, or the International Islamic University) was cooperatively funded by the Malaysian government and several other countries.[182]

During the NEP era, higher education was available mainly in the 6 national universities, one independent International Islamic University, the MARA ("Council of Trust for Indigenous People"), the Institute of Technology and the semi-private Tunku Abdul Rahman College. After the start of the New Development Policy in 1990, two new public universities, the Universiti Malaysia Sarawak in 1993, the Universiti Malaysia Sabah in 1995, and four private universities by 1998 were established.[183]

At the post-secondary and higher education levels, expansion started from a very low base in Malaysia. By 1970 only about 0.6 per cent of the population in the relevant age group were enrolled in tertiary education in Malaysia. Between 1960 and 1985, the participation rate of the population in the relevant age cohort for post-secondary education increased from 0.06 per cent to 7.4 per cent.[184] In the same period, the participation rate for higher education increased from 0.04 per cent to 4.0 per cent.[185]

The expansion in enrollment at the post-secondary and tertiary level in the Independence period 1960 to 1985 is shown in the following Table:

Table 8

Annual Rate of Increase in Enrollment, 1960-1985

(NB: The post-secondary level includes Enrollment in pre-university and matriculation courses and the tertiary level includes Enrollment in teacher training colleges).

Educational Level	1961-1970	1971-1980	1981-1985
Post-secondary	77.6 %	13.1 %	13.0 %
Tertiary	7.7 %	25.0 %	14.5 %

Sources: Malaysia, *Third Malaysia Plan, 1976-1980*, op. cit., Malaysia, *Fourth Malaysia Plan, 1981-1985*, op. cit., and Malaysia, Fifth Malaysia Plan, 1986-1990, op. cit.

Despite the expansion after decolonisation, higher education in the new Malaysian State remained elitist—reflecting the British colonial legacy. In 1980, the percentage distribution of tertiary enrollment in Malaysia was only 1.5 per cent of the total educational enrollment. Upper secondary and post-secondary school enrollment was 8.9 per cent, lower secondary school enrollment was 25.8 per cent and primary school enrollment was 63.8 per cent. Though the total number of university students in 1980 represented a four-fold increase from 1969, about 57 per cent of the qualified applicants did not gain entry into any one of the five universities in 1981.[186] By 1985, tertiary enrollment was 2.4 per cent of the total educational enrollment while upper and post-secondary enrollment formed 10.8 per cent of the total educational enrollment.[187]

As the education system expanded under the impetus of the NEP, educational imbalances among ethnic and socio-economic groups as well as between the sexes were amended significantly. This was particularly conspicuous with regard to ethnic imbalances, which would in consequence change the social composition of the academic profession in the longer term. To ensure that at least 55 per cent of places overall should be filled by *Bumiputeras,* a quota system has been operating. Fees are low and most *Bumiputeras* obtain scholarships.[188]

The following Table shows the enrollment figures for the five universities:

Table 9

Enrollment Rate by Race in Malaysian Universities in 1980

Race/ Institutions	Malay	Chinese	Indian	Other	Total
University of Malaya	4,045 (50.3)	3,162 (39.3)	676 (8.4)	162 (2.0)	8,045 (100.0)
University of Science, Malaysia	1,956 (54.4)	1,354 (37.6)	270 (7.5)	17 (0.5)	3,597 (100.0)
National University of Malaysia	4,997 (86.1)	621 (10.7)	180 (3.1)	9 (0.1)	5,807 (100.0)
Agricultural University of Malaysia	3,025 (87.3)	294 (8.5)	130 (3.8)	14 (0.4)	3,463 (100.0)
Technological University of Malaysia	3,669 (88.2)	348 (8.4)	108 (2.6)	34 (0.8)	4,159 (100.0)
Total Number Percentage	17,692 (70.6)	5,779 (23.1)	1,364 (5.4)	236 (0.9)	25,071 (100.0)

Source: *Fourth Malaysia Plan, 1981-1985*, Kuala Lumpur: Government Printers, pp. 351-352.

As indicated in the Table, through the quota system, the *Bumiputera* share of total enrollment rapidly increased. In 1985, the enrollment rate of *Bumiputeras* was 68.1 per cent at the upper secondary level and 56.9 per cent at the post-secondary level.[189] Furthermore, the participation rate of the *Bumiputera* in higher education in 1988 became 74.9 %, considerably in excess of their proportion in the population, which was 60.1 % in 1988.[190]

In the 1990s, despite the substantial expansion of higher education in Malaysia, the enrollment rate of the 19-24 age cohort in higher educational institutions was 3. 5 per cent, still low in comparison with the developed countries and other East Asian neighbouring countries.[191] In the period 1985 to 1995, the enrollment in certificate, diploma and degree courses in higher education increased by 33 %, 12 % and 59 %, respectively.[192] During the period 1990 to 1995, the enrollment rate of full time students in public institutions of higher education showed an increase of 62.3 per cent. The enrollment rate in science based courses at the first degree level in higher educational institutions showed an increase of 20. 4 per cent while that in the arts courses increased by 54. 5 per cent during the same period.[193] Accordingly, in the output from public institutions of higher education, arts graduates exceeded science and technical graduates.

The overall capacity of public local institutions continued to be limited severely, resulting in only about 50 per cent of applicants being admitted to degree level courses in the Sixth Plan period (1991-1995).[194] As a consequence, a sizeable number of Malaysian students continued their studies abroad, until recently.[195] In 1995, an estimated 50,600 Malaysian students or 20 per cent of students in tertiary education were enrolled in various institutions overseas. Of this total, about 20,000 or 39.5 per cent were Government-sponsored students. Among this group, 18,300 were first degree students, of whom 59.8 per cent pursued science, medicine, engineering and technical-related courses.[196]

Since the Fifth Plan period (1986-1990), private educational institutions have emerged as important avenues to meet the increasing demand for higher education among Malaysians. The Malaysian government has set up five new polytechnics in the period of the Sixth Plan, while also expanding the existing ones. In consequence, the number of private educational institutions has also increased from 280 in 1995 to 354 in 1996 an increase of 79%.[197] The courses offered in the private sector higher education system mainly covered the fields of accountancy, commerce, law, engineering and electronics, computer science and business management.[198] The new polytechnics offer more diploma level courses as well as new courses in the engineering fields, such as electronic communications, computer technology and textile engineering.[199]

The 1990s saw a rapid expansion in student enrollments in the private colleges, and in the scope of courses offered, in conjunction with the corporatisation scheme. On 1 January 1998 the University of Malaya was corporatised and in due course the other eight public universities are expected to be so.[200]

The implementation of the Private Higher Educational Institution Act 1996 also enabled foreign universities to set up branch campuses in the country. The Twinning Programmes in higher education have been active (gradually since 1987), and permission to teach in the English medium in higher education was suggested by the Prime Minister.[201]

Thus, the growth of Malaysian universities has been a direct result of the State's new values and visions in the postcolonial period, in addition to the demographic change in the postwar era—the natural growth of population followed by the increasing social demand for higher education. The postcolonial university education system in Malaysia has been under the direct control of the central government, aiming to achieve national unity and to develop human resources. The institutional forms of higher education have been altered over time, while the initial British influence of the binary model of higher education continued to remain as the basic structure of the higher education system in Malaysia, still reflecting the British colonial legacy of the elitist conception of the university.

Yet, the shift in institutional forms of Malaysian higher education has been visible in the on-going process of Malay-Muslim centred indigenisation since political independence, and in the contemporary trend of internationalisation. The following section will focus on the types of knowledge valued in university education in Malaysia, to attain these two goals.

Valued Knowledge

The book argues that the *Bumiputera* policy within the NEP initially provided a political frame within which certain types of knowledge were valued in Malaysian university education. In the first decade after Independence, the entrance requirements to the university in Malaysia still reflected a colonial inheritance. That is to say, the English-oriented texts were still in use more than a decade after independence. School examinations were also organised on the English pattern. For instance, entry to the national universities in Malaysia has been coordinated by the Unit Pusat Universiti (UPU), which corresponds to the UCCA in the U.K..[202]

The process of indigenisation has been gradual but steady in Malaysia. One of the starting points was an address by Tun Abdul Razak, the Deputy Prime Minister at the 1961 convocation ceremony of the University of Malaya:

> It is the policy of the Alliance Government to make the University of Malaya a bilingual university. It is essential that the University of Malaya be at the apex of the national educational system. In view of the fact that the first Malay pupil will be able to sit for the Federation of Malaya Certificate Examination entirely in Malay in 1962, which is a very proud achievement of the Federation Government, it is necessary to link the school system with the University. In 1963, it is proposed to introduce pre-university courses in the National Language to enable Malay students to proceed direct to the University. It is through this and by concerted efforts at the university level to introduce more and more instruction in Malaya, that the University of Malaya can become more national in scope and bilingual in form. However, every effort will be made to ensure that this change will not result in the lowering of standards of instruction either in the Malay language or in English language.[203]

To build the unity of the new nation-state, it was urgent to produce indigenous teachers as soon as possible. To meet this aim, the Malaysian government offered numerous bursaries to attract Malay-speaking people to the teaching profession: "To meet the acute shortage of graduate teachers and lecturers in training colleges, it is recommended that more bursaries be awarded to help students in their university education, especially those with Malay language at least as a subsidiary subject."[204]

The Malaysian government also began to develop programmes for technical and agricultural education. For instance, the Universiti Sains Malaysia (USM) established in Penang in 1969 has a strong science bias. The university offers courses in biological sciences, chemical sciences, physics, mathematics, applied science, pharmaceutical sciences, housing building and planning, humanities, comparative social sciences, education and medicine. There is also a centre for educational studies within the university. Universiti Pertanian Malaysia (UPM) is the Agricultural University founded in 1971. The university offers courses in agriculture, food science, agricultural engineering, resource economics and agribusiness and educational services which offer only degree courses, and forestry, veterinary medicine, fisheries and science.[205]

The percentage of enrollment in all scientific and technical subjects in Malaysia in 1962 was 31.0% against 69.0 % in all other subjects (including teacher training).[206] In terms of distribution of enrollment by subject in Malaysia in 1962, the figures are Agriculture 156 (1.3 %), Arts 2,711 (23.3 %), Education 4,233 (36.4 %), Engineering 1,343 (11.6 %), Law and Social Science 1,074 (9.3 %), Medicine 771 (6.6 %), Science, 1,339 (11.5%) in total 11,627 (100.0%).[207]

However, the outcome of the *Bumiputera* policy to promote an increase of Malays in higher education, especially in the fields of science and technology, had a relatively low impact on the Malay/non-Malay balance in the occupational categories that the government initially attempted to effect. In the years 1976 to 1980, there was a considerable short-fall of science and technical manpower at the university degree level ranging from 9 per cent in science to 24 per cent in medicine and dentistry to 75 per cent in surveying and other technical services.[208] Enrollments in applied science fields were around 3 per cent and in postgraduate studies only about 4 per cent of total enrollments in the early 1980s. At the same time, there was an oversupply of Arts and Humanities graduates by 41 per cent. In the early 1980s, the government's higher education policy aimed at achieving a target output of 60 per cent science and 40 per cent arts graduates.[209] However, shortages in key technical and scientific areas continued through to 1985.[210]

Ethnic division in higher education was also noticeable in academic faculties. In the early 1970s, the disproportionate number of non-Malays to Malays in the University of Malaya (the only University then) and the concentration of Chinese in the science subjects and Malays in the arts subjects were evident. The majority of the Malay students at the University of Malaya in Kuala Lumpur were enrolled in the faculties of arts, education and economics and administration while the majority of the Chinese students were enrolled in the faculties of science, engineering, agriculture and medicine.[211]

In the process of economic development based on five-year plans, however, *Bumiputeras* began to increase their share of the medical, science and engineering fields in higher education so as to move into the equivalent occupations which used to be dominated by the non-*Bumiputeras*. In 1985, among the students enrolled in the University of Malaysia, 25.7 per cent of students in engineering, 56.8 per cent in medicine and 48.4 per cent in science were *Bumiputeras*.[212]

The output of the university system has gradually reflected the State's project to create *Bumiputera* scientific manpower. In conjunction with the State's advocacy of science and technology, teacher education and vocationally-oriented knowledge have continued to be an important part of the university knowledge profile in Malaysia since the colonial period. The following Table shows the ethnic composition of students in each faculty of the University of Malaya:

Table 10

Ethnic Composition of Students in Each Faculty of the University of Malaya

Year	Ethnic Group	Arts	Economics and Public Administration	Education	Science	Agriculture	Engineering	Medicine
1966 -67	Malays	42.5	36.8	28.3	7.5	30.3	1.6	15.9
	Chinese	39.7	54.2	46.6	81.5	61.6	90.0	73.6
	Others	17.8	9.0	25.1	11.0	8.1	8.4	10.5
	Total	100.0	100.0	100.0	100.0	100.0	100.0	100.0
1968 -69	Malays	47.7	39.0	33.0	12.8	26.2	1.8	18.6
	Chinese	37.2	50.7	49.7	81.2	67.1	92.6	70.6
	Others	15.0	10.3	17.3	6.0	6.7	5.6	10.8
	Total	100.0	100.0	100.0	100.0	100.0	100.0	100.0
1970 -71	Malays	61.1	37.5	53.4	11.5	28.1	1.3	20.3
	Chinese	26.6	48.8	33.3	82.0	64.2	93.1	66.1
	Others	12.3	13.7	13.3	6.5	7.7	5.6	13.6
	Total	100.0	100.0	100.0	100.0	100.0	100.0	100.0

Source: Federation of Malaysia, *Report of the Committee Appointed by the National Operations Council to Study Campus Life of Students in the University of Malaya*, Kuala Lumpur: Government Press, 1971, pp. 35-36.

The Bahasa Malaysia language policy is central to the knowledge policy of the Malaysian State. For instance, Universiti Kebangssan Malaysia (i.e. the National University of Malaysia) established in 1970 provides higher education for students graduating from Malay-medium schools. Thus, the student population of the university is almost 80 per cent Malay. There are faculties of economics and management, Islamic studies, social science and humanities (including education), science, medicine, and an institute of Malay language, literature and culture.[213]

The postcolonial Malaysian knowledge profile also reveals American influence in administrative and academic developments. At the operational level, universities in Malaysia adopted the American system of a 2-semester year and 'credits' and four-year university education. In 1961, Malaya formally recognised degrees from United States institutions only in the fields of engineering, chemistry, mining and fishery—and only from certain selected institutions. All other equivalences are decided on an *ad hoc* basis.[214]

Since the 1980s, the American influence on the Malaysian university system has become more visible through U.S. College-and University-Sponsored Programmes. The programmes covered a wide range of learning—e.g. from general education for first degrees to master's degrees in

Engineering and Applied Science at SUNY Buffalo, in Business Administration at Ohio University, and in Curriculum and Instruction at the College of Education, Michigan State University.[215]

Despite the Malay academic retention of the British colonial academic legacy in its university knowledge profile, and its permeability to the new foreign influence from the United States, the process of cultural indigenisation in Malaysia has also included a resurgence of Islamic knowledge. The International Islamic University was established in Malaysia in 1983 to promote Islamic studies and began to train manpower based on Islamic principles of knowledge with instruction in English and Arabic.[216]

In the Malaysian context, however, it can be suggested that the State would not provoke a fundamentalist Islamic cultural revival. As indicated earlier, the cultural valuation of Islamic knowledge is subordinated to a concern for the *Bumiputera* in Malaysia.

Overall, the types of knowledge valued in the Malaysian higher education system in the postcolonial period are identified in the following Table:

Table 11

Enrollment and Output for First Degree Courses from Local Public Educational Institutions, 1990-2000

Course	Enrollment			Increase		Output	
	1990	1995	2000	6MP	7MP	6MP	7MP
Arts (Arts & Humanities, Economics & Business, Law)	59 %	55 %	49 %	28%	63%	58%	50%
Science (Medicine & Dentistry, Agriculture & Related Sciences, Pure Sciences, Others)	27 %	28%	29 %	54%	90%	27%	31%
Technical (Engineering, Architecture & Town Planning)	14%	17%	22%	88%	134%	15%	19%
Total	100%	100%	100%	100%	100%	100%	100%

Source: *The Seventh Malaysian Plan*, p. 313.

The contemporary decade saw the revival of English as a significant medium of university education in Malaysia, along with the State's internationalisation, and globalisation projects.[217] Simultaneously, the Malaysian government intends to expand and improve further the use of Bahasa Malaysia as the medium of university education. To intensify Malay *Bumiputera* cultural identity in higher education, for instance, all private colleges must conduct their courses in Bahasa Malaysia, and if they want to conduct any course in English, they must teach Malaysian studies (including Islamic and Asian civilisation), Islamic studies (for Muslim students), and moral education (for non-Malay students).[218]

While emphasising the use of Bahasa Malaysia, however, competency in other languages will also be encouraged, particularly the English language which is recognised as an international and commercial language in Malaysia again. The promotion of the English language in Malaysia is led by the private institutions of higher education, which are tightly linked to the industrial sector. As indicated above, Malaysian students enrolled in private higher educational institutions still need to study Bahasa Malyasia, and foreign students studying in Malaysia are also encouraged to learn the language.[219]

In the 1990s, the impact of economic globalisation has been also notable on the university curriculum in Malaysia. In order to increase Research and Development personnel, priority is given to information technology, micro-electronics, advanced materials technology, advanced manufacturing, biotechnology, aerospace, energy and environmental-related technology and communication technology—visible in the ongoing scheme of the Multi-media Super Corridor (MSC).[220]

As reviewed so far, the postcolonial cultural valuation of knowledge in Malaysia stresses the 'pragmatic' application of knowledge of science and technology and adaptation of East Asian values for economic development. Simultaneously, Malaysia has tried to indigenise knowledge, by the recognition of Bahasa Malaysia as the sole national language since 1967 and the official medium of university education by 1984, and by the revival of Malay Islamic cultural tradition since the 1970s. For comparison, the following section will examine the Singaporean State's idea of the University, and struggles over institutional forms and valued knowledge.

Singapore: The State's Idea of the University

After Independence, the University of Singapore with its British colonial origins still maintained the detailed codes of practice developed in the British tradition. The University had strong inducements to conform to British standards and patterns so as to receive recognition as a full university from the British authorities. Up to the mid 1960s before political Independence from Malaya, the University of Singapore maintained the British pattern of a state financed university system to secure academic autonomy.[221]

However, the Singaporean State held a new idea of the university. Although as mentioned earlier, most of the People's Action Party (PAP) leaders had themselves been educated in England[222], the PAP government intended to change the British colonial legacy of the 'idea of the university' in Singapore. In other words, Singapore's education system should "move away from the British-American model—which provides a general liberal education for all—to one akin to the German-Swiss system which stresses technical and/or vocational education for the majority of students."[223]

It is here argued that the newly independent Singaporean State early saw the need for a nationally managed university system under its direct policy guidance and governed by managerial rather than collegial or academic principles. As a result, from the inception of the post-colonial period, the university's relations with government were strained in Singapore. The government of the People's Action Party (PAP) took over the former role of the British colonial government which had initially determined the institutional forms, medium of instruction and student composition of the higher education institutions in Singapore, but started to create a new managed higher education system.[224] Since then, at every stage of the country's political and economic development, the Singaporean State, through its constant interventionist policy, has directly intervened in the higher education system to make the system respond to and adapt to major societal changes and needs.

In the colonial origins of the university in Singapore, there was, arguably, a gap between the idea of the university by English standards and the reality of the university by local standards. The historical relations between the State and the university in Singapore took different forms from the British tradition and created distortions due to the colonial origins of the university in Singapore as analysed in Chapter Three.

In the postcolonial period, two crucial interrelated factors—nation-building and the economic transformation of Singapore—have had an important impact on the character, ethos, and direction of the University—especially after the Deputy Prime Minister, Dr. Toh Chin Chye was also appointed to the Vice-Chancellor of the University of Singapore in April 1968.[225]

The Singaporean State after political independence expressed a critical view of a university culture which had had a Western colonial genesis, and redefined the concept of academic autonomy in a series of conflicts between the expatriate academics and the government in the 1960s. One example was the Enright Affair, in which a foreign academic was severely reproved by politicians for the content of a lecture on "Robert Graves and the Decline of Modernism".[226] Another example of the State's view of academic autonomy is found in the process of introduction of the Suitability Certificate as an amendment to the Internal Security Act in Singapore in 1964.[227] Alarmed by disruptive Maoist activities in the Chinese schools in 1963, the PAP government requested that the university should remove from its admissions list for the next year the names of candidates they thought to be subversive.[228] The then Vice-Chancellor, Dr. B. R. Sreenivasan refused this proposal on the ground that this would make the university a voluntary party to political repression. He was forced to resign in October 1963, on the threat of discontinuance of state financial support.[229] His post was filled by Dr. Toh Chin Chye, then Deputy Prime Minister and Chairman of the PAP.

During the period of Toh Chin Chye's Vice-Chancellorship, the departments of history and political science were combined and headed by another cabinet minister, ensuring that the university should not become the base for political opposition.[230] In 1970, Lee Kuan Yew told students not to take political science, philosophy and sociology but to take more useful subjects such as science, medicine and law. Subsequently, in the following year, the Public Service Commission stopped all bursaries for students taking the subjects that were disliked.[231] This was an official marker that the arts and social science subjects would be less prestigious in Singapore.

PAP party members were inserted at various levels of university administration, faculty and student organisations, and expatriate faculty were marginalised. Foreign academics were strictly forbidden to comment on local issues and some had to be deported.

In the postcolonial period, the Singaporean State has invented various incentives and mechanisms for the academic staff in higher education to perform efficiently to meet the requirements of manpower supply and research goals for the State's modernity projects. For instance, the PAP government has developed a stringent tenure policy; rewards for good teaching and research performance with incentives, and recognition; a favourable staff-student ratio accompanied by well equipped teaching and research facilities; and the provision of staff training to upgrade skills and performance.[232]

The Singaporean State's effort to alter the British colonial legacy of liberal education continued. In 1990, the Government Report, *Building a Firm Foundation*, which came out after a comparative policy study of Japan and Taiwan, recommended a more rigorous streaming process, single session schools, teacher upgrading and stressed the significance of moral education.[233] Accordingly, the PAP government has also continued its interventionist policy in higher education in the 1990s. The State's tight control over the university system as a whole and thus the lack of academic autonomy has been justified in the PAP government's contention that university academics lacked the will to tackle the national economic strategy. Thus, university academics in general have little share in academic decision-making.

Simultaneously, however, some academics could take up both political and academic roles in Singapore. For instance in 1968, as indicated earlier, the government appointed the Deputy Prime Minister Dr. Toh Chin Chye as Vice-Chancellor, who was a former Reader in Physiology in the University of Malaya and a founding member of the PAP. During the period of his Vice-Chancellorship, he was released from his duties as Deputy Prime Minister, but served concurrently as the Minister of Science and Technology and the Chairman of the Board of Governors of the Singapore Polytechnic. Also, the University Council[234] and Senate have always had PAP members who could be appointed to important administrative positions within the Faculties and Departments of both university and polytechnic sectors in Singapore.[235] In terms of the link between the State and the academic profession, local university academics in Singapore have increasingly participated in various national and community activities. A number of academic staff both of the National University of Singapore and Nanyang Technical University have been members of parliament. University academics have been called upon to serve in various government and statutory bodies as well as in key government economic and welfare committees.[236]

As the government provides about 75 per cent of the budget of higher educational institutions, policy guidelines for higher education have been made by the government on selection and admission policy, curriculum design and delivery, examination policy, procedures of staff appointments and promotions, and financial management.[237]

At the national level, all state-managed and financed higher education institutions in Singapore have been coordinated by the Council for Professional and Technical Education (CPTE) since 1979. The CPTE became the main agency responsible for reviewing, planning and projecting the overall middle and high-level manpower requirements of the country. The changing manpower needs for the national economy monitored by the CPTE are quickly translated into policy measures and transmitted to the higher education system to reflect changing needs in research, education and training programmes. CPTE is chaired by the Minister of Trade and Industry and its members are made up of Minister of Education, Senior Minister of State for Education, Permanent Secretary (Labour), Chairman of the Economic Development Board (EDB), the Vice-Chancellor of NUS, the President of Nanyang Technological University, Deputy Secretary-General of the National Trade Union Congress.[238]

Thus, the Singaporean State's idea of the university can be found in its pragmatic intervention and surveillance to ensure the quality of university education and in its search for effective results judged in terms of the national manpower scheme. The struggle is visible in the details of the institutional forms of higher education in Singapore.

Institutional Forms

The original University of Malaya was renamed the University of Singapore in 1962. In addition to the University of Singapore, there were five other tertiary institutions in the 1970s: the Nanyang University, the Singapore Polytechnic, the Ngee Ann Technical College, the Singapore Technical Institute and the Institute of Education was upgraded from being the Teachers' Training College (TTC) in 1973. In 1980, the National University of Singapore (NUS) was newly established through the merger of the former University of Singapore and Nanyang University. The merger was in accordance with the recommendations of Sir Frederick Dainton's Report on *University Education in Singapore of 1979,* in which he stressed the need for Singapore to have a single strong national university.[239]

Since the early 1970s, the Singaporean State has focused on developing an effective and sustainable vocationally-oriented university education system as a major resource for its modernity project.

The total enrollment in higher education has been expanded in Singapore since the Independence period. The university participation rate (of the annual age cohort) steadily increased from 2 per cent in 1960 to 4 per cent in 1978; 6 per cent in 1983 and 13 per cent in 1988.[240] The overall polytechnic enrollment has exceeded university enrollment and the difference grew in the 1980-1990 decade.[241]

In 1991, following the recommendation of the Dainton Report of 1989, the Nanyang Technological Institute[242] became a full-fledged university and was renamed the Nanyang Technological University (NTU). The Institute of Education and the College of Physical Education were also integrated into a single National Institute of Education (NIE) and incorporated into the NTU. From 1992, NTU started awarding its own degrees.[243]

In 1994, the Singapore Institute of Management (SIM) established a new Open University as a private university, with a one-time financial grant and a donation of some land from the Government. This new university belongs to the first layer of the higher education system in Singapore.[244] In 1990, the Temasek Polytechnic was established to complement existing programmes and broaden course options offered by polytechnics. In 1992, the Nanyang Polytechnic was established to pioneer health sciences education and para-medical technology.[245]

The universities, polytechnics and special intermediate-level, vocationally-oriented higher educational institutes were called upon by the State to meet national manpower requirements. Both the universities and polytechnics have established their own in-house institutes and centres to facilitate university-industry R & D cooperation, and consultancy services.[246]

The government's R & D policy has emphasised the university-industry linkage to upgrade the country's technology competence. Within this policy, a scheme has been established to encourage greater university-industry interaction through consultancy and joint R & D projects. Accordingly, engineering students accounted for 48 per cent of total university enrollment in 1980.[247] The total national expenditure on R & D was designed to reach 2 % of GDP by 1995 and the private sector would account for a minimum of 50 % of this total and the ratio of the number of scientists and engineers would amount to 40 % of the labour force.[248]

In the last decade, there has been a major policy shift in the provision of higher education: private higher educational institutions are operating on a full cost-recovery basis and as self-financing.[249] To maintain quality of academic performance, there has been little compromise on the fixed staff-student ratio in Singapore, with an average of 1:10 and a much lower ratio in medicine at 1:6 and dentistry at 1:4.[250] The case of Nanyang Technological Institute, however, shows a higher staff-student ratio average between

1:13.6 to 1: 14.7, due to a shortage of staff. The polytechnics maintain a staff-student ratio of 1:14.[251]

V. Selvaratnam highlights the positive aspect of the State's tight control over the university in Singapore, arguing that the State's control has paradoxically resulted in a diversified and flexible, market-driven university system in Singapore.[252] Clearly, his positive view attributes the nation's economic success to the planned and controlled university system.

In the 1990s, Singapore continues to develop its state-managed and financed higher education system. To ensure Singapore's competitiveness in the market place, the government endorsed a high technology policy in 1986, which targeted 10 per cent of the university population as research students by 1990. To this end, a series of reforms was introduced, including improving staff-student ratios, tripling the research budget for the NUS, increasing international links with leading universities in developed countries, and enhancing university-industry ties.[253]

In summary, the Singaporean State has tried to develop a high-quality, vocationally-oriented and highly-subsidised higher education system as a vehicle to train and use local talents to support and improve its manpower. The Singaporean State has altered the British colonial inheritance of a traditional elite university system into a managed multi-functional and stratified, labour market-driven, tertiary system. The thrust of the State-university relations in Singapore has been to discipline Singaporeans with the right kind of skills, and to equip them with knowledge for use.

The next section will examine types of valued knowledge in the Singaporean higher education system. Arguably Singapore has focused on the principle that technological and economic development should depend both on an elite and on a broader base of educated and skilled persons.

Valued Knowledge

Since Independence, the book argues, the State has made deliberate efforts to promote a Chinese-centred knowledge tradition in the university curriculum in Singapore. This trend has some similarities with the case of Malaysia where the State has promoted Islamic Studies and Bahasa Malaysia.

Another Singaporean characteristic in its cultural valuation of knowledge is that types of knowledge pursued at the university have been prioritised to concentrate on technology, for the State's long-term economic project.

As argued earlier, the colonial legacy of the British conception of university education did not survive long in Singapore.[254] Since the late 1960s, the Singaporean university system has been driven by State objectives. Thus, university education has prioritised the fields of science and technology, complemented by accounting and business management to generate an indigenous supply of manpower.[255]

The development of education at all levels has been ultimately for the purpose of human resource development. From the 1970s, Engineering was emphasised. In the 1973/74 academic year, the Faculty of Arts and Social Sciences which had the second largest number of departments (11) next to the Faculty of Medicine (14), started to show a decline in student enrollment. The new and relatively new faculties such as Engineering with 4 departments, Business Administration and Accountancy with 2 departments rapidly increased their student enrollments.[256]

Table 12

Percentage Changes in Student Enrollment by Faculty

University of Singapore

Sessions 1969/1970 to 1973/1974

Faculties/Schools	Percentage Changes 1973/1974 Over 1969/1970
Law	+37.7
Engineering	+200.0
Business Administration	+110.0
Accountancy	+84.7
Architecture	+108.5
Building and Estate Management	+352.9
Arts and Social Sciences	- 3.9
Science	- 42.1
Medicine	- 5.1
Dentistry	- 9.4
Pharmacy	- 25.7
(University Total)	(+25.0)

Source: University of Singapore Annual Report 1961/62 to 1973/74

Dr. Toh Chin Chye, the new Vice-Chancellor of the University of Singapore from 1968 and also the Chairman of the Board of Governors of the Singapore Polytechnic since 1959, made drastic changes in the knowledge profile of the University of Singapore. In 1969, for instance, three new faculties—the Faculty of Engineering, the Faculty of Architecture and Building, and the School of Accountancy and Business Administration—were created. The Vice-Chancellor also amalgamated the old Faculty of Arts with the relatively newer Faculty of Social Sciences to form the Faculty of Arts and Social Sciences.[257]

In 1969, the university also altered its degree structure. All undergraduates in the Faculty had to take three subjects in the first three years for a BA degree before being selected to read a subject of specialisation for the honours degree given after a further year. This contrasted with the older British model, in which undergraduates used to specialise in one or two subjects from the first year onwards, did not sit for an examination in the second year, and took an honours degree in Arts or in the Social Sciences within three years. [258] The overall changes in the State's valuation of the fields of humanities and social sciences have shifted the university curriculum to the needs of the newly independent Singaporean State and the Southeast Asian region,[259] as part of the process of indigenisation in the postcolonial period.

To meet the particular needs of the State modernity projects, the higher education system in Singapore has developed with three internal strata. Selvaratnam indicates that the first stratum is composed institutionally of two State universities, the National University of Singapore (NUS) and the Nanyang Technological University (NTU). These institutions are required to meet the country's high-level manpower needs including the professional applied research and consultancy needs of both the public and private sectors. The second stratum in knowledge terms is made up of four polytechnics: Singapore, Ngee Ann, Tema sek and Nanyang. These institutions provide the country's technical, management and service middle level skills. The third stratum is made up of the Institute of Technical Education (ITE) and the joint training centres established by the Singaporean government with foreign governments and firms as well as a mixture of institutes and centres established by statutory boards, professional groups and private bodies. These institutions in knowledge terms provide the cutting-edge training programmes as well as responding rapidly to changing needs for upgrading and updating existing workers.[260]

The overall knowledge profile of the Singaporean higher education institutions shows that priority is always in R & D related areas such as management science, medicine, science and technology. The Singapore government has actively influenced the career choices of university graduates to manage the input and output of human resource development and to ensure that there is no undue mismatch between the supply and demand of graduates. Since the postcolonial period began, engineering has received major attention in Singapore. As a result, by 1989, engineering enrollment increased to 62 per cent. By the 1990s, enrollment in the arts and humanities has become less than 30 per cent of the total.[261]

According to Selvaratnam, "Since Singapore does not have a research tradition nor an advantage in fundamental research, it judiciously pursues an R & D policy which concentrates on incremental technology that is beneficial to Singapore's long-term economic strategy".[262]

According to the Singaporean State's higher education policy statements, the improvement of quality and standards is a central goal of all the higher education institutions in Singapore and every effort is made to translate this into operational performance at the institutional level.[263] Accordingly, the State intends to develop NUS, by the year 2000, to the level of the best universities in the world, and for it to be acknowledged as a world leader in the areas of medical care and biotechnology, information technology application, artificial intelligence and expert systems, microelectronics and automation technology, construction technology, plant and animal tissue culture and biomedical engineering.[264] As of 1989, NUS had eight faculties (accountancy and business administration, architecture and building, arts and social sciences, dentistry, engineering, law, medical and science), three postgraduate schools (engineering, management, and medicine), three non-faculty departments, and a number of research institutes.[265] In conjunction with the contemporary policy on the internationalisation of higher educa-tion, the PAP government sets a fixed quota for foreign students' enroll-ment in the Singaporean university system. By this regulation, Singapore provides between 15 and 17 percent of its university places and about 5 to 7 percent of its polytechnic places to foreign students, despite the high com-petition among Singaporeans for university entrance.[266] To maintain inter-nationally acceptable standards[267] and enhance further economic develop-ment, university academics are required to conduct research actively. On the other hand, the polytechnics do not insist that their staff undertake research, but polytechnic staff are encouraged to be involved in applied research and consultancy work. For university staff tenure and promotion, high quality in research output and publication in international journals are regarded as a single measure of merit. As a consequence, the pressure to "publish or perish" is visible in the contemporary Singaporean academ-ic environment, while academic research publication is being used a param-eter to assess the level of internationalisation of the academic profession.

As reviewed so far, there are common themes and issues found in shap-ing the academic profession in these three East Asian countries with differ-ent colonial origins of the university. Given the values and visions of the State and its idea of the university in the respective East Asia countries, as frames within which the academic professions have been shaped, the book will next examine the actual *shape* of the academic profession in these three East Asian countries.

THE SHAPE OF THE ACADEMIC PROFESSION

This section looks at the shape of the academic profession with the sub-themes: academic routes; social composition of the academic profession; and formal ranks of the academic profession. The entry routes to the aca-demic profession continued to mark the former colonial academic links in the three countries. The process of diversification of academic entry routes was slow and gradual, but has become increasingly important under the pressures of 'internationalisation' and 'globalisation' in the con-temporary decade. In terms of social composition, the academic professions have become homogenised in terms of nationality (or ethnicity) as a result of a new political integration in the indigenisation process during the postcolonial period. Along with the expansion of the newly established national education system, and the impact of rapid economic development in this period, the socio-economic background of those in the academic profession has become more diversified compared with the former colonial elitist pattern. With these themes, the case of Korea will be examined first, followed by the cases Malaysia and Singapore.

Korea: The Shape of the Academic Profession

Based on the previous examination of the postcolonial shaping of the academic profession in South Korea, this book here notes the postcolonial shape of the academic profession. The higher education system after political independence rapidly expanded despite the military government's control. The demand for the academic profession increased and accordingly, those teaching at the secondary and upper secondary level and sometimes even at the primary level could be recruited to the academic profession in the early postcolonial period, replacing the former expatriates, and occupying academic positions in newly created higher educational institutions.

As will be examined, however, inbreeding in the university academic profession in South Korea—recruiting from the same prestigious institutions—has become conspicuous in the postcolonial situation. At the same time, there developed new foreign academic routes through the postcolonial political alliance between South Korea and the United States of America, which have replaced the former Japanese colonial routes into the academic profession.

The postcolonial shape of the academic profession is also identified in terms of the intensity of the South Korean State's economic development project. The involvement of the university academics in the political and economic arenas has been clear in the postcolonial and post-Confucian academic environment. In the following sections, the book will first examine the postcolonial entry routes to the academic profession, and then the social composition of the academic profession.

The Entry Routes

In the postcolonial period, it is argued that there emerged a mixture of old and new political legitimation of academic privilege for certain educational routes domestically and internationally.

In Seoul National University—formerly Kyung Sung Imperial University—vacancies left by the Japanese had to be filled by new recruitment. The recruits were often former Kyung Sung Imperial University graduates who used to work for the Japanese government administration, or Korean academics who had been working in the existing private higher educational institutions such as Yonsei, Ewha, and Korea Universities. After political Independence, Kyung Sung Imperial University graduates not only continued to maintain their former colonial political career trajectory in the government, but often combined that with jobs in academe.

As indicated in the Table below, the university academic profession was the most popular career route for Kyung Sung Imperial University graduates after Independence. The number of graduates (533) in the Table covers only those who entered Kyung Sung Imperial University between 1924 and 1941.[268] Those who combined political and academic careers were counted in both sections.

Table 13

Post-colonial Career Routes of Kyung Sung Imperial University Graduates

Occupation	No.	cf.	Occupation	No.	cf.
Politicians	33	Mainly MPs	Journalists	11	
University Academic Profession	134		unknown	69	incl. drop-outs
Legal Profession	44		those who defected to North Korea	100	incl. Abductees
Secondary Schools Principals	22	Incl. one Headteacher	those who died during the studying period	15	
Government bureaucrats	68	Incl. Ministers	those who stayed abroad	8	
Business administrators	62	Incl. Banks, Companies	etc.	15	
			Total	*533*	

Sources: Joung, S. E. 'A Study on the Characteristics of Kyungsung Imperial University' Unpublished Ph.D. book, Department of Education, Yonsei University, Seoul, 1997, p. 144.

In academia, many of the graduates of Kyung Sung Imperial University occupied major administrative posts such as principalships and deanships. According to Joung's research, a third of the Korean graduates chose the academic profession (in Joung's work, this included secondary school principals) as a post-colonial career.[269]

The routinisation of recruitment of candidates graduating from a few prestigious institutions—mainly Seoul National, Yonsei, and Korea University—has been noticeable since the colonial period. (The prestige of these institutions is also linked with their concentration in the capital, Seoul.) In the case of Seoul National University, for instance, 93.3 per cent of faculty members were its own graduates and in the cases of Yonsei and

Korea University, the proportions were 74.5 per cent and 53.0 per cent, respectively, as of October 1992.[270]

Another pattern of academic recruitment was from the foreign educated group who came back from Japan and the U.S.A. after independence. Along with domestic networks in recruiting new personnel, there have been new foreign routes of access to the academic profession in South Korea. These routes which are American, since the period of the USAMGIK (United States Army Military Government in Korea), severed the former Japanese colonial routes [271]

The legal conditions for staffing in higher education was initially based on the Education Public Officials Law of 1953, which set the basic minimum standards. The qualifications of academic staff required for private institutions of higher education are based on the Private School Law.[272] In practice, institutions of higher education, both national and private, have adopted an open recruiting system. Accordingly, the actual standards tend to exceed the legal standards and vary widely from institution to institution. In most universities and colleges, a doctoral degree is regarded as a basic minimum qualification for lecturers.[273] In the assessment of promotion to a higher rank, both research achievements and teaching experience are taken into account.[274]

While maintaining a controlling mechanism for selecting candidates for overseas study,[275] as demand for pursuing higher degrees overseas has constantly increased since 1953, the governmental policy officially encouraged postgraduate students to go abroad for advanced training during the 1970s. To promote advanced science and technology in particular, and to improve the quality of university teaching staff in general, the government began to send academics abroad in 1978 with public money from the education budget. In 1980 overseas study for academics majoring in engineering and business management was initiated under an IBRD loan project. One hundred new academics have benefited from the programme annually.[276]

The Ministry of Education has promoted overseas study with grants since 1978. The academic faculty select the university where they want to pursue research. In 1986, the Ministry of Education provided grants to 1,656 Korean faculty members as illustrated in the Table below. The United States received the majority of such scholars: 61.3 per cent, followed by Japan, with 22.5 per cent, Great Britain with 6.5 per cent and West Germany with 4.1 per cent.[277] A large number of academics have used their study leave for research overseas over the last decade.[278]

Table 14

Korean Academics Studying Overseas by Country in 1986

Country	Number of Academics	Percentage
U.S.A.	1,015	61.3
Japan	373	22.5
Great Britain	108	6.5
West Germany	68	4.1
France	36	2.2
Canada	25	1.5
Austria	8	0.5
Taiwan	6	0.4
Australia	4	0.2
Others	13	0.8
Total	1,656	100

Source: Korean Council for University Education. *Korean Higher Education -Its Development, Aspects and Prospects.* Seoul: KCUE, 1990, p. 84.

As shown in the Table, the major international academic links of the Korean academic profession continue to reflect the earlier overseas routes developed by the first generation of the Korean academic profession since the colonial period.

At the beginning of 1979, approximately 13,300 Korean students were studying abroad. Almost 87 per cent of them chose the United States and West Germany.[279] France and Canada were also favoured. In the 1980s, considerable advance was made in developing indigenous graduate programmes and in diversifying the external sources of the country's expertise. Nevertheless, the United States of America has remained the most favoured country for Koreans to study abroad. From 1961 to 1980, about 6,000 Koreans a year were permitted to attend U.S. colleges or universities. In 1981, when government policy was eased, the annual number climbed to 15,000.[280]

In the 1960s and 1970s, many of the Korean doctorate-holders often remained in the United States. This trend was especially visible in the fields of mathematics, computer science, and engineering. The South Korean government then undertook to attract back Koreans of internationally outstanding calibre who had been working abroad. For instance, when the Korean Institute of Science and Technology (KIST) was established by the government in 1966 to serve the growing needs of high technology, repatriation programmes were successfully organised in the United States, Europe, Japan and Canada in the 1970s and 1980s. Short-term and long-term plans to recruit Korean professors working abroad were established in the early 1980s. Overall 100 academics returned to Korea at a cost of US$ 859,000 in the period 1981 to 1983.[281] By 1991, the Korean government no longer needed to offer permanent repatriation programmes and announced that the brain drain had ceased.[282]

However, in the recruitment process of the academic profession in 1998, U.S. doctoral degree holders were still more successful than any other foreign degree holders. Among the foreign degree holders in the new academic recruitment in 1998, 64.5 per cent of them had taken their Ph.D. in the U.S.A., 13. 7 per cent in Japan, 7.5 per cent in Germany, 4.4 per cent in France, 2.1 per cent in China, and 1.4 per cent in Great Britain.[283]

The proportion of doctoral degree holders in the academic profession has notably increased in the postcolonial period. In 1975, for instance, among the Korean academics who were members of the Korean Political Science Association, only forty-five percent held doctoral degrees, of whom 101 of those doctorates had been awarded by Korean universities (27 % of the doctorate members of the Association); 50 by U.S. universities (13 %); 8 by West German and Austrian universities; 3 by Japanese universities; and one each by British and French universities.[284] In 1988, academics with a doctoral degree were estimated as 7.1 per cent of staff in junior colleges and 42.7 per cent in colleges and universities.[285] In 1997, the proportion of university academics with Ph.D. degrees is estimated at 72.46 per cent as a whole—73.56 per cent in the public sector universities; 72.02 per cent in the private sector.[286]

As reviewed so far, the entry routes to the academic profession in the postcolonial period have been routinised on both the domestic and international levels. The colonial pattern of a few domestically prestigious institutional routes has been reinforced by the postcolonial recruitment pattern in South Korea. On the other hand, the major foreign links were not with Japan, but with America, reflecting South Korean postcolonial international relations. The consequent social composition of the academic profession will be investigated next.

The Social Composition of the Academic Profession

In the process of rapid economic development along with political disruptions, the postcolonial period saw a new socio-economic and cultural pattern and a relatively classless social structure in South Korea.[287] The breakdown of class rigidity, especially at the top, and a steady erosion in the assumption that academic life has nothing to do with economic concerns, has made it easier for people to be upwardly mobile in social class terms.[288]

Thus, the academic profession in South Korea became open to those from a wide range of social backgrounds. Soon after Independence, upgraded secondary school teachers educated in the colonial period, or young graduates, newly equipped with Western technical knowledge after education in the United States were recruited into the academic profession.[289]

At the time of liberation in 1945, gender bias was the single greatest source of inequality in Korean education. In 1975, however, sex parity in primary-school enrollment was reached; 15 years later, male and female students attended high schools in equal numbers. Higher education continued to lag. Since the 1960s the proportion of female students' enrollment in higher education has risen from less than 20% to somewhat over 30%.[290] Despite the increase of female students in higher educational institutions, the low proportion of females in the academic profession has continued; in 1994, the proportion of females in the academic profession was estimated at 21.6 per cent.[291]

In the postcolonial period, the academic profession has been composed mainly of Korean nationals. This highly homogeneous ethnic composition of the academic profession in South Korea can also be linked to the use of Korean as the uniform medium of university education instruction after Independence. In 1995, the proportion of expatriates in the academic profession was estimated only at 1.03 per cent, including short-term visiting scholars as well as the formally recruited foreign academics. (The proportion of expatriates was 0.78 per cent in the public sector of higher education and 1.16 per cent in the private sector).[292]

In short, the composition of the academic profession in the 1990s is still unbalanced in terms of both gender and nationality. In 1997, the total number of academic staff members in four-year universities (excluding Teacher Education Institutes and Open Universities) was 53,300.[293] Among those, 41,180 (77.3 per cent) were male, and 12,120 (22.7 per cent) were female.[294] The figure shows a slight increase of female participation in the academic profession compared with that in 1995.

The Ministry of Education has formulated guidelines for hiring foreign nationals. In the guidelines, the recruitment of foreign academic staff is encouraged primarily in the fields of science, technology and foreign languages and invitations to foreign scholars to be in South Korea for less than a year are encouraged. According to the guidelines, each university is free to appoint foreigners to permanent positions, but the appointments should be reported to the Ministry of Education. In 1986, there were 450 foreign professors employed in Korea as indicated in the Table below.

Table 15
Foreign Professors in Korea in 1986

(in person)

Total		Colleges and Universities		Junior Colleges		Miscellaneous School	
Total	Female	Total	Female	Total	Female	Total	Female
450	134	411	118	22	11	17	4

Sources: Korean Council for University Education. *Korean Higher Education -Its Development, Aspects and Prospects.* Seoul: KCUE, 1990, p. 82.

However, the number of foreign academics (893) in South Korean academe by 1997 was still only 1.7 per cent.[295]

In the 1990s, the expansion of the private sector of higher education continues, with big variations in academic quality among institutions. Some of the newly established private universities sponsored by big enterprises have emerged as outstanding research universities along with prestigious traditional universities. The last decade also saw the rise and fall of family-owned small universities, which are often of low quality and lack proper research facilities.

In summary, the contemporary shape of the academic profession in South Korea is still based on highly exclusive academic networking and the prestige of particular academic backgrounds, including foreign routes—still mainly identified with American institutions. The domestic academic networks in South Korea have been used as effective credentials to gain sponsorship for further overseas higher education and ultimately for future academic careers. The domestically prestigious academic routes which were originally formed in the colonial period have been consolidated through three generations of academic inbreeding since then. Overall, the South Korean academic profession is homogeneous—it is made up of Korean nationals. For comparison, the book now shifts attention to Malaysia.

Malaysia: The Shape of the Academic Profession

Earlier the book examined the postcolonial shaping of the academic profession in Malaysia through the independent State's principle of positive discrimination in favour of *Bumiputeras* in recruitment procedures. It is argued here that on the basis of the legitimated privilege of indigenous Malays (the *Bumiputeras*), the composition of the academic profession in Malaysia has shifted to those with Malay Islamic origins, who replaced the former expatriate and Chinese and Indian academics. The postcolonial entry routes to the academic profession in Malaysia have also become diversified from the former British colonial link. The foreign routes have been expanded to the American universities, through American academic aid and programmes of staff development (as in the case of South Korea), and more recently, the Australian universities and Japanese research institutions. The following section will look at the details of postcolonial entry routes to the academic profession in Malaysia.

Entry Routes

In the early postcolonial period, foreign universities were the major entry route to the academic profession in Malaysia. There was a considerable proportion of Western academic expatriates who undertook teaching, consultancy or research assignment over a fixed period of time. The recruitment of Western expatriates was significant in the initial development of the University of Malaya up to the 1960s.[296] However, as shown in the Table, local academics started to be recruited outnumbering the European expatriates in universities by 1963:

Table 16
Number of Expatriates vs. Locals in the Academic Profession

Year	Expatriates	Locals	Total
1959	20	18	38
1960	17	6	23
1961	26	9	35
1962	17	12	29
1963	14	26	40
1964	23	31	54

Source: ASAIHL, *Seminar on University Organization and Administration,* 20-24 January 1964, Bankok, Association of Southeast Asian Institutions of Higher Learning, 1964, p. 103.

As noted by T. H. Silcock, the regular procedure of recruitment to the academic profession in the University of Malaya, by advertisement and selection, did not attract the most promising Chinese candidates; and suitable Malay candidates were not forthcoming up until the inception of the New Economic Policy.[297] In the NEP era (1970-1990), the government set a 55 per cent enrollment rate for *Bumiputeras,* following an ethnic quota system. A core of young Malay scholars was quickly developed and they were promoted to administrative positions in universities to replace expatriate and other ethnic staff members in the NEP era.[298] In addition to the enrollment and recruitment quotas, the government continued its general policy to support *Bumiputera* staff through a special training scheme (restricted to *Bumiputeras*) for pursuing masters or doctoral degrees.[299]

Given the special provisions for the *Bumiputeras* in the national system of Malaysia and outside through the MARA college and the residential schools, which also allow instruction in English to facilitate movement into higher education overseas, there has been an accusation that there are two standards, one for the *Bumiputeras* and one for the others.[300] In spite of rationales for the quota system in academic recruitment, many non-Malay academics find it difficult to accept the discrimination. The imposition of quotas in academic recruitment and promotion policies has affected non-Malay access to academe. For example, the implementation of the National Language (Bahasa Malaysia) as the medium of instruction requires staff to be proficient in the language.[301] The academic staff training scheme for purposes of pursuing masters or doctoral degrees is also restricted to the *Bumiputeras* only.[302]

As a consequence of this policy, the high proportion of overseas enrollment by Malaysians has been identified with Chinese Malaysians. In 1983, the number of students enrolled in all types of overseas institution was about 58,000, of whom 63.3 per cent were of Chinese origin, whereas 18.9 per cent were *Bumiputera*.[303]

As indicated, the former British colonial academic routes have remained in postcolonial Malaysia, but have catered for Chinese Malaysians in particular, who had to seek overseas routes as a consequence of initial discrimination in domestic university entry. The number of Malaysian students studying in the U.K. has been so far larger than those of other neighbouring countries in Southeast Asia.[304]

Academic staff who are Malaysian citizens are appointed initially on a probationary period of 18 months (for serving employees) or three years (for candidates through direct appointment), with prospects of tenure to the retiring age of 55. These services may be extended to the age of 60. Non-Malaysian staff are appointed on a contract of three years subject to the possibility of further contracts or on visiting arrangements.[305] Those who have received tenure as permanent faculty members of the university are given up to thirty-five days of annual holidays and may be granted study leave for approved research or field work.[306] The following Table shows the rate of university staff recruitment differentiated by the internal academic hierarchy in the early postcolonial period.

Table 17

University of Malaya: Rate of Recruitment of Staff

Year	Professors	Senior Lecturers	Lecturers	Assistant Lecturers
1959	12	1	16	9
1960	2	2	11	8
1961	1	-	21	13
1062	3	1	18	7
1963	7	1	15	17
1964	4	1	31	18

Source: ASAIHL, *Seminar on University Organization and Administration*, 20-24 January 1964, Bankok, Association of Southeast Asian Institutions of Higher Learning, 1964, p. 103.

The patterns of initial recruitment to the academic profession are a mixture of domestic and foreign routes. Two-thirds of the first-degree holders in the academic profession at the University of Malaya were locally qualified, while the majority are graduates of the University of Malaya itself. However, the number of locally qualified doctorates is much less at only 11%. Most of the teaching staff obtained their doctorates from either Europe (37%) or the USA and Canada (35%). Among the European countries, the UK has been the most popular so far. The number of staff with local masters' degrees is 44 per cent. The rest obtained their second degrees from Europe, USA and Canada and a small proportion (13%) gained their degrees in Australia and New Zealand. It is notable that a large portion of the faculty members in both Departments of Education (62%) and Engineering (38%) received their doctoral degrees in the USA and Canada.[307]

In terms of professional qualifications for the formal entry routes to the academic profession in faculties, other than Medicine,[308] normally a Masters degree would be a prerequisite for appointment. Statistics for 1977 indicate that more than half of the academic staff members in the Engineering Faculty and 43% in the Faculty of Education possessed doctoral degrees as compared to the number of Ph.D. and M.Ds in the Medical Faculty (23%).[309]

The contemporary decade—identified with the Sixth Plan period (1991-1995) in Malaysia—saw a new international dimension in academic recruitment routes, through institutional links initiated by the Malaysian government. Advanced skill training institutes were established with the cooperation of the Federal Republic of Germany, France and Japan.[310] As a consequence, foreign academic routes available for the future Malay academic candidates have been diversified. The foreign routes were also extended to American universities which have coordinated Malay staff development programmes as well as providing higher degree courses, and more recently to the Australian universities for twinning programmes.[311]

In the process of indigenisation and diversification of academic routes in Malaysia, the size of the academic profession has been steadily expanded in the postcolonial period—as indicated in Table below, from 109 in 1962 to 1061 in 1977, which is an increase of 880 %:

Table 18
Academic Staffing at University of Malaya 1962 - 1977

1962/63 - 109	1963/64 - 151	1964/65 – 190	1965/66 - 253
1966/67 - 337	1967/68 - 381	1968/69 - 393	1969/70 - 484
1970/71 - 524	1971/72 - 747	1972/73 - 791	1973/74 - 876
1974/75 - 884	1975/76 - 906	1976/77 - 1061	

Source: Regional Institute of Higher Education and Development (RIHED), *Staff and Faculty Development in Southeast Asian Universities*, 1981, p. 9.

In the Seventh Plan period (1996-2000), the capacity and enrollment for post-graduate and post-doctoral courses, particularly in the fields of science and technology, are being expanded to increase R & D activities and to meet the increasing demand for higher qualified teaching staff.[312]

Despite this expansion, the internal hierarchy of the university academic profession has not changed drastically since the 1960s, which has basically remained in the English pattern as indicated in Table 19.[313]

Table 19

Teaching Staff by Academic Rank University of Malaya

Academic Ranks	1965 No	1965 %	1970 No	1970 %	1975 No	1975 %	1977 No	1977 %
Professor	21	10	28	5	38	5	44	5
Associate Professor Senior Lecturer	6	6	36	7	79	11	95	12
Lecturer	107	52	271	52	467	63	474	58
Assistant Lecturer	30	15	76	15	-		-	
Temporary Lecturer	-		12	2	44	6	27	3
Tutor	23	11	82	16	105	14	168	21
Visiting Lecturer/ Visiting Professor	11	6	13	3	4	1	4	1
Total	205	100	518	100	737	100	811	100

Source: Regional Institute of Higher Education and Development Research Series, *Staff and Faculty Development in Southeast Asian Universities,* Hong Kong: Maruzen Asia 1981, p. 10.

The rank of senior lecturer has been redesignated as associate professor. The percentage of professors has declined from 10 % in 1965 to 5 % in 1977. The reverse has been the case for associate professors/ senior lecturers. Their share increased from 6 percent in 1965 to 12 % in 1977. The majority in the academic profession are lecturers, who make up more than half of the academic staff. The proportion of tutors has more than doubled from 11 % in 1965 to 21 % in 1977.[314]

The senior academic staff (professors and associate professors) are normally expected to have a Ph.D. or professional qualifications in their field, whereas the majority of lecturers have only a Master's degree. After joining the university profession, some individuals pursue a higher degree either locally or overseas.[315]

Overall, the Malaysian academic recruitment routes in the postcolonial period have been indigenised as a consequence of the independent State's pragmatic approach to university knowledge. In other words, the academic routes in postcolonial Malaysia have been constructed by the State's political, economic and cultural priorities, in terms of initial access to, and use of knowledge in the university. Both have been identified with Malay Muslim origins, especially in the fields of science and technology. Given these particular Malaysian criteria prioritised by the State, the following section will examine more details of the social composition of the academic profession.

Social Composition of the Academic Profession

As discussed earlier, the one hundred and fifty years of British colonial rule in Peninsular Malaysia (1786-1957) transformed a largely homogeneous Malay society into a multi-ethnic society. By 1957, Malays accounted for 49.8 per cent of the population, Chinese 37.2 percent and Indians 11.3 percent.[316]

As a result of the State's efforts to increase the participation of the *Bumiputera* in higher education, the Malay percentage of university students significantly increased. In 1970, the Malay percentage of university students was 40 per cent (3237 students). By 1975 the percentage had risen to 57 per cent (8153 students), and in 1980 the percentage had further increased to 67 per cent (13,857 students).[317] The *Bumiputera* portion of university students had already risen to a level beyond the percentage of Malays in the whole population, by the late 1990s.

The proportion of ethnic Malays in the academic profession has almost certainly increased, following the *Bumiputera* policy, which has affected the overall ethnic composition of the teaching profession at all education levels, as a consequence of initial recruitment and promotion. As noted by R. Murray Thomas, the State deliberately demoted Chinese and Indians and promoted Malays in the power hierarchies of the Ministry of Education and individual educational institutions.[318] As a result, higher proportions of the *Bumiputeras* than other ethnic groups have probably occupied the academic profession as well as positions as government administrators and teachers.[319]

The existing policy on entry quotas in higher educational institutions among the various ethnic communities is expected to continue in order to generate a larger supply of qualified *Bumiputera* in the professional, managerial and technical categories.[320] In this pro-*Bumiputera* stance, the two decades of the NEP (1970-1990) saw an increase of the *Bumiputera* share of total educational opportunities in all local educational institutions. This share was estimated at 60 per cent by 1990, which reflects their proportion in the population.[321]

In fact, the precise ethnic profile of the university academic profession is not available due to the Official Security Act in Malaysia. However, there is evidence at the anecdotal level that the proportion of *Bumiputeras* in the university academic profession is at around 65 per cent, whereas in the Malay Civil Service, it is at around 85 per cent.[322] Patterns for other occupations are known.[323] It can be anticipated that more *Bumiputera* will continue to have better opportunities to enter the academic profession in the university system than other ethnic groups in the country.

In terms of gender, the academic profession in Malaysia has been typically a male profession. In 1977, only 22 % of the academic profession from the nine faculties of the University of Malaya were women. In the same year, the Education Faculty recorded the highest proportion of female participation (40 %), with the lowest (4%) being in the Engineering Faculty.[324]

The current expansion of the private sector is expected to induce diversification of the ethnic profile of the academic profession through the new recruitment of expatriates, while the local entry routes remain.[325] Overall, since political independence, the Malaysian State has continued to indigenise the academic profession, but more recently the Malaysian government has tried to internationalise the academic profession through the privatisation and corporatisation of universities. In the following section, the book will examine the case of Singapore.

Singapore: The Shape of the Academic Profession

Attention will again be focused on the ways in which the academic profession is composed: the entry routes, the social composition, and university academic ranks. In the early postcolonial period, the education system in Singapore still remained a British colonial legacy on the 'divide and rule' principle—there was no unified national education system in the colonial period. There was little government supervision and no standardisation of curricula or required level of achievement for graduating. In particular, the Chinese-medium educational institutions were outside government supervision.

After political independence from Malaysia in 1965, however, the PAP government accorded education a high priority, seeing education as a fundamental device for the building of a new nation. As indicated, the PAP government established and tightly controlled the new national education system, within which curricula, textbooks, and examinations are all standardised, with an emphasis on languages, mathematics, science, and technology. The PAP government emphasised the creation of technical educational institutions and teacher-training programmes. The government's intention to manage society itself in certain ways meant an educational sorting mechanism, through which, by 1969, students already had to be streamed into academic, technical, and vocational routes after Primary VI.[326]

In late 1986, as part of the major education reform, "Towards Excellence in Schools", the PAP government planned to reintroduce some independent schools with outstanding academic records and on a sound financial status. In the promotion of the government's project for the 'privatization' of education, independent schools have been created to replicate the British and American models of good private schools.

From the beginning of 1987, there was established a single "national educational stream" with English as the only first language and with all mother tongues taught as a second language. This policy, however, would subsequently be amended, with growing emphasis on Asian values. In 1989, the government planned to strengthen mother-tongue instruction for

purposes of values transmission by more than doubling for 1990 the number of primary schools teaching both English and Chinese as first languages. The PAP government's attention has now switched to a
German/Swiss model of education with more emphasis on technical and
vocational education—thus limiting access to university.[327]

Given this background of the State's construction of the education system, the following section will look at the entry routes to the postcolonial
academic profession in Singapore.

Entry Routes

Singapore altered the routes into the academic profession after political
independence. The Singaporean government has pursued the recruitment
of academic staff locally and internationally. Emphasis is given to all
round, high, academic qualifications. Scholars have been recruited to the
academic profession from various parts of the non-Communist world, on
the basis of their ability in their specialised fields, not necessarily for their
proficiency in English.[328] Since 1969, the minimum academic qualification
for staff in the non-professional disciplines has been a Ph.D.[329]

Academic recruitment in the University of Singapore showed a continued British influence in academic background and some privileging of
expatriate academic status in the process of decolonisation.[330] However,
under Lim's Vice-Chancellorship (1966-67), expatriate staff in the
University of Singapore would not get tenure, however long their service.
Instead, they got an offer of a gratuity payment (two months' extra salary
per year of service in lieu of permanence), which initially provided sufficient incentive to foreign staff.[331] These conditions for expatriates changed
again to reduce benefits to new expatriate staff after Dr. Toh Chin Chye
became Vice-Chancellor in 1968. In the new academic contracts after
1968, the expatriate was, for a while, relegated to the status of a temporary academic helper. Also, all new academic staff lost any safeguard
against dismissal: either party, employer or employee could terminate the
agreement on three to six months' notice, or pay in lieu of notice, without
giving any reason for doing so.[332]

The government's policy states that local staff would be "more reliable,
having a commitment to the country that was complete and irrevocable".[333]
Nevertheless, this policy of building a strong nucleus of local academics has
not been successfully implemented. The local academic candidates could
not meet the demand for a wide range of academic specialisations. This
shortage was exacerbated by the deliberate policy of the government of
channelling many of the best local graduates into administrative and political leadership. There has been a strong monetary incentive in the private
sector which attracted bright Singaporeans to take up university courses in
accountancy, business management, law and medicine and to move into the
financially rewarding professions rather than an academic career.[334]

Therefore, to ensure the quality of academic staff in terms of international standards of scholarship, Singaporean universities have had to open the range of academic recruitment, a process which is reviewed regularly by units of senior academics and administrators.[335]

In the late 1970s and 1980s, Singapore benefited from the international academic labour market to recruit highly qualified expatriate academic staff on the basis of three-year contracts.[336] The Singaporean government has offered an attractive salary and benefits package to attract and retain expatriate staff, including the granting of postgraduate scholarships and citizenship or permanent residence status to the foreign academics selected. The recruitment of expatriate academics has been more successful in the science and technology fields than the humanities.[337] This may be related to the PAP government's censorship of critical academic comments on political and social issues, with possible consequences for creativity in the humanities and in the social sciences in Singapore.

The expatriate academics are classified as employment-pass holders, which reveals a discriminatory facet of the Singaporean State policy. That is to say, those employment-pass holders are expatriate professionals and business people, overwhelmingly Caucasian and Chinese middle-class from Malaysia and elsewhere, who are then permitted to bring their families to Singapore, to marry Singaporeans, to use the education system and to join the Central Provident Fund (CPF), an incentive to foreigners who can take out the total amount in cash on departure. (In contrast, however, work-permit holders are working-class manual workers mainly from Malaysia, Thailand, Indonesia, the Philippines and Sri Lanka, who are then stringently controlled and denied the rights accorded employment-pass holders, while working in Singapore.[338])

Another mechanism to maintain high professional standards of academic recruitment in Singapore is a stringent tenure policy, in which only 40 per cent of the staff are tenured in the Singaporean higher education system. The initial condition of academic tenure and promotion is to fulfil two contracts of three years each. The second criterion is favourable judgement of academic qualifications, teaching ability and research publications in professional journals of international and regional standing. Academic publications in international journals have been used as a universal currency to judge academic excellence.[339]

However, the short-term renewable contracts prescribed by the tenure policy in Singapore make many expatriate staff insecure and alienated in terms of a personal career path and growth. For that reason, it is not uncommon that the expatriates are often more committed to their own disciplinary research to gain recognition in the international academic community than to the teaching and research expected locally in Singapore. As a result, it may be difficult in the long term to retain outstanding expatriate staff in Singaporean universities.[340]

The penalty applied to incompetent local academics is not to reward them with salary increments, or tenure. Unsatisfactory expatriate academics can be asked to leave: as indicated earlier their contracts can be quickly terminated.[341]

Like Malaysia, Singapore developed a new model of academic ranks by adapting the American academic ranks to the British model inherited from the colonial period. The academic profession is ranked as follows: Senior Professor—Professor- Associate Professor—Senior Lecturer—Lecturer—Senior Tutor (formerly instructor).[342] Salary scales follow the hierarchy. The polytechnic ranks are different, but again reminiscent of British ranks: Principal lecturer, senior lecturer and lecturer.[343]

Singaporean universities have maintained an English-style labour intensive lecture-tutorial and laboratory-workshop mode as instructional methods, which has led to a constant increase of the academic profession along with the rapid expansion of the higher education system. Average teaching loads, between 9-10 hours a week in the university and 20 hours a week in the polytechnics (with an average of 5 student contact hours a week) is also used as an incentive to academics' own research and consultancy work.[344]

Recently, however, professional skills in teaching and its significance has been newly emphasised so as to achieve excellence in university education. Since 1981, concerted efforts have been made to improve teaching on a university-wide basis.[345] Good university teachers are given incentives through salary increases, promotion, tenure and study leave.[346] The following Table indicates the number of scholarships and bursaries provided for study leave in the selected countries:

Table 20

Scholarships and Bursaries by Country of Study, 1985-1991

Country	1985	1986	1987	1988	1989	1990	1991
Australia	14	12	10	1	19	15	3
NZ	7	4	6	17	14	2	-
UK	40	40	34	38	56	74	75
France	5	3	6	3	2	7	3
Germany	-	3	-	-	-	-	-
Japan	14	5	11	14	8	7	12
Taiwan	5	6	6	6	-	-	1
USA	-	1	3	2	6	7	10
Others	1	-	-	-	-	-	-
Singapore	89	141	174	157	156	134	122
Total	175	215	250	238	261	246	228

Source: *Public Services Commissions*, Singapore, Requoted from Selvaratnam, V., *Innovations in Higher Education, Singapore at the Competitive Edge*, Washington, D. C.: The World Bank, 1994, p. 112

In the 1988/89 academic year, 114 academic staff members of the NUS were pursuing postgraduate degrees overseas. In the 1989/90, the NUS sent 29 staff members to overseas universities for postgraduate studies and 27 successfully completed their postgraduate programmes and resumed their duties. In 1990, a total of 103 staff members were at overseas universities, doing postgraduate studies.[347]

As reviewed so far, the Singaporean State, soon after decolonisation, tried to indigenise the entry routes and recruitment criteria, which used to be favourable to British academic expatriates and the social science faculty following the Carr-Saunders' university model. After political independence from Malaya, the PAP government provided a new direction for nation unity, centred on Chinese Confucian culture, and the PAP simultaneously stressed economic development. Following the indigenised entry and recruitment routes to the academic profession in the postcolonial period, the social composition of the academic profession in Singapore has subsequently changed. This is the theme of the following section.

Social Composition of the Academic Profession

As examined in Chapter Three, there were few indigenous scholars in the academic profession in the colonial period. The social composition of the colonial academic profession in Singapore was expatriate—mainly people from the United Kingdom.[348]

In the process of indigenisation, the University of Singapore immediately after Independence started to give a full incremental credit to the locals who had a Ph.D., or half an incremental credit to those who had not have a Ph.D. to fill the vacancies in the university academic profession created by the departing colonial scholars.

At the time of political independence, the Philosophy Department at the University of Singapore had three Singapore citizens out of six, the others being an American, who was departmental head,[349] and two Englishmen. Political science had only one Singaporean, a Malaysian departmental head, a Canadian, an Englishmen, an Indonesian, an American and a Pakistani. The new Sociology Department had no Singaporean staff.[350]

Overall, the proportion of expatriates in the postcolonial academic profession in Singapore has been by no means small, but the composition of the academic profession has become more diversified, in terms of nationality. For instance, expatriates in the NUS currently comprise between 16 and 20 per cent of the academic staff. The majority of expatriate academics are from the USA, Britain, Australia, Canada, New Zealand, Sri Lanka, India, Hong Kong and Taiwan.[351]

The Singaporean State has maintained the colonial tradition of international academic recruitment along with the pragmatic use of English as the sole medium of university instruction. As indicated, however, academic expatriates in Singapore, who used to enjoy privileged work conditions, had to adapt to a new State's arrangement to reduce the amount of social space within which academics undertook their social roles as 'men of knowledge'.

THE CONCLUSION TO CHAPTER FOUR

In this chapter, the postcolonial shaping and the shape of the academic profession in Korea, Malaysia and Singapore were examined. As in the colonial period, the shaping of the academic profession in the postcolonial period was analysed through the ways in which the respective East Asian States related to their universities in the process of executing their modernity projects. The conclusion to Chapter Four will undertake a comparison of these countries.

The Shaping of the Academic Profession

Values and Visions of the State

In the respective contexts of South Korea, Malaysia and Singapore, the State was again the major actor in shaping the academic profession; though this time it was an independent State whose new political values and visions framed the academic profession in the process of decolonisation.

It is notable that, in all three countries, the independent East Asian government leaders had anti-colonial, anti-communist, and new nationalist values. At the same time, however, the former colonial elite continued to play a major role in the political, economic and academic arenas in these three East Asian States in the postcolonial period.

The first independent South Korean State was officially led by the American-educated President Rhee. However, the new governing elite were recruited from Japanese colonial networks—many of them were former Japanese colonial government officers—and those newly recruited to the Rhee government were often graduates of Kyung Sung Imperial University.[352] Thus, the independent South Korean State retained the former colonial Korean elite trained by the Japanese colonial government. Subsequently, the colonial style of governance was regenerated in the newly independent State, with some copying of a Japanese tradition.[353] In short, the modern bureaucratic structure established in Korea was the replication of the Japanese system which had emerged by 1900—with an American overlay.

In the postcolonial independence period, the political project of South Korea was based on an anti-communist, pro-American stance, especially after the Korean War of 1950-1953. The new Republic of Korea kept close military, political, and economic links with the United States. At the same time, American influence on shaping the postcolonial academic profession was visible through the new stress on the use of English, new models of teacher training, new types of valued knowledge, new academic entry routes, and a new predilection for American-educated Koreans in university academic recruitment.

In contrast, in Malaysia and Singapore, the new political leaders were all from the English-medium academic routes and often educated in British universities. However, again there was an influence from Japan. As noted by Christopher Tremewan, there is a considerable similarity between the Japanese wartime methods of social control in Malaya and the postcolonial system of social control in Singapore in particular: "a pervasive internal security apparatus, a system of collective security of households, wards and districts, constant surveillance of religious organisations and the banning of all others except those officially approved".[354] Similarly, South Korea in the postcolonial period retained social control mechanisms reminiscent of those used by the Japanese. In secondary and tertiary education, military training and anti-communist, national ideological discipline—such as *Yushin*—were imposed as educational requirements on all students. The South Korean military government also implanted military units in the secondary schools and included, in the national curriculum, military studies, compulsory for all students, which also evokes Japanese social control patterns in Korea in the colonial period.

In both Malaysia and Singapore, despite their colonial experience of the British versions of an education system, the postcolonial education systems are more reminiscent of the Japanese model, which is highly centralised under the tight control of the Ministry of Education. In all three cases, South Korea, Malaysia and Singapore, the State and university relations have been influenced by the political leadership, down through the Ministry of Education, to university staff. The South Korean State and university relations show the continuation of the former (Japanese) colonial pattern of educational control, whereas the Malaysian and Singaporean cases deviated from the former British colonial tradition of indirect control over a decentralised education system.

Economically, South Korea has followed the Japanese model of State-led, export- oriented industrialisation dominated by the major conglomerates—*chaebol* in Korean. In Malaysia, also, the adaptation of Japanese values and visions articulated in the contemporary Malaysian Look East Policy can be seen as a partial legacy of the Malayan experience of Japanese domination during the Second World War. More contemporaneously, however, the Look East Policy over the last decade has been the official stance of the Malaysian government to incorporate (contemporary) Japanese cultural values in its economic infrastructure. In the domain of higher education, the Look East Policy includes compulsory third language acquisition, including Japanese, Mandarin, Korean, Vietnamese, or Thai, among which Japanese language learning has been recognised as the most significant. For instance, Universiti Malaysia Sarawak (UNIMAS), which was established in December 1992 to address the new directions of the Look East Policy and Vision 2020, states clearly its aim in compulsory language learning, in the case of Japanese, is not merely to speak Japanese but to gain an understanding of what it means to *be* Japanese.[355]

In parallel with the State's political and social control, South Korea, Malaysia and Singapore have all applied meritocratic principles in education as a strong rationale for modernisation. However, it should be noted that Malaysia has devised its own criteria—the ethnic quota system—to specify meritocratic principles in education. The meritocratic selection process in South Korea and Singapore has been legitimated by the proposition that people were being offered equality of educational opportunity, and are being sorted more or less correctly according to their own abilities, through the State's supervision over the examination and selection process.

In reality, however, the extent of the opportunities offered to individual participants in education has been adjusted to meritocratic criteria defined by the State. As indicated, the State's selection criteria in Malaysia are defined as talent with *Bumiputera* origins and Islamic cultural values; in Singapore, they are defined as talent educated in English, but preferably with Chinese origins, and embracing Confucian cultural values. In the case of South Korea, the social selection criteria tacitly applied as the meritocratic principle are not as overtly defined as in Malaysia and Singapore by ethnicity—but parallel Singapore in the emphasis on examinations. Thus, unlike the other two cases, the South Korean State is homogeneous in terms of ethnicity, language, cultural tradition, and a strong anti-communist political ideology. To express meritocratic principles and equality of educational opportunity, the South Korean State has devised a highly uniform sorting process in education. The emphasis is on mass education rather than elitism—a deviation from the Japanese colonial model.[356]

In Singapore, unlike South Korea, the concept of meritocracy as a central controlling value of the State has legitimated educational elitism, carefully incorporated into the multi-ethnic context of Singapore. In terms of the tight social control by the State's meritocratic ideology, Wilson notes that Singapore is "not so very unlike Plato's perception of the ideal city-state in which 'the wise shall lead and rule, and the ignorant shall follow'."[357] The principle of meritocratic rule reflected in the Singaporean case is also reminiscent of the Confucian model of the State, as reviewed in Chapter Two. Indeed, education in Singapore has become highly selective and competitive, a process which includes channelling the majority into one or other of the technical and vocational streams. In contrast to Singapore, the Malaysian State has created an ethnic quota system in the selection process, giving more educational opportunities to the *Bumiputeras*.

Within these educational selection systems, operated on their own specific definition of meritocratic and mobility principles, in all three countries estimated requirements for doctors, engineers and specialists of all kinds are made, and quotas are drawn up to regulate university admission to the various fields of study, on the criterion of potential contribution to economic development.

Therefore, in all three cases, the academic profession in the postcolonial period has been shaped by these policies which legitimate values prioritised in education and in the selection process. It is suggested that much of the former colonial political and economic systems are reflected in these postcolonial independent East Asian countries. Consequently, despite the East Asian States' efforts to create a new endogenous system of education to expedite decolonisation, their educational systems contain traits still reminiscent of the former colonial patterns. In addition, the systems of State control and surveillance in both Malaysia and Singapore are reminiscent of the Japanese model implanted during the period of occupation. The overall visions and values of these three independent East Asian States have articulated the postcolonial idea of the university, which will be reviewed in the following section.

The Idea of the University

In all three cases, the independent State shifted its priorities in higher education based on new ideas about national development. In the postcolonial period, the university in the three East Asian States was expected to play a significant role in vocational and technical training rather than emphasising cultivation and *Bildung*. Toward the contemporary decade, the idea of the university in all three East Asian countries has focused more on quality control of higher education. Stress has been put on the significance of science and technology, cost effective management, and central control, for the survival and independence of the domestic university system within an increasingly globalised economy.

In the case of South Korea, the postcolonial idea of the university was officially altered from the former Japanese imperial model of elite training to the American model of liberal democratic mass education following principles of equality of opportunity. However, in practice, the Japanese model of university education has survived, in terms of modes of instruction and tight government control over university administration and finance, through which the historical division between the public and the private sectors of higher educational institutions has been maintained.

In Malaysia, the need for technical education and the political significance of Bahasa Malaysia as the only national language were realised early, even before independence, by the Alliance Government in 1955. The new idea of education was spelt out in the Razak Report in 1956, which recommended that technical education should be organised in the Malayan National Language on three levels; first, technical colleges at the postsecondary education level; second, technical institutes at the upper secondary school level; and third, trade schools at the primary school level.[358]

Accordingly, at the time of independence in 1957, education at the primary level was relatively well developed in Malaysia. However, the university sector still remained in the British colonial model of education for an elite minority. Thus, by 1970, only about 0.6% of the population in the relevant age group were enrolled in higher education in Malaysia.[359]

It was only after the inception of the NEP in 1971 that the State's idea of the university in Malaysia has become fully articulated, with its stress on access for the *Bumiputeras* in higher education, business and the professions, which had been dominated by the non-Malays, especially the Chinese since the colonial period. Simultaneously, however, the Malaysian State retained much of the former British colonial configuration of higher education—such as the examination system, the degree granting system, internal academic ranks, and the financial relationship between the State and institutions of higher education.

In Singapore, the postcolonial idea of the university also shifted from the British colonial heritage. The 'idea of the university' in Singapore now stresses elitist, meritocratic values in the educational selection system and the pragmatic application of knowledge in the university. The PAP government maintained the English language as the medium of university education while stressing science and technology in particular.[360]

In the contemporary decade, both NUS and NTU have developed their postgraduate education in the fields of engineering, information technology and business administration. The broad frame of these East Asian States' idea of the university has continued to reflect their colonial legacies in the process of postcolonial indigenisation as they strive to create their own endogenous concepts of the university. The following section will exemplify this theme in the struggles over institutional forms and valued knowledge.

Struggles over institutional forms and valued knowledge

It is suggested here that the newly independent States established a new independent education system, whose form was to some extent a blend of the inherited colonial model of higher educational institutions and the newly adopted foreign models—e.g. the American model in all three countries, the Japanese model in Malaysia, and the German and Swedish model in Singapore.

Colonial institutional forms and valued knowledge continued in the postcolonial period. For example, in South Korea, the independent government continued to sponsor teacher training colleges, and stressed primary education more than tertiary education, as had the Japanese colonial government. Also, the South Korean military government intended to halt the rapid expansion of higher education, as did the Japanese Governor-General during the colonial period. The form of expansion was differentiated by the public and the private division in the sectors of higher education, although the higher education system as a whole was under the direct control of the Ministry of Education, as it had been in the colonial period.

Despite its short fifty year old university history and its direct inheritance of the former Japanese colonial legacy of Kyung Sung Imperial University, Seoul National University has stood at the top of the prestige hierarchy as the first national university in South Korea since its establishment in 1947. Against the prestige of Seoul National University in the public sector, a few private universities (such as Yonsei and Ewha) have a long tradition of liberal university education from the late 19th century under American influence, and they also inherited the older Confucian culture of academic autonomy from the precolonial period.

In the postcolonial independent State's economic and manpower planning, the South Korean government has developed new research institutes such as KIST as well as expanding the enrollment capacities of university faculties and colleges of science, engineering, and technology to produce the required number of experts for the economy. Private enterprise in the business and industrial sectors has also contributed to establishing their own institutions of higher education in the fields of science and technology, among which Pohang University is the most famous.

In the case of Malaysia, the control and administration of education as a whole has become centralised in the process of indigenisation. Like the case of South Korea, uniformity is found in curricula, syllabuses and examinations in schools and colleges as prescribed by the Ministry of Education to promote national unity and meet national manpower planning targets.[361] Accordingly, new higher educational institutions have been established for the promotion of science and technology, which is tightly linked to the *Bumiputera* policy. For example, the MARA Institute of Technology (MIT) was established to enrol the *Bumiputeras* in the field of science and technology. The postcolonial period also witnessed the relatively rapid expansion of tertiary education in Malaysia. Despite the expansion of higher education, the overall demand far exceeded supply in terms of the number of places. As a consequence, a substantial number of student especially those with Chinese ethnic origins, after the beginning of the enrollment quota system, have sought educational opportunities overseas.

In Singapore, the postcolonial development of higher education is also characterised with the government's strong intervention in higher education, to meet the needs of national projects. In undergoing the processes of decolonisation and indigenisation, the PAP government has successfully transformed the higher education system from the traditional British elitist university model to a labour market-driven, structured and stratified national education and training system to produce middle and high level manpower. This pragmatic idea of the university in Singapore has developed on the principle of cost-effectiveness, as in South Korea.

The postcolonial period saw changes in the types of knowledge valued in university education, although the former colonial legacy of valued knowledge was less visible in South Korea than in Malaysia and Singapore. The language of the academic profession in South Korea was replaced by Korean immediately after Independence. Simultaneously, however, the value of English as a major means of acquiring Western knowledge intensified in university education in Korea in the postcolonial period, after the severance of the former academic authority of the Japanese language. This was partly due to American influence, although the Japanese language has, without official encouragement, revived.

In Malaysia, the English version of valued knowledge in the university survived long after political decolonisation, despite the newly independent government's promotion of 'Malayness' in education. This cultural tension over valued knowledge within the university system affected the postcolonial shaping of the academic profession. The British pattern of educational practices in Malaysia included, for example, the English-oriented content of texts still in use up until the late 1970s, and the official recognition of the Cambridge Overseas Certificate (until its abolition in 1978), the UPU—University entrance examination coordination body directly corresponded to the UCCA in the U.K., and at the postgraduate level, British and Australian medical postgraduate qualifications and British postgraduate diploma courses, especially in education. Even though the MARA Institute of Technology is an endogenous invention, as a symbol of the new post-colonial Malay cultural valuation of knowledge,[362] some of its postgraduate degrees in various fields are still granted by professional bodies in the United Kingdom.[363]

In Singapore, the PAP refined the British colonial educational legacy to suit its pragmatic ambitions to combine a new Chinese Confucian-oriented political identity. The national education system became standardised following the English-medium schooling pattern and operated through meritocratic selection mechanisms tightly controlled by the State. The colonial heritage of English-medium education was preserved in Singapore on the grounds that English is the international language and the language of modernity, of science and technology. The PAP leaders also expected benefits from the use of English, through which differences between ethnic groups in Singapore could be overcome to generate an educated middle class which could use English, as well as a new technically skilled working class with English literacy in the postcolonial era. Like Malaysia, Singapore maintained a British version of university enrollment: for instance, in the "O" and "A" levels Singapore-Cambridge Examinations for university entry.[364]

In all these East Asian countries, the practicality of knowledge for immediate use and application to meet economic needs has been stressed. Thus, in all three countries the faculties of science and technology have been prioritised in the university system on the whole. Among the three countries, the clearest pragmatic approach is offered by Singapore where teaching mathematics, science and technical subjects should be delivered in the medium of English at all educational levels, as part of both nation-building and economic modernisation.[365] In all three countries, as a correlate, there has occurred a downgrading of the humanities and liberal arts education.

Under the pressures of internationalisation and globalisation in the contemporary decade, the resurgent significance of English in Malay higher education counter-balances the Malaysian State's earlier effort to indigenise the language of academic discourse in higher education after political independence. The use of English was intensified in South Korea in the process of decolonisation from Japan, confirming a longer-term American influence on Korean academe since the late nineteenth century.

English is now being reconsidered as the principal medium of academic discourse and it is thus internationalising the university and the academic profession in South Korea, Malaysia, and Singapore. In addition to the use of English, the common strategies to meet the demands of internationalisation and globalisation in these three postcolonial East Asian countries are privatisation, corporatisation, and international academic networking, mobility and exchange. It is likely that the number of academic expatriates in the university system of these East Asian countries will increase, altering the current shape of the academic profession in the postcolonial contexts of these three East Asian countries, which is the theme of the next section.

The Changing Shape of the Postcolonial Academic Profession: South Korea, Malaysia and Singapore Compared

In the early postcolonial Independence era, the academic profession was 'nationalised' by the State-driven development of (i) new indigenous academic routes and (ii) the new indigenous (ethnic, religious, or gender-related) social criteria for State sponsorship into the academic profession. The result was a new homogeneity in the social composition of the academic professions.

In all three cases, the prestige of the former colonial university remained important in the postcolonial era, as the most significant route to the academic profession. In South Korea, the major entry point to the academic profession has been Seoul National University, which inherited the prestige of Kyung Sung Imperial University; in Malaysia and Singapore, it has been the University of Malaya and the National University of Singapore, both of which are part of the colonial heritage. In all three cases, the dominant foreign academic links have been altered, to some extent, from Japanese and British links to American links, in the postcolonial period. The American academic links and recruitment routes, as the new major foreign influence on the East Asian academic profession, reflect the international relations of these East Asian States in the postcolonial era, in which the United States has become the most significant international power.

For example, in Korea, university academic recruitment in the postcolonial era shifted from Japan to America. Those with the American higher degrees have become more privileged in university academic recruitment than those from indigenous routes as well as other foreign routes (which used to be mainly Japanese, and less significantly German). It is construed here that the high respect for the American degrees in South Korea is partly due to the short history of the Korean doctorate and the newly risen international academic currency of the American doctorate since 1945. As a consequence of the enhanced economic status of South Korea in the contemporary decade, the foreign academic routes have broadened. The number of South Korean students studying abroad in 1995-1996 was estimated as the third highest (36,231) in the world, next to China (39,613) and Japan (45,531).[366] This indicates the plausibility of a further increase in foreign educated academic personnel in universities in South Korea, as the internationalisation of higher education continues.

In Malaysia, the postcolonial academic routes have been indigenised especially after Bahasa Malaysia became the national language, and soon after, the language of the academic profession.[367] In university academic recruitment, however, preference was given to the local candidates with experience of foreign education especially in British and American institutions.

In the context of internationalisation reflected in forms of employment, rapid and significant changes were most visible in Singapore immediately after Independence. The details of employing expatriates altered after political independence, to curtail their former colonial privileges, but university staffing policy in Singapore has remained international, along with its pragmatic use of English as the language of the academic profession.

In all three cases, the social composition of academic staff in terms of nationality (or ethnicity) became more homogeneous through an influx of new local academics who were recruited to fill the vacancies left by the former colonial expatriates in the academic profession after Independence. In all three cases, the postcolonial academic profession has remained male-dominant.

In South Korea, the changes in social composition of the academic profession were mainly through the rapid expansion of higher education, which occurred immediately after political independence. The majority of those in the first generation of the postcolonial academic profession in South Korea were upgraded from secondary school teaching and lacked academic experience and advanced qualifications. However standards of formal qualifications have notably risen during the postcolonial period, e.g. on the measure that about 73% of those in the academic profession possessed a doctorate in 1997.[368] The academic profession in South Korea is male dominated.[369]

In Malaysia, the academic profession was indigenised by "positive discrimination" principles, to expand the participation of the *Bumiputeras* in the major professions, government work, and in the business and industrial sector. Female participation in the Malaysian academic profession has also been low.[370]

The changing social composition of the academic profession in Singapore was noted through the recruitment and work contracts of expatriates in the university academic profession. The proportion of female academics in the Singaporean higher education system also confirms the general pattern of a male profile of the academic profession.

In summary, the postcolonial shape of the academic profession in these three East Asian countries has been altered by rapid expansion and by specific State visions of higher education development which directly focused on the practical use of knowledge for industrialisation and on vocational and professional training, even more so than in the colonial period.

Second, the postcolonial shape of the academic profession in these three East Asian countries has been constructed through two integrative principles: homogenisation of the national, or ethnic, composition of the profession, and an increasing recognition of local doctoral degrees in academic recruitment. In all three cases, a new strong foreign influence on the entry routes to the academic profession came from the United States, as a consequence of American diplomatic and cultural policy in the postcolonial era. However, despite the new American impact on the shape of the academic profession, the favoured foreign routes to the academic profession in Malaysia and Singapore remained linked with British traditions. Among the Southeast Asian countries, Malaysia still sends the largest number of students to the U.K. for university education.

Overall, the shape of these academic professions can be described in relatively simple terms. There are certain routes into the academic profession (which change over time). There is a particular social composition of the academic profession at a given moment, though this changes over time and can be demonstrated (except in the case of contemporary Malaysia, where the Official Security Act blocks access to the official records of the ethnic composition of the academic profession). And there is an internal structuring of the academic profession which in these three cases shows the colonial origins of (and the subsequent foreign influences on) the academic profession.

Similarly the shape of the academic profession is heavily influenced by major shifts (often in the postcolonial period, expansions) in its institutional base and knowledge patterns, which are in turn affected by the political and economic concerns of a State's modernity projects, and often its international political relations.

These changing patterns have, of course, a historical dynamic linked to the shift from a colonial to a postcolonial condition. One way to interpret these shifts is to emphasise the social construction of a 'meritocratic principle'.

Thus the entry route to the academic profession reveals the social criteria as well as formal educational excellence (such as success in examinations) through which academic candidates for the university profession are selected.

The postcolonial period saw newly defined meritocratic principles shaping the academic profession. In all three cases, the State interpreted the meritocratic principle to favour academic candidates in the fields of science and technology. In South Korea, the State's definition of meritocratic principles to shape the academic profession emphasised Korean nationality, the Korean language, and particular local networks at home, with the addition of American networks. In Malaysia, meritocratic principles were framed by the emphasis on *Bumiputera* cultural identity, whereas in Singapore the emphasis was on academic training in English and cultural education in Chinese. The internal stratification of the academic profession defines not only a rejection of some foreign influences and acceptance of other foreign influences but also the shift from stratified to more open academic professions.

The next chapter, Chapter Five, will focus on the comparative dimensions of the academic profession including the continuities and the discontinuities of the Japanese and British colonial legacies in East Asia.

NOTES

1. Morris, P. and A. Sweeting, "Human Resource Development in East Asia." *Asia Pacific Journal of Education* Vol. 17, No. 11, 1997, pp. 7-26; McGinn, N. *Education and Development in Korea*, Cambridge, Mass.: Harvard University Press, 1980; Preston, P. W., *Rethinking Development : Essays on Development and Southeast Asia,* London & New York: Routledge & Kegan Paul, 1987.

2. Morris, P. and A. Sweeting. "Human Resource Development in East Asia." *Asia Pacific Journal of Education* 17, no. 11 (1997): 7-26; Ogawa, Naohiro, Gavin W. Jones, G. Jeffrey, and (eds). *Human Resources in Development along the Asia-Pacific Rim.* Singapore: Oxford University Press, 1993; Ihm, Chun-Sun. "Education, Human Resources and Development in Korea: Achievement and Challenges." In *Issues in Education in Asia and the Pacific: an International Perspective*, edited by OECD, 104-113. Paris: OECD, 1994; Ismail, M. Zawawi. "Human Resource Development: Meeting the Challenges of the Future." In *The New Wave University: A Prelude to Malaysia 2020*, edited by G. Ismail and M. Mohamed. Selangor: Pelanduk Publication, Universiti Malaysia Sarawak, 1997.

3. Anderson, B., *Imagined Communities: Reflections on the Origins and Spread of*

Nationalism, London: Verso, 1983.

4. Cole, D. C. and P. N. Lyman, Korean Development, Cambridge, Mass.: Harvard University Press, 1971.

5. Cummings, Bruce, 'The Origins and Development of the Northeast Asian Political Economy: Industrial Sectors, Product Cycles, and Political Consequences' International Organization Vol. 38, No. 1, 1984, p. 41.

6. Sakong, Il, Korea in the World Economy, Washington, D. C.: Institute for International Economics, 1993.

7. The American military government policy in Korea was epitomised as indirect rule. As a result, the number of Korean officers in the American military government organisations rapidly increased from 56 %, in 1946 to over 90 % within three years after decolonisation. In recruiting Koreans to the American military government bureaucracy, preference was given first to the Koreans with English proficiency, second, to the former Japanese bureaucrats still residing in Korea, and the Korean colonial collaborators with the former Japanese government, and third, to anti-communist political activists. (For details, see Jhin, Duck Kyu, 'A Study on the Power Structure of the Korean Political Society' Doctoral thesis. Dept. of Political Science, The Graduate School, Yonsei University, 1977; Chung, H. K. 'A Study on the Establishment of Seoul National University in Usamgik', Doctoral thesis. Department of Education, The Graduate School. Yonsei University, Seoul, 1997.)

8. The period of Syngman Rhee's regime ended in economic and political crisis, engendered by its inept and corrupt administration. The Second Republic started with a civilian government led by Chang Myon, the successor of Rhee, but was overthrown by a military coup within a year. General Park Chung Hee legitimated his military coup in 1961 by invoking national security and economic survival.

9. There was antagonism between the new political elite and traditional civilian elites. In the beginning, Korean intellectuals disapproved of the military regime. As Kim Kwang-ok notes, however, what he called "the Confucian literati group" in Korean society eventually accepted President Park as the patriarchal head of a nation perceived as a family. The traditional Confucian respect for the high position of the teacher and its particular combination with the paternalistic role of the ruler also helped to justify the authoritarian government of President Park, whose academic background was from the Japanese colonial teacher training system. Thus, many Korean Confucianists started to collaborate with the government on the grounds that the authority of the government was necessary to achieve national security and economic prosperity, although some liberal Christian intellectuals still criticised the deterioration in human rights and democracy. (For details see Kim, I. J. & Kihl, Y. W. (eds). Political Changes in South Korea, New York: Paragon House, 1988, pp. 22-43; Kim, K. S. 'From neo-mercantilism to globalism:

the changing role of the state and South Korea's economic prowess' in M. T. Berger and D. A. Borer (eds). *The Rise of East Asia: Critical Visions of the Pacific Century*, London & New York: Routledge, 1997, p. 93; Kim, Kwang-ok, 'The Reproduction of Confucian Culture in Contemporary Korea' in Tu Wei-ming (ed). *Confucian Traditions in East Asian Modernity*, Cambridge, Mass.: Harvard University Press, 1996, p. 217.)

10. The South Korean government formulated three Five-Year Economic Development Plans aimed at the structural improvement of the economy and high economic growth through export promotion, and made subsequent institutional reforms. The annual growth rate of GNP was raised to 7.8 per cent during the First Five-Year Plan period (1962-1966), and increased to 10.5 per cent in the Second Five-Year Plan (1967-1971). In spite of adverse world economic conditions in the early 1970s, rapid growth continued in South Korea during the four years of the Third Five-Year Plan (1972-1974), averaging 10.0 per cent per annum. In this period, economic development focused on the mining and manufacturing sector. (For details, see McGinn, N. et al., *Education and Development in Korea*, Cambridge, Mass., Harvard University Press, 1980, pp. 99-110.)

11. In the postcolonial period, South Korea (i.e. the Republic of Korea) has been also characterised as a "strong state", or " interventionist state". These terms capture the highly authoritarian South Korean State's power implemented through a centralised bureaucracy, which can be partly attributed to the Confucian legacy in Korean political culture. The traditional Confucian political culture in Korea has been characterised as "familism", where the fundamental framework of politics remained a communal one. This Korean Confucian political culture survived after early modernisation of the State administrative systems in the late nineteenth century, and was intensified by the Japanese colonial state. The independent Korean government of Syngman Rhee, after the first free elections in 1948, succeeded the U.S. military government, but soon reinforced authoritarian rule for the sake of national security—especially after the Korean War. (For details, see Il Sakong, op. cit.; Kim, K. S., op. cit., 1997; Hahn, Bae-ho, 'The State and Culture in Korean Development' in Hirano, K. (ed). *The State and Cultural Transformation: Perspectives from East Asia*, Tokyo & New York & Paris: United Nations University Press, 1995, pp. 232-64.)

In terms of the Confucian characteristics of the State's organisation, Korea has been described as family-oriented, or extended-family-oriented State centering around "filial piety", while Japan has been noted as a nuclear family-oriented State, based on "loyalty". In this analogy, collective group identity at the level of State administration in Korea can be compared with that in Japan. The collective tendency is strong in both countries. But in Korea, such a collective orientation is toward families, relatives, and other consanguine groups, whereas in Japan, it centers around small groups. In terms of the Confucian tradition of paternalism, Korea shares more similarity with China, where "consanguine groups" or "clans" are organised as the basis of the paternal social structure. In Japan, there is no paternal system; the field in which an individual belongs (such as one's office or the village) carries great importance since it becomes an index of belongingness to a collectivity. In Korea, social interactions and human relations structured within the Confucian paternal group are more flexible and fluid than in Japan. Initial bonds formed by the paternal consanguine relationship work in favour of one's activity and one's social status.

The use of nepotic ties in the realm of public administration in Korea appears stronger than in Japan. In both Korea and Japan, school alumni networks have a powerful effect on group-oriented social relations. The word *hakbol* (in Korean) and *gakubatsu* (in Japanese) are often used to indicate its significance. However, the word in Japan is applied more widely to a sphere of influence than in Korea where the word denotes individual educational background or social status achieved by a certain school education. Both in Korea and Japan, seniors of school/university alumni strive to recruit graduates from the same school/university to their university academic positions, government office and organisations so as to perpetuate the influence of the school alumni group. However, in Korea, there is another layer of influence in the practice of group-oriented recruitments, which is from the family clan network. The word *munbol* (literati family clan group in Korean) marks that the influence of familism and nepotism which has continued in the State systems in Korea. (For details of the Confucian legacy in the Korean political, administrative culture, see Kim, M. K. 'The Administrative Culture of Korea: A Comparison with China and Japan' in Caiden, G. E. and Kim, B. W. (eds). *A Dragon's Progress: Development Administration in Korea*, Connecticut: Kumarian Press, Inc., 1991, pp. 26-42; Hirano, K. op. cit.; Tai, Hung-chao (ed). *Confucianism and Economic Development: an Oriental Alternative?*, Washington, D.C.: The Washington Institute Press, 1989; Appelbaum, R. P. & Henderson, J. (eds)., op. cit. In the comparative literature on the State, the Korean state has often been compared to the bureaucratic authoritarian state described in G. A. O'Donnell, *Modernization and Bureaucratic-Authoritarianism in South American Politics*, Berkeley: University of California Institute for International Studies, 1973.)

12. Kim, K. S. op. cit., p. 89.

13. Bedeski, R.E., *The Transformation of South Korea: Reform and reconstitution in the Sixth Republic under Roh Tae Woo, 1987-1992*, London & New York: Routledge, 1994, p. 79.

14. Ibid.

15. Kim, K. S. op. cit., p. 97.

16. At the end of 1993, South Korea's per capita GDP was ranked 13th in the world. This growing economic importance in the global economy led South Korea successfully to join the Organization for Economic Cooperation and Development

(OECD) in 1996. (For further details of the economic growth of South Korea in the early 1990s, see Republic of Korea. "Investment in Korea: An Introduction to One of the Most Promising Investment Opportunities of the 21st Century." Seoul: The Ministry of Finance, 1994, p. 13.)

17. Ibid., pp. 81-105.

18. At the beginning of the Independence period, the Korean economy immediately after political liberation from Japan had to deal with the aftermath of the complete withdrawal of Japanese manpower which used to fill most of the managerial, professional, technical, and even some labour positions during the colonial period. According to Il Sakong, almost one-fifth of total manufacturing employment was Japanese; and the Japanese constituted over 80 per cent of technicians and engineers in Korea in 1943. (For details, see Sakong, I. op. cit., p. 2.)

19. Amsden, A. H. op. cit., 1989, Chapter 3.

20. Jones, L. P. and I. Sakong. *Government, Business, and Entrepreneurship in Economic Development: The Korean Case.* Cambridge, Mass.: Council on East Asian Studies, Harvard University Press, 1980; Amsden, A. H., *Asia's Next Giant: South Korea and Late Industrialization,* Oxford: Oxford University Press, 1989.

Table C
Annual Growth Rates in Real GNP

Government	Period	%
Park	1965-69 average 1970-74 average 1975-79 average	10.0 9.1 10.1
Transition	1980	-5.2
Chun	1981-86 average	7.3
Roh	1987-92 average	8.3
Kim	1993-94 average	5.6

Sources: Economic Planning Board and the Bank of Korea

The military *coup d'état* led by General Park Jung Hee in 1961 was a turning point in the South Korean State's rapid economic modernisation. The successful land reforms prior to industrialisation in the 1950s contributed to an equitable income distribution (by international standards) in the process of rapid industrialisation. The new economic structure designed by the military regime sponsored by the United States continued to nurture the former Japanese collaborators from colonial times. C. J. Eckert points out that the economic elites "have historically been the recipients of a cornucopia of special privileges and favours from the State". Since 1972, "the government has generally continued to provide special emergency loans to *chaebols* threatened by bankruptcy." (For details, see Eckert, C. J. 'The South Korean Bourgeoisie: A Class in Search of Hegemony' in Hagen Koo (ed). *State and Society in Contemporary Korea*, Cornell University Press, 1993, p. 126.)

21. Kim, K. S. op. cit., pp. 82-105.

22. Ibid., p. 96; For a comparative perspective on the bureaucratic authoritarian state, see O'Donnell, G. A. *Modernization and Bureaucratic-Authoritarianism in South American Politics*. Berkeley: University of California Institute for International Studies, 1973.

23. In March 1946, there was a meeting for the 'Recommendation of the United States Office of Education Regarding Educational Reconstruction in Korea', which involved 6 Korean educational experts, with advanced degrees from America, and who were spending more than three months for the mission in America. In the recommendations made through the meeting, there was a suggestion that 300 Koreans should be sent to America to train for the academic profession after return to South Korea.

Through the Program for Educational Aid from America devised during the period of the American military government (1945-1948), 100 Korean educators were initially sent to the USA for short term training; 10 American educational experts were invited to South Korea; the Educational and Informational Survey Mission to Korea with American experts was sent to Korea before the start of educational aid. Subsequently, 289 Korean students were sent to the USA for university education; 100 American teachers were invited to teacher training colleges in South Korea for one year; and library and laboratory equipment was also donated to South Korea. (For details, see Wilson, Howard E., "Education, Foreign Policy, and International Relations." In *Cultural Affairs and Foreign Relations*, edited by Columbia University The American Assembly. Englewood Cliffs, N. J.: Prentice-Hall, 1963; Requoted from Chung, Hwan-kyu. "A Study on the Establishment of Seoul National University in Usamgik.", Doctoral thesis. Dept. of Education, Graduate School, Yonsei University, 1997, pp. 36-39).

American educational aid in Korea was diverse, ranging from direct financial support, and training university administrators until the 1950s—through the International Cooperation Administration, the Agency for International Development Programme devised after the Marshall Plan in 1948, and the Point Four Program in 1949. American educational aid to South Korea included the urgent provision of English education for Koreans as well as the exchange of educational experts between South Korea and the United States. As a result, the new experts qualified through the programme started to occupy the major positions in academe and industry as well as the governments in each country which benefited from the American aid. (For details, see, Chung, H.-k., op. cit. pp. pp. 35-44.)

24. Hung-chao Tai points out the general characteristics of individuals' group identity in East Asian Confucian culture, where individuals seek identity not so much in

terms of who they are as in terms of whom they are associated with. With this group identity, individuals are supposed to uphold the interest of the group—ranging from the family to the nation—above their own. For details, see Tai, Hung-chao, 'The Oriental Alternative: An Hypothesis on Culture and Economy' in Hung-chao Tai (ed)., op. cit., 1989, p. 17.

25. The Charter of National Education:

We have been born into this land, charged with the historic mission of regenerating the nation. This is the time for us to establish a self-reliant posture within and contribute to the common prosperity of mankind without, by revitalising the illustrious spirit of our forefathers. We do hereby state the proper course to follow and set it up as the aim of our education.

With a sincere mind and strong body, improving ourselves in learning and arts, developing the innate faculty of each of us, and overcoming the existing difficulties for the rapid progress of the nation, we will cultivate our creative power and pioneer spirit. We will give the foremost consideration to public good and order, set a value on efficiency and quality, and, inheriting the tradition of mutual assistance rooted in love and respect and faithfulness, will promote the spirit of fair and warm cooperative activities, and in that national prosperity is the ground for individual growth, we will do our best to fulfil the responsibility and obligation attendant upon our freedom and right, and encourage the willingness of the people to participate and serve in building the nation.

The love of country and fellow countrymen together with the firm belief in democracy against communism is the way for our survival and the basis for realising the ideals of the free world. Looking forward to the future when we shall have the honourable fatherland unified for the everlasting good of posterity, we, as an industrious people with confidence and pride, pledge ourselves to make new history with untiring effort and collective wisdom of the whole nation.

(Source: UNESCO, *Educational Innovation in the Republic of Korea,* Paris: The UNESCO Press, 1974, pp. 18-19.)

26. Ibid., p. 19.

27. The South Korean government advanced the doctrine that as a Confucian society, South Korea did not need the Western style of confrontational labour-management relations. In 1980, the South Korean government established labour-management councils which were expected to achieve the ideal of harmony by bringing together labour representatives and management officials in a highly paternalistic context. As a consequence, by 1983, the labour unions had lost their capacity to challenge the allied forces of management and government, and union membership was down by almost 20 per cent. (For details, see Pye, Lucian. *Asian Power and Politics: The Cultural Dynamics of Authority.* Cambridge, Mass.: Harvard University Press, 1985, pp. 226-227.)

28. That is to say, communal divisions along rural-urban lines have been overlaid with occupational divisions. The Malays were overwhelmingly kampong dwellers, working as padi (rice) planters, fishermen and small rubber plantation holders, while the Chinese have generally been urban city dwellers, engaged in trade or commerce, or as workers in the tin mines. Most Indians worked in the rubber estates of the public works department, though some were teachers, clerks, lawyers and medical doctors. This clear ethnic division of labour has meant that each group came to be identified with specific economic functions, a British colonial legacy which has proved one of the most divisive rules and the base of communal tension. (For details, see Hashim, W. *Race Relations in Malaysia*. Kuala Lumpur: Heinemann, 1983, p. 62).

29. In the concept of 'the ethnic State', the force of politicised ethnicity is perceived as powerful enough to shape political outcomes independently of class structure. S. Majstorovic used Walker Connor's definition of ethnicity. In this definition, ethnicity is manifested by the dimensions of language, religion and class. (For details, see Walker Connor, 'Ethnonationalism' in Weiner and Huntington (eds). *Understanding Political Development*, Boston, Mass.: Little, Brown & Company, 1987; Walker Connor, 'Eco-or Ethno-Nationalism' *Ethnic and Racial Studies* Vol. 7, No. 3, 1984, pp. 342-359; Walker Connor, 'Nation-Building or Nation-Destroying?' *World Politics*, No. 24, 1972, pp. 319-355; Majstorovic, S. "Malaysia: The Evolution of an Ethnic State." in *The Journal of Pacific Studies,* Vol. 17, No. 1-2, December 1993, pp. 161-189. For a major discussion of the ethnohistorical antecedents of nations and states, see Smith, Anthony D., *The Ethnic Origins of Nations*, Oxford: Basil Blackwell, 1986; Benedict Anderson's influential work on national identity, *Imagined Communities: Reflections on the Origins and Spread of Nationalism*, 1991, is especially useful on how ideas and myths can drive ethno-national mobilisation.)

Although the Malaysian State's values and visions are not treated as a case of some type of 'ethnic determinism', it is accepted that the Malaysian State's political and economic modernity projects had the major theme of a new Malay-Muslim cultural and national identity in the postcolonial period. In post-independence Malaysia, the retention in power of the traditional rulers, the Sultans was linked, paradoxically, to Chinese interests. In the Malay Peninsula the hereditary rulers have become a force for maintaining the status quo and have not tampered with the rule of law and Constitution. Although the sultans were originally conceived of as champions of Malay interests and defenders of Islam as the state religion, they have acted as a moderating force after political independence, by checking Malay radicalism which might easily have induced Malay enmity toward the Chinese. The Sultans had enough economic self interest to be sympathetic toward Chinese commercial activities. Simultaneously, the conservative Chinese leaders did not want to provoke ideas of socialism in the younger and more radical Chinese, for the Malays might then decide to nationalise private industry by expropriating Chinese interests and dividing their wealth among the Malays. (For details, see Pye, Lucian. op. cit., p.

256.)

30. For a discussion of the differences between civic and ethnic nationalisms, see Safran, W. 'Ethnic Mobilization, Modernization, and Ideology: Jacobinism, Marxism, Organicism and Functionalism' in *The Journal of Ethnic Studies*, Vol.15, No. 1, 1987, pp. 1-31.

31. Ethnic relations in Malaysia have been shaped by 150 years of British colonisation and then by the subsequent difficulties of nation-state building after Independence in 1957. The term *Bumiputera* literally means 'sons of the soil' and refers to the Malays and other indigenous people of the country. In 1985, Malays comprised roughly 85 % of the *Bumiputera* population. The concept of *Bumiputeras* is a politically potent term because it represents the paramount political position of the indigenous Malays over the non-Malay population. (For details, see, Vasil, R. K., *Ethnic Politics in Malaysia*, New Delhi: Radiant Publishes, 1980.)

32. Many other postcolonial States—e.g. the Burmese, the Indonesian, and a number of African States—had significant conflict in the process of decolonisation. However, independence came to Malaysia gradually and the British members of the Malayan Civil Service (MCS) stayed even after Independence, working with Malaysian politicians in the newly independent State's political system replicating the Westminster system in Britain. (For details, see Pye, Lucian, op. cit., pp. 256-257.)

33. Esman notes that the Tengku believed "living the good life is not only a virtue in itself but that 'wining, gambling, and womanizing', horse racing, sports, and beauty contests, however offensive to intellectuals, help to keep politics in their proper pragmatic perspective." (For details, see Esman, Milton J., *Administration and Development in Malaysia*, Ithaca, N.Y.: Cornell University Press, 1972, p. 36.)

34. Pye notes his governing style: to preside at the top "by leaving technical matters to the civil servants, showing respect to the sultans, and acting as a wise man for the Malay masses, and by being friendly to the non-Malays". (Pye, Lucian. op. cit., p. 261.)

35. The ethnic riots on 13th May 1969 was taken as a 'collective symbol of the political sanctity of Malay nationalism' by the Malays. (For details, see Lee, R. L. M. "The State, Religious Nationalism and Ethnic Rationalisation in Malaysia." *Ethnic and Racial Studies* Vol. 13, No. 4, 1990, pp. 491-492. For an extensive discussion of the Malay ethnic state, see Majstorovic, S. op. cit., 1993, pp. 161-189; Majstorovic, S. "The Politics of Ethnicity and Post-Cold War Malaysia: the Dynamics of an Ethnic State." In Berger, M. T. & D. A. Borer, op. cit., 1997, pp. 147-168.)

36. For instance, the government started to favour economic and educational

opportunities for the *Bumiputeras* on the basis of the New Economic Policy (NEP) in 1971. The "positive discrimination" policy throughout the postcolonial period has been helped by the rapid and continuous economic growth which Malaysia enjoyed—in the order of 7 per cent per annum—until recently. Malaysia, *Second Malaysia Plan, 1971-75*, Kuala Lumpur: Government Press, 1971; Malaysia, *Fourth Malaysia Plan 1981-1985*, Kuala Lumpur: Government Printers, 1980.

37. After the inception of the NEP, the changes in the Malay concepts of power were significant. In 1981, Mahathir bin Mohamad became Prime Minister. The political slogan then was "Clean, Efficient, and Trustworthy". As indicated, the Malay Civil Service has the British colonial origins. The British created a highly centralised bureaucracy in the Malayan colonial government, staffed with general administrators of high professional competence. In the new government's attempt to reform the British Malayan administrative culture, the Mahathir government replaced older generalist administrators with younger technocrats. Mahathir's criticism of the traditional Malay style of easy-going administration was extended to his perception of the Malay ethnic traits as elucidated earlier in his book, *The Malay Dilemma* published in 1970. In the book, Mahathir notes that "[the Malay economic backwardness] is the result of the clash of racial traits. They are easy-going and tolerant.... [On the other hand], the Chinese especially are hard-working and astute in business. When the two came in contact, the result was inevitable." Subsequently, there developed a notion of inner ethnic friction in the process of administrative reform led by Mahathir. Some Malays criticising Mahathir argued he had gone beyond seeking equality for the Malays and was determined to "transform Malays into Chinese", which were unacceptable to those conservative Malay Muslims. (Quoted from Mohamad, Mahathir bin. *The Malay Dilemma*, Singapore: Donald Moore Asia Press, 1970, p. 85; For further comments, see Pye, Lucian W., op. cit., p. 263)

38. The series of National Plans aimed to (i) reduce and eventually eradicate poverty; (ii) restructure society to eliminate the identification of race with economic function; (iii) create a *Bumiputera* commercial and industrial community so that 30 per cent of the modern sector would by 1990 be owned and managed by it. (For details, see Majstorovic, S., op. cit., 1997, p. 158; Rudner, M. *Nationalism, Planning & Economic Modernisation in Malaysia: the Politics of Beginning Development*. Beverly Hills: Sage Publications, 1975.)

39. Malaysia, *Mid-Term Review of Second Malaysia Plan*, Kuala Lumpur: Government Printers, 1973; Malaysia, *Third Malaysia Plan 1976-1980*, Kuala Lumpur: Government Printers, 1975.

40. Prime Minister Mahathir wrote in 1970 that there was a need for the Malays to "break away from custom and to acquire new ways of thinking and a new system of values. Urbanisation will do this to a certain extent; but there must also be a conscious effort to destroy the old ways and replace them with new ideas and val-

ues." (Mohamad bin Mahathir, op. cit., 1970, p. 113.) Since he took office in 1981, Mahathir has designed a series of new ideas, policies and slogans to transform Malaysia as a modern state, by changing the national economic and cultural infrastructure. His 'Look East' policy is not restricted to simply emulating Japanese and South Korean economic development strategies but their attitudes and priorities stemming from their own cultural values.

41. Malaysia, *Fifth Malaysia Plan, 1986-1990*, Kuala Lumpur: National Printing Department, 1986.

However, there has been criticism of the prioritisation of ethnic balance in the State's industrial development plans. For instance, Steve Majstorovic points out that Malaysian developmental expenditures are in fact being used to mollify distributional ethnic demands instead of to attain developmental goals. Ethnic considerations vitiate assumptions about economic rationality. In the contemporary decade, the Malaysian State started to reduce its formerly stringent intervention on the inter-ethnic redistribution of wealth, and to consolidate further the industrialisation and growth-oriented policy reforms of the mid-1980s. (For details, see Malaysia, *Sixth Malaysia Plan, 1991-1995,* Kuala Lumpur: National Printing Department, 1991; Majstorovic, S. op. cit. 1997, p. 161; Bowie, A. 'Redistribution with Growth? The Dilemmas of State-Sponsored Economic Development in Malaysia' in C. Clark and J. Lemco (eds). *State and Development*, New York: E. J. Brill, 1988.)

42. The year 1990 was a turning point in the Malaysian modernity projects when the Malaysian government announced the end of the First Outline Perspective Plan (OPP1), 1971-90. The Malaysian Prime Minister, Mahathir Mohamad, has set the year 2020 as the target for Malaysia to attain the level of the developed nations in the world. He urges that Malaysia should be "fully developed in terms of national unity and social cohesion, in terms of our economy, in terms of social justice, political stability, system of government, quality of life, social and spiritual values, national pride and confidence." (For details, see Mahathir bin Mohamad, *Malaysia: The Way Forward*, London: Weidenfeld & Nicolson, 1998.)

43. Dato'Seri Dr. Mahathir bin Mohamad, *Vision 2020, Malaysia: Towards Establishing a Fully Developed Nation,* Malaysia, Kementerian penerangan, 1997, pp. 22-23.

The New Development Policy (NDP) signals the beginning of a new era in the effort to make Malaysia a fully developed nation by the year 2020. The objective of the NDP is "to attain a balanced development of the economy in order to establish a more united and just nation." (Malaysia, *The Second Outline Perspective Plan 1991—2000*, Kuala Lumpur: Government Press, 1991, p. v) For stable and sustained growth of the economy, the government would continue to be:

flexible and pragmatic in the implementation of its policies and programmes so as to create a favourable climate for private investment and for exports to expand, which is a fundamental requirement for the economy to move towards higher levels of industrialization. (ibid., p. vi)

In this new vision, economic restructuring is given emphasis though the Prime Minister continues to emphasise "the inculcation of the right value system" to carry out the NDP:

With the globalization of the world economy, and the rapid changes taking place in the international environment, the economy must be made more resilient to meet these challenges. Economic resilience can only be attained through higher levels of productivity and efficiency and a broad-based industrial spread...Quality and excellence must become the hallmark of our nation. These values coupled with our strong moral and spiritual values will enable Malaysia to achieve the target...towards becoming a developed nation by the year 2020. (ibid., p. vii)

44. 80 % of the Malaysian exports is reportedly made up of manufactured goods. (See Mahathir bin Mohamad, *Vision 2020, Malaysia: Towards Establishing a Fully Developed Nation,* op. cit., 1997.

45. Ibid., p. 13.

46. The Seventh Malaysia Plan 1996-2000 covers the second phase of the Second Outline Perspective Plan (OPP2), 1991-2000. OPP2 projected an increase of 30,000 engineers alone to the current stock for the period 1991-2000. Projected demands for managers and teachers were even higher. In 1989, the total R & D manpower was estimated at 5,337, or about 3.2 researchers per 10,000 population. While this may be a tenfold increase since the seventies, it is still far behind the figure of South Korea which possessed about 56,545 researchers in 1988, or 13.4 researchers per 10,000 population. Only 7 per cent of the current workforce received upper secondary and above training in 1996. Less than half of university applicants secure places in the Malaysian university system annually—10,652 or 42.2 % and 10,668 or 41.3 % in 1990 and 1991 respectively. Moreover, Malaysia has a low percentage of age-group in tertiary education, only 7 per cent . In comparison, the figures for South Korea, Japan, Germany, United States are 36 %, 28 %, 30 % 60 % respectively in 1987. To achieve 5 researchers per 10,000 population requires 6,000 researchers added to the current supply. (For details, see Mohamad, M. bin, op. cit., 1997; Ismail, M. Zawawi, 'Human Resource Development: Meeting the Challenges of the Future' in Ismail, Ghazally, and Murtedza Mohamed (eds). *The New Wave University: A Prelude to Malaysia 2020.* 2nd ed. Selangor: Pelanduk Publication, Universiti Malaysia Sarawak, 1997, p. 54; p. 67.)

47. Rudner, M. op. cit.

48. Majstorovic, S. op. cit., 1997, pp. 148-168.

Education has been perceived as crucial instrument for modernisation in several reports: for example, the Barnes Report of 1951, the Fen-Wu Report of 1951, the Razak Report of 1959, the Rahman Talib Report of 1961, as well as in the five-year development plans. (For details, see Hashim, Shafruddin, 'Muslim Society, Higher Education and Development: the case of Malaysia' in Ahmat, Sharom & Siddique, Sharon (eds). *Muslim Society, Higher Education and Development in Southeast Asia,* Singapore: Institute of Southeast Asian Studies, 1987, p. 45.)

49. Hashim, Shafruddin, op. cit., p. 45.

50. In 1970, an examination in Bahasa Malaysia was made a requirement for SPM (Sijil Pelajaran Malaysia). In 1971, the Abdul Majid bin Ismail Report (Report of the Committee Appointed by the National Operations Council to Study Campus Life of Students of the University of Malaya) proposed an ethnic quota for university admission. In 1979, the Report of the Cabinet Committee (Mahathir Report) reviewed the implementation of education policy. In 1980, the MCE examination—an English-medium examination equivalent to GCSE- was converted into SPM (Sijil Pelajaran Malaysia), which is a Malay medium-examination as the secondary school certificate. As a consequence, Malaysia saw a complete reversal of status of the Malay and English languages in education by 1982. (For details, see Hashim, Shafruddin, op. cit., p. 50; Singh, Jasbir, Sarjit & Mukherjee, Hena, *Education and National Integration in Malaysia: Stocktaking Thirty Years after Independence,* Kuala Lumpur: University of Malaya, 1990, p. 3.)

51. As defined by Muzaffar, the Islamic resurgence refers to "the endeavour to re-establish Islamic values, Islamic practices, Islamic institutions, Islamic laws, indeed Islam in its entirety, in the lives of Muslims everywhere." The Malay notion of Islamization, however, cannot be viewed as simply an expression of international Islamic influences. (Muzaffar, C. *The Islamic Resurgence in Malaysia,* Petaling Jaya: Penerbit Fajar Bakti Sdn Bhd, 1987, p. 2.)

52. Mauzy, D. K. & Milne, R. S. 'The Mahathir Administration in Malaysia: Discipline through Islam' in *Pacific Affairs,* Vol. 56, No. 3, 1983-4, p. 636.

53. *Foreign Affairs Malaysia,* At the 5th ASEAN-Japan Symposium in Kuala Lumpur, 24 August 1982, p. 228.

54. The LEP was officially set forth in a speech at the 5th Joint Annual Conference of the Malaysia-Japan and the Japan-Malaysia Economic Association in 1982. The 5th Joint Annual Conference of the Malaysia-Japan and the Japan-Malaysia Economic Associations Speech, 1 February, 1982, p. 40.

55. *New Straits Times,* 16 June, 1982.

56. The British Council. *Higher Education Market Survey Malaysia.* London: The British Council, October 1984, p. 13.

57. In the governmental system of educational administration, there are the Islamic Education Division and the Advisory Council for the Coordination of Islamic Education (Lembaga Penasihat Penyelarasan Pelajaran dan Pendidikan Agama Islam), better known as LEPAI. (For details, see Hashim, R., *Educational Dualism in Malaysia: Implications for Theory and Practice,* op. cit., 1996, pp. 70-71.)

58. Although the Look East Policy is rather elusive in its definition of various Asian values, it has epitomised the contemporary Malaysian State's intention to adopt, implicitly, East Asian Confucian values for its modernity project. This ambivalent political and cultural stance of the Malaysian government and the appeals for a better work ethic and more diligence and productivity among Malay Muslims has induced stresses into Malay society. Accordingly, there has been a subtle cultural backlash in the form of Malay Islamic resurgence during the last decade. Pye notes that "For many Malays the only alternative to becoming more "like Chinese" was to become more truly Muslim." (Pye, Lucian. op. cit., p. 264.)

59. Gopinathan, S. 'Singapore' in P. Morris and A. Sweeting (eds). *Education and Development in East Asia,* New York & London: Garland Publishing, Inc., 1995, p. 79.

60. Tremewan, C. *The Political Economy of Social Control in Singapore.* London: Macmillan Press Ltd. in association with St. Antony's College, Oxford, 1994, pp. 6-29.

On the route to political power, Lee Kuan Yew's ambition was for the bourgeois Chinese nationalists to share State power with the Malay upper class and not to engage in the anti-imperialist movement which involved most Chinese in Malaya. He intended to establish a mutual interest in defeating the anti-imperialist communist movement and in consolidating a relationship with the British.

In 1979 Lee Kuan Yew recalled:

Our primary concern was how to muster a mass following. How did a group of English- educated nationalist -graduates of British universities—with no experience of either the hurly-burly of politics or the conspiracies of revolution, move people whose many languages they did not speak and whose problems and hardships they shared only intellectually?

(Minchin, James, *No Man is an Island,* Sydney: Allen & Unwin, 1986, p. 66; Quoted in Tremewan, C. op. cit., p.l8.)

61. Shee Poon Kim, 'Political Leadership and Succession in Singapore' in Chen, Peter S. J. (ed). *Singapore Development Policies and Trends*, Singapore: Oxford University Press, 1983, pp. 173-196.

62. In retrospect, Lee Kuan Yew admitted:

Did we, an English-educated bourgeois group, with no organization, and little ability to communicate with the Chinese dialect speaking masses or the Mandarin speaking educated elite, believe we could cope with Chinese pride in Chinese language, culture, history, in a period of intense resurgence, and stand up to the MCP (Malayan Communist Party), the protege of the CCP? In all honesty, we did not think in those terms; we wanted the British out; we believed nationalism to be a more potent force than communism; we pressed on regardless of the horrendous risks because our visceral urges were stronger than our cerebral inhibitions.

(Lee Kuan Yew, *Leadership in Asian Countries*, Singapore: Ministry of Culture, September 1967, p. 5.)

63. Quah, Jon S. T., 'Singapore's model of development: is it transferable?' in Rowen, Henry S. (ed). *Behind East Asian Growth: The Political and Social Foundations of Prosperity*, London & New York: Routledge, 1998, p. 106.

Although the PAP leaders did not adopt the welfare state model, the government has provided public housing to satisfy basic needs and ultimately to achieve harmony in a multiracial, multi-religious society. In June 1976, Goh Keng Swee, then the Deputy Prime Minister and Minister of Defence, identified the negative consequences of welfare state policies: "But nothing is for free in this world and the end result of indiscriminate welfare state policies is bankruptcy". (Goh, K. S. *The Practice of Economic Growth*, Singapore: Federal Publications, 1977, p. 166.) The government feared that the State's provision of social welfare might lead to "an unhealthy dependence on the State and sap individual initiative and enterprise, thereby also undermining growth". (Lim, Linda Y. C., 'Social Welfare' in Kernial S. Sandhu and Paul Wheatley (eds). *Management of Success: The Moulding of Modern Singapore*, Singapore: Institute of Southeast Asian Studies, 1989.) The Singaporean State's policy was to reduce welfare to the minimum and restrict it to only those who are handicapped or old. The Central Provident Fund (CPF) contributed significantly to the success of the Home Ownership for the People Scheme. The provision of social welfare by the new Singaporean State relied on the Central Provident Fund (CPF), created by the colonial government in 1955 to provide social security for the working population. (For details, also see Quah, Jon S. T., op. cit. pp. 114-115.)

64. George, T. J. S. *Lee Kuan Yew's Singapore*. Singapore: Eastern University Press, 1984, p. 137; Tremewan, C. op. cit., p. 92.

65. Quah, Jon S. T., op. cit., p. 113.

66. The PAP government's emphasis on meritocracy began early. In 1959, it adopted a policy of selective retention of senior civil servants. By this policy, expatriate civil servants who were competent and due for retirement could stay on while those incompetent were retired prematurely. Efficiency as the sole criterion for retaining or retiring a senior civil servant was reinforced by de-emphasising seniority in promotions. (For details, see Quah, Jon S. T., op. cit., p. 111.)

To prevent corruption, the pay of civil servants has been repeatedly increased since political independence. A White Paper on "Competitive Salaries for Competent and Honest Government" issued in October 1994 reveals these principles. The salaries of ministers and senior civil servants are comparable to the average salaries of the top four earners in six private sector professions: accounting, banking, engineering, law, local manufacturing companies and multinational corporations. The long-term formula suggested in the White Paper ensured the building of "an efficient public service and a competent and honest political leadership". (For details, see Quah, Jon S. T., op. cit., p. 109.)

The majority of new recruits in the 1968 General Election in Singapore were formerly professionals (including university academics, architects, medical doctors, and journalists, as well as technocrats, businessmen and trade unionists. Up to the end of the 1970s, the new recruits were from professional, managerial and bureaucratic elite backgrounds. Since the 1976 General Election in particular, there has been a tendency to co-opt directly top bureaucrats as Ministers. For instance, among the five new recruits in the 1970 By Election, there were three university lecturers, one civil servant and one technician. More local born candidates were elected as political leaders of the second generation in the parliament in the 1970s and onwards whereas the majority of the 'old guard' were born abroad. In the 1976 General Election, previous occupations of the eleven new recruits vary but mainly professional, managerial and administrative sectors, for example, three of them economists, one businessman, one teacher, one political scientist, one journalist, one manager, one civil servant, two trade unionist. (For details, see She Poon Kim, op. cit.)

To guarantee the recruitment of the most talented to the Singapore Civil Service, the government has been offering attractive undergraduate scholarships to university applicants with excellent results in the Cambridge General Certificate of Education Advanced Level examination to study at the two local universities or prestigious universities abroad. After graduation, such persons should serve the SCS for a number of years. The most prestigious scholarship is the President's Scholarship; 134 President's Scholars were selected from 1966 to 1994. Thus Singaporean civil servants and politicians have been regarded among the brightest of their generation having distinguished themselves academically by winning competitive scholarships to study in England. (For details, see Quah, Jon S. T., op. cit., p. 111.)

67. Ezra Vogel describes Singaporean meritocracy as "more than a procedure for selecting talent; it creates a special awe for the top leaders and provides a basis for discrediting less meritocratic opposition almost regardless of the content of its arguments. This special awe enabled the first generation of meritocatic, impeccably honest heroes to establish what might be called a macho-meritocracy." (Vogel, Ezra, F. "A Little Dragon Tamed in Kernial S. Sandhu and Paul Wheatley (eds) *Management of Success: The Moulding of Modern Singapore,* Singapore: Institute of Southeast Asian Studies, pp. 1049-66; Requoted from Quah, Jon S. T., op. cit., p. 112.)

68. In October 1988 First Deputy Prime Minister Goh Chok Tong (who succeeded Lee Kuan Yew as Prime Minister in November 1990) suggested developing a "national ideology" to evolve and anchor a Singaporean identity embracing all different races and faiths in the country. (For details, see Kuo, Eddie C. Y. 'Confucianism as Political Discourse in Singapore: The Case of an Incomplete Revitalization Movement' in Tu Wei-Ming (ed). *Confucian Traditions in East Asian Modernity: Moral Education and Economic Culture in Japan and the Four Mini-Dragons* Cambridge, Mass. & London, England: Harvard University Press, 1996, p. 308.)

69. Islam and Hinduism are the dominant religions of the Malays and Indians in Singapore. In 1980, Muslims and Hindus comprised 16 per cent and 4 per cent of the population respectively. Virtually all Malays (99.4 per cent) are Muslims, but some 10 per cent of Muslims are of Indian and other non-Malay origin. Hinduism represents the religion of the Indians, who comprise 6.4 per cent of the Singaporean population. (For details, see *Singapore 1983,* Singapore: Ministry of Communication and Information, 1983.)

70. Tremewan, C. op. cit., pp. 118-119.

71. Ibid.

72. Ibid.

73. This was a reversal of the earlier position supported by Goh Seng Kwee that Confucianism as a political ideology must be distinguished from Confucianism as an ethical system to be promoted as the basis for moral growth and the building of character. As noted by Eddie C. Y. Kuo, the reinterpretation of Confucianism in Singapore has been officially completed, its relevance redefined in the contemporary decade. (*The Straits Times,* 16 January 1991, Quoted in Tremewan, C. op. cit., p. 146.)

74. The 1959 Annual Report states that "the economy of the State can no longer

be sustained by entrepôt trade alone. In the re-orientation of the economic policy of the State, industrialisation is vital". Ministry of Education (MOE). *The Annual Report 1959*. Singapore: Government Printing Office, 1961, p. 1.

75. Lim, C.-Y. *Education and National Development*. Singapore: Federal Publications, 1983, p. 37.

76. Gopinathan, S. 'Singapore' in Morris, P. and A. Sweeting (eds). *Education and Development in East Asia*, New York & London: Garland Publishing, Inc., 1995, p. 81.

77. World Bank, *The East Asian Miracle: Economic Growth and Public Policy*, New York: Oxford University Press, 1993.

78. Quah, J. S. T. op. cit., p. 105.

79. The Economic Planning Committee, *The Strategic Economic Plan: Towards a Developed Nation*, Singapore: Ministry of Trade and Industry, 1991, p. 2.

80. However, this system of educational sorting for maximising human resources has become clogged by its own mechanism of selection. By 1978, it had already become evident that except for the highly selected small elite, the rest of the participants in the educational process were failing. In 1979, an Educational Study Team chaired by Deputy Prime Minister Goh Keng Swee presented a Report focused on 'educational wastage': failure to achieve expected standards and premature school-leaving. The problem was found at both ends of the educational spectrum. The academic-stream students after graduation often had not achieved the high educational standard expected and, similarly the students in vocational and technical education were still insufficiently skilled, linguistically (in English) and technically, to meet the changing demands of industrialisation. In this situation, the Singaporean State's economic project was not maximising its major resource, people. (For details, see Seah, C. M., and L. Seah. 'Education Reform and National Integration' in Chen, P. S. J. (ed). *Singapore Development Policies and Trends*. Singapore: Oxford University Press, 1983, p. 250.)

The selection process of universal examinations ensured that the Chinese working class and other ethnic minorities were denied significant opportunities for upward social mobility, thus remaining available for training as wage labour.

Also, as noted by Tham, the education system was discriminating against students outside the English-medium background, i.e. those from Chinese working class or ethnic minority backgrounds. The ideology of meritocracy in educational practices and its sorting function had maximised the advantages of the wealth and linguistic heritage of the upper class while simultaneously reproducing a skilled, docile middle class in Singapore. While the meritocratic education system has reproduced the Chinese working class, the geopolitically marginalised Malay underclass has been excluded even from the core of the working class. (For details, see Tham, S. C. 'The

Perception and Practice of Education' in Sandhu, K. S. and Wheatley, P. (eds). *Management of Success: The Moulding of Modern Singapore*, Singapore: Institute of Southeast Asian Studies, 1989, pp. 477-502; Tremewan, C. op. cit.,pp. 132-151.)

81. Only 71 per cent of pupils passed the Primary School Leaving Examination according to a 1978 government report. Of these only 35 per cent completed secondary school while the remaining 36 per cent failed or dropped out. Thus, 65 per cent of primary school entrants did not successfully complete secondary education. Among the 35 per cent who completed secondary education, only 15 per cent entered pre-university level and only 9 per cent then went on to tertiary study—four per cent to university, five per cent to polytechnic or teachers' college. (For details, see Gopinathan, S. 'Towards a National Education System' in Hasan, R. (ed). *Singapore: Society in Transition*, Kuala Lumpur: Oxford University Press, 1976, p. 75.)

82. Rodan, G. *The Political Economy of Singapore's Industrialization: National State and International Capital*. Kuala Lumpur: Forum Enterprise, 1991, p. 149.

83. Tremewan, C., op. cit., p. 105.

84. As noted by Tremewan, the legitimation of the results of educational sorting by meritocratic ideology has been consummated by an ideology of multiracialism which features Malay failure as an unavoidable by-product in achieving the common good. (ibid.)

85. Lim, C. 'The Role of English in the Development of a National Identity in a Multilingual Setting: the Singapore Dilemma' paper presented at The International Conference on Language Learning: Theory into Practice, Kuala Lumpur, 1989, p. 1.

86. However, Benjamin suggests that the most significant legacy of British colonial rule may have been not so much the institutionalisation of the English language as the institutionalisation of the notion of race. Singapore's multiracial national ideology insists that each person must belong to one of four races—i.e. Chinese, Malay, Indian (Tamil) and Eurasian. These categories are marked on each Singaporean's identity card. With this racial identity come both a culture and a language, inherited through the paternal side. Benjamin argues that there are a number of consequences of this form of multiracialism, as race becomes the principal division of culture in Singapore. (Benjamin, G. 'The Cultural Logic of Singapore's "Multiracialism"' in Hassan, R. (ed) op. cit., 1976.)

Similarly, J. Clammer argues that the Singapore ideology is "to a great extent bound up with *classifying* things, people, events, attitudes and relationships and that this pervasive classificatory activity is closely bound up with strong feelings for the necessity of *order*: tidiness, the fear of 'social pollution', and that this ideology is expressed symbolically through conservative dress, short hair, anti-litter campaigns, the language policy, urban renewal (intolerance of villages and other 'untidy' zones in the city) and the self-image of the 'rugged society.'" (For details, see Clammer, J. *Singapore: ideology, society, culture.* Singapore: Chopmen Publishers, 1985, p. 165.)

However, Chua Beng-Hua and Kuo suggest that the promotion of a disciplined workforce was given precedence over the promotion of ethnic culture from the outset of independence and that the principle has remained in place. (Beng-Huat, C., and E. Kuo. 'The Making of a New Nation: Cultural Construction and National Identity in Singapore' paper presented at the Cultural Policy and National Identity Workshop East-West Center, Honolulu, Hawaii, 1990, p. 7.)

Thus, the disciplining, classifying and standardising effects of a pragmatic culture have been closely entwined with meritocracy in Singapore. After legalising abortion and sterilisation in 1970, the then Prime Minister Lee Kuan Yew gave a speech to argue that intelligence was genetically based and determined by socioeconomic level, children of professionals and executives having higher IQs than those of manual workers. (*The Mirror,* 5 January 1970. Cited by Pennycook, A. *The Cultural Politics of English as an International Language.* London & New York: Longman, 1994, p. 244.)

Lee Kuan Yew intended to correct a general tendency that those in the low socioeconomic class often have larger families, which can leave "our society with a number of the physically, intellectually and culturally anaemic" by organised family planning at the national level. The government set up the Social Development Unit (SDU) to match couples of similar educational backgrounds. The government gave priority to women who had graduated from university in enlisting their children in the primary school of their choice, and women of lower educational achievements were given a cash grant of S$10,000 to dissuade them from having more than two children. (ibid.)

87. As noted by Alastair Pennycook, the overall cultural project of Singapore has revealed a strong tendency towards defining boundaries and maintaining conformity, leading in turn to a tendency towards dichotomising e.g. East/West; Chinese-educated/English-educated, etc. The bilingual structure of Singapore society has supported the divisions between the East and the West, and between culture and technology, by using English for instruction in science, mathematics and technological subjects, and the mother tongues for civics, humanities, and the like. (Pennycook, A., op. cit., pp. 238-240.)

88. Education Minister Dr. Tony Tan quoted in *The Sunday Times,* 10 March 1991, Cited by Pennycook, A., op. cit., p. 222.

89. Tremewan, C., op. cit., pp. 90-91.

90. Clammer, J., op. cit., 1985, p. 168.

91. Within this cultural project, Malay alienation and resentment has continued to remain at a high level. Tremewan notes that "The British pre-War communalist strategy of building links with the Malay aristocracy in Malaya and largely ignoring the welfare of Chinese migrant labour in Singapore had to change when confronted with the popular surge towards self-government. The separation of Singapore from its Malayan hinterland and emphasising its special character as a predominantly Chinese-city state was an important part of the British strategy to keep Singapore as a separate strategic colony.... The British worked to consolidate pro-British forces and to minimise the contradiction between them so that the suppression could be effected over the long term after the end of direct colonial rule. The colonial state therefore wished to take control of the Chinese education system in order to remove a major institutional base for Chinese ideological formation and anti-colonial mobilisation." (Tremewan, C., op. cit., pp. 76-77.)

Furthermore, the State's process of building a new nation, centered on the new English-speaking Singaporean Chinese culture, produced unexpected contradictions. For instance, the use of English in education for the middle class Singaporean Chinese has opened access to liberal democratic ideas and to the international media. In the already highly centralised system of social control in Singapore, signs of social dissent started to appear in the 1980s. Western liberal democracy developed out of the liberal state and capitalist society. The type of liberal democracy was bequeathed to Singapore by British colonialism. In the process of decolonisation and subsequent Singapore's political independence, the English-educated elite led by Lee Kuan Yew gained political power through an alliance with the British. Its main opposition was the anti-colonial mass movement of the lower classes with which it initially made an accommodation. (For details, see Tremewan, C., op. cit., pp. 176-186.)

Lee Kuan Yew's Confucian, authoritarian approach to politics has alienated some university academics in the humanities and social sciences, who have complained about their government (much as Chinese intellectuals in Malaysia complain about theirs). (For the details of the authoritarian dimensions of the Singaporean State, see George, T. J. S. op. cit., Chapt. 6 & 7.)

92. Korean Council for University Education, *Study and Life in Korea: Korean Universities and Colleges*, Seoul: KCUE, 1998, p, 116.

93. Pye argues that the rather shrill advocacy of a purified form of Islam in Malaysia seems to be a kind of compensation for difficulties in competing with non-Malays in secular pursuits. (For details, see Pye, Lucian W., op. cit., pp. 264-265.)

94. In Singapore, there was a deliberate governmental policy to develop a 'nation-

al ideology' through the schooling system. The rationale behind this policy was that academic 'knowledge' would lend legitimacy to the government's attempt to inscribe 'Confucianism' as the essential 'nature/truth' of the Chinese. This 'truth' was to be revitalised through the school curriculum. The government provided resources to advance the investigation and accumulation of knowledge of Confucianism. In 1979, the Prime Minister Lee Kuan Yew's response was that in educating Singaporeans, "Confucianist ethics, Malay traditions and the Hindu ethos must be combined with sceptical Western methods of scientific inquiry, the open discursive methods in the search for truth; more specifically, students 'must be made to place group interests above individual interests" (*The Straits Times*, 15 March, 1979) "Indicative of the absence of Confucian tradition in Singapore, overseas scholars, primarily expatriate Taiwanese scholars in the U.S., were engaged to develop teaching materials and to extend Confucian teachings to the entire Chinese population through public lectures. A well endowed Institute of East Asian Philosophy was established to bring the best in the tradition to conferences and research". (Chua Beng Huat, 'Culture, Multiracialism and National Identity in Singapore' Department of Sociology Working Papers' No. 125, 1995, p. 19).
However, a new strategy to create a national ideology, the so-called 'Asianisation', was set up in the 1990s. By virtue of its multi-ethnic populations composed of Chinese, Malays and Indians, Singapore is presenting its national image as the inheritor of three major Asian traditions of Chinese/Confucian, Malay/Islamic, and Indian/Hindu-Buddhist. For further details, see Chua Beng Huat, op. cit.

95. OECD. *Liberalisation of Trade in Professional Services*. Paris: OECD, 1995; OECD. *Internationalisation of Higher Education*. Paris: OECD, 1996.

96. Lee, Molly N. N. 'Corporatization and Privatization of Malaysian Higher Education' in *International Higher Education, The Boston College Center for International Higher Education* No. 10, Winter 1998, p. 8.

97. Mason, E.S., Kim, M.J., Kim, K.S. and Cole, D.C., *The Economic and Social Modernization of the Republic of Korea*, Cambridge, Mass., Harvard University Press, 1980, p. 344.

98. Ibid.

99. Ibid., p. 345.

100. Selth, A. *The Development of Public Education in the Republic of Korea: an Australian Perspective*. Edited by Don McMillen. 46 vols, *Australia Asia Papers*. Nathan: Centre for the Study of Australian-Asian Relations, Griffith University, 1988, p. 11.

101. According to a Ministry report, "since 1945 higher education in Korea has mushroomed..., the Presidential Decree was quite timely". (Quoted from Ministry

of Education, *Education in* Korea, 1970, Seoul: the Government Press, 1971, p. 21.)

102. Snodgrass, Donald R., 'Education in Korea and Malaya' in Rowen, H. S. (ed)., op. cit., p. 170.

103. KCUE, op. cit., 1998, p. 36; Snodgrass, D. R., op. cit., p. 171.

104. Ihm, Chun-Sun, 'Education, Human Resources and Development in Korea: Achievement and Challenges' in OECD, *Issues in Education in Asia and the Pacific: an International Perspective,* Proceedings of a Conference in Hiroshima, Paris: OECD, 1994, P. 104.

105. Jayasuriya, J. E. *Education in Korea: A Third World Success Story.* Seoul: Korean National Commission for UNESCO, 1983, p. 86.

106. Ministry of Education, *Education in Korea 1970,* Seoul: The Government Press, 1971, p. 24.

107. Ministry of Education, *Education in Korea 1971,* op. cit., 1972, p. 21.

108. KCU E, op. cit., 1990, pp. 37-39.

109. Selth, A. op. cit., p. 10.

110. Ryee, J. C., 'Republic of Korea' in Uchida, T. (ed). *Political Science in Asia and the Pacific: Status Reports on Teaching and Research in Ten Countries,* Bangkok: UNESCO Regional Office for Education in Asia and the Pacific, 1984, p. 59.

In 1971, the Ministry of Education began to review higher education. The Bureau of Higher Education within the Ministry of Education and the 38 member Higher Education Committee of the Educational Policy Council in the Ministry of Education worked together on the overall direction of higher educational reforms. The Higher Education Committee of the Ministry of Education was chaired by Dr. Joong-hwi Kwon, former President of Seoul National University. Other members were drawn from administrators and faculties in higher education institutions throughout the country, members of the National Assembly, and editors of leading newspapers. The University Council and the Board of Trustees for national higher education played a role in making a balance between governmental control and university autonomy in South Korea in the 1970s. (For details, see UNESCO, op. cit., 1974, p. 24.)

111. KCUE, op. cit., p. 43.

112. In the Table below, the relatively limited expansion of the public sector is indicated by the rate of enrollment in the public higher educational institutions in the

period 1965 to 1975:

Table D
Percentage of Students in the Public Sector

Types of Institutions	1965	1970	1975
Junior College	3.2	0	0
Junior Technical	55.0	50.0	32.0
Junior Teaching	100.0	100.0	100.0
College and University	27.4	24.6	27.2
Graduate School	42.9	39.1	30.5

Source: Ministry of Education, Statistical Yearbooks of Education 1965, 1970, 1975.
McGinn et al., op. cit., p. 8.

113. As an inter-institutional organisation, the KCUE is composed of the Presidents of 125 colleges and universities in South Korea. The Council conducts independent research for the development of college and university education in the country, including evaluation of the management of academic affairs, exchange programmes of academic staff and the flow of information among institutions. (KCUE, op. cit. 1990, p. i; 54.)

114. Ministry of Education, Republic of Korea, *Education in Korea 1997-1998*, Seoul: The Government Press, 1998, p. 42.

115. The chairman and members of the Commission are the Prime Minister and Ministers of government departments related to education including the Ministry of Education and academic specialists in education. There were 15 university academics among the total 25 members who served during the first term (1994-96). Overall, the Commission consists of 25 members. On 5 September 1994, the Commission advised the President on 11 education reform proposals for the expansion of educational finance, the inducement of international competitiveness in university education, and an increase of autonomy and accountability in the private sector. (For details, see The Presidential Commission on Education Reform. *Education Reform for the 21st Century—To Ensure Leadership in the Information and Globalization Era*, PCER Report. Seoul, The Republic of Korea, Nov. 1997.)

The involvement of university academics in the governmental decision making process has been common in Korea. In this centralised university system under direct government supervision, the postcolonial period saw a collaborative relationship between the government officials and the university academic profession in South Korea. For instance, under the Park regime (1961-1979), some political scientists left the academic profession to occupy high positions in the government and seats in the National Congress between 1973 and 1979 and some political scientists in the academic profession were appointed to positions in the Blue House, as special assistants, counsellors to the President, etc.. (For details, see Ryee, J.C., 'Republic of Korea', in Uchida, T. (ed). op. cit., p. 59)

The active link between academia and the political arena in South Korea is reminiscent of the role of the Confucian scholar mandarin reviewed earlier in Chapter Two.

116. According to statistical sources by the Ministry of Education, there were about 74,280 applicants who failed to be admitted to Korean colleges in 1970. This figure had increased to almost 300,000 in 1980.

117. KCUE, op. cit., 1990, pp. 40-41.

118. Ihm, C. S. op. cit.,1994, pp. 106-107.

119. Adams, D. & Gottlieb, E. E., *Education and Social Change in Korea*, New York & London: Garland Publishing Inc. 1993, pp. 65-66. The following Table shows the increasing enrollment rates of higher educational institution between 1970 and 1996.

Table E
Changes in Enrollment Rates in Higher Educational Institution by Year

Year	Enrollment Rates of Higher Education Institution
1975	9.7
1980	17.0
1985	37.2
1990	37.4
1995	57.9
1996	61.8

Source: *Korean Education Indicators 1996*, Seoul: KEDI,1996, p. 32.

The Table below also shows the rapid expansion of higher education in South Korea in the postcolonial period.

Table F
Expansion of Higher Education, 1945-1997

Year\ Classification	1945	1960	1970	1980	1990	1997
Schools	19	85	232	357	556	950
Index	100	450	1,220	1,879	2,926	5,000
Academic Staff	1,490	3,808	10,435	20,900	41,920	69,157
Index	100	260	700	1,400	2,813	4,641
Students	7,819	101,041	201,436	615,452	1,490,809	2,792,410
Index	100	1,290	2,586	7,871	19,066	35,713

Source: *Education in Korea 1997-1998,*op. cit., p. 32.

As indicated in both Tables, the governmental effort to control the expansion of higher education in the long term was unsuccessful due to its inconsistent policy direction and also to the public demand for higher education.

120. Ministry of Education. *Education in Korea 1997-1998*. Seoul: Ministry of Education, Republic of Korea, 1998, p. 68.

Table G
Students per Teacher in Higher Educational Institutions

Classification	Junior College			College & University		
	Total Private	National	Public	Total Private	National	Public
1975	20.1	15.2	25.3	20.7	16.4	23.0
1980	28.9	20.0	32.7	27.9	25.2	29.1
1985	37.8	23.9	40.2	35.4	29.1	38.6
1990	43.9	28.1	46.2	31.0	24.5	34.2
1995	54.9	35.7	56.1	26.3	23.4	27.5
1996	55.8	37.9	56.8	26.1	23.6	27.0

Source: *Korean Educational Indicators 1996*, Seoul: KEDI, 1996 p. 45.

121.There has been a regular international comparison to reveal relatively poor academic conditions in Korea in comparison with the industrialised countries. The annual international comparison of academic condition by UNESCO often focuses on the weakness of Korean academic provisions compared with those industrialised countries, in terms of for instance a high student and staff ratio, many hours of teaching, a limited number of university library books per head of the academic population, physical facilities, and percentage of GDP allocated to higher education. (For details, see McGinn, N. (ed). *Education and Development in Korea.* Cambridge, Mass.: Harvard University Press, 1980; Mason, E.S., Kim, M.J., Kim,

K.S. and Cole, D.C. op. cit.)

The Ministry of Education wanted to raise the quality of higher education through improving working conditions and enhancing the quality of academic staff. As the government plans to reduce the present number of students per academic to 20 by the year 2000, the number of academics in the institutions of higher education has been expected to increase. (Ministry of Education. *Education in Korea 1997-1998.* op. cit., pp. 69-70.)

122. Despite the highly centralised higher education system under the direct control of the Ministry of Education, the financial resources of higher education in South Korea come from students' tuition fees, especially in the case of private institutions. As indicated in the Table below, the percentage of higher education finance borne by the government was only 13.3 per cent in 1985. Endowments are less than 1 per cent of the total revenue of higher education in South Korea.

Table H
Revenues of Higher Education Institutions (1985)

Classification	Total (%)	National & Public (%)	Private (%)
Total	1,439 (100.0)	392 (100.0)	1,047 (100.0)
Tuition & Fees	1,055 (73.4)	194 (49.6)	861 (82.3)
Government Aid	191 (13.3)	181(46.1)	11 (1.0)
Grants & Research Contracts	58 (4.0)	-	58 (5.5)
Endowments	12 (0.8)	-	12 (1.1)
Fees & Income	10 (0.7)	0.1 (0.0)	10 (1.0)
Other Income	112 (7.8)	17 (4.3)	96 (9.1)

Sources: KCUE, op. cit., p. 68.

The vast discrepancy between the public and private sectors is determined by the proportion of government aid in budgets, as shown in the Table above. (For details, see KCUE, op. cit., pp. 67-68.)

Institutions in the public sector of higher education take 46 per cent of their budgets from government aid whereas those in the private sector receive nominal amounts of government aid—1 percent of the total budget. In the expansion of higher education, the South Korean case was different from the conventional model of higher education development which in general requires public funding arranged by the State. The cost-effectiveness of Korean (higher) education has been high. Korean families have had to carry most of the financial load, paying fees even in public institutions and relying heavily on the private sector, when the government was slow to expand the capacity of the public educational institutions as discussed above. In that sense, private education in Korea has played a major role historically in the development of higher education—let alone primary and secondary education. (In the 1880s western educational influences were initiated by Protestant and Catholic missionaries in Korea. Prior to that time, private education was fostered by influences from Confucian and Buddhist sects and philosophers. The tradition of private education remained as a counterbalance to the control of education during the Japanese colonial period. (For details, see Mason, E.S., Kim, M.J., Kim, K.S. and Cole, D.C., op. cit., p. 361.)

123. Bedeski, R.E. op. cit., 1994, p. 109.

124. KCUE, op. cit., p. 80.

125. Ministry of Education, *Education in Korea 1989-1990.* op. cit., p. 114.

126. Ibid., p. 112.

127. Kim, T., 'The evaluation of the higher education system in the Republic of Korea' in Cowen, R. (ed). *The Evaluation of Higher Education Systems, World Yearbook of Education 1996,* London: Kogan Page, 1996, pp. 119-121.

128. Ibid.

129. Cowen, R. (ed). op. cit., 1996.

130. Gannon, P. J., *The Republic of Korea: A Study of the Educational System of the Republic of Korea and a Guide to the Academic Placement of Students in Educational Institutions of the United States,* American Association of Collegiate Registrars and Admissions Officers, 1985, pp. 6-11.

131. Yonsei University, *The 100 -Year History of Yonsei University 1885-1985,* Vol. I, op. cit., 1985.

132. KCUE, op. cit.,1990, p. 35.

The institutions included colleges and universities offering four year programmes leading to a bachelor's degree. Medicine and dentistry are six-year programmes. To be considered a university, an institution must have three or more colleges. Colleges and universities may have graduate programmes. Teachers' Colleges are all national institutions with a four-year programme for training primary and secondary teachers leading to a bachelor's degree. National primary teacher colleges were formerly junior colleges. Graduate Schools within Colleges and Universities offer a two year programme for Master's Degree and a three- or-more-year programme for the Ph.D.. Junior Vocational Colleges offer two-year vocational/technical programmes and three-year nursing programmes. The Korea Correspondence University delivers curriculum via radio and TV, and correspondence education leading to a bachelor's degree mainly for adult working students. The Open College offers two year technical and commerce programmes leading to a diploma and four year technical or commerce programmes leading to a bachelor's degree. 'Miscellaneous Schools' are regarded as post secondary level educational institutions, and they are predominantly theological seminaries in South Korea. The diplomas issued by these schools, however, are not recognised by the Ministry of Education as bachelor degrees. (For details, see Gannon, P. J., op. pp. 6-9.)

133. "As the largest research organization in the Far East, KIST is dedicated to national development and the advancement of science and technology through the conduct and encouragement of scientific research and development." (Quoted from Ministry of Culture and Information, *A Handbook of Korea,* Third Edition, Seoul: the Government Press, 1979, p. 647.)

134. The government placed major emphasis on a two year Master of Science programme in engineering and applied science as a high priority for Korean industry. A doctor of science degree was also instituted in the KIST "to prepare individuals to do research and advanced development in Korean industry and in government institutes." (Park, Joseph D., 'The Why of 'KAIS' in Korean Education' in Park, Tae Sun (ed). *Innovation in Higher Education,* Seoul, 1972, pp. 140-141.)

135. Ibid., p. 140.

136. Ibid.

137. Adams, D. & Gottlieb, E.E. op. cit., pp. 133-7; 140-1.

138. In August 1948, there was established the Teacher Training Centre within the Medical College in Seoul National University. In February 1946, the American Language Institute was established by the Bureau of Cultural Affairs in the American military government and soon transferred to the Bureau of Education in October 1946. For details, see Kim, Sung Hack. *'Mikookei Daehan Kyoyook Wonjo-e kwanhan Kyoyook Sawhoijuck Yonkoo'* [Research on the American Educational Aid to South Korea: an educational sociological approach]." Doctoral thesis. Graduate School, Yonsei University, Seoul, 1988.

139. Adams, D. 'Problems of Reconstruction in Korean Education' in *Comparative Education Review* Vol. 3, 1959-60, p. 27.

For instance, American behavioural political science, Keynesian economics, and Theodore Schultz's human capital theories became a major part of the knowledge profile in political science and the study of economics in South Korea. In the 1980s, however, criticism by Korean academics became notable in the fields of social sciences with the charge that Korea had simply exchanged masters. (For details, see Kim, In Whoe, *Hankook Kyoyook-eyu Yerksa-wa Moonje* (History of Korean Education and its problem), Seoul: Moon-eum Sa, 1993; Gil San Lee, *Ideological Context of American Educational Policy in Occupied Korea, 1945-1948,* Doctoral dissertation, University of Illinois, 1989, p. 12, Quoted by Weinberg, M. op. cit., p. 85.)

140. For instance, in examining legal education in Korea in 1967, Jay Murphy notes that the post-war young generation of university academics in the legal field often found it almost "indispensable to read Japanese literature since there was so little Korean literature on Law, and since the legacy of Japanese legal studies was so important for the present day Korean academics of law". (For details, see Murphy, J., *Legal Education in a Developing Nation*, Seoul & New York: Seoul National University Press & Oceana Publications, Inc., 1967, p. 65.)

141. Eckert, C. J. et. al. op. cit., 1990, p. 392.

142. Kim, Y. C., *Educational Contribution to the Economic Development in Korea*, Seoul: Korean Educational Development Institute, 1986.

143. The government's promotion of scientific knowledge in academe starts before the tertiary level. For example, by 1997, the government has set up 15 Science High Schools where youngsters with scientific talent are admitted and then can be selected, two years after study, to enter the bachelor's programme at the Korea Advanced Institute for Science and Technology. (For details, see *Education in Korea 1997-1998*. op. cit., p. 66.)

144. Ministry of Education, *Education in Korea 1997-1998*. op. cit., p. 71.

145. Selth, A. op. cit., p. 11.

146. The overall education policy of the postcolonial period was first set out in two reports—*the Report of the Education Committee* (the Razak Report) and *the Report of the Education Review Committee* (the Rahman Talib Report). The Razak Report attempted to set up a national education system acceptable to the various ethnic groups, having regard to the intention of making Bahasa Malaysia the national language of the country. (Aziz, U. A., S. B. Chew, K. H. Lee, and B. C. Sanyal. *University Education and Employment in Malaysia*. op. cit., 1987, pp. 76-77; Malaya, *Report of the Education Committee*, Kuala Lumpur: Government Printer, 1956.)

147. Hashim, Shafruddin, op. cit., 1987, p. 47.

148. Malaysia, *Report of the Higher Education Committee*, Kuala Lumpur: Government Printer, 1967.

149. Ibid.

150. Malaysia, *Report of the Committee appointed by the National Operations*

Council to Study Campus Life of Students in the University of Malaya, Kuala Lumpur: Government Press, 1971, pp. 44-45.

151. Hashim,Shafruddin, op. cit., p. 51.

152. Ibid.

153. Ibid.

154. Ibid.

155. Mukherjee, H. and J. S. Singh, op. cit., 1995, p. 169.

156. Omar, Elyas, 'Policy Analysis and Development in Malaysia' in Colloquium on Policy Analysis and Development, Kuala Lumpur: Asian Centre for Development Administration, 25-28 November 1974, p. 15.

157. Phillips, J. A., 'Staff and Faculty Development in the University of Malaya' in Staff and Faculty Development in Southeast Asian Universities, Hong Kong: Maruzen Investment Ltd., 1981, p. 6.

158. Ibid.

159. Ibid., p. 5.

160. Mukherjee, H., and J. S. Singh, op. cit., 1995, p. 169.

161. Singh, J. S., 'Education and Society Equity in Peninsular Malaysia' in EDC Occasional Papers, No.3, London: Department of Education in Developing Countries, University of London, Institute of Education, 1982; Mohamad, M. bin. The Malay Dilemma, op. cit.; Rudner, M., 'Education, Development and Change in Malaysia' in South East Asian Studies, Vol. 15, no. 1, 1977, pp. 23-62.

162. Loh Kok Wah, 'The Socio-Economic Basis of Ethnic Consciousness: The Chinese in the 1970s' in S. H. Ali, Ethnicity, Class and Development: Malaysia, Kuala Lumpur: Persatuaan Sains Social Malaysia, 1984, p. 99.

163. Reid, L. J. "The Politics of Education in Malaysia." Monograph Series, University of Tasmania, 1988, pp. 70-71.

164. Enloe, Cynthis H., 'Issues and Integration in Malaysia' in Pacific Affairs, 51, 1968, p. 374.

165. According to Amir Awang, Malaysia has not yet developed sufficient sophistication to permit total freedom and autonomy of the academic profession com-

pared to the Western countries. (For details, see Awang, Amir, 'Staff and Faculty Development in the Universiti Sains Malaysia' in *Staff and Faculty Development in Southeast Asian Universities,* op. cit., 1981, p. 59.)

166. Ibid., p. 62.

167. Accordingly, university education has received an increasingly larger share of the total educational expenditure. The expenditure on university education increased from 7.1 per cent in 1970 to 15. 9 per cent in 1975. In 1985, the total educational expenditure comprised 6.2 per cent of the country's GNP and university education absorbed about 15.6 per cent of the total educational expenditure. (For details, see Aziz, U. A., S. B. Chew, K. H. Lee, and B. C. Sanyal, op. cit., 1987, p. 101.)

168. Considering the university as the valued producer of high-level manpower and the principal mechanism for enabling *Bumiputeras* to move upward in the socio-economic stratification system, the Malaysian State has increased its investment in the university system. Expenditure on higher education has grown relative to other sectors of education in the Independence period. During the period of the Second Malaysia Plan (1971-75), university development expenditure accounted for 14.0 per cent of the total development expenditure on education. During the Third Malaysia Plan Period (1976-80), its share rose to 25.3 per cent. During the Fourth Malaysia Plan Period (1981-85), it accounted for 22. 4 per cent. In 1985, Malaysia was spending 6. 9 per cent of its GNP on education overall, with 15. 6 per cent of it disbursed to higher education. (For details, see Mukherjee, H., and J. S. Singh. 'Malaysia' in: *Education and Development in East Asia,* op. cit., 1995, p. 168; Aziz, U. A., S. B. Chew, K. H. Lee, and B. C. Sanyal, op. cit., p. 103)

The 1975 amendment to the Universities and University Colleges Act of 1971 provided for more personnel from government departments to serve as members of university governing bodies. The amendment was made to ensure that the universities were conforming to the State's projects and to coordinate the decisions of the universities. Given that over 90 per cent of the Universities' funds are derived from central government and each University Council contains a majority of government officials, it is difficult for the universities to maintain any serious degree of administrative autonomy.

In addition to the funds channelled by the Ministry of Education, Public Development Expenditure for Education and Training is provided by the Ministry of Labour, the MARA Training Division, the National Institute of Public Administration (INTAN) and the Ministry of Culture, Youth and Sports. MARA is the government body charged with advancing *Bumiputeras* professionally and economically, partly through training institutions in Malaysia and partly through the provision of scholarships and loans for overseas training. In the period of the Fourth Malaysia Plan (1981-85), these governmental branches collectively allocated about M$1 billion, however over 80 per cent of the sum was reserved for MARA. (For details, see The British Council, *Higher Education Market Survey Malaysia*, London: The British Council, 1984, pp. 11-13.)

The major source of funds for the six Malaysian national universities is the government budget. The Universities and University Colleges Act of 1971 provides for parliament to make grants-in-aid to the universities. The national budget provides, in some cases, up to 95 per cent of the needed funds. The Universiti Islam Antarabangsa/International Islamic University is funded both by the Malaysian government and the government of other Islamic nations. (For details, see *Commonwealth Universities Yearbook 1984*, London: Association of Commonwealth Universities, 1985, p. 1,886.)

169. Singh, J. S. & Mukherjee, H., *Education and National Integration in Malaysia: Stocktaking Thirty Years after Independence*, Kuala Lumpur: University of Malaya, 1990, p. 3.

170. Malaysia, *Mid-Term Review of Second Malaysia Plan*, Kuala Lumpur: Government Printers, 1973; *Third Malaysia Plan 1976-1980*, 1975; *Fourth Malaysia Plan 1981-1985*, 1980.

Table I
Membership of Registered Professional by Ethnic Group, 1990

Profession	Bumiputera	(%)	Chinese	(%)	Indian	(%)	Others	(%)	Total	(%)
Architects	231	2.0	728	3.2	12	0.2	8	1.1	979	2.4
(%)	23.6		74.4		1.2		0.8		100.0	
Accountants	627	5.3	4,524	20.0	346	6.5	77	10.3	5,574	13.8
(%)	11.2		81.2		6.2		1.4		100.0	
Engineers	7,018	59.7	11,741	51.9	1,065	19.9	342	45.6	20,166	49.8
(%)	34.8		58.2		5.3		1.7		100.0	
Dentists	406	3.5	847	3.7	396	7.4	21	2.8	1,670	4.1
(%)	24.3		50.7		23.7		1.3		100.0	
Veterinary Surgeons	242	2.1	160	0.7	250	4.7	23	3.1	675	1.7
(%)	35.9		23.7		37.0		3.4		100.0	
Lawyers	705	6.0	1,575	7.0	836	15.6	37	4.9	3,153	7.8
(%)	22.4		50.0		26.5		1.2		100.0	
Surveyors	573	4.9	636	2.8	48	0.9	26	3.5	1,283	3.2
(%)	44.7		49.6		3.7		2.0		100.0	
Total	11,750	100.0	22,641	100.0	5,363	100.0	750	100.0	40,507	100.0
(%)	29.0		55.9		13.2		1.9		100.0	

Source: Professional Associations and Institutions, covering both the public and private sectors, Malaysia, *The Second Outline Perspective Plan, 1991-2000*, Kuala Lumpur: Government Press, 1991, p. 120.

Although the non-Malay growth in education and employment has slowed down as a result of the State's official regulations to put Malays in favoured positions in education and employment—by means of the language of instruction, admission requirements and financial support—the Chinese participation in the professional occupational classifications has continued to be higher than the *Bumiputera*. The Table indicates the proportion of the *Bumiputera* in the classification of the professional occupations.

As indicated in the Table above, the Chinese still occupy 55. 9 per cent of the professions available in Malaysia as of 1990, which is attributed to the fact that the growth of the *Bumiputera* in these categories had slowed down during the 1980s. (Lim, M. H. 'Affirmative Action, Ethnicity and Integration: The Case of Malaysia' *Ethnic and Racial Studies* Vol. 8, No. 2, 1985, p. 259.)

171. Malaysia, *The 6th Malaysian Plan 1991-1995*, Kuala Lumpur: Government Press, 1991. pp. 175-76.

172. Mukherjee, H. and J. S. Singh, op. cit., 1995, p. 170.

173. Director General, Economic Planning Unit., Prime Minister's Department, *The Seventh Malaysia Plan 1996-2000*, Kuala Lumpur, Malaysia, 1996, p. 339.

174. According to the Seventh Plan, the teaching and R & D capabilities of tertiary institutions are expected to be strengthened through the allocation of increased resources. A Science and Technology Human Resource Fund of RM 300 million has been set up to provide scholarships for post-graduate and post-doctoral studies as well as fellowships for graduate research. (ibid., p. 20.)

175. This corporatization permits greater autonomy of higher education institutions in management. Institutions can seek their own revenue sources, increase their capacity for consultancy services and can commercialise research findings and more flexibly recruit and remunerate teaching staff. (*The Seventh Malaysian Plan (1996-2000)*,op. cit., p. 333.)

176. Ibid.

177. The central governmental control of the higher education system in the 1990s is directly through the Department of Higher Education. As an umbrella branch of the Department of Higher Education, the National Council on Higher Education was established in 1996. The functions of the Council are: to plan, develop and determine the national policy and strategy for the development of higher education; to develop and facilitate the growth of higher learning institutions. This newly established Higher Education Council with members from both the public and private sectors will ensure greater coordination in planning and development of tertiary education during the Seventh Plan period. The Council will provide policy directions as well as plan and coordinate the development of all public and private institutions of higher learning. In addition, the Department of Higher Education, established in 1995, will be strengthened with relevant expertise to provide the necessary support to the Council.

The Private Education Department takes responsibilities to determine the policies and direction of the private education; to coordinate the applications for the establishment and registration of private education institutions; to ensure that the education offered by the private sector is of quality and international standard; to export education.

The Department of Islamic and Moral Education is responsible for managing all matters concerning the formulation of policies related to Islamic Education, Moral Education and the Arabic Language in the national school system. The new curriculum emphasises the building of character and the development of values which are based on *tauhid* as well as practising, appreciating and understanding the concept of *ibadat* in Islam. This new approach intends to make the teaching and learning of Islamic Education more attractive. The National Accreditation Board will be established to provide guidelines and standards for quality control to ensure that facilities and teaching are of high quality. (For details, see Malaysia, *Malaysia Official Yearbook 1997*, Kuala Lumpur: Department of Information, Malaysia, 1997, p. 163; *The Seventh Malaysian Plan*, op. cit., pp. 333-337.)

178. The ethno-centric New Economic Policy has not brought adequate economic benefits to the Malay masses at large, especially in the rural areas. Instead, the NEP has helped to increase the wealth of a "closed circle" of upper-class Malays in both urban and rural areas and created a small class of new rich and privileged and powerful bureaucrats and technocrats, who are mainly products of the University. What has in effect happened and is happening is that the University has to some extent contributed to the creation and perpetuation of a local bourgeoisie, a bureaucratic and technocratic elite in association with local and foreign economic interest. (For details, see Thomson, Kenneth W., Barbara R. Foger and Helen E. Danner (eds). *Higher Education and Social Change*. New York: Praeger Publishers, 1977, pp. 239-248.)

179. Hayden, H., *Higher Education and Development in South-east Asia,* Paris: UNESCO and the International Association of Universities, 1967, p. 60.

180. Wong Hoy Kee, Francis and Ee Tiang Hong. *Education in Malaysia.* op. cit., 1975, pp. 160-161.

181. Hashim, Shafrudd, op. cit., p. 51; Marimuthu, Thangavelu. *Student Development in Malaysian Universities, RIHED Occasional Paper No. 19.* Singapore: Regional Institute of Higher Education and Development, 1984, pp. 16-19.

182. Hashim, Shafrudd, op. cit., p. 51.

183. Between 1996 and 1998, there have been established four private universities: Universiti Telekom (The Telecom University); Multi Media University—linked to the Multi-media Super Corridor project, Universiti Tenaga Nasional (The National

Energy University), and Universiti Tun Abdul Tazak—the first visual university in Malaysia, as equivalent to Open University in the U. K..

184. Aziz, U. A., S. B. Chew, K. H. Lee, and B. C. Sanyal, op. cit., 1987, p. 104.

185. Ibid., p. 85.

186. Marimuthu, Thangavelu, op. cit., 1984, pp. 17-18.

187. Aziz, U. A., S. B. Chew, K. H. Lee, and B. C. Sanyal, op. cit., p. 84.

188. The British Council, op. cit., 1984, p. 62.

189. Ibid., p. 85.

190. Mukherjee, H., and J. S. Singh. 'Malaysia', op. cit., 1995, p. 160.

191. Malaysia, *The 7th Malaysian Plan*, op. cit., p. 312.

192. Malaysia, *The 6th Malaysian Plan 1991-1995*, op. cit., 1991, p. 163.

193. Ibid.

194. Malaysia, *The 7th Malaysian Plan*, op. cit., p. 312.

195. A substantial growth of Malaysian student enrollment in overseas higher education was notable in the 1980s. However, the total enrollment started to decline in 1990, as a consequence of higher fees imposed by overseas institutions and the increasing number of local private institutions offering twinning programmes. (Malaysia, *The 6th Malaysian Plan 1991-1995*, op. cit., p. 163.)

196. Malaysia, *The 7th Malaysian Plan*, op. cit., p. 315.

The overall percentage ratio of the output of arts to science/technical graduates at the degree level remained at about 53: 47 while at the diploma level, the percentage ratio was about 50: 50. Almost 50 % of the arts graduates at the degree and diploma levels were from the applied arts courses which included accountancy, business and law. At the certificate level, however, the percentage ratio of arts to science and technical graduates was 15:85. (Malaysia, *The 6th Malaysian Plan 1991-1995*, op. cit., p. 163.)

197. Malaysia, *Malaysia Official Yearbook 1997*, op. cit., p. 163.

198. Malaysia, *The 6th Malaysian Plan 1991-1995*, op. cit., pp. 166-167.

199. Ibid., p. 174.

200. Lee, Molly N. N., 'Corporatization and Privatization of Malaysian Higher Education', op. cit., 1998, p. 7.

201. Singh, J. S. & H. Mukherjee, op. cit., 1990.

202. The conditions of university entry include the Sijil Pelajaran Malaysia (SPM) or the Malaysian Certificate of Education (MCE) with credits in at least 5 subjects as basic educational requirements. For higher education entry, candidates must obtain the Sijil Tinggi Persekolahan (STP) or the Higher School Certificate (GSC) or the Sijil Tinggi Persekolahan Malaysian (STPM) not later than 2 years after obtaining the SPM or MCE. STP/HSC is a pass in the General Paper and 2 subjects at Principal level or one subject at Principal level and two subjects at subsidiary level. STPM is a pass in the General Paper and 2 subjects with at least Grade E and 2 subjects with Grade R. (For details, see The British Council, op. cit., 1984, pp. 62-63.)

203. Reference Papers on the Federation of Malaya, *Teacher Training and Higher Education,* 1961, p. 3; Quoted in Wong Hoy Kee, Francis and Ee Tiang Hong, op. cit., 1975, pp. 80-81.

204. *Report of the Education Review Committee,* Kuala Lumpur: Government Printers, 1960, p. 46.

The shortage of teachers soon after political independence in Malaysia was eased to a certain extent by the help from the British Voluntary Service Overseas. The first group of these volunteers arrived in Malaya in September 1961. There were other organisations like the Colombo Plan and the American Peace Corps which relieved the shortage of trained teachers, especially for science and mathematics. Malaysia also benefited from various teacher exchange programmes, such as the International Teacher Development Programme offered in some American universities, and the Commonwealth Teacher Training Bursary, which offers one year training at various institutions in Britain. (Wong Hoy Kee, Francis and Ee Tiang Hong, op. cit., 1975, pp. 142-144.)

Arguably, it was through this British provision of teacher training that the English types of valued knowledge have been regenerated in Malaysia, despite the efforts of examining bodies, such as the Cambridge Local Examination Syndicate, to adapt syllabuses to Malaysian needs. Such attempts and the freedom to propose new syllabuses were frustrated by the conservatism or inertia of local teachers rather than by the obduracy of the examining body, as the Malaysian government abolished the Cambridge Overseas Certificate in 1978. (Hayden, H., op. cit., 1967, p. 37.)

205. The British Council, op. cit., p. 63.

206. Hayden, H., op. cit., p. 70.

207. Ibid., pp. 71-72.

208. Singh, J. S. 'Scientific Personnel, Research Environment and Higher Education in Malaysia' in P. G. Altbach (ed). *Scientific Development and Higher Education in Newly Industrialised Nations*, New York & London: Praeger Publishers, 1989.

209. The British Council. op. cit., 1984, p. 14.

210. Jasbir Singh notes that even though the output of science graduates has been expanded, they have largely concentrated in generalist science disciplines rather than the professional and technical fields. (Singh, J. S. & H. Mukherjee, op. cit., 1990, p. 11.)

211. Aziz, U. A., S. B. Chew, K. H. Lee, and B. C. Sanyal, op. cit., 1987, p. 89.

212. Singh, J. S. 'Scientific Personnel, Research Environment and Higher Education in Malaysia', op. cit., 1989.

213. The British Council, op. cit., p. 64.

The language policy in Malaysia, however, failed in terms of its ultimate aim of national unity. There has been a critical line of analysis that the use of the single official national language has served to solidify the ethno-politicisation of the non-Malayan groups. For instance, Martina Ting and Lee Yong Leng provide statistical evidence that indicate knowledge of Malay by non-Malays has decreased between 1972 and 1978; and intra-ethnic communication has continued to decline toward the 1990s. (For details, see Ting, M. and L. Y. Leng, 'Language and National Cohesion in Malaysia' *Asia Profile,* Vol. 14, No. 6, 1986, p. 522.)

214. Hayden, H., op. cit., p. 83.

The four-year duration of university education, however has now shortened to three years. The Department of Higher Education announced in the beginning of the 1996/97 academic year that all public universities should shorten their undergraduate programmes from four to three years, except the fields of medicine, dentistry, pharmacy and architecture. The reduction in the length of their courses was aimed to enable graduates to enter the workforce earlier and thus contribute to the national economic development. (Malaysia, Ministry of Education. *Laporan Tahunan (Annual Report 96)*. Kuala Lumpur: Ministry of Education, Malaysia, 1996, p. 56.)

215. Stedman, Joann Bye, *Malaysia, A Study of the Educational Systems of*

Malaysia and a Guide to the Academic Placement of Students in Educational Institutions of the United States, The American Association of Collegiate Registrars and Admissions Officers, The International Education Activities, 1986, pp. 120-28.

The initial American influence in Malaysia's academic development was through Harvard University's Development Advisory Service (DAS). (ibid) Within this, Milton J. Esman (of Pittsburgh University) and John Montgomery (of Harvard University) conducted in 1966 a Ford Foundation-funded study which proposed the creation of a Development Administration Unit (DAU) which was immediately undertaken by the Malaysian government. The Montgomery-Esman Report called for the creation of, and support for, an undergraduate and graduate programme in development administration at the University of Malaya for the training of civil service officers. Esman, who was then a senior adviser to DAU, was asked again to design the curriculum of the new Division of Public Administration by the Dean of the Faculty of Economics and Administration in the University of Malaya. (ibid., p. 137) Esman also coordinated study visits of Malaysian planners to US institutions such as Harvard, Pittsburgh, Southern California and Cornell. A Harvard's DAS assessment on the role of American advisors on Malaysia's planning recognises the politico-academic influence of the USA in Malaysian development:

Both the First (1956-60) and the Second (1961-65) Plans, as well as the Interim Report of 1963, were almost exclusively the work of foreign advisors. However, with the creation of EPU (Economic Planning Unit) and other key planning organizations, Malaysian participation in plan formulation increased rapidly. Roughly one-half of the FMP (First Malaysia Plan 1965-70) was drafted by indigenous personnel, the other half by DAS experts.

(Quoted from Sarvanamuttu, J., L. Kamaluddin, and P. Chung-Nyap, 'Malaysia' in *Political Science in Asia and the Pacific: Status Reports on Teaching and Research in Ten Countries,* edited by UNESCO, op. cit., 1984, p. 186.)

In the immediate post-independence period, British advisors continued to influence Malaysia but soon after US-influenced planners were more involved in the formation of Malaysia's administrative and academic profile.

As a result, the discipline of political science in Malaysia has its roots in Western social sciences especially in the American tradition of political science. Even though the Malaysian university education system in general has still retained strong British influence, according to the UNESCO report of 1984 the subject of political science itself was an American import at least in the initial phases of disciplinary development. (ibid., p. 184) F. Galiano explains "In a significant shift from Malaysia's almost exclusive prior reliance upon the United Kingdom, Razak chose to initiate the reforms under American auspices and thereby opened the door for political science institutionally to enter Malaysia". (Galiano, F. 'Political Science', in J. Lent (ed). *Social Science Research in Malaysia,* De Kalb: Northern Illionois University,

1978, p. 136.)

216. Lim, T. G. 'Malaysian and Singaporean Higher Education: Common Roots but Differing Directions; in A. H. Yee (ed). *East Asian Higher Education, Traditions and Transformations*, Oxford: Pergamon, 1995, p. 73.

217. Malaysia, *The Seventh Malaysia Plan 1996-2000*, op. cit., p. 129.

218. Lee, Molly N. N. 'Corporatization and Privatization of Malaysian Higher Education', op. cit., 1998, p. 8.

219. Malaysia, *The Seventh Malaysian Plan*, op. cit., p. 334.

220. Ibid., p. 332.

221. Puccetti, R. 'Authoritarian Government and Academic Subservience: The University of Singapore' in *Minerva*, 19, 1972, pp.223-241.

222. The then Prime Minister Lee Kuan Yew holds a starred double first from Cambridge University; Dr. Goh Keng Swee, former Defence Minister and later Minister of Finance holds a Ph.D. from the London School of Economics. See Puccetti, R. op. cit., p. 224.

223. *Straits Times Weekly*, 28 July 1990. Quoted in Tremewan, C., op. cit., pp. 127-128.

224. Singapore has a 6-4-2-(3) school system: six years of primary education, four years of secondary education, two or three years of post-secondary [Junior College] and three or more years of university education. As a young country with a median age of the resident population at 30.2 years, Singapore has experienced a steady, voluntary incorporation of the school-age population into the education system. The total enrollment increase between 1965 and 1990 was 65 per cent. For details, see Selvaratnam, V. *Innovations in Higher Education: Singapore at the Competitive Edge*. Washington, D. C.: The World Bank, 1994, p. 23; Gopinathan, S., op. cit., p. 79.

225. Lim, C.-Y. *Education and National Development*. Singapore: Federal Publications, 1983, p. 36.

226. For instance, when D. J Enright, as newly appointed Johore professor of English, delivered his inaugural lecture on "Robert Graves and the Decline of Modernism" on 17 November 1960, his topical remarks on culture caused a strong governmental reaction.

"The next morning, Professor was called in (with passport) by the Acting Minister for Labour and Law, Ahmad bin Ibrahim, who described him as a "mendicant" and "beatnik professor" who thought he was free to participate in local politics "from the superhuman heights of European civilisation". Prof. Enright was told that if ever again he dared enter the heat and the dust of the political arena, his professional visit permit would be cancelled and he would have to leave the country. However, due to the students' disapproval of this political interference in academic freedom of speech and the traditional Chinese expression of regret over such harsh treatment of a distinguished guest in the country, the Prime Minister reassured students that academic freedom was secure so long as foreigners did not mingle in local politics and face was saved all around. Professor Enright remained for another nine years before resigning to return to England".

(Quoted from Puccetti, R. "Authoritarian Government and Academic Subservience: The University of Singapore." op. cit., 1972, pp. 224-225.)

The government reacted promptly to the inaugural lecture of Prof. D. J. Enright, an expatriate Professor of English on "Robert Graves and the Decline of Modernism" by accusing him of meddling in the country's internal affairs. The former Prime Minister argued:

How are we to know where the bound of academic freedom end and the boundaries of political issues begin?...If you are an authority on Greek literature but a non-citizen then you would be wise to leave the question of whether or not Malay should be the only language to those who are citizens...the best thing is to stick to your subject...

(Quoted in S. Gopinathan, "University Education in Singapore: The Making of National University" in P. G. Altbach and V. Selvaratnam (eds). *From Dependence to Autonomy: The Developments of Asian Universities*, London: Kluwer Academic Publishers, 1989, p. 214.)

227. Puccetti, R. op. cit.

228. Ibid.

229. Ibid.

230. Tremewan, C. op. cit., p. 93.

231. Clammer, J. *Singapore: ideology, society, culture.* Singapore: Chopmen Publishers, 1985, p. 160.

232. Selvaratnam, V., op. cit., 1994, p. 5.

233. *Straits Times Weekly,* 4 August 1990. Quoted in Tremewan, C., op. cit., p. 127.

234. The University Council comprises 17 members who are representatives from the University including the Vice-Chancellor, the Government including the Permanent Secretary of the Ministry of Education and a Member of Parliament, and the private sector. (For details, see Selvaratnam, V., op. cit., 1994, pp. 69-70.)

235. Ibid., p. 73.

236. Some of them have been on secondment to serve either as Ministers or Ministers of State, Ambassadors, representatives at the United Nations or in other political and social arenas outside the University. (For details, see Selvaratnam, V. op. cit., 1994, p. 68.)

237. Ibid., p. 70.

238. Ibid., p. 25.

239. Dainton, Lord, *Report on University Education in Singapore of 1979,* Singapore.

240. Selvaratnam, V., op. cit., 1994, p. 33.

241. Ibid.

242. The Nanyang Technological Institute (NTI) was established in 1981 as a new engineering institute on the former campus of the Nanyang University to produce the "highly skilled manpower needed for the sophisticated, capital-intensive, high value added industries that will figure predominantly in Singapore's economy in the 1990s". (Chan, M. "Report on Tertiary Education in Singapore" RIHED Bulletin, Vol. 10 (1), January-March 1983, p. 5.)

The Institute started with three schools: Mechanical and Production Engineering, Civil and Structural Engineering, and Electrical and Electronic Engineering. The role of the NTI focused on training practice-oriented engineers to complement the output of the more academically-oriented engineers from the NUS. The NIT had functioned as an integral part of NUS so that the graduates of the NIT had been awarded NUS degrees until 1991. (Selvaratnam, V. op. cit., 1994, p. 27)

243. Selvaratnam, V., op. cit., 1994, p. 27.

244. Ibid., p. 28.

245. Ibid., p. 29.

246. Lim, T. G. 'Malaysian and Singaporean Higher Education: Common Roots but Differing Directions' op. cit., 1995, p. 77.

247. Ibid.

248. Selvaratnam, V., op. cit., 1994, p. 5.

249. Ibid., p. 2.

250. Ibid., pp. 52-53.

251. Nanyang Technological Institute, *10th Annual Report 1990-91*,p. 7.

252. Selvaratnam suggests that "Singapore's good practices and emerging issues has important lessons for small nation states as well as for larger developed and developing countries that have increasingly to depend on a highly competitive global market for their survival in the 1990s and beyond". (For details, see Selvaratnam, V., op. cit., 1994.)

253. Lim, T. G. 'Malaysian and Singaporean Higher Education: Common Roots but Differing Directions' op. cit., 1995, p. 77. For a detailed analysis of the policies and programmes developed by the Singaporean government to foster a R & D environment and the role of the NUS in implementing the policy on science and technology, see Pang Eng Fong and S. Gopinathan, op. cit., 1989, pp. 137-176; Tham and Mani, op. cit., 1991, pp. 504-505.

254. Nevertheless, the British model of the infrastructure of university enrollment system has been maintained: for instance in the "O" and "A" levels Singapore-Cambridge Examinations, required before university entry.

255. Selvaratnam, V., op. cit., 1994, p. 1.

256. In 1973, the Faculties and Schools at the University of Singapore were as follows:

Table J
Faculties and Schools at the University of Singapore

Faculties/Schools	Departments of Study
Medicine	14
Arts and Social Sciences	11
Science	5
Engineering	4
Architecture and Building	3
Dentistry	2
Accountancy and Business Administration	2
Law	1
Pharmacy	1
Total	44

Source: Lim, C.-Y. *Education and National Development.* op. cit., 1983, p. 37.

257. Lim, C.-Y., op. cit., p. 36.

258. Another notable change in the curriculum structure was made to integrate the courses of Arts and Social Sciences with those of Natural Science for the first two years of undergraduate study. (By the curriculum reform, students enrolled in Arts and Social Sciences course would have to follow a specially designed course in the natural sciences offered in the Faculty of Science for the first two years of their study. In turn, students in the Science Faculty would have to select one of the six specially designed courses provided by the Faculty of Arts and Social Sciences in the second and third year of study.) All students from the Faculty of Engineering, the Faculty of Science and the School of Accountancy and Business Administration who have not reached a desired level of English proficiency have to attend an English Language course in the first year of their study. Those who have met the proficiency level then have to follow a specially structured course in the humanities offered by the Faculty of Arts and Social Sciences. (For details, see Lim, C.-Y.,op. cit., p. 39)

259. "We must from time to time review our curriculum so that our graduates will be equipped with the skills and versatility which will help them in good stead in our part of the world where prosperity and stability are hinged on a strong interaction between politics, economics and technology...Restructuring of the University undergraduate curriculum by itself is already a challenge to faculties to make university education more relevant and meaningful to our young men and women who will come in to study, and will leave to participate in the organisation and running of our political, business and economic lives." (Extract from June 1968 Convocation Address by the Vice-Chancellor, Dr. Toh Chin Chye. Requoted from Lim, C.-Y., op. cit., p. 39.)

260. Selvaratnam, V., op. cit., 1994, p. 2.

261. Ibid., p. 77.

262. Selvaratnam, V., op. cit., 1994, p. 60.

263. Ibid., p. 57.

264. National University of Singapore, *A Decade of Achievement 1980-90*, Singapore: NUS University Liaison Office, July 1990, p. 2. (Requoted from Selvaratnam, V. op. cit., 1994, p. 57.)

265. Lim, T. G. op. cit., p. 76.

266. Ibid., p. 4.

267. For instance, NUS and NTU professional degrees have become recognised by the international professional organisations operated by leading industrialised countries such as the USA and Britain. All NUS and NTU degrees are also by and large recognised by most English-speaking universities for postgraduate studies. (ibid., p. 57.)

268. Lee, Choong-woo, *Kyung Sung Jekook Daehack* [Kyung Sung Imperial University], Seoul: Darackwon, 1980, pp. 266-297, requoted from Joung, Sun Ei. "*Kyung Sung Je-kook Dae-hack* [A Study on the Characteristics of Kyung Sung Imperial University].", Doctoral thesis. op. cit., 1997, p. 144.

269. Joung, S. E., op. cit., pp. 143-145.

270. Yonsei University Development Committee, Yonsei 21st century Planning Report [*Yonsei 21 Segi Gae-whaeck*], Seoul: Yonsei University, September 1993, p. 96.

271. In 1967, for instance, many Korean academics in the legal field already held American degrees in Law. The Dean and the Associate Dean of the Graduate School of Law at Seoul National University both gained J. S. D. degrees from Yale Law School in the U.S.A. and a Professor of Seoul National University College of Law gained an M. C. L. from Columbia and an LL. M. from Yale, and a part time lecturer at Seoul National University College of Law also had a J. S. D. from Yale and a professor of Yonsei University College of Law received an LL. B. degree from Harvard University School of Law. (For details, see Murphy, J., op. cit., p. 65.)

272. KCUE, op. cit., 1990, p. 54.

273.

Table K
Official Qualification Requirements for Faculty Members

Classification	College graduate & equivalent		
	Research Achievement	Teaching Experience	Total
College Professor	4	10	6
Associate Professor of College or Professor of Junior College	3	7	4
Assistant Professor of College or Associate Professor of Junior College	2	4	2
Full-time Lecturer of College or Assistant Professor of Junior College	2	3	1
Full-time Lecturer of Junior College	2	2	0

Source: KCUE, *Korean Higher Education - Its Development, Aspects and Prospects*, op. cit., 1990, p. 55.

274.

Table L
Qualification Requirements for Academic Staff

Classification	Research Achievement	Teaching Experience	Total
University Professor	4	6	10
Associate Professor Or Professor of Junior College	3	4	7
Assistant Professor or Associate Professor of Junior College	2	2	4
Full-time lecturer or Assistant Professor of Junior College	2	1	3
Full-time lecturer of Junior College	2	0	2

Source: KCUE, op. cit., 1990, pp. 54-55.

275. The demand was so high that the government authorities intervened to slow it down. One controlling mechanism was to require stiff examinations to select candidates for studying abroad. Thus, applicants for overseas study were required to pass a special qualifying examination set by the Ministry of Education. Those with a record of anti-governmental activities were excluded. (KCUE, op. cit.)

276. KCUE, op. cit., p. 58.

277. Ibid., p. 83.

278. University academics are also given the opportunity to study abroad by the Colombo Plan, UNESCO, the International Atomic Energy Association (IAEA), Fulbright Scholarships and invitations from the French government. (ibid.)

279. Selth, A., op. cit., 1988, p. 11.

280. Hong, Sah-myung, 'All about Koreans Studying Overseas' *Koreana* 5, 1991, p. 81.

281. KCUE, op. cit., p. 57.

282. Bang-Soon L. Yoon, 'Reverse Brain Drain in South Korea: State-led Model' *Studies in Comparative International Development*, 27 Spring 1992, p. 7.

283. *The Academic Newspaper*, 23 March 1998, Seoul, p. 5.

284. Ryee, J.C., 'Republic of Korea' in Uchida, T. (ed). op. cit., 1984, pp. 56-57.

285. KCUE, op. cit. p. 56.

286. Korean Council for University Education (KCUE). *University Education Development Indicators.* Edited by Hyung-chung Lee and Young-hack Lee. Seoul: KCUE, 1997, p. 128.

287. Cole, D. C. and P. N. Lyman *Korean Development,* Cambridge, Mass.: Harvard University Press, 1971, p. 17.

288. Hahn, Bae-ho, 'The State and Culture in Korean Development' in Hirano, K. (ed)., op. cit., 1995, pp. 232-264.

289. Chung, Hwan-kyu. "A Study on the Establishment of Seoul National University in Usamgik.", op. cit., 1997.

290. Adams, D. and E. E. Gottlieb, *Education and Social Change in Korea,* op. cit., 1993, p. 171.

291. OECD, *Education at a Glance,* Paris: OECD, 1996.

292. KCUE, op. cit., 1997, p. 34.

293. Ministry of Education, Republic of Korea, *Annual Report on Education Statistics,* April 1, 1997.

294. Ibid.

295. Ibid.

296. In 1965, expatriates were 11; 6 % of the teaching staff at the University of Malaya. By 1977, they numbered only 4 (down to 1%). (For details, see Phillips, J. A. 'Case Study of University of Malaya', op. cit., 1981, p. 11.)

297. Silcock, T. H. 'The Development of Universities in South-East Asia to 1960', *Minerva* Vol. II, no. 2, 1964, p. 190; Despite efforts to improve the ethnic structure of employment, in the private sector, the *Bumiputera* are still underrepresented in the higher levels of occupations such as the professional, managerial and executive positions. On the other hand, the non-*Bumiputera* are underrepresented in the public sector appointments such as the middle and senior levels of the civil services. (For details, see Malaysia, *The Second Outline Perspective Plan, 1991-2000,* Kuala Lumpur: Government Press, 1991, p. 115.)

298. Lim, T. G. op. cit., p. 73.

299. Phillips, J. A. op. cit., 1981, p. 26.

300. Singh, J. S. & H. Mukherjee, op. cit., p. 9.

301. Ibid., p.40.

302. Ibid., p. 26.

In conjunction with staff development schemes, a concern about the improvement of teaching skills started growing as early as 1975. Mahathir Mohammed, then the Minister of Education in Malaysia, emphasises this aspect:

No other profession permits its members to engage in their responsibilities without some form of formal preparation and guidance. The one important criterion for selection as a university teacher is academic qualifications. It is almost as if teaching at the university level requires no skills. It is therefore urged that certain consideration be given to this issue to ensure that in the long run, university teachers can effectively contribute to optimal student development.

(Mahathir Mohamad, Malaysian Minister of Education, *New Straits Times*, 7 November 1975; Requoted from Phillips, J. A., op. cit., p. 29.)

303. Malaysia, *Mid-Term Review of Fourth Malaysia Plan: 1981-83*, Kuala Lumpur: Government Press, 1984, p. 3,547.

304. Last year, more than 16,5000 Malaysians enrolled at British universities, more than twice the number from any other East Asian country. This trend is changing rapidly now, as a consequence of the Asian financial crisis. The MARA (the Malaysian government-funded agency for preparing and sponsoring higher education students) has decided just 50 Malaysian students—down from 5,000—can study in Britain this year (1998). Currently, those coming from Malaysia to study in the U. K. will have to be privately funded and thus more likely to be Chinese Malaysians. (For statistical details, see *Times Higher Education Supplement*, 13 November 1998, p. 4.)

305. Chan, P. 'Malaysia' in *Economics in Asia: Status Report on Teaching and Research in Nine Countries*, op. cit., 1985, p. 205.

306. *Commonwealth Universities Yearbook 1984*, op. cit., 1985, p. 1,887.

307. The high concentration of North American higher degrees in Education and Engineering can be attributed to the U. S. College-and University Sponsored Programmes in Malaysia, which were available in the fields of Education and Technology, Engineering in response to the knowledge valued in the university system in Malaysia examined earlier in this book. (Phillips, J. A., op. cit., pp. 12-13.)

308. The Medical Faculty has the highest percentage (66%) of teachers with first degrees. This is because the recruitment system permits the employment of first-degree holders (i.e. M.B.B.S.) with some years of experience as lecturers in the Medical Faculty.

309. Those with doctorates are largely from the Department of Biochemistry, Microbiology, Parasitology, and Pathology. One out of every four engineers in the Faculty of Engineering at the University of Malaya possessed a fellowship or membership of the Institute of Engineers, such as the Institute of Civil Engineers, Mechanical Engineers, etc. In the Medical Faculty, beside the qualification of M.B.B.S., 39 % of the doctors were either Fellows or Members of Royal Colleges such as the Royal Colleges of Medicine, Surgeons, Pathologists, Obsterics and Gynaecology, etc. In the Faculty of Education, all members of the teaching staff had a teaching qualification, either a Diploma in Education or a Teaching Certificate from a teacher training college as a prerequisite. (ibid.)

Staff development was also perceived as the "expertization" of professional skills. At one level, academics are encouraged to develop skills as practitioners of their specialities, as well as teaching. At the Faculty of Engineering at the University of Malaya, for instance, leave is provided for staff to gain practical experience in local industries. It is notable that almost all academic staff in the Faculty of Education at the University of Malaya were school teachers before taking up appointment in the academic profession at the university. At another level of the staff development scheme, academics are encouraged to update their professional knowledge and skills by participating in conferences, seminars, workshops, in their area of specialisation both locally and abroad. (For details, see Phillips, J. A., op. cit., p. 31.)

310. The German-Malaysian Institute (GMI), established in 1992, offered advanced training, particularly in production technology and industrial electronics. The Institute, with a maximum enrollment capacity of 450 trainees, produced its first batch of 57 graduates in 1995. The Malaysia-France Institute, which began operation in October 1995, had a capacity for 600 trainees and offered courses in areas such as the maintenance of automated mechanical systems and electrical equipment installation and welding technology. In addition, the establishment of the Japan-Malaysian Technical Institute (JMTI) was at the planning stage. (Malaysia, *The 7th Malaysian Plan,* op. cit., p. 319.)

311. Australian universities have established Malaysian twinning operations. Earlier this year, in 1998, Monash University became one of the first foreign higher educational institutions to be given a licence to establish a full off-shore campus in Kuala Lumpur.

312. According to the Plan, enrollment at post-graduate level in local public institutions of higher learning is expected to increase from 11.5 per cent of total enroll-

ment at the degree level in 1995 to at least 14 per cent in the year 2000. Of the total post-graduate students, 41.5 per cent will be in science and technology. (ibid, p. 333.)

313. Therefore, the official leader of the university in Malaysia is the Chancellor, who is appointed by the constitutional monarch of Malaysia for a term of seven years. The chief executive and principal academic officer is the Vice-Chancellor, whose term is variable and who is appointed by the constitutional monarch on advice from the Minister of Education and with the recommendation of the University Council. The faculties within each university are headed by Deans appointed by the Vice-Chancellor for renewable two-year terms. The university has three governing bodies: a court, a council and a senate. The Court is the formal legislative body and meets once a year to receive the annual report of the university from the Vice-Chancellor and the report of the audited accounts and new statues enacted during the year. The Council, which meets monthly, is the executive body of the university that rules on all matters of the university except academic affairs. The senate of the university meets once a month to consider the academic affairs of the institution. It is chaired by the Vice-Chancellor and comprises the Deans of Faculties, Institutes of Schools; Directors of Centres; Heads of Departments or Chairmen of Divisions and academic representatives as members. (*Commonwealth Universities Yearbook 1984*, op. cit., 1985.)

A master's degree in the relevant discipline is the minimum requirement for recruitment as a lecturer; however, the university can employ teachers with other qualifications in special areas such as languages (Bahasa Malaysia and English). The detailed categories of academic hierarchies and related conditions are listed below:

Professors: Receive tenure on appointment and teach until they are fifty-five with possible extensions to the age of sixty; women have mandatory retirement at age fifty.

Associate Professors: Receive a three-year contract and then a contract to age of retirement.

Readers: Teach and do research (may be recruited locally or from abroad).

Lecturers and Assistant Lecturers: Receive a three-year contract and are then considered for promotion to the next level in the faculty track.

Tutors: Assist with teaching while reading for higher degrees; receive a one-year or two-year appointment with one-year extensions and are   recruited locally.

(For details, see Stedman, Joann Bye, *Malaysia, A Study of the Educational System of Malaysia and a Guide to the Academic Placement of Students in Educational Institutions of the United States,* The American Association of Collegiate Registrars and Admission Officers, The International Education Activities, 1986, p. 57.)

314. Phillips, J. A., op. cit., p. 10.

315. Chan, P. 'Malaysia', op. cit., 1985, pp. 205-206.

316. Lee Kiong Hock, 'Socio-Economic Framework of the Country' in Ungku A. Aziz (ed)., op. cit., 1987, p. 38.

317. Malaysia, *Fourth Malaysia Plan 1981-1985*, op. cit., p. 352; *Third Malaysia Plan 1976-1980*, op. cit., p. 401.

318. Thomas, R. Murray, 'Malaysia: Cooperation versus Competition or National Unity versus Favoured Access to Education' in R. Murray Thomas (ed). *Politics and Education: Cases from Eleven Nations*, Oxford: Pergamon Press, 1983, p. 163.

319. Aziz, U. A., S. B. Chew, K. H. Lee, and B. C. Sanyal, op. cit., 1987, pp. 157-159.

320. Malaysia, *The Second Outline Perspective Plan, 1991-2000*, op. cit., 1991, p. 114.

321. According to 1985 figures for the whole of Malaysia, which includes Peninsular Malaysia, Sabah, and Sarawak, the ethnic composition of the population in Malaysia consisted of *Bumiputeras* (60.1 per cent), Chinese (30.9 per cent), and Indians and others (8.4 per cent). In Peninsular Malaysia, the distribution was 56.6 per cent *Bumiputeras*, 32.7 per cent Chinese and 10.7 per cent Indians and others. For details, see Singh, Jasbir Sarjit, 'Malaysia' in Altbach, P. G. (ed). *International Higher Education: an Encyclopedia*, Vol I., New York: Garland Publishing, Inc., 1991, p. 511; ft.1 (p. 522); Mukherjee, H., and J. S. Singh. 'Malaysia', op. cit., 1995, p. 160.

322. This source is a Malay from the University of Malaya who is at present doing doctoral research at the Institute of Education, University of London.

323. The impact of the NEP on social restructuring can be traced through the changes in the ethnic distribution at different educational and occupational levels. As indicated, significant changes in the educational structure were visible, as more *Bumiputeras* moving into the higher education sector from 21.7 per cent in 1970 to 40.5 per cent in 1990. Accordingly, the *Bumiputera* share of professional and technical occupations increased from 47 per cent to 60 per cent and among service workers their share rose from 44 per cent to 61 per cent during the NEP phase of development. (Mukherjee, H. and J. S. Singh. 'Malaysia' op. cit., 1995, p. 171.)

Table M

Employment by Occupation and Ethnic Group 1990

Occupation	Bumiputera (%)		Chinese (%)		Indian (%)		Others (%)		Total	(%)
Professional & technical	350.4	9.2	178.6	8.2	44.8	8.0	7.0	13.8	580.8	8.8
(%)	60.3		30.8		7.7		1.2		100.0	
Teachers & Nurses	148.7		54.9		13.7		1.2		218.5	
(%)	68.1		25.1		6.3		0.5		100.0	
Administrative & Managerial	54.1	1.4	95.3	4.4	8.6	1.5	4.4	8.7	162.4	2.5
(%)	33.3		58.7		5.3		2.7		100.0	
Clerical	354.7	9.3	238.1	10.9	50.5	9.0	2.6	5.1	645.9	9.8
(%)	54.9		36.9		7.8		0.4		100.0	
Sales	274.2	7.2	429.8	19.7	49.7	8.8	7.6	15.0	761.3	11.5
(%)	36.0		56.5		6.5		1.0		100.0	
Service	473.9	12.4	207.7	9.5	81.8	14.5	6.9	13.6	770.3	11.6
(%)			27.0		10.6		0.9		100.0	
Agricultural	1,431.1	7.4	295.1	13.5	31.4	23.4	14.9	29.4	1,872.5	28.3
(%)	76.4		15.8		7.0		0.8		100.0	
Production	887.0	23.2	737.6	33.8	195.9	34.8	7.3	14.4	1,827,8	27.6
(%)	48.5		40.4		10.7		0.4		100.0	
Total	3,825.4	100.0	2,182.2	100.0	562.7	100.0	50.7	100.0	6,621.0	100.0
(%)	57.8		32.9		8.5		0.8		100.0	

Source: Labour Force Surveys, 1980-88 and EPU estimates

324. Phillips, J. A., op. cit., p. 11.

325. Malaysia, Ministry of Education. *Laporan Tahunan (Annual Report 96)*. Kuala Lumpur: Ministry of Education, Malaysia, 1996.

326. Milne, R. and Mauzy, D. *Singapore: The Legacy of Lee Kuan Yew*. Boulder, CO.: Westview Press, 1990, p. 18.

327. Ibid., p. 21.

328. Lim, C.-Y., op. cit., p. 60.

329. Selvaratnam, V., op. cit., 1994, p. 55.

330. For instance, the new Vice-Chancellor after Independence was Prof. Lim Tay Boh who was a Singaporean citizen and professor of economics holding the degrees of B.A., Ph.D. from London in economics. Before Lim Tay Boh, Toh Chin Chye had a Ph.D. from the University of London, was a Reader in Physiology in the University of Singapore and then took a governmental post. As indicated earlier, before accepting the vice-chancellorship, Toh Chin Chye was serving as Deputy Prime Minister. (For details, see Puccetti, R. op. cit., 1972, pp. 227-228.)

331. After three years' service, expatriate staff members could sign another three-year contract with six months' leave between contracts with passage paid for them and their immediate family to their home plus six months' extra salary. In the case of senior staff members among expatriates, this offer could lead to successive contracts up to retirement age or beyond as there was often no local academic eligible for the post in the early Independence period. (For details, see ibid., pp. 226-227.)

332. The official retirement age of 55 has not changed since colonial times. (ibid.)

333. National University of Singapore Student's Union, 1980, p. 9. (Requoted from Selvaratnam, V. op. cit., 1994, p. 53.)

334. Ibid.

335. Overseas recruitment offices in London and New York also help recruit Western expatriate academics, and other academics from countries in the ASEAN (Association of Southeast Asian Nations). For overseas recruitment of academic staff, Singaporean higher education institutions routinely send recruiting units to Australia, Britain, and North America to interview potential candidates. (ibid.)

336. Selvaratnam, V. op. cit., 1994, p. 54.

337. Lim, T. G. op. cit., p. 76.

338. Tremewan, C. op. cit., p. 126.

339. Selvaratnam, V. op. cit., 1994, pp. 53-54.

340. Ibid., p. 55.

341. Ibid.

342. Unlike the Malaysian model, in which the rank of Associate Professor and that of Senior Lecturer are equal, the Singaporean case puts the rank of Associate Professor higher than that of Senior Lecturer in the academic hierarchy. (ibid., p. 54.)

343. Ibid.

344. Ibid., p. 53.

345. NUS and NTU have a Centre for Educational Technology and Centre for Educational Development respectively to improve teaching and learning. The NTU has also introduced a special training programmes for new lecturers to train them as better teachers and tutors since July 1993. In addition, more advanced academ-

ic development schemes conducted by senior staff members and visitors are operated to upgrade and refine teaching skills. Also, all qualified local staff members recruited at the senior tutor level are sent under the staff training scheme to an overseas university in North America, Britain, Australia, New Zealand for doctoral training. Once in every 5 years, tenured staff can have study leave. (For details, see Selvaratnam, V. op. cit., 1994, p. 57.)

346. Yen, Chen Ai 'Trends and Issues in Improving University Teaching' in *Higher Education Research and Development* Vol. 7 No. 1, 1988, p. 49.

347. National University of Singapore, *10th Annual Report 1989-1990,* Singapore: NUS press, 1990, p. 21.

348. Lee, Edwin, and Tan Tai Yong. *Beyond Degrees: The Making of the National University of Singapore.* Singapore: Singapore University Press, 1996, pp. 81-110.

349. Prof. K. J. Ratnam, B.A., M.A. (UBC), Ph.D. (London), expert on Southeast Asian Politics. He resigned to become Dean of Social Science in Penang University, Malaya. (For details, see Puccetti, R. op. cit.)

350. The first holder of the chair, M.C. Groves, B. A. (Melb.), Ph.D. (Oxon) was an Australian and resigned after receiving a letter from the new Vice-Chancellor, Dr. Toh, who accused him of meddling in internal affairs as he criticised the Vice-Chancellor's way of conducting faculty business. Prof. Groves later moved to the Sociology Department in the University of Hong Kong. (For details, see Puccetti, R. op. cit.)

351. Ibid.

352. Among 533 Kyung Sung Imperial graduates (in the period of 1924-1941), 33 people went to political careers (mainly MP), 44 went to the legal profession, 68 became government bureaucrats, 8 diplomats. For details, see the Table below:

Table N
Postcolonial Career Development Trends of Kyung Sung University Graduates after Independence

Occupation	Number	Details	Occupation	Number	Details
Politicians	33	Mainly MP	Journalists	11	
University Academic profession	134		Unknown	69	Including Drop out
Legal profession	44		Absconder to North Korea	100	Including Abduction
Principals and teachers of Secondary Schools	22 (+3)		Death during the period of studying	15	
Government Bureaucrats	68	Including Ministers	Living abroad	8	
Business career and Industrialist	62	Including Banking	Etc.	15	
				533 Total	

353. It was from the Meiji period that education and examinations in Japan started to be used as tests of capacity for lower and upper civil service roles. From the mid-1870s, those who continued to hold government offices in Japan sought to utilise the administrative role as the basis for the creation of a systematic structure of governance. They created an emperor whose powers were limitless and who was defined by his embodiment of the public interest. At the same time, the putative leaders sought to show that they alone were capable of serving this divine embodiment of Japanese society before whom all men were equal. In terms of the selection mechanism, the modern Japanese civil service examination system reflected the older Confucian State mandarin system in Korea as reviewed in Chapter Two and Three. In both the Korean Confucian State and in Meiji Japan, the public legitimacy of governance was derived from the requirement that officials were trained experts. (For details, see Silberman, B. S. *Cages of Reason*, Chicago & London: The University of Chicago Press, pp. 221-222.)

354. Tremewan, C., op. cit., p. 11.

355. Ismail, G. and Mohamed, M. (eds). *The New Wave University: A Prelude to Malaysia 2020*. 2nd ed. Selangor: Pelanduk Publication, Universiti Malaysia Sarawak, 1997, pp. 15-22.

356. The strong government control and constant surveillance to assure educational quality and equality in fact overturned the historical trait of educational elitism and instead focused on educational matters for mediocrity who would be produced in this highly standardised education system as homogeneous educated mass. It is suggested here that the experience of meritocratic but in the standardised uniform educational sorting process has produced some ideological effect to indoctrinate participants that they were being sorted correctly according to their own abilities.

357. Wilson, H. E. *Social Engineering in Singapore*. Singapore: Singapore University Press, 1978, pp. 238-239; Tremewan, C. op. cit., pp. 94-95.

358. *Report of the Education Committee* (The Razak Report), Kuala Lumpur: Government Printers, 1956, p. 1.

359. Aziz, U. A., Sing Buan Chew, Kiong Hock Lee, and Bikas C. Sanyal, op. cit., 1987, p. 104.

360. The consequence of that was an alteration of the colonial legacy of the Carr-Saunders' university model, which valued economics as the most central knowledge discipline.

361. According to the *Report of the Committee on Curriculum Planning and Development* in 1967, "It is not our intention that everything should be centrally controlled but rather that, in the present circumstances, central operations will

make the most effective use of existing manpower." (*Report of the Committee on Curriculum Planning and Development*, Kuala Lumpur: Dewan Bahasa dan Pustaka, 1967, p. 7.)

362. As indicated, the establishment of the MIT legitimates the privilege of the *Bumiputera* in promoting the fields of science and technology in Malaysia.

363. The MARA Institute gradually started to grant its own diplomas and undergraduate degrees from the early 1980s. However, some of its postgraduate degrees (e.g. Law and Business studies) are still awarded by the professional bodies and universities (e.g. the University of Kent) in the U. K. in the 1990s.

364. Selvaratnam, V., op. cit., p. 37.

365. In 1966 mathematics and science were required to be taught in English in the first-year classes of non-English-medium primary schools. By 1969 all pupils were streamed into academic, technical or vocational schools after their primary education, essentially on the basis of their aptitude in English. By 1975 all schools, regardless of language medium, were required to teach mathematics and science in English at all levels while other subjects, e.g. history, civics and geography, could be taught in the second language. For details, see Seah, C. M., and L. Seah. 'Education Reform and National Integration' in Chen, P. S. J., *Singapore Development Policies and Trends*, Singapore: Oxford University Press, 1983, p. 242.

366. KCUE, *The University Education Development Indicators*, op. cit., 1997, p. 100.

367. A start had been made in 1958 to provide secondary education in the Malay medium by attaching classes for this purpose to former government English schools. The Certificate of Education Examination in Malaysia was conducted in the National Language for the first time in November 1962. From 1965 onwards, entrance into the university was not entirely through the Cambridge School Certificate and Higher School Certificate, which up to then were conducted only in English except for certain language subjects. Such examination could be conducted in Malay from 1965. Accordingly, the first batch of students from the Malay-medium secondary schools entered the University of Malaya and received instruction in Malay in 1965. (For details, see Wong Hoy Kee, F. and Ee Tiang Hong, op. cit., 1975, pp. 78-81.)

368. KCUE, op. cit., p. 128.

369. OECD, *Education at a Glance 1996*; KCUE, *International Indicators of Higher Education*, Seoul: KCUE, 1997, p. 61.

370. Phillips, J. A. op. cit., 1981, pp. 1-44.

CHAPTER FIVE

The Conclusion

This book originally expressed dissatisfaction with the existing literature on the academic profession, notably with the 1994 Carnegie Foundation Report. The starting point of the Report was the "convergence that has fostered in recent years a stronger, more professionally connected, international community of scholars".[1] With that as the assumption, the Carnegie research was an empirical investigation in fourteen countries of the role perceptions of academics. Thus the international analysis of the multi-site Carnegie survey did not address the historical formation of academic professions, nor did it contextualise them comparatively. I have attempted to redefine what may be taken as problematic about the academic profession.

Operationally, the book contextualised the academic profession in the three East Asian countries through a comparative treatment over time of the colonial and postcolonial relations of the State and the university. In Chapter Three and Chapter Four, I analysed the shaping of the academic profession through the values and visions of these States in their respective modernity projects and the States' ideas of the university expressed in the struggles over institutional forms and valued knowledge. The shape of the academic profession was sketched for each period, by examining the ways in which entry routes to, and the social composition of, the academic professions changed in and after the colonial periods.

In this Conclusion to the book, reflections will be offered on the ways in which the three East Asian academic professions have changed over time. Second, an effort will be made to analyse the significance of the 'ideas of the university' which began to be articulated in the colonial period. Third, some of the material in the book will be reinterpreted through the theme of the changing 'meritocratic principles' which have shaped the postcolonial academic professions. Fourth, the changing cultural identity of the academic profession will be analysed by tracing the patterns of destruction and construction of the cultural values of the academic professions expressed in the language(s) of professional work and kinds of valued knowledge which resulted from different foreign influences. Fifth, I will reinterpret some of the material in the book in terms of cultural 'importations'; and the autonomy and the expected social role of the academic profession. Finally some reflections about the contemporary pressures on 'the academic profession' will be offered.

In other words, I shall try to avoid a simple reprise of the material already set out in detail in the early chapters. The conclusion makes an effort to re-think the significance of the earlier narrative. However, the conclusion begins with a couple of simple points and then moves to points of greater complexity.

THE CHANGING SHAPE OF THE ACADEMIC PROFESSIONS

In all three cases, after political independence and in the process of decolonisation, the academic professions expanded with the expansion of higher education.

In South Korea, the number of higher educational institutions went from 19 in 1945 (including tertiary institutions newly upgraded after political independence) to 950 in 1997. There were 46 State universities and 135 private universities; 129 graduate schools in the State universities and 475 graduate schools in the private universities; 11 junior colleges in the public sector and 144 in the private sector in 1997.[2] In 1945, the number of university academic staff was estimated at 753, while the number of academic staff in the higher education sector as a whole was estimated at 1,490 in the same year. The size of the academic profession increased to 3,808 in 1960; 10,435 in 1970; 20,900 in 1980; 41,920 in 1990 and 69,157 in 1997, with the institutional expansion of higher education.[3]

In Malaya, the University of Malaya was founded in 1949.[4] The number of academic staff in the University of Malaya between 1949 and 1958 (a year after Independence) increased from 58 to 195. After the Kuala Lumpur branch opened in 1959, the number of academic staff increased to 239.[5] Although between 1959 and 1969 there was only one university in Malaysia, six new universities had been created by 1986.[6] In 1998, there are 8 public universities, 1 International Islamic university, and 4 private universities.[7] The size of the academic profession also expanded along with the increasing number of universities. By 1996, the number of academics in the public universities and the International Islamic Universities was estimated at 9,114.[8]

In Singapore, the expansion of higher education has also continued since political independence from Malaya in 1965. By 1994, there had been established two State Universities, a new private Open University established by the Singapore Institute of Management, and four polytechnics.[9] In 1997, the number of academic staff in the NUS was estimated at more than 2,470—more than two-thirds of which are Ph.D. holders.[10]

The expansion was linked with a changing balance of nationalities in the academic professions. In the colonial period, expatriates occupied almost all the positions in the university academic profession in both Korea and Malaya. In Kyung Sung Imperial University in Korea, the number of Korean academics was insignificant and professorships were given only to Japanese nationals.[11] In Malaya, the majority of the academic posts in the University of Malaya were filled with expatriates from Britain and white Commonwealth countries. For instance, at the time of political independence, the number of locally born academics was estimated at 103, less than the number of expatriates (estimated at 136). Among the expatriates, the majority recruited to the University of Malaya were still from the British Empire: 63 British academics and 49 Commonwealth academics. The number of 'other nationals' was about 24 in the late 1950s.[12]

After Independence, the balance of nationalities in the academic professions altered. In all three cases, locally born, indigenous academics have occupied the major posts in the university academic profession in the post-colonial period. However, unlike South Korea and Malaysia, Singapore has kept and continued to recruit a considerable number of overseas academics in the postcolonial period.

Although Singapore has maintained a more international profile in terms of the academic profession than Malaysia and South Korea, the PAP government's stated policy has also focused on creating a strong nucleus of local academics, on the grounds indicated earlier: "a community of local staff would be more reliable, having a commitment to the country."[13] It is this principle which has meant that the main ethnic composition of the academic profession in Singapore has increasingly become identified with the Singaporean Chinese. This has not occurred through an official affirmative action policy, as used in Malaysia, but through the political promotion of the Chinese-Confucian cultural identity.

However, foreign influences on the shape of the academic profession have also continued in the postcolonial period. In terms of the changing size of the university academic profession, South Korea has explicitly followed the American pattern of expansion toward a mass system of higher education, deviating from the former Japanese colonial elitist university system. On the other hand, Malaysia and Singapore have maintained the older British pattern of an elitist university system, still small in comparison with the American pattern—and its exported versions—of mass higher education. These shifts in the shape of the academic profession – its expansion and its nationality principles – can be given a broader treatment: the shifts also reflect the respective States' 'ideas' of the university.

'IDEAS OF THE UNIVERSITY' AND STRUGGLES OVER INSTITUTIONAL FORMS

These 'ideas of the university' are first visible in the Japanese and British establishment of a Colonial University for different reasons in Korea and Malaya.

The Japanese colonial State introduced into Korea its model of Imperial Universities, already pioneered in Japan from 1886.[14] Japan legitimated Kyung Sung Imperial University in 1926 as the only university in Korea throughout the colonial period. In principle, the Imperial University demonstrated the new Japanese 'Enlightenment' policy in Korea. In practice, the University was to meet the increasing demand for higher education from the Japanese residents in Korea as well from a few, selected, Koreans. The University was to carry through the Japanese vision of colonial assimilation: to make Korea a part of the Japanese Empire, including training a Korean elite to be recruited into the Japanese colonial civil service.

Unlike the Japanese State's provision of university education mainly for the Japanese residents in Korea, the British State did not establish universities for its own people in the colonies.[15] Even the English-medium secondary education system available in Malaya was for selecting an elite among the colonised rather than for the British residents. The process of establishing a university was a long-term development which was organised by the British government and British universities at home—not by the British colonial government.

Given these versions of the University, there were political struggles over the institutional forms of higher education in both Korea and Malaya from colonial times. In Korea, private institutions sought to gain official recognition from the colonial State and upgrade their status to university level. As the private sector of higher education was run by American Christian missionary organisations as well as by Korean nationalists, the institutional forms in that sector developed on the American rather than the imported Japanese model.

Thus, the private sector of higher education provided a separate academic route into the academic profession for local Koreans as well as expatriates mainly from the United States and Canada, rather than Japan, during the colonial period. In the late colonial period, private institutions of higher education were forced to recruit more Japanese academics. In these ways, the Japanese tried to control most of the entry routes into the academic profession in Korea at that time. In Malaya, struggles over the legitimisation of private higher education were also visible in the Chinese community, as shown by the establishment of Nanyang University in Singapore in 1956, a year before the Independence of Malaya. In contrast with Korea, however, there was no major effort by the Malays in the colonial period to establish their own vernacular university in parallel with the English-medium University set up by Britain. The main entry routes to the university academic profession in Malaya were through English-medium academic institutions and universities overseas. The entry route to the Chinese Nanyang University was through Chinese-medium institutions of higher education overseas, especially in China itself.

Thus, the academic professions have been defined not merely by expansion and by nationality principles but by States' modernity projects and struggles over institutional forms in the colonial period. It is the institutional patterns in higher education which provide a central framing of the locus of the academic profession: which institutions will be under the rather direct control of the State; and which will not.

Again, however, this point may be broadened. The struggles over institutional forms contain and to some extent disguise an extra layer of interpretation. It is suggested that sociologically what was occurring was definitions and re-definitions of 'meritocratic principles', socially constructed and re-constructed over time, which directly shaped the academic profession.

THE SOCIAL CONSTRUCTION OF MERITOCRATIC PRINCIPLES

It is suggested that what was taken as 'merit'[16] – the legitimation of putative 'excellence' in the academic profession – was defined and then was re-defined by these East Asian colonial and postcolonial States. Thus, entry routes to the academic profession and the definitions of knowledge to be valued and tested in the selection of academic candidates can be taken not merely as descriptive categories but as comparative parameters which reveal changing definitions of socially acceptable 'merit'.

For example, the meritocratic principles operated by the Japanese colonial State in Korea legitimated the Japanese academic network as the official route into the university academic profession, which reproduced a Japanese model of the profession and a Japanese cultural valuation of knowledge: the knowledge on offer was appropriate for the colonial State's projects. In Malaya, the meritocratic principle used by the British colonial State legitimated an English-literate academic, formed through a 'weak' version of the English tradition of liberal education and selected on the elitist principles that informed selection to the civil service – here the British Colonial Civil Service.

In the postcolonial period, the social re-construction of meritocratic principles continued, but the principles were shifted by the aspirations of the respective independent East Asian States to achieve political and cultural unity and economic modernisation.

New criteria of 'merit' were legitimated in the processes of decolonisation and indigenisation. In South Korea, the meritocratic principles were redefined in the new mass higher education system on the basis of educational performance in the national examination system,[17] affected by newly introduced American ideas, such as equality of opportunity and democracy in mass education. However, the Confucian themes in the selection of 'merit'—in the stress on examinations—also continued to be visible after political independence. Other Korean Confucian elements continued—violating the meritocratic principles formally defined and operated by the State—such as academic networking and academic nepotism as a major criterion for elite sponsorship.

In Malaysia, meritocratic principles were also altered, specifically to sponsor *bumiputeras* for upward social mobility in the process of decolonisation and indigenisation. By the late 1990s, the *bumiputera*-Muslim identity has emerged as a fundamentally ascriptive meritocratic principle for all major educational and even occupational mobility. In Singapore, the socially constructed meritocractic principles reflect a unique combination of Platonic elitism, Confucian examination principles and contemporary academic pragmatism. In both Malaysia and Singapore, the former colonial meritocratic practices in educational selection have also continued in the domestic examination systems, where the British example continues to be influential.

In other words, what is being suggested here is that for the academic profession (and indeed for the educational systems) there was no fixed universal definition of 'merit', educational or social. The respective States intervened to define and to change the concept of 'merit' which they wanted socially supported and socially rewarded. Such a series of definitions and re-definitions was an intervention in culture, an intervention in educational culture, and an intervention in the culture of universities and the academic profession.

Again that theme of interpretation of culture can be broadened. At the intersection of State power, the idea of the university and the social role of the 'man of knowledge', there were struggles over other major definers of culture, such as language and valued knowledge.

CULTURAL IDENTITY: LANGUAGE

In the colonial period, the language of the university academic profession was the language of the colonisers in both Korea and Malaya. Thus, the language of the academic profession in Kyung Sung Imperial University in Korea was Japanese throughout the colonial period. The language of the academic profession in the University of Malaya was English in both Malaysia and Singapore even after decolonisation in 1957. The British colonial State used English literacy as a basic criterion in sponsoring academic candidates in Malaya.

This principle has continued in Singapore: despite the indigenisation process in the postcolonial period, the language of the academic profession has continued to be English. However, unlike the British definition of English as the language of the privileged in Malaya, the Singaporean State has used English as the medium of official mass communication rather than as an academic symbol of elite status. In other words, Singapore has maintained a pragmatic approach to English as the language of the academic profession. This permits its academics to keep up with advanced research done elsewhere, and to participate in international academic discourse directly.

On the other hand, in both South Korea and Malaysia domestic academic discourse has relied on the native language in the postcolonial period, a result of the processes of indigenisation and decolonisation of the academic profession. Nevertheless, in South Korea, the significance of English academic literacy (along with Korean) has increased in importance in academic selection and elite mobility—replacing Japanese academic literacy. In contrast, the multi-lingual legacy of colonial Malaya is being cancelled in Malaysia by Bahasa Malaysia as the single legitimate national language.[18] At present, there is no English-medium primary and secondary schooling in Malaysia.

However, despite the stress by the State on particular languages, the issue is so important that resistance has sometimes occurred. There was contestation in the private sector against the imposition of the State's preferred language in the academic domain in both colonial and postcolonial times. For instance, in Korea the language of the academic profession in the private sector was Korean up until 1938 although, as indicated earlier, the Japanese towards the end of the colonial period imposed the use of Japanese in the private sector of higher education. In the case of Malaya, Nanyang University established by the Chinese community in Singapore in 1956 used Chinese as the language of instruction, in contrast to the English-medium University of Malaya. The Chinese effort to set up a Chinese-medium university—Merdeka University—continued to be visible even after independence in Malaysia (up until 1982).

In the last two decades, there has been increasing pressure to adopt English in academic discourse. In both South Korea and Malaysia, the use of English as the language of the academic profession has become more extensive, following the 'internationalisation' of higher education outlined in Chapter Four. The cultural identity of the academic profession over time has also been altered by the changing patterns of knowledge valued in East Asia. The struggle has been between old knowledge traditions and new ones, which have reflected continuities and discontinuities in academic cultures in these East Asian contexts.

CULTURAL IDENTITY: KNOWLEDGE

The types of knowledge valued for the cultural identity of the academic profession reflect the destruction of knowledge traditions inherited from pre-colonial times and the construction of colonial and postcolonial knowledge traditions. Both the destruction and construction of knowledge traditions are related to the changing foreign influences on the shape of the academic profession.

For instance, in Korea, the epistemic pattern created in Kyung Sung Imperial University during the colonial period was based on German traditions indirectly imported by Japanese professors. On the other hand, in the private sector of higher education in colonial Korea the epistemic pattern was directly imported from American academe by Western missionaries.

In Korea, the types of knowledge which were valued replicated those institutionalised in the Imperial Universities in Japan. For instance, the Faculty of Law and Humanities was as central in Kyung Sung Imperial University as it was in Tokyo Imperial University.[19] The knowledge valued in Kyung Sung Imperial University was not however designed to produce highly skilled Korean scientists and technicians. Those roles were taken by the Japanese sent from Japan. As a consequence, it was only in 1938 during the War that the Faculty of Engineering was added in Kyung Sung Imperial University. Simultaneously, as indicated earlier, struggles to form a new nascent "Korean" academic profession in the colonial period were visible in the private sector of higher education, which developed different patterns of knowledge, reflecting the American missionary model as well as the Korean national epistemic tradition.

Unlike the Korean case, where Western patterns of valued knowledge had been indirectly and selectively imported via Japan, Malaya was exposed to the direct importation of an English epistemic pattern carried by the British academic expatriates. Even before the establishment of the University of Malaya, the types of knowledge transmitted in the English-medium schooling system already duplicated the English elite school curriculum in Britain. The knowledge profile of the academic profession in the University of Malaya after its establishment in 1949, followed the British civic university model—especially Carr-Saunders' LSE model. Accordingly, economics became the prime subject of university education, combined with other subjects considered as subsidiaries in Malaya at that time.[20] Despite this direct importation, the colonial university in Malaya stressed vocational preparation. Thus, there was a discrepancy between the colonial 'university' in Malaya and the original English model in Britain, as Channon lamented in his Memorandum.

In the postcolonial period, the colonial legacy of the pragmatic valuation of knowledge continued in South Korea, Malaysia and Singapore. However, American influence has become significant in all these East Asian countries—especially in South Korea, through educational aid and academic sponsorship at both the governmental and individual levels. The American influence was expressed in the idea of the 'research university' and the stress on useful knowledge in science and technology. Under American influence, all these three East Asian States have used their major national universities to carry out R & D projects for national economic development. The earlier severance of the indigenous knowledge tradition and the creation of an R & D capacity reflect colonial academic legacies, new external political forces, and new patterns of international academic relations. In summary, in all three East Asian countries, it was during the colonial period that the academics became involved in the State's modernisation projects. 'Modernisation' since the establishment of the colonial university has been the official charge to the new academic professions in East Asia.

Against the common pursuit of modernisation as the official doctrine of the State since colonial times, the theme of cultural conflict can again be broadened. These are new complexities which can be identified in the cultural shaping of the academic professions in these countries. These themes are (i) 'importations' and (ii) the relative autonomy and the expected social role of academics.

CULTURAL IMPORTATIONS AND ADAPTATIONS

The theme of cultural clash was, it will be recalled, sharply visible in colonial Korea. Japanese colonialism in Korea stressed "assimilation" to make Korea a subordinate part of Japan. However, this Japanese colonial and modernity project was a modification of ideas borrowed from Europe: i.e. the French examples of colonial assimilation policy and the Prussian model of State-led modernisation, which began with the establishment of a national education system and its subsequent control. Based on Western examples of colonial domination and modernisation, the cultural dimension of Japanese colonialism in Korea was to infuse Japanese cultural traditions and to transmit Western concepts of modernity—as these were translated by the Japanese—to Korea.

In this colonial condition, Korea had to undergo a complex process of cultural importation and adaptation. The cultural process was simultaneously one of Japanisation and Westernisation. Thus, the academic profession in Korea was shaped in, at least, a doubly-divided culture. In academe, there were different channels for absorbing Western knowledge in the Imperial University and in the private institutions of higher education. The Japanese academics in Kyung Sung Imperial University in Korea were transmitters of knowledge created by their Western counterparts. Japanese uniqueness as the first non-western country in attaining modernisation is marked by Japan's own conflict over Japanisation and Westernisation. Unlike Korea, however, the Japanese State had some power over what to adopt and what to reject.

The Japanese position is often identified with the slogan 'Eastern spirit, Western science' in its definition of the modernity project. Korea however was faced with a more complex proposition in absorbing foreign influences: i.e. Eastern (Japanese) spirit and Western science, as these were imported by the Japanese. Variations on the theme are visible in contemporary Singapore where Western science is located in a culture concerned to define and to establish 'East Asian' values. A similar struggle is going on in Malaysia—although this struggle is still working itself out, rather dramatically at the time of writing.

Thus, the colonial origins of the East Asian academic profession have altered the patterns of knowledge in East Asia in three ways: first, the importation—indirectly in the case of South Korea—of the "Western" epistemic tradition and particular new knowledge, and second, the pragmatic use and valuation of such knowledge (e.g. engineering) for the State's modernity projects—within, thirdly, a careful construction in all three cases of variants on the concept of 'Eastern spirit'. The processes of cultural importation and adaptation have been complex, difficult and even dangerous, for example, in terms of political stability and social cohesion. It is partly within this context that the autonomy and the social role[21] of the academic professions in these countries can be construed. The autonomy and social role of the academic profession is another version of cultural conflict and of continuities and discontinuities.

AUTONOMY AND THE CHANGING SOCIAL ROLE OF THE ACADEMIC PROFESSION

It has been argued that it was the colonial States that created 'modern' universities in these countries. Very early, the colonial States developed a tight collaborative relation with the university academic profession, reflecting the concerns of the colonising States to utilise colonial resources and the new academic professions for their modernisation projects. In these contexts, classic ideas of academic autonomy in the European university knowledge tradition—such as those outlined by Newman, or carried in the Humboldtian tradition reflected later by Jaspers—were inapplicable in reality from the beginnings of university education in the colonies.

In both Korea and Malaya, the Japanese directly and British indirectly defined the University as a State institution. The role of the university academic profession was to be part of the State's modernity project. In both cases, university education was focused on training a selected colonial elite as assistants to the major professions and for the colonial civil service. Given this colonial interest in a strong vocational bias in university education, liberal knowledge and education for cultivation were given little emphasis.

Thus, East Asian academics' involvement with the contemporary State's modernity projects can be traced back to the colonial origins of their universities. This involvement has remained as a colonial legacy in State and university relations in East Asia, within which the practice of academic inquiry in the university is legitimated by and linked to the purposes of government. Thus, the academic role of the East Asian university profession is defined within the 'social space'[22] left to it by the State. The State has intervened politically to define the social role of these East Asian university professions.

In addition, culturally, in the postcolonial period, the social role of the academic profession has been affected by the Confucian tradition in South Korea and Singapore, and also in Malaysia (by the new definition of *being a Malay*, since the New Economic Policy started in 1971). For example, in Korea, despite the immediate negation of the Confucian State apparatus after the 1894 Kabo Reform, Confucian ideas about social prestige and privilege, attached to the State examination system, survived through the colonial period.[23] The role of the Confucian scholar mandarin was inherited by the academics in the Imperial University. They were involved in the colonial civil service examination and selection process and the government's projects in general. On the other hand, the autonomous role of an academic in the Confucian sage tradition was preserved in the private sector and was further legitimated by the newly imported Western conception of university academic autonomy and freedom at that time.

Similarly, the postcolonial academic profession in South Korea has displayed both aspects of the Confucian tradition. Members of the university academic profession have been invited into State politics, through serving in official governmental positions—often as ministers or senior advisers to key policy makers. Simultaneously, university academics have taken an autonomous role as critical opinion leaders in South Korean society. Since the colonial period, the academics who have played the role of autonomous intellectual leaders have often been critics of the legitimacy of the political ruling elite of the time. In short, as an influential cadre for the State and in civil society, Korean university academics have continued to take up both Confucian social roles: as State-mandarins and roles as a Confucian sage.

The Confucian-centred 'Asian Values' in Singapore and the *Bumiputera*-centred Malay-Asian cultural values are the new political frame for the contemporary postcolonial social role of the academic profession in these countries. The involvement of university academics in the political arena has also been visible in Singapore, whose case is arguably conforming to the Confucian scholar mandarin tradition consistently exalted by the PAP after political Independence. However, the PAP government in Singapore has deliberately sought out non-British models in higher education. Ideas have been also borrowed from the USA, Taiwan, Japan, and more recently Switzerland and Germany. In the extensive pursuit of efficient and pragmatic ways of modernisation, Singapore revived 'Asian values', which have been asserted in various statements and explicitly in a national ideology known as the "Shared Values", publicly marked in a Parliamentary White Paper in 1991. These Chinese-Confucian "Shared Values" would sustain the nation's socio-economic and cultural modernisation process.[24] Yet, it is contended that the Singapore government's use (or abuse) of 'Asian values' does not follow the tradition of the Confucian State and the Confucian sage. Lee Kuan Yew's political visions of modernity and the political tests for academics in Singapore diminish the social space for academic autonomy and frame very narrowly the expected social role of academics.

In Malaysia, the implementation of the NEP in Malaysia as subsequently articulated in the 'Look East' Policy expresses a concerted effort of the State to invent a new national cultural identity and consensus. Malaysia's NEP was an application of affirmative action (claimed to be based on the US example[25]) to combine racial equity with economic growth. It was justified as an instance where the end legitimates the means.[26] The political views of the Prime Minister, Mahathir bin Mohamad and the former Deputy Prime Minister, Anwar Ibrahim[27] have had a significant impact on current academic discourse in Malaysia. As in Singapore, there is an emerging notion of endogenous academic resistance to Western cultural domination in Malaysia. In the attack on Western notions of globalisation, academic perspectives in Malaysia tend to use the new 'Asian' values discourse, which was initially promoted by the government. The legitimacy of this Malaysian political and cultural perspective has subsequently been strengthened by the work of indigenous Malaysian academics. For instance, the Malaysian Chandra Muzaffar has attacked the very notion of human rights as the most evolved form of Western imperialism.[28] Lately, South Korean academics also started to use Asian values discourse in both national and international contexts.[29]

Noting the similarities and differences illustrated here, it is unclear yet how far the academic professions in these three East Asian countries are being shaped by a new cultural definition of the scholar mandarin, carefully adapted to new economic contexts, as these were examined in Chapter Four. The possibility is intriguing, not least because of other powerful interrelationships between academics and the State.

East Asian academics have been under the careful surveillance of the State since the colonial period. Surveillance is taken here to mean the State's control over and intervention in knowledge transmission (i.e. teaching and publication) and in the supervision of the social and political activities of academics as intellectual leaders. In all three societies, as indicated in Chapter Four, academics either in the university or in the process of their selection for scholarships, are subject to political approval. That was part of the colonial legacy of State-university relations, especially in Korea.

In addition, the elaborate machinery of governmental planning and the actual conduct of the State's modernity projects in these countries mean that academics have been called upon to build nations, to strengthen economies and to create (State-approved) collective values. As a result, possibilities for an independent role of the academic profession have been limited. Even university academic autonomy in research has been recognised only in pragmatic terms in East Asia. Overall, policy makers in these three East Asian countries have perhaps underestimated the significance of liberal knowledge in university education for revitalising cultural values; they have constantly stressed science and technology for rapid industrial development and modernisation in the postcolonial period. East Asian academics have been kept busy: staying in touch with new scientific and technological developments.

However, in a continuation of the common colonial legacy, the East Asian States have not only defined the role of university academics in terms of their political usefulness as State technocrats but also in terms of their social usefulness as guardians of cultural stability. They have also been used—as in Singapore—to re-invent social (Confucian) traditions. This is an extension of the Japanese and British colonial models of the academic profession, as social guardians and as civil servants—not only working within the boundaries of the States' modernity projects, but inventing those boundaries.

This surveillance by the State and the restricted social space for the university academic contrast sharply with the classic ideas of the university and the social space for the man of knowledge expected by Newman and Jaspers and Confucius in their respective traditions. In the Confucian tradition, the social role of 'the academic' was identified as a State-mandarin and as an autonomous sage – a man of knowledge. As reviewed through the ideal typical model of the Confucian University in Chapter Two, the two distinctive roles used to be unified by the social role of *sonbi* in the Korean Confucian State apparatus. These roles became separated in the modern bureaucratic Japanese colonial State apparatus. This cultural division of the academic profession, demarcated by the public and private sectors of higher education in the colonial period, has continued in the contemporary tensions over the social role of the academic in South Korea.

In Malaya, the social role of the academic as (an English version of) the scholar mandarin began with the establishment of the University of Malaya, where all academics were officially appointed with the status of a civil servant. This colonial university tradition has continued in the postcolonial period in both Malaysia and Singapore. In both societies, the State has shown little hesitation about redefining academic contracts and conditions of work, about insisting on the limits of academic freedom, and about demanding in quite formal ways proofs of political correctness.

It is thus suggested that the expected social role of the academic profession in contemporary East Asia is a mixture of (the revived, or transplanted, or occasionally corrupted Confucian tradition of) the social role of scholar mandarins and the contemporary version of scholar technocrats where academics should, indeed sometimes must, be involved in and agree with the State's modernity projects.

Overall, then, in this book, the shapes of the East Asian academic professions have been re-contextualised through an analysis of the changing relationships between the State and the University, where the colonial origins were treated as a significant frame of reference. One major colonial impact on and continuity in the shape of the East Asian academic professions is recognised in the maintenance of the initial colonial institutional

framing of the university and the forms of valued knowledge. These continuities in the colonial legacy of State and university relations have tightly
limited the social and political and economic role of the academic profession. Accordingly, East Asian academics have been subject to utilitarian
valuations of their roles in contributing to economic modernisation, and
have been strongly guided and supervised by their States. This is also true
in countries such as the U. K. and Australia and the U. S. A. *for very different reasons.* Thus—given the very different historical contexts of East
Asia—a simple convergence theory does not hold.

This supervision and guidance has meant that these States in East Asia
have been central in determining the meritocratic principles which shape
the academic profession. These meritocratic principles constructed by the
respective East Asian States have stressed both nationality and ethnicity
(while perhaps undervaluing gender). However, following the 'internationalisation' of higher education as outlined in Chapter Four, the 'nationality'
of the academic profession is likely to become more diversified because of
international knowledge competition and an increase in expatriate academic staff.

As convergence theorists might suggest, it is also likely that the exigen-
cies of developing national economies, to compete in the new international order, will induce an increasing emphasis on short-term rather than long-
term objectives of academic performance in the university and on the economic rate of returns of university education and research for both individuals and for States.

However, again, this would be partly to underestimate the historical
context, by stressing only one likely development. Perhaps the most significant historical impact on the shape of the contemporary East Asian academic professions is their initial acceptance of the Western paradigm of
knowledge and their remaining position as recipients of advanced knowledge. An international academic community may exist in the form of networks, but it still exists in a steep hierarchy, within which the ownership of
epistemic authority is located outside of East Asia. It is in this context that
the respective East Asian State's common policy on the internationalisation
of the university and the academic profession needs to be understood. Of
course, the East Asian universities are responding to global pressures, but
they are doing so from a unique historical position which includes:

• the ambivalent position of Japan, as the first non-western
modernising colonisers, in transmitting Western "modernity" to its
East Asian colonies;30

• the long-term impact of multiple importations of knowledge
and its cultural values on the East Asian academic discourse in the
postcolonial period (for example, Islamic, English, American and
Japanese influences in Malaysia);

- the contemporary attempt to re-define modernity from both academic sites of the East and the West; and

- the centrality in these three States of the search for a clear Asian cultural identity.

It is these themes which, it is finally suggested, can constitute a perspective and a subsequent research agenda to locate and reinterpret the academic professions of Asia, and the kind of intellectual work they do—not merely in the countries already described here but in Japan, Taiwan, Hong Kong, Thailand, the Philippines and so on. Such comparative work on the variations in the social space permitted to the university and the academic professions offers an exciting intellectual agenda.

In such contexts, 'the academic profession' is under stranger (and more complex) pressures than those assumed (or dreamt of) by the Carnegie Commission.

NOTES

1. Boyer, E. L., P. G. Altbach, and M. Whitelaw. *The Academic Profession: an International Perspective*. Princeton, NJ.: The Carnegie Foundation for the advancement of Teaching, 1994, p. 1.

2. Ministry of Education, Republic of Korea. *Education in Korea 1997-1998*. Seoul: The Government Press, 1998, p. 32; Korean Council for University Education (KCUE). *University Education Development Indicators*. Seoul: KCUE, 1997, p. 138.

3. Joung, Sun Ei. "*Kyung Sung Je-kook Dae-hack* [A Study on the Characteristics of Kyung Sung Imperial University].", Doctoral thesis, Yonsei University, Seoul, 1997; Chung, Hwan-kyu. "A Study on the Establishment of Seoul National University in Usamgik.", Doctoral thesis, Yonsei University, Seoul, 1997; Ministry of Education, ROK, op. cit.; KCUE, op. cit.

4. Before the establishment of the University of Malaya in 1949, there existed only two higher educational institutions: King Edward VII School of Medicine founded in 1905, and Raffles College, founded in 1928. These two institutions were merged to form the nucleus of the University of Malaya in Singapore. The first University in Malaya in Singapore was designed by the Carr-Saunders' Committee on the basis of the model of London University, especially the LSE (London School of Economics).

5. The number of students rose from 645 to 1,615. (For details, see Carr-Saunders, A. M. *New Universities Overseas*. London: George Allen & Unwin Ltd., 1961, p. 61; p. 174.)

6. University of Science, Malaysia (USM), National University of Malaysia (UKM), Agricultural University of Malaysia (UPM), Technical University of Malaysia, the International Islamic University (IIU), Northern University of Malaysia.

7. Between 1996 and 1998, there have been established four private universities: Universiti Telekom (The Telecom University); Multi Media University—linked to the Multi-media Super Corridor project, Universiti Tenaga Nasional (The National Energy University), and Universiti Tun Abdul Tazak—the first visual university in Malaysia, which is equivalent to the Open University in the U. K..

8. In 1996, the number of the academic staff was estimated at 1,689 in the University of Malaya, 1,857 in the University of Science Malaysia, 1,675 in the National University of Malaysia, 1,311 in the University of Technology, 968 in Universiti Pertanian (recently renamed as Putera) Malaysia (Agricultural University of Malaysia), 454 in Universiti Utara Malaysia (Northern University of Malaysia), 280 in Universiti Malaysia Sarawak; 72 in Universiti Malaysia Sabah, 808 in the International Islamic University Malaysia, Ministry of Education. (For details, see *Laporan Tahunan (Annual Report 96)*, Kuala Lumpur: Ministry of Education, Malaysia, 1996.)

9. By the 1990s, the two national universities are the National University of Singapore and Nanyang Technical University. A new Open University was established by the Singapore Institute of Management as the first self-financing private institution indicating a major shift in the provision of higher education by the contemporary Singapore Government. The four polytechnics are Singapore Polytechnic, Ngee An Polytechnic, Institute of Education, and College of Physical Education). The size of the university student population has seen a seven fold increase in the last three decades from 3,502 in 1960 to 25,307 in 1990. Student enrollments in the polytechnics have also increased from 4,669 in 1960 to 31,265 in 1990. For details, see Selvaratnam, V. *Innovations in Higher Education: Singapore at the Competitive Edge*. Washington, D. C.: The World Bank, 1994, p. 3.

10. NUS. *The National University of Singapore: General Information 1996-7*. Singapore, 1996, p. 4.

11. As examined in Chapter Three, the number of Korean students in Kyung Sung Imperial University had to be limited to a third of the total enrollment.

12. Carr-Saunders, A. M., op. cit., p. 174.

13. National University of Singapore Student's Union, The Student Report on University Education in Singapore, *Student Undergrad*, Vol. 13 (1), 1980; Requoted in Selvaratnam, V., op. cit., 1994, p. 53.

14. Tokyo Imperial University was established in 1886, and was developed from Tokyo University established in 1877, which was the first State University in Japan to teach modern Western knowledge in four faculties: the Faculty of Law, Faculty of Humanities, Faculty of Science, and Faculty of Medicine. For details, see Joung, Sun Ei. op. cit., pp. 36-40.

15. It was a convention in the British Empire that British residents in the colonies would go back home to Britain to receive university education. (For details, see Rich, P. J. *Elixir of Empire*. London: Regency Press Ltd., 1989.)

16. The normal assumption in educational writing, that merit is the same as academic excellence, or a combination of academic excellence and personal virtue, is less useful here than seeing 'merit' as a social construction to understand how the State affects the composition of the academic profession. According to *The Oxford English Dictionary*, 'merit' is defined as the "quality of deserving well; something that entitles one to reward or gratitude; the condition of being valued or honoured; a commendable quality, an excellence; chiefly in recent terms denoting rewards for proficiency in school work, or prizes for skill in some athletic pursuit".

17. This combination shaped the academic profession. The entry routes to the academic profession became wider with the absorption of secondary and upper secondary teachers into the tertiary institutions and social upward mobility in rapid economic development. The new Korean political culture after political independence has manifested this opportunistic mode of meritocratic education selection, which was tightly controlled by the State, so as to sustain political power whenever State legitimacy and credibility were questioned. Unlike Singaporean elitism promoted through both education and politics, Korean political culture has been led by populist demand. Accordingly educational selection has stressed serving the populist political concerns such as the absolute standardisation of quality in schooling and conformity in teaching the national curriculum.

18. Through the New Economic Policy, the language of the university academic profession became Bahasa Malaysia, in 1977.

19. At Kyung Sung Imperial University, there were only two faculties: the Faculty of Law and Humanities, and the Faculty of Medicine. University education was then focused on liberal arts education and traditional professional training such as Law to produce the skilled groups who would then be recruited to the colonial government or to the professions.

20. The University of Malaya did not initially have a Faculty of Law, but began with three faculties: Medicine, Arts and Science. Later, the University of Malaya was expanded into other fields—Education in 1950, Engineering in 1955, Law in 1957 and Agriculture in 1960 (after Independence).

21. The concept of 'social role' is here interpreted to include the performativity expected of and statuses given to academics in political, economic and cultural arenas. The term 'social' is chosen precisely because it can be used to cover all three dimensions of expected performativity and the award of 'social honour' (in Max Weber's terms).

22. For the concept of "social space", see Cowen, R. 'The State, Civil Society and Economies: the University and the Politics of Space' Unpublished paper presented in the CESE Conference in Gröningen, the Netherlands, July 1998.

23 The Japanese State's systemic control over the formation of the governing elite in liaison with the Imperial University academics was a Japanese adaptation of the traditional Confucian State mandarin system to the recruitment of government officers. Japan implanted this modern civil service system in her colony, Korea, where the historical Confucian State mandarin system had been already abolished in the 1894 *Kabo* Reform.

24 Lee, K. Y., 'Confucian Values Helped Singapore Prosper' *Straits Times,* Oct. 6, 1994; Quoted by Gopinathan, S. "Globalisation, the State and Education Policy in Singapore." op. cit., p. 71.

25 Mahathir bin Mohamad writes, "The NEP was roughly the embodiment of the affirmative action approach formulated in the USA." (Quoted from Mohamad, Mahathir bin. *The Way Forward*. London: Weidenfeld & Nicolson, 1998, p. 85.)

26 Mahathir bin Mohamad assures that "Having admitted that the distribution of wealth between the different races in the country was unfair, we were willing to be unfair, in order to achieve fair results and the equitable distribution of wealth." (ibid)

27 Mohamad, M. bin. *The Malay Dilemma*, Singapore: Donald Moore Asia Press, 1970; "Look East." *New Perspectives Quarterly* 9, no. 1 (1992): 16-19; *Vision 2020, Malaysia: Towards Establishing a Fully Developed Nation.* Kementerian Penerangan, Malaysia: Dicetak oleh Zizi Press Sdn Bhd., 1997; *The Way Forward.* op. cit., 1998; Anwar Ibrahim, *The Asian Renaissance,* Kuala Lumpur: Times Books, 1996.

28 Muzaffar, Chandra, *Human Rights and the New World Order,* Penang: Just World Trust, 1993. Malay Islamic academic identity seems to be supported by the establishment of the International Islamic University in Kuala Lumpur. According to Shabbir Akhtar, who taught philosophy at the IIU, "academics in the International Islamic University in Malaysia were united in their hatred of the West.... Students and faculty alike are obsessed with the defense of Islam against western Christian and secular liberal accusation," which evinces to some extent the

resurgence of the pan-Arabic ecumenical Islamic movement. (For details, see *Times Higher Education Supplement,* 13 February 1998.)

29. For example, see *Jontong-kwa Hyundai,* Summer Special Issue on Confucianism and Asian Values edited by Ham Jae-bong, Seoul, 1998; *Jonton-kwa Hyundai* has organised meetings of the International Forum for Democratic Studies held in both South Korea and the USA in 1998, with specific reference to Confucian democracy, Confucian capitalism, and Asian values discourse.

30. In Chapter Four, I already stressed the Japanese impact on the postcolonial education systems in Malaysia and Singapore, as well as South Korea. That is, despite the experience of British colonialism, both Malaysia and Singapore have developed highly centralised national education systems under the tight control and surveillance of the Ministry of Education in the postcolonial period, which is more reminiscent of the Japanese model than the British version. Malaysia articulates further the Japanese connection in its new direction of modernity projects, namely the Look East Policy and Vision 2020. For example, the State established Universiti Malaysia Sarawak in December 1992, with clear aims to gain the cultural knowledge of what it means to *be* Japanese as well as to learn the language. (For detailed discussion, see the Conclusion to Chapter Four in this book.)

Bibliography

Adams, D. "Problems of Reconstruction in Korean Education" *Comparative Education Review* 3 (1959-60).

Adams, D. and E. E. Gottlieb. *Education and Social Change in Korea.* New York & London: Garland Publishing Inc., 1993.

Ahmad, Z. (ed). *Government and Politics of Malaysia.* Singapore: Oxford University Press, 1987.

Ahn, C-S. "Democratization and Political Reform in South Korea: Development, Culture and Institutional Change." *Asian Journal of Political Science* 1, no. 2 (1993): 93-110.

Alastair, L. "Early History" In *Malaysia: a survey* edited by Gungwu Wang, Singapore: Donald Moore Books, 1964.

Alatas, H. S. *Intellectuals in Developing Societies.* London: Frank Cass, 1977.

Alatas, H. S. *The Myth of the Lazy Native: a Study of the Image of the Malays, Filipinos and Javanese from the 16th to the 20th Century and its Function in the Ideology of Colonial Capitalism,* London: Cass, 1977.

Ali, S. H. (ed). *Ethnicity, Class and Development: Malaysia.* Kuala Lumpur: Persatuaan Sains Malaysia, 1984.

Alisjahbana, S. T. (ed). *The Cultural Problems of Malaysia in the Context of Southeast Asia,* Kuala Lumpur: The Malaysian Society of Orientalists, 1966.

Allington, N. F. B. and N. J. O'Shaughnessy. *Light, Liberty and Learning: the Idea of a University Revisited.* Oxford: The Education Unit, 1992.

Altbach, P. G. (ed). *Comparative Perspectives on the Academic Profession.* New York: Praeger Publishers, 1977.

Altbach, P. G. "Patterns in Higher Education Development: Toward the Year 2000." In *Emergent Issues in Education: Comparative Perspectives,* edited by R. F. Arnove, P. G. Altbach and G. P. Kelly, New York: State University of NewYork Press, 1992.

Altbach, P. G., C. H. Davis, T. O. Eisemon, et. al. *Scientific Development and Higher Education, The Case of Newly Industrializing Nations,* New York: Praeger, 1989.

Altbach, P. G. and G. P. Kelly (eds). *Education and Colonialism.* London: Longmans, 1978.

Altbach, P. G. (ed). *International Higher Education: an Encyclopedia.* Vol. I. New York: Garland Publishing, Inc., 1991.

Altbach, P. G. and G. P. Kelly (eds). *New Approaches to Comparative Education,* Chicago: The University of Chicago Press, 1986.

Altbach, P. G. and V. Selvaratnam (eds). *From Dependence to Autonomy: The Development of Asian Universities,* London: Kluwer Academic Publishers, 1989.

Amsden, A. H. *Asia's Next Giant: South Korea and Late Industrialization.* Oxford: Oxford University Press, 1989.

Anchor, R. *The Enlightenment Tradition,* New York: Harper & Row, 1967.

Anderson, B. *Imagined Communities: Reflections on the Origins and Spread of Nationalism.* London: Verso, 1983.

Anderson, R. D. "The Formation of National Elites: The British Case." In *University and Nation: The University and the Making of the Nation in Northern Europe in the 19th and 20th Centuries,* edited by M. Norrback & K. Ranki. Helsinki: SHS, 1996.

Applebaum, R. P. and J. Henderson. *States & Development in the Asian Pacific Rim.* Newbury Park: Sage, 1992.

Arnove, R. F. "Comparative Education and World System Analysis." *Comparative*

Education Review 24, (1980): 48-62.

Arnove, R. F., P. G. Altbach, and G. P. Kelly (eds). *Emergent Issues in Education: Comparative Perspectives.* New York: SUNY Press, 1992.

Ashby, E. "The Future of the Nineteenth Century Idea of a University." *Minerva* VI, no. 1, (1967): 3-17.

Ashby, E. "Universities under Siege." *Minerva: A Review of Science Learning and Policy* I, no. 1, (1962): 18-29.

Ashby, E. *The Academic Profession,* Oxford: Oxford University Press for the British Academy, 1969.

Ashby, E. *Universities: British, Indian, African: A Study in the Ecology of Higher Education.* Cambridge, MA.: Harvard University Press, 1966.

Ashton, S. R. and S. E. Stockwell. *Imperial Policy and Colonial Practice 1925-1945, Part II Economic Policy, Social Policies and Colonial Research.* edited by S. R. Ashton and S. E. Stockwell, *British Documents on the End of Empire.* London: HMSO, 1996.

Asquith Commission, The. *Report of the Commission on Higher Education in the Colonies,* London: HMSO, June 1945.

Association of Commonwealth Universities. *Commonwealth Universities Yearbook 1984.* London: Association of Commonwealth Universities, 1985.

Awang, Amir. "Staff and Faculty Development in the Universiti Sains Malaysia." In *Staff and Faculty Development in South Asian Universities,* RIHED. Hong Kong: Maruzen Asia Ltd., 1981.

Aziz, U. A., S. B. Chew, K. H. Lee, and B. C. Sanyal. *University Education and Employment in Malaysia.* IIEP Research Report Vol. 66. Paris: IIEP, 1987.

Barber, E. G., P. G. Altbach and R. G. Myers, *Bridges to Knowledge: foreign students in comparative perspective,* Chicago: The University of Chicago Press, 1984.

Barnett, R. and R. Middlehurst. "The lost profession." *Higher Education in Europe* 18, (1993): 110-28.

Barnett, R. (ed). *Academic Community: Discourse or Discord?* London: Jessica Kingsley Publishers, 1994.

Bartholomew, J. R. "Science, bureaucracy and freedom in Meiji and Taisho Japan." In *Meiji Japan: Political, economic and social history 1868-1912 Vol. IV. The End of Meiji and Early Taisho*, edited by P. Kornicki. London: Routledge, 1998.

Bauman, Z. *Intimations of Postmodernity,* London: Routeledge, 1992.

Bauman, Z., *Legislators and Interpreters: on modernity, post-modernity and intellectuals,* Cambridge: Polity Press, 1987.

Becher, T. *Academic Tribes and Territories: Intellectual Enquiry and the Cultures of Disciplines.* Milton Keynes: Society for Research into Higher Education & Open University Press, 1989.

Becher, T. "The Disciplinary Shaping of the Profession." In *The Academic Profession: National, Disciplinary, and Institutional Settings*, edited by B. R. Clark. Berkeley: University of California Press, 1987.

Becher, T. and M. Kogan. *Process and Structure in Higher Education.* 2nd ed. London & New York: Routledge, 1992.

Becher, T. (ed). *Governments and Professional Education.* Buckingham: Society for Research into Higher Education & Open University Press, 1994.

Beck, U. *Risk Society: towards a new modernity.* London: Sage, 1992.

Becker, H. S. "The Nature of a Profession: The Debate. The Symbol. The Reality. Implications for Education." In *Education for the Professions*, edited by Nelson B. Henry. Chicago: University of Chicago Press, 1962.

Bedeski, R. E. *The Transformation of South Korea: Reform and reconstitution in the Sixth Republic under Roh Tae Woo, 1987-1992.* London & New York: Routledge, 1994.

Bedlington, S. S. *Malaysia & Singapore: the Building of New States.* Ithaca, N. Y.: Cornell University Press, 1978.

Benjamin, G. "The Cultural Logic of Singapore's "Multiracialism"." In *Singapore: society in transition*, edited by R. Hassan. Singapore: Oxford University Press, 1976.

Berger, M. T. and D. A. Borer (eds). *The Rise of East Asia: Critical Visions of the Pacific Century.* London and New York: Routledge, 1997.

Berger, P. L. and H.-H. M. Hsiao (eds). *In search of an East Asian Development Model.* New Brunswick, N. J.: Transaction Publishers, 1988.

Berman, M. *All that is Solid Melts into Air: the experience of modernity,* London: Verso, 1983.

Bhabha, Homi K. (ed). *Nation and Narration,* London: Routledge, 1990.

Binsbergen, P. H. de Boer, and F. van Vught. "Comparing Governance Structure of Higher Education Institutions: towards a conceptual framework." In *Comparative Policy Studies in Higher Education,* edited by L. Goedegebuure and F. van Vught. Utrecht: Lemma, 1994.

Black, C. E. *The Dynamics of Modernisation: A Study in Comparative History.* New York: Harper & Row, 1966.

Bledstein, B. J. *The Culture of Professionalism,* New York: Norton, 1976.

Bloom, A. *The Closing of the American Mind: How Higher Education Has Failed Democracy and Impoverished the Souls of Today's Students.* New York: Simon & Schuster, 1987.

Blumenthal, P., C. Goodwin, A. Smith, and U. Teichler (eds). *Academic Mobility in a Changing World: Regional and Global Trends.* London & Bristol, Pennsylvania: Jessica Kingsley Publishers, 1996.

Bocock, R. *Hegemony.* London & New York: Tavistock Publications, 1986.

Bowen, H. R., and J. H. Schuster. *American Professors: A National Resource Imperiled.* Oxford: Oxford University Press, 1986.

Bowie, A. "Redistribution with Growth? The Dilemmas of State-Sponsored Economic Development in Malaysia" In *State and Development,* edited by C. Clark and J. Lemco, New York: E. J. Brill, 1988.

Bown, L. (ed). *Towards a Commonwealth of Scholars: A New Vision for the Nineties.* London: Commonwealth Secretariat, Marlborough House, 1994.

Boyd, D. *Elites and their Education: the educational and social background of eight elite groups,* New York: Humanities Press Inc., 1973

Boyd, W. *History of Western Education.* 12th ed. Lanham, Md.: Barnes & Noble, 1995.

Boyer, E. L., P. G. Altbach, and M. J. Whitelaw. *The Academic Profession: an International Perspective*. Princeton, NJ.: The Carnegie Foundation for the Advancement of Teaching, 1994.

Brah, A., *Cartographies of Diaspora: contesting identities*, London: Routledge, 1996.

Braibanti, R. *Asian Bureaucratic Systems Emergent from the British Imperial Tradition*. Durham, North Carolina: Duke University Press, 1966.

Brandt, V. S. R., "Chapt. 8. Korea", In *Ideology and National Competitiveness: An Analysis of Nine Countries*, edited by G. C. Lodge and E. F. Vogel, Boston: Harvard Business School Press, 1987.

Brauer Jr., G. C. *The Education of a Gentleman: Theories of Gentlemanly Education in England, 1660-1775*. New Haven, Conn.: College & University Press, 1959.

British Council, The. *Higher Education Market Survey Malaysia*. London: The British Council, Oct. 1984.

Brody, C. M. and J. Wallace (eds). *Ethical and Social Issues in Professional Education*. Albany, New York: State University of New York Press, 1994.

Brook, T. and Hy V. Luong (eds). *Culture and Economy: The Shaping of Capitalism in Eastern Asia*. Michigan: The University of Michigan Press, 1997.

Brooker, P. and P. Humm. *Dialogue and Difference: English into the Nineties*, London: Routledge, 1989.

Buczynska-Garewicz, H. "Jaspers and University Self-Governance." In *The Tasks of Truth*, edited by G. J. Walters. Frankfurt am Main: Peter Lang, 1996.

Burgen, A. (ed). *Goals and Purposes of Higher Education in the 21st Century*. Higher Education Policy Series, no. 32. Edited by Maurice Kogan. London: Jessica Kingsley Publishers, 1996.

Burger, T. *Max Weber's Theory of Concept Formation: History, Laws and Ideal Types*. Durham, NC.: Duke University Press, 1976.

Burrage, M. "Practitioners, Professors and the State in France, the USA and England." In *Education for the Professions: Quis custodiet...?*, edited by Sinclair Goodlad. Guildford, Surry: SRHE & NFER-NELSON, 1984.

Burrage, M. and R. Torstendahl (eds). *Profession in Theory and History: Rethinking the Study of the Professions in Europe and North America,* London, 1990.

Caiden, G. E. and B. W. Kim (eds). *A Dragon's Progress: Development Administration in Korea.* Connecticut: Kumarian Press, Inc., 1991.

Caplow, T. and R. J. McGee. *The Academic Marketplace.* New York: Basic Book, Inc., 1958.

Capra, F. *The Turning Point: Science, Society and the Rising Culture.* London: Flamingo Fontana Paperbacks, 1982.

Carey, J. *The Intellectuals and the Masses: Pride and Prejudice among the Literary Intelligentsia, 1880-1939.* London: Faber and Faber, 1992.

Carnoy, M. "Education and the State: From Adam Smith to Perestroika." In *Emergent Issues in Education,* edited by R. Arnove, P. G. Altbach and G. P. Kelly. New York: SUNY Press, 1992.

Carnoy, M. *Education as Cultural Imperialism: a Critical Appraisal.* New York: David McKay, 1974.

Carnoy, M. "Universities, Technological Change, and Training in the Information Age." In *Revitalizing Higher Education,* edited by J. Salmi and A. M. Verspoor. Washington, D. C.: The World Bank, IAU Press, Pergamon, 1994.

Carr-Saunders, A. M. *New Universities Overseas.* London: George Allen & Unwin Ltd., 1961.

Carr-Saunders, A. M. and P. A. Wilson. *The Professions.* London: Frank Cass, 1933, New edition 1964.

Castells, M. "Four Asian Tigers with a Dragon Head: a Comparative Analysis of the State, Economy and Society in the Asian Pacific Rim." In *States and Development in the Asian Pacific Rim,* edited by R. P. Appelbaum and J. Henderson. Newbury Park: Sage, 1992.

Castells, M. *The Developmental City State in an Open World Economy: The Singapore Experience.* Berkeley: University of California, Berkeley Roundtable on the International Economy, 1988.

Castells, M. *The Rise of the Network Society.* Vol. 1, *The Information Age: Economy, Society and Culture.* Oxford: Blackwell Publishers, 1996.

Chai, H-C. *The Development of British Malaya 1896-1909*. Oxford: Oxford Univeristy Press, 1964.

Chan, H. C. "The Political System and Social Change." In *Singapore: Society in Transition*, edited by R. Hassan. Singapore: Oxford University Press, 1976.

Chan, P. "Malaysia." In *Economics in Asia: Status Report on Teaching and Research in Nine Countries*, edited by UNESCO. Bangkok: UNESCO, 1985.

Chang, Y-S. "Planned Economic Transformation and Population Change." In *Korea's Response to Japan: The Colonial Period 1910-1945*, edited by C. I Eugene Kim and Doretha E. Mortimore. Michigan: Western Michigan University, 1974.

Channon, H. J. "Some Observations on the Development of Higher Education in the Colonies: Memorandum by Professor H.J. Channon [Extract]." In *Imperial Policy and Colonial Practice 1925-1945, Part II: Economic Policy, Social Policies and Colonial Research*, edited by S. R. Ashton and S. E. Stockwell. London: HMSO, Jan. 1941.

Chapman, J. W. (ed). *The Western University on Trial*. Berkeley, CA.: University of California Press, 1983.

Chee M. S. (ed). *Asian Values and Modernisation*. Singapore: Singapore University Press, 1977.

Chelliah, D. D. *A History of the Educational Policy of the Straits Settlements with Recommendations for a New System Based on Vernaculars*. Kuala Lumpur: The Government Press, 1947.

Chen, P. S. J. "The Cultural Implications of Industrialisation and Modernisation: with Special Reference to Southeast Asia." In *Culture and Industrialisation: an Asian Dilemma*, edited by Rolf E. Bente and Peter S. J. Chen. Singapore: McGraw-Hill, 1980.

Chen, P. S. J. "Asian Values and Modernisation: A Sociological Perspective." In *Asian Values and Modernisation*, edited by Chee Meow Seah. Singapore: Singapore University Press, 1977.

Chen, P. S. J. (ed). *Singapore Development Policies and Trends*. Singapore: Oxford University Press, 1983.

Chen, P. S. J. and H.-D. Evers (eds). *Studies in ASEAN Sociology: Urban Society and Social Change*, Singapore: Chopmen Enterprises, 1978.

Cheng, C-y. *New Dimensions of Confucian and Neo-Confucian Philosophy*. New York: State University of New York Press, 1991.

Childs, P. and P Williams. *An Introduction to Post-colonial Theory*. London: Prentice Hall Europe, 1997.

Ching, L. Y. "Academic Exchange Schemes in Malaysia." In *Towards a Commonwealth of Scholars: A New Vision for the Nineties*, edited by L. Bown. London: Commonwealth Secretariat, Marlborough House, 1994.

Chua, B-H. *Communitarian Ideology and Democracy in Singapore*. London & New York: Routledge, 1995.

Chua, B-H. *Culture, Multiracialism and National Identity in Singapore*, Department of Sociology Working Papers, No. 125. Singapore: National University of Singapore, 1995.

Chua, B-H. "Pragmatism of the People's Action Party Government of Singapore: a critical assessment." *Southeast Asian Journal of Social Science* 13, no. 2 (1985): 29-46.

Chua, B-H, "Taking Asia Out of 'Asian Values' Discourse', Unpublished paper presented at Pacific Asia Cultural Studies Forum Conference on "Globalising Cultural Studies?", held at Goldsmiths College, University of London, on 25 June 1998.

Chung, B. M. "Education for Development and Beyond: A Korean Perspective" In *Asia and the Pacific: Issues of Educational Policy, Curriculum and Practice*, edited by D. C. Wilson, D. L. Grossman and K. J. Kennedy. Calgary, Alberta: Detseling Enterprises Ltd., 1990.

Chung, H-k. "A Study on the Establishment of Seoul National University in Usamgik.", Doctoral Thesis, Dept. of Education, Graduate School, Yonsei University, Seoul, 1997.

Chung, Y-i. "The Impact of Chinese Culture on Korea's Economic Development." In *Confucianism and Economic Development*, edited by Hung-chao Tai. Washington, D.C.: The Washington Institute Press, 1989.

Clammer, J. "Religion and Language in Singapore." In *Language and Society in Singapore*, edited by E. Afendras and Kuo. Singapore: Singapore University Press, 1980.

Clammer, J. *Singapore: Ideology, Society, Culture*. Singapore: Chopmen Publishers, 1985.

Clark, B. R (ed). *The Research Foundations of Graduate Education: Germany, Britain, France, United States, Japan.* Berkeley: University of California Press, 1993.

Clark, B. R. (ed). *The Academic Profession: National, Disciplinary, and Institutional Settings.* Berkeley: University of California Press, 1987.

Clark, B. R. and G. R. Neave (eds). *The Encyclopedia of Higher Education.* Oxford: Pergamon Press, 1992.

Clark, D. N. (ed). *Christianity in Modern Korea.* New York: Asia Society, 1986.

Clarke, J. and J. Newman. *The Managerial State.* London: Sage Publications, 1997.

Clegg, S. R. *Frameworks of Power.* London: Sage Publications, 1989.

Coffield, F. (ed). *Higher Education in a Learning Society.* Durham: School of Education, University of Durham on behalf of DFEE, ESRC and HEFCE the co-funders of the Seminar held in St. Edmund Hall, Oxford, 26-26 June 1995.

Cohen, S. *Visions of Social Control.* Cambridge: Polity Press, 1985.

Colclough, C. "Structuralism versus Neo-liberalism: an Introduction." In *States or Markets?: Neo-liberalism and the Development Policy Debate*, edited by C. Coclough and J. Manor. Oxford: Clarendon Press, 1991.

Cole, D. C. and P. N. Lyman. *Korean Development.* Cambridge, Mass.: Harvard University Press, 1971.

Committee appointed by His Excellency the Governor. *Official Report on Education in the Straits Settlements and the Federated Malay States 1870-1939 (The Firmstone Report)*, London: HMSO, 1919.

Committee on Malay Education. "Report of the Committee on Malay Education, Federation of Malaya." Kuala Lumpur: The Government Press, 1951.

Connor, W. "Ethnonationalism." In *Understanding Political Development*, edited by M. Weiner and S. Huntington. Boston, Mass.: Little, Brown & Company, 1987.

Corbett, Jack. "The Internationalization of Professional Education." In *Ethical and Social Issues in Professional Education*, edited by C. M. Brody and J. Wallace. New York: State University of New York Press, 1994.

Cowen, R. "Late Modernity and the Rules of Chaos: an Initial Note on Transitologies and Rims." In Alexander, R., P. Broadfoot & D. Phillips, *Learning from Comparing: new directions in comparative educational research,* Oxford: Symposium Books, 1999.

Cowen, R. "Last past the post: comparative education, modernity and perhaps post-modernity." *Comparative Education* 32, no. 2 (1996): 151-170.

Cowen, R. "The Utilitarian University." In *Higher Education in a Changing World: The World Yearbook of Education 1971/72,* edited by B. Holmes, D. Scanlon. London: Evans Brothers Ltd., 1971.

Cowen, R. (ed). *The World Yearbook of Education: The Evaluation of Higher Education Systems.* London: Kogan Page, 1996.

Cowen, R. "The State, Civil Society and Economies: the University and the Politics of Space." Paper presented in the CESE Conference in Gröningen, July 1998.

Cummings, B. "The Origins and Development of the Northeast Asian Political Economy: Industrial Sectors, Product Cycles, and Political Consequences." *International Organization* 38, no. 1 (1984).

Cummings, W. K. and P. G. Altbach (eds). *The Challenge of Eastern Asian Education: Implication for America.* Albany, N.Y.: SUNY, 1997.

Cummings, W. K., and Kuo Amano. "The Changing Role of the Japanese Professor." In *Changes in the Japanese University: a Comparative Perspective,* edited by W. K. Cummings, K. Amano and K. Kitamura. New York: Praeger, 1979.

Cummings, W. K, I. Amano, and K. Kitamura (eds). *Changes in the Japanese University.* New York: Praeger, 1979.

Cummings, W. K., S. Gopinathan, and Y. Tomoda (eds). *The Revival of Values Education in Asia and the West.* Oxford: Pergamon, 1988.

Cummings, W. K. and N. McGinn (eds). *Handbook of Development and Education: Past and Future.* New York: Garland, 1997.

Currie, J. "Globalization Practices and the Professoriate in Anglo-Pacific and North American Universities." *Comparative Education Review* 42, no. 1, (February 1998): 15-29.

Cutts, R. L. *An Empire of Schools: Molding of a National Power Elite.* Armonk, New York & London, England: An East Gate Book, 1997.

Davis, W. "Religion and Development: Weber and the East Asian Experience." In *Understanding Political Development*, edited by M. Weiner and S. P. Huntington. Boston, Mass.: Little, Brown & Company, 1987.

de Bary, W. T. "Confucian Education in Premodern East Asia." In *Confucian Traditions in East Asian Modernity: Moral Education and Economic Culture in Japan and the Four Mini-Dragons*, edited by Tu Wei-ming. Cambridge, Mass.: Harvard University Press, 1996.

de Bary, W. T. *Confucianism as an Aspect of East Asian and World Civilizations*. Singapore: Institute of East Asian Philosophies, 1986.

de Bary, W. T. *Neo-Confucian Orthodoxy and the Learning of the Mind-and-Heart*. New York: Columbia University Press, 1981.

de Bary, W. T. and J. W. Chaffee (eds). *Neo-Confucian Education: The Formative Stage*. Berkeley: University of California Press, 1989.

de Bary, W. T. and JaHyun Kim Haboush (eds). *The Rise of Neo-Confucianism in Korea*. New York: Columbia University Press, 1985.

Deyo, F. C., (ed). *The Political Economy of the New Asian Industrialism*. Ithaca: Cornell University Press, 1987.

Dill, D. D. and B. Sporn (eds). *Emerging Patterns of Social Demand and University Reform: Through a Glass Darkly*. Oxford: Pergamon, published for the IAU Press, 1995.

Dingwall, R. and P. Lewis (eds). *Sociology of the Profession*, London: Macmillan, 1983.

Dong, W. "Japanese Colonial Policy and Practices in Korea, 1905-1945: A Study in Assimilation." Doctoral thesis, Georgetown University, 1965.

Doraisamy, T. R. (ed). *150 Years of Education in Singapore*, Singapore: Teachers' Training College, 1969.

Dunn, J. *The Political Thought of John Locke*. Cambridge: Cambridge University Press, 1969.

Dyson, K. *The State Tradition in Western Europe*. Oxford: Martin Robertson, 1980.

Easton, D. and C. S. Schelling (eds). *Divided Knowledge: Across Disciplines, Across Cultures*. London: Sage, 1991.

Eckert, C. J., K-b Lee, Y. I. Lew, et. al. *Korea Old and New. A History*. Seoul: Ilchokak, 1990.

Economic Planning Committee, The. *The Strategic Economic Plan: Towards a Developed Nation*. Singapore: Ministry of Trade and Industry, 1991.

Elias, N. *State Formation and Civilization*. Oxford: Blackwell, 1982.

Emerson, R. *Malaysia: A Study in Direct and Indirect Rule* (reprint). Kuala Lumpur: University of Malaya Press, 1964.

Enders, J. and U. Teichler. "A Victim of its Own Success? Employment and Working Conditions of Academic Staff in Comparative Perspective." In *Higher Education* 34, no. 1, Special Issue on the International Survey of the Academic Profession edited by A. Welch. (1997).

Engel, A. "Emerging Concept of the Academic Profession." In *The University in Society, Vol. I, Oxford and Cambridge from the 14th to the Early 19th Century*, edited by L. Stone. Princeton: Princeton University Press, 1974.

Engel, A. J. *From Clergyman to Don: the Rise of the Academic Profession in Nineteenth-Century Oxford*. Oxford: Clarendon, 1983.

Esman, M. J., *Administration and Development in Malaysia*, Ithaca, N.Y.: Cornell University Press, 1972.

Etzkowitz, H. "Entrepreneurial Scientists and Entrepreneurial Universities in American Academic Science." *Minerva* 21 (1983): 198-233.

Evans, P. *Embedded Autonomy: State and Industrial Transformation*. Princeton: Princeton U. P., 1995.

Evans, P., D. Rueschemeyer, and T. Skocpol (eds). *Bringing the State Back In*. Cambridge: Cambridge University Press, 1985.

Everman, R. *Between Culture and Politics: Intellectuals in Modern Society*. Cambridge: Polity Press, 1994.

Evers, H.-D. (ed). *Modernisation in Southeast Asia*. Kuala Lumpur: Oxford University Press, 1973.

Featherstone, M., S. Lash and R. Robertson. *Global Modernities*. London: Sage, 1995.

Fenn, W. P. and The Yao Wu. *Chinese Schools and the Education of Chinese Malayans*. Kuala Lumpur: The Government Press, 1951.

Fishman, J.A., A. W. Conrad and A. Rubal-Lopez (eds). *Post-Imperial English, Status Change in Former British and American Colonies, 1940-1990*, Berlin & New York: Mouton de Gruyter, 1996.

Fong, P. E. *Education, Manpower and Development in Singapore*. Singapore: Singapore University Press, 1982.

Freidson, E. *Professional Powers: A Study of the Institutionalization of Formal Knowledge*. Chicago: University of Chicago Press, 1986.

Freidson, E. *Professionalism Reborn: Theory Prophecy and Policy*. Cambridge: Polity Press, 1994.

Galtun, J. *The True Worlds, A Transnational Perspective*. New York: The Free Press, 1980.

Gannon, P. J. *The Republic of Korea: A Study of the Educational System of the Republic of Korea and a Guide to the Academic Placement of Students in Educational Institutions of the United States*, World Education Series: American Association of Collegiate Registrars and Admissions Officers, 1985.

Gellert, C. *Structural and Functional Differentiation: remarks on changing paradigms of tertiary education in Europe*. London: Jessica Kingsley, 1993.

Gellert, C. (ed). *Higher Education in Europe*. Higher Education Policy Series no. 16. London: Jessica Kingsley Publisher, 1993.

George, T. J. S. *Lee Kuan Yew's Singapore*. Singapore: Eastern University Press, 1984.

Giddens, A. *The Consequences of Modernity*. Cambridge: Polity Press, 1990.

Giddens, A. *The Nation-State and Violence*. Volume Two of a Contemporary Critique of Historical Materialism. Cambridge: Plity Press in Association with Blackwell, 1987.

Glassick, C. E., M. T. Huber, and G. I. Maeroff. *Scholarship Assessed: Evaluation of the Professoriate*. San Francisco, California: Jossey Bass Publishers, 1997.

Goedegebuure, L., F. Kaiser, P. Maassen, L. Meek, F. van Vught, and E. de Weert. *Higher Education Policy: an International Comparative Perspective, Issues in Higher Education*, Centre for Higher Education Policy Studies (CHEPS), University Twente, The Netherlands. Oxford & New York & Seoul & Tokyo: Pergamon Press, 1994.

Goedegebuure, L. and F. van Vught (eds). *Comparative Policy Studies in Higher Education*. Utrecht, The Netherlands: Centre for Higher Education Policy Studies (CHEPS), 1994.

Goh, S. K. *The Practice of Economic Growth*. Singapore: Federal Publications, 1977.

Gong, G. W. *The Standard of 'Civilization' in International Society*. Oxford: Clarendon, 1984.

Goodchild, L. F. and H. S. Wechlsler (eds). *The History of Higher Education*. Needham Heights, MA.: Simon & Schuster Sustom Publishing, 1997.

Goodlad, S. (ed). *Education for the Professions: Quis custodiet...?*, Papers presented to the 20th annual conference of the Society for Research into Higher Education 1984. Guildford, Surrey: SRHE & NFER-NELSON, 1984.

Gopinathan, G. "Open to Talent: Higher Education in Singapore." In *Towards a Commonwealth of Scholars*, edited by L. Bown. London: Commonwealth Secretariat, Marlborough House, 1994.

Gopinathan, S. "Being and Becoming: education for values in Singapore." In *The Revival of Values Education in Asia and the West*, edited by W. Cummings, S. Gopinathan and Y. Tomoda. Oxford: Pergamon Press, 1988.

Gopinathan, S. "Education." In *Government and Politics of Singapore*, edited by J. S. T. Quah, H. C. Chan and C. M. Seah. Singapore: Oxford University Press, 1985.

Gopinathan, S. "Educational Development in a Strong-developmentalist State: The Singapore Experience." In *Handbook of Education and Development*, edited by W. K. Cummings and N. McGinn. New York: Garland Press, 1997.

Gopinathan, S. "Education and State Development: Lessons for the United States?" In *The Challenge of East Asian Education: Implication for America*, edited by W. Cummings and P. G. Altbach. Albany, N. Y.: SUNY, 1997.

Gopinathan, S. "Globalisation, the State and Education Policy in Singapore." In *Education and Political Transition: Perspectives and Dimensions in East Asia*, edited by W. O. Lee and M. Bray. Hong Kong: Comparative Education Research Centre, The University of Hong Kong, 1997.

Gopinathan, S. "Singapore." In *Education and Development in East Asia*, edited by P. Morris and A. Sweeting. New York & London: Garland Publishing, Inc., 1995.

Gopinathan, S. "Towards a National Education System." In *Singapore: Society in Transition*, edited by R. Hassan. Singapore: Oxford University Press, 1976.

Gopinathan, S. *Towards a National System of Education in Singapore 1945-1973*. Singapore: Oxford University Press, 1974.

Gopinathan, S. "University Education in Singapore: The Making of National University." In *From Dependence to Autonomy: The Developments of Asian Universities*, edited by P. G. Altbach and V. Selvaratnam. London: Kluwer Academic Publishers, 1989.

Government General of Chosen. *Annual Report on Administration of Chosen 1930-32*. Seoul, December 1932.

Green, A. *Education and State Formation: The Rise of Education Systems in England, France and the USA*. New York: St. Martin's Press, Inc., 1990.

Gullick, J. M. *Indigenous Political Systems of Western Malaya*. London: The Athlone Press, 1965.

Gundara, J. S., D. Coulby, and C. Jones. *World Yearbook of Education: Intercultural Education*. London: Kogan Page, 1997.

Gundara, J. S. "Societal diversities and the issue of 'the other'." *Oxford Review of Education* 16 (1990): 97-109.

Gundara, J. S. "Intercultural Knowledge in the University: Common Values in a Civil Society." Paper presented at the University and Multicultural Societies, Alexandropupolis, June 1997.

Guttsman, W. L. (ed). *The English Ruling Class*. London: Weidenfeld and Nicolson, 1969.

Guy, K. R. *The Emperor's Four Treasuries: Scholars and the State in the Late Ch'ien-Lung Era*. Cambridge, Mass.: Harvard University Press, 1987.

Hall, S. "The West and the Rest: Discourse and Power." In *Formations of Modernity*, edited by S. Hall and G. Bram. Cambridge: Polity Press in association with the Open University, 1992.

Hall, S. and G. Bram (eds). *Formations of Modernity*. Cabridge: Polity Press, 1992.

Halsey, A. H. *Decline of Donnish Dominion: The British Academic Professions in the Twentieth Century*. Oxford: Clarendon Press, 1992.

Halsey, A. H. "Dons' Decline Reviewed." In *Higher Education in a Learning Society*, edited by Frank Coffield. Durham: School of Education, University of Durham, 1995.

Halsey, A. H. and M. Trow. *The British Academics*. London: Faber & Faber, 1971.

Han, J-H. "Education and Industrialization: The Korean Nexus in Human Resources Development." *Education Economics* 2, no. 2 (1994): 169-185.

Han, S. S. "Republic of Korea." In *Economics in Asia; Status Reports on Teaching and Research in Nine Countries*, edited by UNESCO. Bangkok: UNESCO, 1985.

Haron, I. "The role of government in higher education in Malaysia." In *The Role of Government in Asian Higher Education Systems: Issues and Prospects*, edited by Hiroshima University Research Institute for Higher Education. Hiroshima: Hiroshima University, 1988.

Hashim, R. *Educational Dualism in Malaysia: Implications for Theory and Practice*. Kuala Lumpur: Oxford University Press, 1996.

Hashim, S. "Muslim Society, Higher Education and Development: The Case of Malaysia." In *Muslim Society, Higher Education and Development in Southeast Asia*, edited by S. Ahmat and S. Siddique. Singapore: Institute of Southeast Asian Studies, 1987.

Hashim, W. *Race Relations in Malaysia*. Kuala Lumpur: Heinemann Educational Books, Ltd., 1983.

Haskell, T. L., "Justifying the Rights of Academic Freedom in the Era of "Power/Knowledge"" In *The Future of Academic Freedom*, edited by Louis Menand. Chicago & London: The University of Chicago Press, 1996.

Haskins, C. H. *The Rise of Universities*. Ithaca, New York: Cornell University Press, 1957.

Hassan , R. (ed). *Singapore: society in transition*. Singapore: Oxford University Press, 1976.

Hayden, H. *Higher Education and Development in South-east Asia*. Vol. I. Paris: UNESCO The International Association of Universities, 1967.

Held, D. *Democracy and the Global Order: From the Modern State to Cosmopolitan Governance*. Cambridge: Polity Press, 1995.

Held, D. *Prospects for Democracy: North, South, East, West*. Cambridge: Polity Press, 1993.

Held, D. (ed). *States & Societies*. Oxford: Martin Robertson in association with the Open University, 1983.

Henderson, G. *Korea: The Politics of the Vortex*. Cambridge, Mass.: Harvard University Press, 1968.

Henkel, M. and B. Little (eds). *Changing Relationships between Higher Education and the State*. Edited by M. Kogan, *Higher Education Policy 45*. London: Jessica Kingsley Publishers, 1998.

Henry, N. B. *Education for the Professions*. Edited by The Yearbook Committee. Vol. Part II, *The Sixty-first Yearbook of the National Society for the Study of Education*. Chicago, Illinois: The University of Chicago Press, 1962.

Hill, M. and Kwen Fee Lian. *The Politics of Nation Building and Citizenship in Singapore*. London: Routledge, 1995.

Hirano, K. (ed). *The State and Cultural Transformation: Perspectives from East Asia*. Tokyo & New York & Paris: United Nations University Press, 1995.

Ho, Wing Meng. *Asian Values and Modernisation: a critical interpretation*. Singapore: Chopmen Enterprises, 1976.

Hobbes, T. *Leviathan*. Edited by C. B. Macpherson. London: Penguin, 1968.

Hopkins, T. K. & Wallerstein, I. (eds). *The Age of Transition: Trajectory of the World System, 1945-2025*. London: Zed Books, 1996.

Horio, T. *Educational Thought and Ideology in Modern Japan*. Translated by Platzer, Steven. Tokyo: University of Tokyo Press, 1988.

Hoyle, E. and P. John. *Professional Knowledge and Professional Practice*. New York: Cassell, 1995.

Hsü, L. S. *The Political Philosophy of Confucianism, an Interpretation of the Social and Political Ideas of Confucius, His Forerunners, and His Early Disciples.* London: George Routledge & Sons, Ltd., 1932.

Hunter, G. *Higher Education & Development in South East Asia Vol. 3, Part 1: High-level Manpower for Development.* Edited by UNESCO. Paris: UNESCO, International Association of Universities, 1967.

Hunter, I. "Personality as a vocation: the political rationality of the humanities." In *Foucault's New Domains*, edited by M. Gane and T. Johnson. London & New York: Routledge, 1993.

Hurrell, A. "Regionalism in Theoretical Perspective." In *Regionalism in World Politics: Regional Organisation and International Order*, edited by Louise Fawcett and Andrew Hurrell. Oxford: Oxford University Press, 1995.

Ihm, C-S. "Education, Human Resources and Development in Korea: Achievement and Challenges." In *Issues in Education in Asia and the Pacific: an International Perspective*, edited by OECD. Paris: OECD, 1994.

Inglis, C. "Educational Policy and Occupational Structures in Peninsular Malaysia." In *Issues in Malaysian Development*, edited by J. C. Jackson and M. Rudner. Singapore & Kuala Lumpur: Heinemann Educational Books (Asia) Ltd., 1979.

International Seminar on Asian Higher Education. *Higher Education Expansion in Asia.* Hiroshima: Hiroshima University, 1985.

Islam, I. "Manpower and Educational Planning in Singapore." In *Human Resource Planning: The Asian Experience*, edited by Rashid Amjad. New Delhi: International Labour Organization, Asian Employment Programme (ARTEP), 1987.

Ismail, G. and M. Mohamed (eds). *The New Wave University: A Prelude to Malaysia 2020.* 2nd ed. Selangor: Pelanduk Publication, Universiti Malaysia Sarawak, 1997.

Ismail, M. Z. "Human Resource Development: Meeting the Challenges of the Future." In *The New Wave University: A Prelude to Malaysia 2020*, edited by G. Ismail and M. Mohamed. Selangor: Pelanduk Publication, Universiti Malaysia Sarawak, 1997.

Jackson, J. C. and M. Rudner (eds). *Issues in Malaysian Development.* Singapore & Kuala Lumpur: Heinemann Education Books (Asia) Ltd., 1979.

Jacobs, N. *The Korean Road to Modernization and Development.* Urbana: University of Illinois Press, 1985.

Jaspers, K. *The Idea of the University.* London: Peter Owen, 1960.

Jaspers, K. *Man in the Modern Age.* London: Routledge and Kegan Paul, 1951.

Jaspers, K. *Philosophy and the World.* Chicago: Regnery, 1963.

Jaspers, K. *Truth and Symbol.* New York: Twayne, 1959.

Jayasuriya, J. E. *Education in Korea: A Third World Success Story.* Seoul: Korean National Commission for UNESCO, 1983.

Jesudason, J. V. "Statist Democracy and Limits of Civil Society in Malaysia." *Journal of Commonwealth and Comparative Politics* 33, no. 3 (1990): 335-356.

Jhin, D. K. "A Study on the Power Structure of the Korean Political Society." Doctoral Thesis, Dept. of Politics, Graduate School, Yonsei University, Seoul, 1977.

Johnson, R. K. "Political Transitions and the Internationalisation of English: Implications for Language Planning, Policy-making and Pedagogy." In *Education and Political Transition: Perspectives and Dimensions in East Asia*, edited by W. O. Lee and M. Bray. Hong Kong: Comparative Education Research Centre, University of Hong Kong, 1997.

Jomo, K. S. (ed). *Malaysia's New Economic Policies,* Kuala Lumpur: Malaysian Economic Association, 1985.

Jomo, K. S. *Growth and Structural Change in the Malaysian Economy.* London: Macmillan, 1990.

Jones, L. P. and I. Sakong. *Government, Business, and Entrepreneurship in Economic Development: The Korean Case.* Cambridge, Mass.: Council on East Asian Studies, Harvard University Press, 1980.

Joung, S. E. "*Kyung Sung Je-kook Dae-hack* [A Study of the Characteristics of Kyung Sung Imperial University].", Doctoral Thesis, Yonsei University, Seoul, 1997.

Kahn, J. S. "Class, Ethnicity and Diversity: Some Remarks on Malay Culture in Malaysia." In *Fragmented Vision: Culture and Politics in Contemporary Malaysia*, edited by Joel S. Kahn and Francis Loh Kok Wah. Honolulu: University of Hawaii Press, 1991.

Kang, W. J. "Religion and Politics under Japanese Rule." In *Korea's Response to Japan: the Colonial Period 1910-1945*, edited by C. I. Eugene Kim and Doretha E. Mortimore. Michigan: The Centre for Korean Studies, Western Michigan University, 1177.

Kalberg, S. *Max Weber's Comparative-Historical Sociology*. Cambridge: Polity Press, 1993.

Kang, T. H. "The changing nature of Korean Confucian personality under Japanese rule." In *Korea's Response to Japan: the Colonial Period 1910-1945*, edited by C. I. Eugene Kim and D. E. Mortimore. Michigan: The Centre for Korean Studies, Western Michigan University, 1977.

Keep, E. and K. Sisson. "Owning the Problem: Staffing the System in the 1990s." In *Higher Education, Expansion and Reform*, edited by D. Finegold, E. Keep, D. Miliband, D. Robertson, K. Sisson and J. Ziman, 1992.

Kehoe, M. "Notes and Comments: Higher Education in Korea." *Far Eastern Quarterly* 8, no. 2 (February 1949).

Kehoe, M. "Report from Korea." *Common Ground* (Winter, 1949).

Kerr, C. *The Uses of the University*. 4th ed. Harvard: Cambridge University Press, 1995.

Kibre, P. *Scholarly Privileges in the Middle Ages, the Rights, Privileges and Immunities of Scholars and Universities at Bologna, Padua, Paris and Oxford*. London: Mediaeval Academy of America, 1962.

Kim, C. I. E. and D. E. Mortimore (eds). *Korea's response to Japan: the colonial period 1910-1945*. Michigan: The Centre for Korean Studies, Western Michigan University, 1977.

Kim, H. K (ed). *Japanese Civil Service & Economic Development: Catalysts of Change*. Oxford: Oxford University Press, 1994.

Kim, I. J. and Y. W. Kihl (eds). *Political Changes in South Korea*. New York: Paragon House, 1988.

Kim, I. W. *"Hankook Kyoyook: Kwager, Hyunjae, Mirae* [Korean Education: its past, present and future]." *Sa sang* 1 (1989).

Kim, I. W. *Hankook Kyoyook-eyu Yerksa-wa Moonje [History of Korean Education and Its Problem].* Seoul: Monn-eum Sa, 1993.

Kim, I. W. *Hankook Moosock Sasang Yonku [A Research on Shamanistic Ideology in Korea].* Jipmoon-dang, 1988.

Kim, J-c. *Education and Development: Some Essays and Thoughts on Korean Education.* Seoul: Seoul National University Press, 1985.

Kim, K-o. "The Reproduction of Confucian Culture in Contemporary Korea: an Anthropological Study." In *Confucian Traditions in East Asian Modernity: Moral Education and Economic Culture in Japan and the Four Mini-Dragons,* edited by Tu Wei-Ming. Cambridge, Mass. & London, England: Harvard University Press, 1996.

Kim, K. S. "From neo-mercantilism to globalism: the changing role of the state and South Korea's economic prowess." In *The Rise of East Asia: Critical Visions of the Pacific Century,* edited by M. T. Berger and D. A. Borer. London & New York: Routledge, 1997.

Kim, M. K. "The Administrative Culture of Korea: A Comparison with China and Japan." In *A Dragon's Progress: Development Administration in Korea,* edited by G. E. Caiden and B. W. Kim. Connecticut: Kumarian Press, Inc., 1991.

Kim, S. H. *"Mikookei Daehan Kyoyook Wonjoe kwanhan Kyoyook Sawhoijuck Yonkoo* [Research on the American Educational Aid to South Korea: an educational sociological approach]". Doctoral Thesis, Yonsei University, Graduate School, 1988.

Kim, S. H. *Seokoo Kyoyookhack Doip-ey Kiwon-kwa Chungae [The Origins and Development of Western Educational Studies in Korea].* Seoul: Mooneum-sa, 1996.

Kim, S. P. "Political Leadership and Succession in Singapore." In *Singapore Development Policies and Trends,* edited by Peter S. J. Chen. Singapore: Oxford University Press, 1983.

Kim, T. "The Evaluation of the Higher Education System in the Republic of Korea." In *The Evaluation of Higher Education Systems, World Yearbook of Education 1996,* edited by R. Cowen. London: Kogan Page, 1996.

Kim, Y-c. *Educational Contribution to the Economic Development in Korea*. Seoul: Korean Educational Development Institute, 1986.

Kingsley, J. D. *Representative Bureaucracy: an Interpretation of the British Civil Service*. Ohio: The Antioch Press, 1944.

Knorr-Cetina, K. and A. V. Cicourel. *Advances in Social Theory and Methodology*. Boston: Routledge & Kegan Paul, 1981.

Kogan, M., I. Moses, and E. El-Khawas. *Staffing Higher Education: Meeting New Challenges*. London & Paris: Jessica Kingsley Publishers, OECD, 1994.

Koh, B. I. "Confucianism in Contemporary Korea." In *Confucian Traditions in East Asian Modernity: Moral Education and Economic Culture in Japan and the Four Mini-Dragons*, edited by Tu Wei-Ming. Cambridge, Mass. & London, England: Harvard University Press, 1996.

Koo, H. (ed). *State and Society in Contemporary Korea*, Ithaca, N. Y.: Cornell University Press, 1993.

Korea Foundation, The. *Korean Cultural Heritage Thought & Religion Vol. II*. Edited by Joungwon Kim. Seoul: The Korea Foundation, 1996.

Korean Council for University Education (KCUE). *Korean Higher Education - Its Development, Aspects and Prospects*. Seoul: KCUE, 1990.

Korean Council for University Education (KCUE). *University Education Development Indicators*. Edited by Hyung-chung Lee and Young-hack Lee. Seoul: KCUE, 1997.

Kornicki, P. (ed). *Meiji Japan: Political, Economic and Social History 1868-1912, Vol. I: The Emergence of the Meiji State, Vol. II: The Growth of the Meiji State, Vol. III: The Mature Meiji State, Vol. IV: The End of Meiji and Early Taisho*. London: Routledge, 1998.

Kubota, A. "The Political Influence of the Japanese Higher Civil Service." *Journal of Asian and African Studies* 15, no. 3-4, 1980: 273-284.

Kuo, E. C. Y. "Confucianism as Political Discourse in Singapore: The Case of an Incomplete Revitalization Movement." In *Confucian Traditions in East Asian Modernity: Moral Education and Economic Culture in Japan and the Four Mini-Dragons*, edited by Tu Wei-Ming. Cambridge, Mass. & London, England: Harvard University Press, 1996.

Larrain, J. *Theories of Development: Capitalism, Colonialism and Dependency*.

Cambridge: Polity Press, 1989.

Larson, M. S. *The Rise of Professionalism: A Sociological Analysis.* Berkeley: University fo California Press, 1977.

Lasch, C. *The Revolt of the Elites and the Betrayal of Democracy.* New York: W W Norton, 1995.

Latouche, S. *The Westernization of the World.* Cambridge: Polity Press, 1996.

Lee, E. and Tan Tai Yong. *Beyond Degrees: The Making of the National University of Singapore.* Singapore: Singapore University Press, 1996.

Lee, J. J., D. Adams and C. Cornbleth. "Transnational transfer of curriculum knowledge: a Korean case study." *Journal of Curriculum Studies* 20, no. 3 (1988): 233-246.

Lee, K. "Past, Present and Future Trends in the Public and Private Sectors of Korean Higher Education." In *Public and Private Sectors in Asian Higher Education Systems: Issues and Prospects.* Hiroshima: Research Institute for Higher Education, Hiroshima University, 1987.

Lee, K-b. *A New History of Korea.* Translated by Edward W. Wagner Edward J. Shultz. Cambridge, Mass.: Harvard University Press, 1985.

Lee, K. H. "Socio-Economic Framework of the Country." In *Higher Education and Employment in Malaysia,* edited by Ungku A. Aziz, S. B. Chew, K. H. Lee, and B. C. Sanyal. Paris: IIEP, 1987.

Lee, Kuan Yew, *Leadership in Asian Countries,* Singapore: Ministry of Culture, September 1967.

Lee, M. N. N. "Education and the State: Malaysia after the NEP." *Asia Pacific Journal of Education* 17, no. 11 (1997): 27-40.

Lee, M. N. N. "Corporatization and Privatization of Malaysian Higher Education." *International Higher Education, The Boston College Center for International Higher Education* 10, (Winter, 1998).

Lee, R. "Structures of Knowledge." In *The Age of Transition: Trajectory of the World-System 1945-2025,* edited by T. K. & Wallerstein Hopkins, I. (eds), 197. London: Zed Books, Ltd., 1996.

Lee, R. L. M. "The State, Religious Nationalism and Ethnic Rationalization in Malaysia." *Ethnic and Racial Studies* 13, no. 4 (1990).

Lee, Sungho. "The emergence of the modern university in Korea." *Higher Education* 18, no. 1 (1989): 87-116.

Lee, Sungho. *Hankookeuy Daehack Kyosoo [The Korean Academic Profession]*. Seoul: Hack-ji Sa, 1992.

Lee, W. O. *Social Change and Educational Problems in Japan, Singapore and Hong Kong*. London: Macmillan, 1991.

Lee, W. O and M. Bray (eds). *Education and Political Transition: Perspectives and Dimensions in East Asia*. Hong Kong: Comparative Education Research Centre, The University of Hong Kong, 1997.

Lee, Y-h. *The State, Society and Big Business in South Korea*. London: Routledge, 1997.

Lent, J. A. (ed). *Cultural Pluralism in Malaysia: Polity, Military, Mass Media, Education, Religion and Social Class*. Vol. Special Report Number 14. Illinois: The Center for Southeast Asian Studies, Northern Illinois University, 1977.

Leslie, L. L. "What drives higher education management in the 1990s and beyond?: The new era in financial support." *Journal of Higher Education Management* 10 (1996): 5-16.

Leslie, L. L. and P. T. Brinkman. *The Economic Value of Higher Education*. New York: American Council on Education and Macmillan, 1988.

Leslie, L. L. and H. F. Miller. "The Market Model and Higher Education." *Journal of Higher Education* 15 (1974): 1-20.

Lewis, L. and P. G. Altbach. "The Professoriate in International Perspective: Who They Are and What They Do." *Academe* 82, no. 3 (May-June 1996): 29-33.

Lieberman, M. *Education as a Profession,* Englewood Cliffs, N. J.: Prentice-Hall, Inc., 1956.

Light, A. "Two Cheers for Liberal Education." In *Dialogue and Difference: English into the Nineties*, edited by P. Brooker and P. Humm. London: Routledge, 1989.

Lim, C. "The Role of English in the Development of a National Identity in a Multilingual Setting: the Singapore Dilemma." Paper presented at the International Conference on Language Learning: Theory into Practice, Kuala Lumpur, 17-19 July 1989.

Lim, C. Y. *Education and National Development*. Singapore: Federal Publications, 1983.

Lim, L. Y. C., 'Social Welfare' In *Management of Success: The Moulding of Modern Singapore*, edited by Kernial S. Sandhu and Paul Wheatley, Singapore: Institute of Southeast Asian Studies, 1989.

Lim, M. H. "Affirmative Action, Ethnicity and Integration: The Case of Malaysia." *Ethnic and Racial Studies* 8, no. 2 (1985).

Lim, M. H. and W. Canak. "The Political Economy of State Policies in Malaysia." *Journal of Contemporary Asia* 11, no. 2 (1981): 208-224.

Lim, S-B. "Educational Policy Changes in Korea: Ideology and Praxis." In *Dynamic Transformation: Korea, NICS and Beyond*, edited by Gill-Chin Lim and Wook Chang: Consortium on Development Studies, 1990.

Lim, T. G. "Malaysian and Singaporean Higher Education: Common Roots but Differing Directions." In *East Asian Higher Education, Traditions and Transformations*, edited by A. H. Yee. Oxford: Pergamon, 1995.

Little, I. M. D. "The Experience and Causes of Rapid Labor-Intensive Development in Korea, Taiwan Province, Hong Kong, and Singapore and the Possibilities of Emulation." In *Export-Led Industrialisation and Development*, edited by A. R. Kahn. Geneva: ILO, 1981.

Lodge, G. C. and E. F. Vogel (eds). *Ideology and National Competitiveness: an analysis of nine countries*. Boston, MA.: Harvard Business School Press, 1987.

Loh, K. W. "The Socio-Economic Basis of Ethnic Consciousness: The Chinese in the 1970s." In *Ethnicity, Class and Development: Malaysia.*, edited by S. H. Ali. Kuala Lumpur: Persatuaan Sains Malaysia, 1984.

Loh, P. F. S. *Seeds of Separatism: Education Policy in Malaya 1894-1900*. Kuala Lumpur: Oxford University Press, 1975.

Low, L., Mun Heng Toh and Tech Wong Soon. *Economics of Education and Manpower Development: Issues and Policies in Singapore*. Singapore: McGraw-Hill Book Co., 1991.

Lubeck, P. M. "Malaysian Industrialisation, ethnic divisions and the NIC model: the Limits to replication." In *States and Development in the Asian Pacific Rim*, edited by R. P. Appelbaum & J. Henderson. Newbury Park: Sage Publications, 1992.

Lyotard, J.-F. *The Postmodern Condition: A Report on Knowledge*. Minneapolis: University of Minnesota Press, 1984.

Maassen, P. A. M. and Frans A. van Vught (eds). *Inside Academia: New Challenges for the Academic Profession*. Utrecht, The Netherlands: Centre for Higher Education Policy Studies (CHEPS), 1996.

Macdonald, K. M. *The Sociology of the Professions*, London: Sage, 1996.

Maclean, I., A. Montefiore and P. Winch. *The Political Responsibility of Intellectuals*. Cambridge: Cambridge University Press, 1990.

Majstorovic, S. "Malaysia: The Evolution of an Ethnic State." *The Journal of Pacific Studies* 17, no. 1-2 (December 1993): 161-189.

Majstorovic, S. "The Politics of Ethnicity and Post-Cold War Malaysia: the Dynamics of an Ethnic State." In *The Rise of East Asia*, edited by Mark T. Berger and Douglas A. Borer. London & New York: Routledge, 1997.

Malaya. *Report of the Lemon Committee on Technical and Industrial Education in the Federated Malay States*, Kuala Lumpur: The Government Press, 1918.

Malaya. *Report of the Carr-Saunders Commission on University Education in Malaya*. Kuala Lumpur: The Government Press, 1948.

Malaya. *Report of the Education Committee*. Kuala Lumpur: Government Printer, 1956.

Malaysia. *Akta Pendidikan 1996* (Education Act 1996 (ACT550)). Kuala Lumpur: International Law Book Services, 1996.

Malaysia, Ministry of Education. *Laporan Tahunan (Annual Report 96)*. Kuala Lumpur: Ministry of Education, Malaysia, 1996.

Malaysia. *Report of the Higher Education Committee*. Kuala Lumpur: Government Printer, 1967.

Malaysia. *Report of the Committee appointed by the National Operations Council to Study Campus Life of Students in the University of Malaya*. Kuala Lumpur: Government Press, 1971.

Malaysia. *Mid-Term Review of Second Malaysia Plan*. Kuala Lumpur: Government Printers, 1973.

Malaysia. *Third Malaysia Plan 1976-1980*. Kuala Lumpur: Government Printers, 1975.

Malaysia. *Fourth Malaysia Plan 1981-1985*. Kuala Lumpur: Government Printers, 1980.

Malaysia. *Fifth Malaysia Plan, 1986-1990*. Kuala Lumpur: National Printing Department, 1986.

Malaysia. *Malaysia Official Yearbook 1997*. Kuala Lumpur: Department of Information, Malaysia, 1997.

Malaysia. *Mid-Term Review of Fourth Malaysia Plan: 1981-83*. Kuala Lumpur: Government Press, 1984.

Malaysia. *Sixth Malaysia Plan, 1991-1995*. Kuala Lumpur: National Printing Department, 1991.

Malaysia. *The Second Outline Perspective Plan 1991-2000*. Kuala Lumpur: Government Press, 1991.

Malaysia. *The Seventh Malaysia Plan 1996-2000*. Kuala Lumpur, Malaysia: Economic Planning Unit, The Government Press, 1996.

Mangan, J. A. *The Games Ethic and Imperialism*. Harmondsworth: Viking, 1986.

Mani, L., and R. Frankenburg. "The Challenge of Orientalism." *Economy and Society* 14, no. 2 (1985).

Manrakhan, J. *Autonomy and Freedom in Academe*. Singapore: Kin Keong Printing Ltd., published for The University of Mauritius, 1991.

Marimuthu, T. *Student Development in Malaysian Universities*, RIHED Occasional Paper No. 19. Singapore: Regional Institute of Higher Education and Development, 1984.

Marshall, B. K. "Professors and Politics: the Meiji Academic Elite." In *Meiji Japan: Political, economic and social history 1868-1912 Vol. IV. The End of Meiji and Early Taisho*, edited by P. Kornicki. London: Routledge, 1998.

Mason, E. S., M. J. Kim, K. S. Kim, and D. C. Cole. *The Economic and Social Modernization of the Republic of Korea*. Cambridge, Mass.: Harvard University Press, 1980.

Massy, W. F. and R. Zemsky. *The Dynamics of Academic Productivity*. Denver: State Higher Education Officers, 1990.

Mauzy, D. K. and R. S. Milne. "The Mahathir Administration in Malaysia: Discipline through Islam." *Pacific Affairs 56*, no. 3 (1983-4).

McClelland, C. E., *State, Society, and University in Germany 1700-1914*, Cambridge, 1980.

McCord, W. *The Dawn of the Pacific Century: Implications for Three Worlds of Development*. New Jersey: Transactions Publishers, 1991.

McDaniel, O. C. "The Paradigms of Governance in Higher Education Systems." *Higher Education Policy 9*, no. 2 (June 1996): 137-158.

McEvilley, T. *Art & Otherness: Crisis in Cultural Identity*, New York: McPherson & Company, 1992.

McGinn, N. F. (ed). *Education and Development in Korea*. Cambridge, Mass.: Harvard University Press, 1980.

McGrew, A. "A Global Society?" In *Modernity and its Futures*, edited by S. Hall, D. Held, and T. McGrew (eds). Cambridge: Polity Press in association with the Open University, 1992.

McGrew, A. "Conceptualising Global Politics." In *Global Politics: Globalization and the Nation-State*, edited by Anthony G. McGrew and Paul G. Lewis. Cambridge: Polity Press, 1992.

McLennan, G., D. Held and S. Hall (eds). *The Idea of the Modern State*, Milton Keynes: Open University Press, 1984.

McLean, M., *The Promise and Perils of Educational Comparison*, London: Institute of Education, Tufnell Press, 1992.

McNay, I. "From the Collegial Academy to Corporate Enterprise: The Changing Cultures of Universities." In *The Changing University?*, edited by Tom Schuller. Buckingham: SRHE & Open University Press, 1995.

Means, G. P. *Malaysian Politics: The Second Generation*. Singapore: Oxford University Press, 1991.

Mehmet, O. and Y. H. Yip, *Human Capital Formation in Malaysian Universities*, Kuala Lumpur: Institute of Advanced Studies, University of Malaya, 1986.

Menand, L. *The Future of Academic Freedom*. Chicago & London: The University of Chicago Press, 1996.

Metzger, T. A. *Escape from Predicament: Neo-Confucianism and China's Evolving Political Culture*. New York: Columbia University Press, 1977.

Middlehurst, R. "Professionals, Professionalism and Higher Education for Tomorrow's World." In *Higher Education in a Learning Society*, edited by F. Coffield. Durham: School of Education, University of Durham, 1995.

Migdal, J., A. Kohli, and V. Shue (eds). *State Power and Social Forces*. Cambridge: Cambridge U. P., 1994.

Miller, H. *The Management of Change in Universities, State & Economy in Australia, Canada and the U.K.* Buckingham: Open University Press & SRHE, 1995.

Milne, R. and D. Mauzy. *Singapore: The Legacy of Lee Kuan Yew*. Boulder, CO.: Westview Press, 1990.

Milne, R. S. and D. K. Mauzy. *Politics and Government in Malaysia*. Vancouver: University of British Columbia Press, 1980.

Milner, A. *The Invention of Politics in Colonial Malaya: Contesting Nationalism and the Expansion of the Public Sphere*. Cambridge: Cambridge University Press, 1994.

Ministry of Culture and Information. *A Handbook of Korea*. 3rd ed. Seoul: The Government Press, 1979.

Ministry of Education. *Education in Korea 1989-1990*. Seoul: Ministry of Education, Republic of Korea, 1990.

Ministry of Education. *Education in Korea 1997-1998*. Seoul: Ministry of Education, Republic of Korea, 1998.

Ministry of Finance. *Economic Report 1997/98*. Kuala Lumpur: Ministry of Finance, Malaysia, 1997.

Mitchell, R. H. "The Rise of the Surveillance State, 1900-1917." In *Meiji Japan: Political, economic and social history 1868-1912 Vol. IV: The End of Meiji and Early Taisho*, edited by P. Kornicki. London: Routledge, 1998.

Mohamad, M. bin. *The Malay Dilemma*, Singapore: Donald Moore Asia Press, 1970.

Mohamad, M. bin. "Look East." *New Perspectives Quarterly* 9, no. 1 (1992): 16-19.

Mohamad, M. bin. *The Way Forward*. London: Weidenfeld & Nicolson, 1998.

Mohamad, M. bin. *Vision 2020, Malaysia: Towards Establishing a Fully Developed Nation*. Kementerian Penerangan, Malaysia: Dicetak oleh Zizi Press Sdn Bhd., 1997.

Morley, D. and K. Robins. *Spaces of Identity: Global Media, Electronic Landscapes and Cultural Boundaries*. London & New York: Routledge, 1995.

Morris, P. "Asia's Four Little Tigers: A Comparison of the Role of Education in Their Development." *Comparative Education* 32, no. 1 (March 1996): 95-109.

Morris, P. and A. Sweeting. "Human Resource Development in East Asia." *Asia Pacific Journal of Education* 17, no. 11 (1997): 7-26.

Morris, P. and A. Sweeting (eds). *Education and Development in East Asia*. New York: Garland Publishing, Inc., 1995.

Morsy, Z. and P. G. Altbach (eds). *Higher Education in International Perspective Toward the 21st Century*. New York: UNESCO, 1993.

Mukherjee, H. and J. S. Singh. "Malaysia." In *Education and Development in East Asia*, edited by P. Morris and A. Sweeting. New York & London: Garland Publishing, Inc., 1995.

Müller, R. A. "Student Education, Student Life." In *A History of the University in Europe*, edited by Hilde De Ridder-Symoens. Cambridge: Cambridge University Press, 1996.

Murphey, R. *East Asia: A New History*. New York: Longman Inc., 1996.

Murphy, J. *Legal Education in a Developing Nation, Korea Law Study Series No. 1*. Seoul & New York: Seoul National University Press & Oceana Publications, Inc., 1967.

Mutalib, H. *Islam and Ethnicity in Malay Politics*. Singapore: Oxford University Press, 1990.

Muzaffar, C. *Islamic Resurgence in Malaysia*. Petaling Jaya: Penerbit Fajar Bakti Sdn Bhd, 1987.

Muzaffar, C. *Human Rights and the New World Order*, Penang: Just World Trust, 1993.

Nahm, A. (ed). *Korea under Japanese Colonial Rule: Studies of the Policy and Techniques of Japanese Colonialism*. Kalamazoo: Western Michigan University Press, 1973.

Nakayama, S. *Academic and Scientific Traditions in China, Japan and the West*. Tokyo: University of Tokyo Press, 1974.

National University of Singapore. *10th Annual Report 1989-1990*. Singapore: NUS Press, 1990.

National University of Singapore, *The National University of Singapore 1996-7, General Information*, Singapore: Singapore University Press, 1996.

Neave, G. "Education and social policy: Demise of an ethic or change of values?" *Oxford Review of Education* 14 (1988): 273-83.

Neave, G. and G. Rhoades. "The Academic Estate in Western Europe.", edited by B. R. Clark, 211-270. Berkeley: University of California Press, 1987.

Neave, G. and F. A. van Vught. *Prometheus Bound: the changing relationship between government and higher education in Western Europe*. Oxford: Pergamon Press, 1991.

Neave, G. and F. A. van Vught (eds). *Government and Higher Education Relationships Across Three Continents The Winds of Change*, London: Pergamon, 1994.

Newman, J. H. *The Idea of a University*. Edited by F. M. Turner. New Haven & London: Yale University Press, 1996.

Norman, E. 'Newman's Social and Political Thinking' in *Newman after a Hundred Years*, edited by I. Ker and A.G. Hill, Oxford: Clarendon Press, 1990.

O'Donnell, G. A. *Modernization and Bureaucratic-Authoritarianism in South American Politics*. Berkeley: University of California Institute for International Studies, 1973.

OECD. *Education at a Glance: Analysis*. Paris: OECD, 1996.

OECD. *Education at a Glance: OECD Indicators*. Paris: OECD, 1997.

OECD. *Internationalisation of Higher Education.* Paris: OECD, 1996.

OECD. *Issues in Education in Asia and the Pacific: an International Perspective, Proceedings of a Conference in Hiroshima.* Paris: OECD, 1994.

OECD. *Knowledge Bases for Education Policies, Proceedings of a Conference held in Maastricht, The Netherlands on 11-13 September 1995.* Paris: OECD, Centre for Educational Research and Innovation, 1996.

OECD. *Liberalisation of Trade in Professional Services.* Paris: OECD, 1995.

OECD. *Lifelong Learning for All.* Paris: OECD, 1996.

OECD. *Universities under Scrutiny.* Paris: OECD, 1987.

Ogawa, N., G. W. Jones and G. Jeffrey (eds). *Human Resources in Development along the Asia-Pacific Rim.* Singapore: Oxford University Press, 1993.

O'Hear, A. "Academic Freedom and the University." In *Academic Freedom and Responsibility,* edited by Malcolm Tight. Milton Keynes: The Society for Research into Higher Education & Open University Press, 1988.

Ohmae, K. *End of the Nation State: The Rise of Regional Economies.* London: Harper Collins, 1996.

Omar, E. "Policy Analysis and Development in Malaysia" In *Colloquim on Policy Analysis and Development,* Kuala Lumpur: Asian Centre for Development Administration. November 1974.

Pang, E. F. and S. Gopinathan. "Scholarly Exchanges and Collaboration: the Experience of Singapore." In *North-South Scholarly Exchange: Access, Equity and Collaboration,* edited by G. L. Shive, S. Gopinathan and W. K. Cummings. London and New York: Mansell Publishing Ltd., 1988.

Pang, E. F. and S. Gopinathan. "Public Policy, Research Environment, and Higher Education in Singapore." In *Scientific Development and Higher Education: the case of newly industrializing nations,* edited by P. G. Altbach. New York: Praeger, 1989.

Patterson, O. *Ethnic Chauvinism: The Reactionary Impulse.* New York: Stein and Day, 1977.

Paulston, R. G. (ed). *Social Cartography: Mapping Ways of Seeing Social and Educational Change.* New York: Garland, 1996.

Pennycook, A. *The Cultural Politics of English as an International Language*. London & New York: Longman, 1994.

Perkin, H. *Key Profession: The History of the Association of University Teachers*. London: Routledge & Kegan Paul, 1969.

Perkin, H., *The Third Revolution, Professional Elites in the Modern World*, London: Routledge, 1996.

Peters, M. "Performance and Accountability in "post-industrial society": The crisis of British universities." *Studies in Higher Education* 17 (1992): 123-39.

Peterson, M. A. *Korean adoption and inheritance: case studies in the creation of a classic Confucian society*. Ithaca, New York: East Asia Program, Cornell University Press, 1996.

Phillips, J. A. "Staff and Faculty Development in the University of Malaya." In *Staff and Faculty Development in Southeast Asian Universities*, RIHED, Hong Kong: Maruzen Asia Ltd., 1981.

Phillipson, R. "Linguicism: structures and ideologies in linguistic imperialism." In *Minority Education*, edited by Tove Skutnabb-Kangas and Jim Cummins. Clevedon: Multilingual Matters Ltd., 1988.

Picht, R. "Cultural Dimensions of Regionalization." In *Academic Mobility in a Changing World: Regional and Global Trends*, edited by P. Blumenthal, C. Goodwin, A. Smith and U. Teichler. London: Jessica Kingsley, 1996.

Pieterse, J. N. and B. Parekh (eds). *The Decolonization of Imagination: Culture, Knowledge and Power*, London: Zed Books Ltd., 1995.

Piper, D. W. *Are Professors Professional? The Organisation of University Examinations*. Edited by Maurice Kogan, *Higher Education Policy 25*. London: Jessica Kingsley Publishers, 1994.

Platt, J. T. and H. Weber. *English in Singapore & Malaysia: Status, Features, Functions*. Kuala Lumpur: Oxford University Press, 1980.

Pluvier, J. *South-east Asia from Colonialism to Independence*. Kuala Lumpur: Oxford University Press, 1974.

Pong, S-L. "Access to Education in Peninsular Malaysia: Ethnicity, Social Class and Gender." *Compare* 25, no. 3 (1995): 239-252.

Pott, W. S. A. *Chinese Political Philosophy*. New York: Alfred A Knopf, 1925.

Pratt, J. "Unification of higher education in the United Kingdom." *European Journal of Education* 27 (1992): 29-43.

Presidential Commission on Education Reform, The Republic of Korea. *Education Reform for the 21st Century - To Ensure Leadership in the Information and Globalization Era, PCER Report.* Seoul: The Government Press, November 1997.

Preston, P. W. *Pacific Asia in the Global System.* Oxford: Blackwell, 1998.

Preston, P. W. *Rethinking Development : Essays on development and Southeast Asia.* London & New York: Routledge & Kegan Paul, 1987.

Puccetti, R. "Authoritarian Government and Academic Subservience: The University of Singapore." *Minerva* 19, no. 2 (1972): 223-241.

Purcell, V. *The Chinese in Southeast Asia,* 2nd ed. London: Oxford University Press, 1965.

Pye, L. W. *Asian Power and Politics: The Cultural Dynamics of Authority.* Cambridge, Mass.: Harvard University Press, 1985.

Pye, L. W. and A. L. Singer Jr. "Higher Education and Politics in Singapore." *Minerva* 2, no. 4 (1964): 321-335.

Quah, J. S. T. "Singapore's Model of Development: Is it transferable?" In *Behind East Asian Growth: The Political and Social Foundations of Prosperity,* edited by Henry S. Rowen. London & New York: Routledge, 1998.

Ramirez, F. O. and J. Boli. "The political construction of mass schooling: European origins and worldwide institutionalization." *Sociology of Education* 60 (1987): 2-17.

Reich, R. B. *The Work of Nations.* New York: Vintage Books, 1992.

Reid, L. J. "The Politics of Education in Malaysia." Monograph Series, University of Tasmania, 1988.

Republic of Korea. "Investment in Korea: An Introduction to One of the Most Promising Investment Opportunities of the 21st Century." Seoul: The Ministry of Finance, 1994.

Republic of Korea, *Korean Overseas Information Service,* Seoul: The Government Press, 1994.

Republic of Korea, Ministry of Education. *Education in Korea 1997-1998*. Seoul: The Government Press, 1998.

Rhoades, G. *Managed Professionals: Restructuring Academic Labor in Unionized Institutions*. Albany, N. Y.: State University of New York Press, 1997.

Rich, P. J. *Elixir of Empire*. London: Regency Press Ltd., 1989.

Ridder-Symoens, H. de (ed). *A History of the University in Europe, Vol. I & II*. Vol. II. Cambridge: Cambridge University Press, 1996.

Ringer, F. K. *The Decline of the German Mandarins: The German Academic Community, 1890-1933*. Cambridge, MA.: Harvard University Press, 1969.

Rodan, G. *The Political Economy of Singapore's Industrialization: National State and International Capital*. Kuala Lumpur: Forum Enterprise, 1991.

Rorty, R. "Does academic freedom have Philosophical Presuppositions?" In *The Future of Academic Freedom*, edited by Louis Menand. Chicago & London: The University of Chicago Press, 1996.

Roth, G. and C. Wittich (eds). *Economy and Society*. Vol. 2. California: University of California Press, 1979.

Rothblatt, S. *The Modern University and its Discontents: the fact of Newman's legacies in Britain and America*. New York: Cambridge University Press, 1997.

Rothblatt, S. and B. Wittrock. *The European and American University since 1800*. Cambridge: Cambridge University Press, 1993.

Rothchild, J. *Ethnopolitics: A Conceptual Framework*. New York: Columbia University Press, 1981.

Rowbotham, A. H. "The Impact of Confucianism on Seventeenth Century Europe." *The Far Eastern Quarterly* 4, no. 3 (1935).

Rowen, H. S. "The Political and social foundations of the rise of East Asia : an overview." In *Behind East Asian Growth: the Political and Social Foundations of Prosperity*, edited by Henry S. Rowen. London & New York: Routledge, 1998.

Rowen, H. S. (ed). *Behind East Asian Growth: The Political and Social Foundations of Prosperity*. London & New York: Routledge, 1998.

Rudner, M. "Education, Development and Change in Malaysia." *South East Asian Studies* 15, no. 1 (1977): 23-62.

Rudner, M. *Nationalism, Planning & Economic Modernisation in Malaysia: the Politics of Beginning Development.* Beverly Hills: Sage Publications, 1975.

Rust, V. D. "Postmodernism and its Comparative Education Implications." *Comparative Education Review* 35 (1991): 610-626.

Ryee, J. C. "Republic of Korea." In *Political Science in Asia and the Pacific: Status Reports on Teaching and Research in Ten Countries,* edited by Takeo Uchida. Bangkok: UNESCO Regional Office for Education in Asia and the Pacific, 1984.

Sadlack, J. and P. G. Altbach (eds). *Higher Education Research at the Turn of the New Century: Structures, Issues and Trends.* New York & Paris: Garland Publishing and UNESCO, 1997.

Said, E. W. *Orientalism,* London: Routledge & Kegan Paul, 1978.

Said, E. W. *Culture and Imperialism.* London: Chatto & Windus, 1993.

Said, E. W. *Representations of the Intellectual.* London: Vintage, 1994.

Said, E. W. "Identity, Authority and Freedom: The potentate and the Traveller" In *The Future of Academic Freedom,* edited by Louis Menand. Chicago & London: The University of Chicago Press, 1996.

Sakong, I. *Korea in the World Economy.* Washington, D.C.: Institute for International Economics, 1993.

Salleh, I. M. and S. D. Meyanathan. *Lessons of East Asia: Malaysia: Growth, Equity and Structural Transformation.* Washington, D. C.: World Bank, 1993.

Salmi, J. and A. M. Verspoor (eds). *Revitalizing Higher Education.* Washington, D. C.: The World Bank, IAU Press, Pergamon, 1994.

Salter, B., and T. Tapper. *The State and Higher Education.* Ilford: Woburn Press, 1995.

Sandhu, K. S. and P. Wheatley (eds). *Management of Success: the Moulding of Modern Singapore.* Singapore: Institute of Southeast Asian Studies, 1989.

Sarvanamuttu, J., L. Kamaluddin, and P. Chung-Nyap. "Malaysia." In *Political Science in Asia and the Pacific: Status Reports on Teaching and Research in Ten Countries*, edited by UNESCO. Bangkok: UNESCO Regional Office for Education in Asia and the Pacific, 1984.

Schein, Edgar H. , and Diane W. Kommers. *Professional Education: Some New Directions*. Berkeley, CA.: The Carnegie Commission on Higher Education, 1972.

Schilpp, P. A. (ed). *The Philosophy of Karl Jaspers*. New York: Tudor, 1957.

Schultz, T. W. "The Economic Importance of Human Capital in Modernization." *Education Economics* 1, no. 1 (1993): 13-19.

Scott, A. (ed). *The Limits of Globalization; Cases and Arguments*. London: Routledge, 1997.

Seah, C. M. and L. Seah. "Education Reform and National Integration." In *Singapore Development Policies and Trends*, edited by Peter S. J. Chen. Singapore: Oxford University Press, 1983.

Seidman, S. *Contested Knowledge: Social Theory in the Postmodern Era*. Oxford: Blackwell, 1994.

Selth, A. *The Development of Public Education in the Republic of Korea: an Australian Perspective*. Edited by Don McMillen. Vol. 46, A Series Australia Asia Papers. Nathan: Centre for the Study of Australian-Asian Relations, Griffith University, 1988.

Selvaratnam, V. "Change amidst continuity: University Development in Malaysia." In *From Dependency to Autonomy: The Development of Asian Universities*, edited by P. G. Altbach and V. Selvaratnam. Dordrecht: Kluwer Academic Publishers, 1989.

Selvaratnam, V. "Dependency, Change and Continuity in a Western University Model: The Malaysian Case." *Southeast Asian Journal of Social Science* 14, no. 2 (1986): 29-51.

Selvaratnam, V. *Ethnicity, Inequality and Higher Education in Peninsular Malaysia*. Singapore: National University of Singapore, 1987.

Selvaratnam, V. *Innovations in Higher Education: Singapore at the Competitive Edge*. Washington, D. C.: The World Bank, 1994.

Selvaratnam, V. "Singapore." In *The Encyclopedia of Higher Education*, edited by Burton R. Clark and Guy R. Neave. Oxford: Pergamon Press, 1992.

Shamsul, A. *From British to Bumiputera rule*. Singapore: Oxford University Press, 1990.

Shattock, M. "Thatcherism and British Higher Education: Universities and the Enterprise Culture." *Change* 21 (1989): 31-39.

Shinohara, M. *The Japanese and Korean Experience in Managing Development*. Washington, D.C.: The World Bank, 1983.

Shivadas, P. C. and F. F. Chuilin. *University of Malaya 1949-1989*. Kuala Lumpur: University of Malaya, 1989.

Shive, G. L., S. Gopinathan, and W. K. Cummings (eds). *North-South Scholarly Exchange: Access, Equity and Collaboration*. London and New York: Mansell Publishing Ltd., 1988.

Shuster, G. N. "The Nature and Development of U. S. Cultural Relations." In *Cultural Affairs and Foreign Relations*, edited by Columbia University The American Assembly. Englewood Cliffs, N. J.: Prentice-Hall, 1963.

Siegrist, H. "The Professions, State and Government in Theory and History." In *Government and Professional Education*, edited by T. Becher. Buckingham: SRHE & Open University, 1994.

Silcock, T. H. "The Development of Universities in South-East Asia to 1960." *Minerva* II, no. 2 (1964): 169-196.

Simon, R., "The Intellectuals" In *Gramsci's Political Thought*, by R. Simon, London: Lawrence & Wishart, 1991.

Simone, V. and A. T. Feraru. *The Asian Pacific: Political and Economic Development in a Global Context*. London: Longman Group Ltd., 1995.

Singapore. *Report of the Commission of Inquiry on the University of Malaya*. Singapore: Government Printer, 1957.

Singh, J. S., "Education and Society Equity in Peninsular Malaysia" In *EDC Occasional Papers*, No.3, London: Department of Education in Developing Countries, University of London, Institute of Education, 1982.

Singh, J. S. "Higher Education and Development: The Experience of Four Newly Industrializing Countries in Asia." *Prospects* 21, no. 3 (1991): 386-400.

Singh, J. S. "Higher Education and Development: The Experience of Four Newly Industrializing Countries in Asia." *Prospects* XXI, no. 3 (1991): 142-156.

Singh, J. S. "Malaysia" In *International Higher Education: an Encyclopedia,* Vol I, edited by Philip. G. Altbach. New York: Garland Publishing, Inc., 1991.

Singh, J. S. "Scientific Personnel, Research Environment and Higher Education in Malaysia." In *Scientific Development and Higher Education, The Case of Newly Industrializing Nations,* edited by Philip G. Altbach, C. H. Davis and T. O. Eisemon, New York: Praeger Publishers, 1989.

Singh, J. S. and H. Mukherjee. *Education and National Integration in Malaysia: Stocktaking Thirty Years after Independence.* Kuala Lumpur: Institute for Advanced Studies, University of Malaya, 1990.

Skilbeck, M. and H. Connel. "International education from the perspective of emergent world regionalism: the academic scientific and technological dimension." In *Academic Mobility in a changing world: regional and global trends,* edited by P. Blumenthal, C. Goodwin, A. Smith and U. Teichler. London: Jessica Kingsley, 1996.

Skutnabb-Kangas, K. and Jim Cummins (eds). *Minority Education,* Multilingual Matters 40, Series Editor: Derrick Sharp, Clevedon: Multilingual Matters Ltd., 1988

Slaughter, S. "Introduction to Special Issue on Retrenchment." *Journal of Higher Education* 64, no. 3 (May/June 1993).

Slaughter, S. and L. L. Leslie. *Academic Capitalism: Politics, Policies, and the Entrepreneurial University.* Baltimore & London: The Johns Hopkins University Press, 1997.

Smith, A. and F. Webster (eds). *The Postmodern University? Contested Visions of Higher Education in Society.* Buckingham: SRHE & Open University Press, 1997.

Smith, A. D. *The Ethnic Origins of Nations.* Oxford: Basil Blackwell, 1986.

Smith, A. D. *Nations and nationalism in a global era.* Cambridge: Polity Press, 1995.

Smith, W. W. *Confucianism in Modern Japan: A Study of Conservatism in Japanese Intellectual History.* Tokyo: Hokuseido Press, 1959.

Snodgrass, D. R. "Education in Korea and Malaysia." In *Behind East Asian Growth: the Political and social foundations of prosperity*, edited by Henry S. Rowen. London & New York: Routledge, 1998.

Snodgrass, D. R. *Inequality and Economic Development in Malaysia*. Oxford: Oxford University Press, 1980.

So, A. Y. *Social Change and Development: Modernization, Dependency, and World-System Theories*. London: Sage Publications, 1990.

Sohn, P-k (ed). *The History of Korea*. Seoul: Jung-min Sa, 1970.

Solomon, J. S. *The Development of Bilingual Education in Malaysia*. Selangor, Malaysia: Pelanduk Publications, 1988.

Son, In-su. *Hanguk Kundae Kyoyuksa [A Modern History of Korean Education]*. Seoul: Yonsei University Press, 1971.

Soon, T. W., and C. S. Tan. *Lessons of East Asia: Singapore: Public Policy and Economic Development*. Washington, D. C.: World Bank, 1993.

Spaulding, R. M. Jr. *Imperial Japan's Higher Civil Service Examinations*. Princeton, NJ: Princeton University Press, 1967.

Spengler, O. *The Decline of the West*. Edited by Abridged Edition by Helmut Werner. Abridge Edition 1961 ed. London: George Allen & Unwin Ltd., 1961.

Spitzberg, I. J. Jr. (ed). *Universities and the International Distribution of Knowledge*, New York: Praeger, 1980.

Spybey, T. *Social Change, Development and Dependency: Modernity, Colonialism and the Development of the West*. Oxford: Polity Press, 1992.

Stedman, J. B. *A Study of the Educational System of Malaysia and a Guide to the Academic Placement of Students in Educational Institutions of the United States*. N. Y.: American Association of Collegiate Registrars and Admissions Officers, 1986.

Stephens, M. D. (ed). *Universities, Education and the National Economy*. London & New York: Routledge, 1989.

Stevenson, R. *Cultivators and Administrators: British Educational Policy towards the Malays, 1875-1906*. Kuala Lumpur: Oxford University Press, 1975.

Stone, L. *The University in Society, Vol. I, Oxford and Cambridge from the 14th to the Early,* Princeton: Princeton University Press, 1974.

Stone, L. "Education and Modernization in Japan and England." *Comparative Studies in Society and History* IX, no. 2 (1966-7): 208-232.

Swettenham, Sir F. A. *British Malaya: an Account of the Origin and Progress of British Influence in Malaya.* London, 1906.

Symonds, R. *Oxford and Empire: The Last Lost Cause?* London: Macmillan, 1986.

Tai, H. C. (ed). *Confucianism & Economic Development: an Oriental Alternative?* Washington, D. C.: The Washington Institute Press, 1989.

Tapper, T. R., and B. G. Salter. "The Changing Idea of University Autonomy." *Studies in Higher Education* 20, no. 1 (1995): 59-71.

Tapper, T. R. and B. G. Salter. *Oxford, Cambridge and the Changing Idea of the University: The Challenge to Donnish Domination.* Buckingham: Open University Press/ SRHE, 1992.

Teather, D. (ed). *Higher Education in a Post-binary Era.* Higher Education Policy 38. A Series edited by Maurice Kogan, London: Jessica Kingsley, 1998.

Teichler, U. *Changing Patterns of the Higher Education System: The Experience of Three Decades, Higher Education Policy 5.* London: Jessica Kingsley Publishers, 1988.

Teichler, U. "The State of Comparative Research in Higher Education." *Higher Education* 32, no. 4 (1996).

Tham, S. C. *Malays and Modernization: A Sociological Interpretation.* Singapore: Singapore University Press, 1977.

Tham, S. C. (ed). *Modernization in Singapore.* Singapore: University Education Press, 1972.

Tham, S. C. "The Perception and Practice of Education." In *Management of Success: The Moulding of Modern Singapore,* edited by K. S. Sandhu and Paul Wheatley. Singapore: Institute of Southeast Asian Studies, 1989.

Tham, S. C. "Staff and Faculty Development in Singapore." In *Staff and Faculty Development in Southeast Asian Universities,* edited by RIHED. Singapore: Maruzen Asia Ltd., 1981.

Tham S. C. and A. Mani. "University Education in Singapore in the 1990s." In *University Education in the Nineties,* edited by H. Abdullah and A. Samad Hadi. Bangi: Universiti Kebangsan Malaysia Press, 1991.

Thievandran, R. "Foreign Researchers in Malaysia." In *North-South Scholarly Exchange: Access, Equity and Collaboration,* edited by G. L. Shive, S. Gopinathan and W. K. Cummings. London and New York: Mansell Publishing Ltd., 1988.

Thomas, N. *Colonialism's Culture: Anthropology, Travel and Government.* Cambridge: Polity Press, 1994.

Thomas, R. M. "Malaysia: Cooperation versus Competition or National Unity versus Favoured Access to Education." In *Politics and Education: Cases from Eleven Nations,* edited by R. Murray Thomas. Oxford: Pergamon Press, 1983.

Thomas, R. M. *Politics and Education: Cases from Eleven Nations.* Oxford: Pergamon Press, 1983.

Thomas, R. M. and T. N. Postlethwaite (eds). *Schooling in East Asia: Forces of Change.* Oxford: Pergamon Press, 1983.

Thomson, K. W., B. R. Foger and H. E. Danner (eds). *Higher Education and Social Change: Promising Experiments in Developing Countries.* Vol. 2: Case Studies, Chapter 14. University of Malaya, Malaysia. New York: Praeger Publishers, 1977.

Tight, M. (ed). *Academic Freedom and Responsibility.* Milton Keynes: The Society for Research into Higher Education & Open University Press, 1988.

Tight, M. "Crisis, What Crisis? Rhetoric and Reality in Higher Education." *British Journal of Educational Studies* XXXXII, no. 4 (1994): 364-374.

Torstendahl, R. and M. Burrage (eds). *The Formation of Professions: Knowledge, State and Strategy.* London: Sage Publications, 1990.

Tregonnig, K. G. "Tertiary Education in Malaya: Policy and Practice 1905-1962." *Journal of the Malaysian Branch of the Royal Asiatic Society* LXIII, no. 1 (1990): 1-14.

Tremewan, C. *The Political Economy of Social Control in Singapore.* London Macmillan Press Ltd. in association with St. Antony's College, Oxford, 1994.

Trow, M. "Managerialism and the Academic Profession: the case of England." *Higher Education Policy* 7, no. 2 (1994): 11-18.

Trow, M. "On the Accountability of Higher Education in the United States." In *Inside Academia: New Challenges for the Academic Profession*. Utrecht, The Netherlands: Centre for Higher Education Policy Studies (CHEPS), 1996.

Trow, M. and T. Nybom (eds). *University and Society: Essays on the Social Role of Research and Higher Education*. Edited by Maurice Kogan, *Higher Education Policy 12*, 1991.

Tu, Wei-Ming. *Confucian Ethics Today: The Singapore Challenge*. Singapore: Curriculum Development Institute of Singapore, Federal Publications, 1984.

Tu, Wei-ming. "A Confucian Perspective on the Rise of Industrial East Asia." *Bulletin of the American Academy of Arts and Sciences* 43, no. 6 (1990).

Tu, Wei-ming. *Humanity and Self-Cultivation: Essays in Confucian Thought*. Berkeley: Asian Humanities Press, 1979.

Tu, Wei-ming. *Way, Learning, and Politics: Essays on the Confucian Intellectual*. Singapore: Institute of East Asian Philosophies, 1989.

Tu, Wei-Ming, (ed). *Confucian Traditions in East Asian Modernity: Moral Education and Economic Culture in Japan and the Four Mini-Dragons*. Cambridge, Mass. & London, England: Harvard University Press, 1996.

Tu, Wei-ming (ed). *The Triadic Chord: Confucian Ethics, Industrial East Asia, and Max Weber, The Conference on Confucian Ethics and the Modernization of Industrial East Asia*. Singapore: Institute of East Asian Philosophies, 1991.

Turnbull, C. M. *A History of Singapore, 1819-1975*. Kuala Lumpur: Oxford University Press, 1977.

Turner, B. "Outline of a theory of citizenship." *Sociology* 24, no. 2 (1990): 187-217.

Turner, D. "Changing Patterns of Funding Higher Education in Europe." *Higher Education Management* 8, no. 1 (March 1996): 101-111.

Uchida, T. "Perceptions of the state in post-war Japan." In *The State and Cultural Transformation: Perspectives from East Asia*, edited by Ken'ichiro Hirano. Tokyo &New York & Paris: United Nations University Press, 1995.

Uchida, T. (ed). *Political Science in Asia and the Pacific: Status Reports on Teaching and Research in Ten Countries*, Bangkok: UNESCO Regional Office for Education in Asia and the Pacific, 1984.

UNESCO. *Academic Freedom and University Autonomy.* Bucharest: CEPES, UNESCO European Centre for Higher Education, 1993.

UNESCO, *Domination or Sharing? Endogenous Development and the Transfer of Knowledge*, Paris: UNESCO, 1981.

UNESCO (ed). *Economics in Asia; Status Reports on Teaching and Research in Nine Countries*, Bangkok, UNESCO, 1985.

UNESCO. *Educational Innovation in the Republic of Korea.* Vol. Experiments and innovations in education No. 12. Paris: The UNESCO Press, 1974.

UNESCO (ed). *Political Science in Asia and the Pacific: Status Reports on Teaching and Research in Ten Countries.* Bangkok: UNESCO Regional Office for Education in Asia and the Pacific, 1984.

UNESCO, *Social Sciences in Asia and the Pacific*, Paris: UNESCO, 1984.

University of Malaya. *The University of Malaya: an Introduction.* Kuala Lumpur: Public Relation Office, University of Malaya, 1994.

Vasil, R. K. *Ethnic Politics in Malaysia.* New Delhi: Radiant Publishes, 1980.

Vogel, E. *The Four Little Dragons: The Spread of Industrialization in East Asia.* Cambridge, MA.: Harvard University Press, 1991.

Vogel, E. F. "A Little Dragon Tamed." In *Management of Success: the Moulding of Modern Singapore*, edited by K. S. Sandhu and P. Wheatley. Singapore: Institute of Southeast Asian Studies, 1989.

Waley, A. *Three Ways of Thought in Ancient China.* reprint ed. Garden City, N. Y.: Doubleday, Anchor Book, 1956.

Wallerstein, I. "Liberalism and Legitimation of Nation-States: an Historical Interpretation." *Social Justice* XIX, no. 1 (1991): 22-33.

Wallerstein, I. *The Modern World System.* San Diego: Academic Press, 1974.

Walters, G. J. (ed). *The Tasks of Truth.* Frankfurt am Main: Peter Lang, 1996.

Wang, B.-L. C. "Positive Discrimination in Education: A Comparative Investigation of its Bases, Forms and Outcomes." *Comparative Education Review* 27 (June 1983): 191-202.

Wang, Gungwu "Traditional Leadership in a new nation: The Chinese in Malaya and Singapore." In *The Cultural Problems of Malaysia in the Context of Southeast Asia,* edited by Alisjahbana, S. Takdir, Kuala Lumpur: The Malaysian Society of Orientalists, 1966.

Wang, Gungwu (ed). *Malaysia: a survey*. Singapore: Donald Moore Books, 1964.

Watkins, J., L. Drury and D. Preddy. *From Evolution to Revolution: The Pressures on Professional Life in the 1990s*. Bristol: University of Britstol Press, 1992.

Watson, B. and L. Y. Andaya. *A History of Malaysia*. London: The MacMillan Press, 1982.

Watson, K., C. Modgil and S. Modgil (eds). *Educational Dilemmas: Debate & Diversity - Vol. 3 Power & Responsibility in Education,* London: Cassell, 1997.

Watson, K., C. Modgil and S. Modgil (eds). *Educational Dilemmas: Debate & Diversity - Vol. 4: Quality in Education,* London: Cassell, 1997.

Watson, K. (ed). *Education in the Third World*. London & Canberra: Croom Helm, 1982.

Watson, K. "Education and Colonialism in Peninsular Malaysia." In *Education in the Third World*, edited by K. Watson. London & Canberra: Croom Helm, 1982.

Watson, K. "Educational Neocolonialism - the Continuing Colonial Legacy." In *Education in the Third World*, edited by K. Watson. London & Canberra: Croom Helm, 1982.

Watson, K. "Rulers and Ruled: Racial Perceptions, Curriculum and Şchooling in Colonial Malaya and Singapore" In *The Imperial Curriculum: Racial Images and Education in the British Colonial Experience*, edited by J. A. Mangan, London: Routledge, 1993.

Watson, K., "Dependence or Independence in Education?: two cases from post-colonial South-East Asia" *International Journal of Educational Development* 5, no. 2 (1985): 83-94.

Watson, K. "Memories, Models and Mapping: the Impact of Geopolitical Changes on Comparative Studies in Education." *Compare* 28, no. 1 (1998): 5-31.

Watson, K. "Technical and Vocational Education in Developing Countries: Western Paradigms and Comparative Methodology." *Comparative Education* 30, no. 2

(1994): 85-97.

Watson, K. and K. King. "From Comparative Studies to International Studies in Education: Towards the Coordination of a British Resource of Expertise." *International Journal of Educational Development* 11 (1991): 245-253.

Weber, M. *Die Protestantische Ethik und der 'Geist' des Kapitalismus,* [*The Protestant ethic and the spirit of capitalism*]. Translated by Talcott Parsons. London: Allen and Unwin, 1976.

Weber, M. *The Religion of China: Confucianism and Taoism.* Translated by H. H. Gerth. New York: Free Press, 1964.

Weber, M. *From Max Weber: Essays in Sociology,* Edited by H. H. Gerth and C. Mills, and C. Wright, London: Routledge & Kegan Paul, 1974.

Weinberg, M. *Asian-American Education: Historical Background and Current Realities.* Mahwah, NJ. & London: Lawrence Erlbaum Associates, Publishers, 1997.

Weiner, M. and S. Huntington (eds). *Understanding Political Development.* Boston, Mass.: Little, Brown & Company, 1987.

Weiss, L. *The Myth of the Powerless State.* Cambridge: Polity Press, 1998.

Welch, A. R. "The Internationalisation of Higher Education: Retrospect and Prospect." *Forum of Education* 52, no. 1 (1997).

Welch, A. R. "The Peripatetic Professor: The Internationalisation of the Academic Profession." *Higher Education (Special Issue on the International Survey of the Academic Profession ed. A. Welch)* 34, no. 1 (1997).

Welch, A. R. "All Change? The Professoriate in Uncertain Times." *Higher Education* 34, Special Issue on the International Survey of the Academic Profession (1997).

Welch, A. R. "The End of Certainty? The Academic Profession and the Challenge of Change." *Comparative Education Review* 42, Special Issue on the Academic Profession (1998).

Werth, R. "Educational Developments under the South Korea Interim Government." *School and Society* 69, no. 1793 (April 1949).

White, G. (ed). *The Developmental States in Asia.* New York: St. Martin's, 1988.

Wilke, A. S. (ed). *The Hidden Professoriate: Credentialism, Professionalism and the Tenure Crisis.* Westport, Conn.: Greenwood Press, 1979.

Wilkinson, E. *Japan versus the West: A History of Misunderstanding.* Harmondsworth: Penguin, 1983.

Wilkinson, R. *Gentlemanly Power.* Oxford: Oxford University Press, 1964.

Wilkinson, R. *The Prefects: British Leadership and the Public School Tradition, A Comparative Study in the Making of Rulers.* London: Oxford University Press, 1964.

Wilkinson, R. (ed). *Governing Elites: Studies in Training and Selection.* New York: Oxford University Press, 1969.

Williams, B. R. "University Values and University Organisation." *Minerva* X, no. 2 (1972): 259-279.

Williams, G. "Longer Term Prospects for British Higher Education." . London: Centre for Higher Education Studies, Institute of Education, 1994.

Williams, G. L. *Changing Patterns of Finance in Higher Education.* London: Society for Research into Higher Education and Open University Press, 1992.

Williams, P. and L. Chrisman. *Colonial Discourse and Post-Colonial Theory.* New York: Harvester Wheatsheaf, 1993.

Wilshire, B. *The Moral Collapse of the University: Professionalism, Purity and Alienation.* Albany, NY: State University of New York Press, 1990.

Wilson, H. E. "Education, Foreign Policy, and International Relations." In *Cultural Affairs and Foreign Relations*, edited by Columbia University The American Assembly. Englewood Cliffs, N. J.: Prentice-Hall, 1963.

Wilson, H. E. *Social Engineering in Singapore.* Singapore: Singapore University Press, 1978.

Winstedt, R. O. "The Educational System of Malaya." In *International Yearbook of Education.* New York: Columbia University, 1931.

Wong, F. H. K. and Gwee Yee Hean. *Perspectives: The Development of Education in Malaysia and Singapore.* Kuala Lumpur: Heinemann Education Books, 1972.

Wong, F. H. K., and Yee Hean Gwee. *Official Reports on Education: Straits Settlements and the Federated Malay States 1870-1939*. Singapore: Pan Pacific Book Distributors, Ltd., 1980.

Wong, H. K. F. and Ee Tiang Hong. *Education in Malaysia*. 2nd ed. Kuala Lumpur: Heinemann Educational Books (Asia) Ltd., 1975.

Wong, S. T. *Singapore's New Education System: Education Reform for National Development*. Singapore: Institute of Southeast Asian Studies, 1988.

World Bank, The. *The East Asian Miracle: Economic Growth and Public Policy*. Washington D. C.: The World Bank, 1993.

Wragg, T. (ed). *Education A Different Vision: an Alternative White Paper*. London: Institute for Public Policy Research, 1993.

Wyatt, J. *Commitment to Higher Education*. Buckingham: SRHE & Open University Press, 1990.

Wyatt-Walter, A. *Regionalism, Globalisation and World Economic Order*. Edited by Louise Fawcett and Andrew Hurrell, *Regionalism in World Politics: Regional Organisation and International Order*. Oxford: Oxford University Press, 1995.

Yen, C. A. "Trends and Issues in Improving University Teaching." *Higher Education Research and Development* 7, no. 1 (1988).

Yen, C-h. *A Social History of the Chinese in Singapore and Malaya*. Singapore: Oxford University Press, 1986.

Yip, S. K. and W. K. Sim (eds). *Evolution of Educational Excellence: 25 Years of Education in the Republic of Singapore*. Singapore: Longman, 1994.

Yonsei University. *The 100 -Year History of Yonsei University 1885-1985*. Vol. I. Seoul: Yonsei University Press, 1985.

Yonsei University Development Committee, Yonsei 21st century Planning Report [*Yonsei 21 Segi Gae-whaeck*], Seoul: Yonsei University, September 1993.

Young, K., W. C. F. Bussink and P. Hasan. *Malaysia: Growth and Equity in a Multi-Racial Society*. Baltimore: Johns Hopkins University Press, 1980.

Young, R. *White Mythologies: Writing, History and the West*. London: Routledge, 1990.

Yu, K-h. "Characteristics of Korea's view of the outside world in the late Choson period (1392-1910)." In *The State and Cultural Transformation: Perspectives from East Asia*, edited by Hirano Ken'ichiro. Tokyo & New York & Paris: United Nations University Press, 1995.

Ziman, J. "The College System at Oxford and Cambridge." *Minerva: A Review of Science, Learning and Policy* I, no. 2 (1963): 191-208.

Znaniecki, F. *The Social Role of the Man of Knowledge*. New York: Octagon Books, Inc., 1965.

Index